MUSIC IN CHOPIN'S WARSAW

Music in Chopin's Warsaw

Halina Goldberg

OXFORD
UNIVERSITY PRESS

2008

OXFORD
UNIVERSITY PRESS

Oxford University Press, Inc., publishes works that further
Oxford University's objective of excellence
in research, scholarship, and education.

Oxford   New York
Auckland   Cape Town   Dar es Salaam   Hong Kong   Karachi
Kuala Lumpur   Madrid   Melbourne   Mexico City   Nairobi
New Delhi   Shanghai   Taipei   Toronto

With offices in
Argentina   Austria   Brazil   Chile   Czech Republic   France   Greece
Guatemala   Hungary   Italy   Japan   Poland   Portugal   Singapore
South Korea   Switzerland   Thailand   Turkey   Ukraine   Vietnam

Published by Oxford University Press, Inc.
198 Madison Avenue, New York, New York 10016

www.oup.com

Oxford is a registered trademark of Oxford University Press

Library of Congress Cataloging-in-Publication Data
Goldberg, Halina, 1961–
Music in Chopin's Warsaw / Halina Goldberg.
    p.   cm.
Includes bibliographical references and index.
ISBN 978-0-19-513073-7
1. Music—Poland—Warsaw—19th century—History and criticism.
2. Music—Social aspects—Poland—Warsaw—History—19th century.
3. Chopin, Frédéric, 1810–1849.   I. Title.
ML297.4.G65 2007
780.9438′41—dc22   2007004794

This volume is published with generous support from the Dragan Plamenac
Publication Endowment Fund of the American Musicological Society.

1   3   5   7   9   8   6   4   2

Printed in the United States of America
on acid-free paper

ACKNOWLEDGMENTS

I owe boundless gratitude to the many people who assisted me and lent me their support while I was working on this book. The personnel at the various Polish institutions never cease to surprise me with their willingness to share their expertise and their enthusiasm in assisting and advising me. I am especially indebted for their generous help in locating sources and illustrations to Paweł Bagnowski, Mariola Nałęcz, and Włodzimierz Pigła at the Biblioteka Narodowa in Warsaw; Magdalena Jamroży, Anna Ryszka-Komarnicka, Teresa Lewandowska, and Weronika Witczak at the Muzeum Fryderyka Chopina w Towarzystwie im. Fryderyka Chopina in Warsaw; Andrzej Spóz at the Biblioteka Warszawskiego Towarzystwa Muzycznego in Warsaw; Małgorzata Biłozór-Salwa at the Gabinet Rycin of the Biblioteka Uniwersytetu Warszawskiego in Warsaw; Dorota Hager and Jolanta Lenkiewicz at the Biblioteka XX Czartoryskich in Kraków; Sylwia Heinrich at the Biblioteka Jagiellońska in Kraków; and Stanisław Hrabia and Wanda Rutkowska-Łysoń at the Biblioteka Muzykologii, Uniwersytet Jagielloński in Kraków. I am also grateful to George Platzman of the University of Chicago, Marita Alban Juarez of the Narodowy Instytut Fryderyka Chopina in Warsaw, Jolanta Guzy-Pasiak of the Instytut Sztuki at the Polska Akademia Nauk in Warsaw, and the staff of the Muzeum Teatralne at the Teatr Wielki in Warsaw for their willingness to assist me with my questions and searches.

In preparing the manuscript I had the help of the superb team at Oxford University Press, especially Suzanne Ryan, Norman Hirschy, and Robert Milks. I am also grateful to Leslie Evans for the maps; Michał Świderski, Barbara Świderska, and Randy Goldberg for the musical examples; and Lisa Cooper Vest and Kristen Strandberg for the preparation of the index. The publication of this volume was made possible in part through the financial assistance of the Indiana University Russian and East European Institute through their Andrew W. Mellon Foundation Endowment, and a subvention from the Dragan Plamenac Publication Endowment Fund of the American Musicological Society.

I would like to thank for the help and support I received from my colleague friends in Poland: Maciej Gołąb for many suggestions and advice, Jerzy Gołos for answering my numerous questions, and Benjamin Vogel for reading and commenting on a draft of the chapter on musical instruments. I truly appreciate the hospitality of Alicja Jarzębska and Zofia Helman for making available to me the resources of Instytut Muzykologii of the Uniwersytet Jagielloński and of Uniwersytet Warszawski respectively. I am grateful to Charles Burkhart, Raymond Erickson, Rufus Hallmark, Edward Lerner, Roy Nitzberg, and Drora Pershing for their support in the early stages of this project. I also greatly appreciate the encouragement and help I got from my colleague friends at Indiana University: the late A. Peter Brown, J. Peter Burkholder, Denise Gardiner, Marianne Kielian-Gilbert, Daniel Melamed, Massimo Ossi, and David Ransel.

To my dearest friends in Poland—Ewa Pikulska and her daughter Zuza, Renata Smolarska and her son Bazyl, Basia Grabowska and Zbyszek Pankiewicz, Jacek Piwkowski and his mother Bożena, Małgosia and Marek Rogoziński, Jadzia and Wojtek Konopacki—I owe the gratitude for opening their homes and hearts to me; for providing me with a home away from home. I also greatly appreciate the continuous acts of kindness from Asia Kraska and Renia Pawlak. I am particularly indebted to my wonderful friends in New York: Michael Spudic for his continuous willingness to help me through various obstacles and to David Richards for his steadfast faith in me and his undying support and enthusiasm for this project.

These acknowledgements would be incomplete without thanking my feline friends—Kicia, Fisia, Artie, and Calie (who is cuddled up against me as I am writing these words)—for their calming presence. They provided me with affection, companionship, and welcome distraction through the various stages of this project.

To my husband, Mark Eckhardt, I owe my gratitude for his enthusiastic support and patience. To him, my mother, Maria Goldberg, and my late father, Zenon Goldberg, I dedicate this book with love.

CONTENTS

MUSIC IN CHOPIN'S WARSAW

INTRODUCTION

Among the many works devoted to Fryderyk Chopin, none fully addresses the musical environment in which the composer spent his formative years. In his 1997 biography of Chopin, Jim Samson calls attention to this lacuna: "The weakest sections of most existing biographies (at least by non-Polish authors) concern the Warsaw years. Even where Polish sources have been carefully researched, the tendency has been to give inadequate measure to the shaping influence of Warsaw's social and cultural world."[1] To rectify the situation, Samson included an informative chapter on Chopin's early years, followed by insightful examination of the early musical style. Several of Samson's observations coincide with the points I make in this book; since the musical environment of Chopin's Warsaw is not the focus of his book, however, he treats the subject in a general manner.[2] Samson excepted, the topic has not received much consideration in English. Frederick Niecks's monumental, two-volume 1888 study of Chopin gives some attention to the cultural circumstances of his childhood, but the information is neither

---

[1] Jim Samson, *Chopin* (New York: Schirmer Books, 1997), vi.

[2] Having to rely on flawed published information, he also introduces several inaccuracies into the chapter. Some needed corrections are: General Mokronowski was no longer alive during the 1820s, and his widow's salon was not famed for patriotic promotion of Polish values (10); Walerian Krasiński was not a writer, though he participated in salon gatherings; the writer who rightfully belongs in the company of these great names is his younger relative Zygmunt Krasiński, whose father's name was Wincenty (10); the famous musical soirées took place in the home of the Cichockis, not Cichowskis, who were also Chopin's acquaintances (28); Koźmian's name was Kajetan, not Kalenty (10); Izabela Grabowska was the minister's sister, not wife (18); and Eugeniusz Skrodzki was not a boarder with the Chopins but their neighbor (7).

extensive nor dependable.[3] The most exhaustive Polish study of Chopin's Warsaw is Frączyk's *Warsaw of Chopin's Youth*.[4] Published in 1961, it is significantly dated and does not approach the subject from a musicological perspective. Frączyk concentrates on the general milieu of Warsaw: the physical appearance and demographics of the city, vacationing spots frequented by its dwellers, and its institutions (schools, art galleries, and book publishers) but does not address musical issues. Among Polish and foreign sources concerning Chopin's musical environment there are tomes of related material, yet there is no authoritative study that draws all the data together. In light of this pressing need, my goal is to bring the scattered information previously published in different contexts and entirely new research into a single-volume, comprehensive study of the musical world of Chopin's youth.

To some degree, outside Poland, the lack of knowledge on this subject comes from a lack of appreciation of Warsaw's cultural importance. According to Samson, Chopin was personally troubled by this presumption, and "later in life he was often at pains to counter suggestions that Warsaw was a musical backwater."[5] Yet even in the most recent studies, Poland's cultural milieu is ignored, and Samson's book, based on the belief that "Warsaw was hardly a leading cultural capital, but equally it was not the provincial backwater it has sometimes been labeled,"[6] is among the few that attempt to change this outlook. Indeed, it is not my intention to argue that Warsaw could compete with Paris or Vienna, but that, during the period under consideration, it certainly compared well with many major European cities.

Despite the political situation, Warsaw retained the status of a center of Polish culture expected of a capital. It was a vibrant European city that was home to an opera house, various smaller theaters, one of the earliest modern conservatories in Europe, several societies that organized concerts, musically active churches, spirited salon life, music printers and bookstores, instrument builders, and for a short time even a weekly paper devoted to music. Rather than finding a dormant, peripheral town, one encounters a city that is not only aware of and in tune with the most recent European styles and fashions in music but also the cradle of a vernacular musical language that was initiated by the generation of Polish composers before Chopin and found its full realization in his work.

Significantly, this period of cultural revival in the Polish capital coin-

---

[3] Frederick Niecks, *Frederick Chopin as a Man and Musician* (1888; reprint, New York: Cooper Square, 1973).

[4] Tadeusz Frączyk, *Warszawa: Młodości Chopina* [Warsaw of Chopin's youth] (Kraków: Polskie Wydawnictwo Muzyczne, 1961)

[5] Samson, *Chopin*, 12.

[6] Samson, *Chopin*, 23.

cided with the duration of Chopin's stay there—from his infancy in 1810 to his final departure from his homeland in 1830. An uncanny convergence of political, economic, social, and cultural circumstances generated the dynamic musical, artistic, and intellectual environment that nurtured the developing genius. Had Chopin been born a decade earlier or a decade later, the capital, devastated by warfare and stripped of all cultural institutions, could not have provided support for his talent. The young composer would have been compelled to seek musical education abroad and thus would have been deprived of the specifically Polish experience so central to his musical style.

There is a large amount of Polish scholarship that pertains directly or marginally to my research. Many of these studies are first-rate, but ultimately they present a fragmented picture of the subject. One must also consider the role of several ideological interferences in the shaping of the Polish Chopin narratives: the Romanticized perspectives, the nationalist frameworks through which native culture was perceived, and the ideology imposed in the last century by the communist authorities. The Polish intellectual landscape of the nineteenth century was dominated by the need to uphold Polish sovereignty, channeled into ceaseless efforts at the construction of national identity. Consequently, for nineteenth-century writers, Chopin and his music became principal icons of native Polishness, which was seen as rooted in the culture of the peasants and Catholic Christianity, imbued with native language and customs, and exclusive of any other influences. In the early decades of the twentieth century, the vocabulary of Polish nationalism became intertwined with the prevailing racial theories, metaphorically and literally placing the composer and his oeuvre within imagined biological Polishness. The political climate in post–World War II Poland prompted scholarly dishonesty and during the first years produced pages of Stalinist "newspeak" concealing important factual information. The preferred line of thinking again emphasized the indebtedness of Chopin's music to Polish folklore, but this time as an artist connected to working-class people. These ideologies had obvious impact on the Chopin narratives: they shaped research into his ancestry, the selective memory of the ethnic makeup of his environment, and, most significantly, the perception of his musical environments—the neglect of the role of middle-class, urban entertainment as opposed to peasant folklore on his musical language, and the role salon music played in his musical education.

The demand for unambiguous Polishness, as defined by the successive "-isms," played a role in several aspects of Chopin historiography. The myth of Chopin's Polish peasant patrilineal descent constitutes a primary such example. The communist political agenda perpetuated this myth to support an ideologically acceptable class lineage; the theory, however, that the Chopin family descended from a Polish emigrant to France named

Szop had already been advanced in the second half of the nineteenth century. By the beginning of the twentieth century, the "all-Polish Chopin" narrative was unfolding against the backdrop of nationalist and racial ideologies, which provided biological basis for perceiving his musical style as "racially" Polish.[7] The same ideologies gave rise to the lengthy dispute over whether Chopin's teacher, Józef Elsner, was Polish. Ironically, it was Elsner, a "non-ethnic Pole," who nearly single-handedly rejuvenated Polish musical culture and guided it toward intense Polish patriotism.

Humiliated by military and political defeats and succumbing to the Herderian trends in defining statehood, Poland downplayed the multiethnic and multireligious character of its population. The many groups that made up the population of Poland were gradually written out of Polish history—those living in Poland for centuries and the new immigrants alike—even though many considered themselves Polish enough to devote their lives to the reestablishment of Polish cultural and political sovereignty. The milieu of Chopin's Warsaw rings with a host of foreign names: Żywny, Czapek, Jawurek, and Würfel from Bohemia; Elsner, a German-speaking Silesian who claimed Swedish ancestry; and Soliva, from Milan, were among Chopin's many mentors of foreign ancestry who earnestly participated in Warsaw's musical scene. Several of the immigrants had Polish spouses, and some of them, or their Polish-born children, got caught up in Polish battles. The piano builder Wilhelm Troschel fought in the November Uprising in 1830 as a sergeant of the National Guard.[8] His colleague Jan Kerntopf was wounded in the same uprising.[9] Later in the century, during the January Uprising of 1863, Adolf Jan Wernitz, from the dynasty of Warsaw's trumpet builders, was arrested for selling supplies to the insurgents.[10] A similar fate befell another famous trumpet builder, Wilhelm Glier.[11] Viewing Chopin's Warsaw through the nationalistic lens, and thus failing to recognize that Chopin's formative years took place in the enlightened environment of a cosmopolitan, multiethnic and multireligious European capital, has removed a crucial dimension of Chopin's upbringing and obscured a vital set of influences on his personality and musical language.

Then again, the inflated Polish national pride was in part a defensive reaction to the contemptuous and arrogant treatment that Poland had

[7] For an in-depth study of this problem, consult Maja Trochimczyk, "Chopin and the 'Polish Race': On National Ideologies and the Chopin Reception," in *The Age of Chopin: Interdisciplinary Inquiries*, ed. Halina Goldberg (Bloomington: Indiana University Press, 2004), 278–313.

[8] Beniamin Vogel, *Instrumenty muzyczne w kulturze Królestwa Polskiego: Przemysł muzyczny w latach 1815–1918* [Musical instruments in the culture of the Polish Kingdom: music industry during the years 1815–1918] (Kraków: Polskie Wydawnictwo Muzyczne, 1980), 214.

[9] Vogel, *Instrumenty muzyczne w kulturze Królestwa Polskiego*, 176.

[10] Vogel, *Instrumenty muzyczne w kulturze Królestwa Polskiego*, 217.

[11] Vogel, *Instrumenty muzyczne w kulturze Królestwa Polskiego*, 164.

continuously received from abroad, including some irresponsible and degrading statements found in foreign works on Chopin. Niecks's biography of this composer abounds in absurd assertions, some stemming from Liszt's fanciful descriptions: "Their [the Poles'] oriental mellifluousness, hyperbolism, and obsequious politeness of speech, as well as the Asiatic [*sic!*] appearance of their features and dress, have been noticed by all travelers in Poland. . . . [K]nives, forks, and spoons were conveniences unknown to [Polish] peasants."[12]

But even in more recent works on Chopin, one finds plenty of ridiculous claims. Arthur Hutchings sprinkles a valid and thought-provoking statement with arrogant errors:

> Since Chopin was an infant when his father took up a teaching appointment and the family moved to the very middle of Warsaw, we stretch imagination by savoring any rural background to his music. None of it is directly evocative of the village on the Skarbeck [*sic*] estate, or of the somewhat dull countryside of Poland. Chopin's father was French; polite society in Russia and Poland conversed in French. . . . Yet the Polish element in Chopin's music is as urbane as the Hungarian element in Liszt's, and Chopin's Polish background is not of paramount importance.[13]

Alternatively, Arthur Hedley, through statements like "Nicholas Chopin appears to have had all the best characteristics of his race [French] and type [peasant]: manly, hard-working and careful,"[14] indulges again in old-fashioned racial typology. In all fairness, I must point out that Hedley also shows some generosity toward the Poles, acknowledging that "whatever charges of instability might then be brought against the Poles, no one could deny their mental alertness."[15]

One can only imagine the reaction on the part of Polish writers to

[12] Niecks, *Frederick Chopin*, 1:10 and 1:6. It should be noted that in the early nineteenth century, such conveniences were unknown to peasants elsewhere in Europe as well. On the construction of the "exotic Pole" see Larry Wolff, *Inventing Eastern Europe: The Map of Civilization on the Mind of the Enlightenment* (Stanford; Stanford University Press, 1994).

[13] Arthur Hutchings, "Frédéric Chopin: The Historical Background," in *The Chopin Companion: Profiles of the Man and the Musician*, ed. Allan Walker (1966; reprint, New York: Norton, 1974), 26. Some of the errors of fact and implication in this statement are the following: that anyone ever claimed that Chopin's contact with Polish peasant culture took place during his infancy on the Skarbek family estate, rather than during his annual summer holidays in the countryside; that Chopin's father was simply French, when he lived his entire adult life in Poland; that both the Russian and Polish elite continued to speak French even after the Napoleonic wars, during the period of the establishment of Polish identity; and that the remarkable geological variety of the Polish landscape could be considered dull.

[14] Arthur Hedley, "Chopin: The Man," in Walker, *Chopin Companion*, 4–5.

[15] Hedley, "Chopin: The Man," 4–5.

these and similar statements: for example, the celebrated Polish historian Ferdynand Hoesick was clearly infuriated, and justifiably so, by the statements made by Niecks.[16] The response of Poles to such marginalization was predictable: to intensify the Polishness of the Polish.

An assessment of Chopin's music must remain incomplete without inquiry into the salon culture of the early nineteenth century as a cradle for Chopin's style. In Poland, during the post–World War II period, it was preferable to downplay the contribution of intelligentsia and aristocracy to the Polish culture. Salon culture was scorned by the communist regime as representative of bourgeois decadence and the aristocratic abuse of wealth. In Russian scholarship, the Communist Party–approved vocabulary can be found even in as recent an article as the 1989 version of Semenovskij's "Russian Acquaintances and Friends of Chopin," where the author still refers to the "bourgeois biographers of Chopin."[17] But on a larger scale, at the core of this implied contempt are matters concerning gender, aesthetics of high art, and politics. This already complex nexus of perceptions concerning the salon is further intensified by the centuries-long cultural conflict between the French and the Germans and its effect on music and musicological discourse. Once art music became enshrined in the concert hall and the salon became unequivocally vilified as the home of the trivial, no place was left for the exploration of Chopin's art in its native salon contexts: to be worthwhile, Chopin's music had to be removed from the salon. Only in recent decades is the multifaceted character of the salon culture being explored, including studies concerning Chopin's participation in the Parisian salon and the associated gender stigmas surrounding his person.[18] One of this book's aims is to investi-

---

[16] Ferdynand Hoesick, *Warszawa: Luźne kartki z przeszłości syreniego grodu* [Warsaw: Loose leaves from the past of the "mermaid city"] (Poznań: Księgarnia Św. Wojciecha, 1920), 37–38 and 173–175.

[17] S. A. Semenovskij, *"Russkie znakomye i druz'ja Šopena"* [Russian acquaintances and friends of Chopin], in *Venok Šopenu* [A wreath for Chopin], ed. Leonid S. Sidel'nikov (Moscow: Muzyka, 1989), 64.

[18] Andreas Ballstaedt and Tobias Widmaier, *Salonmusik: Zur Geschichte und Funktion einer bürgerlichen Musikpraxis* (Stuttgart: Steiner Verlag Wiesbaden, 1989); Andreas Ballstaedt, "Chopin as Salon Composer," in *Chopin Studies 2*, ed. John Rink and Jim Samson (Cambridge: Cambridge University Press, 1994); Peter Gradenwitz, *Literatur und Musik im geselligem Kreise: Geschmacksbildung, Gesprächsstoff und musikalische Unterhaltung in der bürgerlichen Salongesellschaft* (Stuttgart: Steiner Verlag, 1991); Petra Wilhelmy, *Der Berliner Salon im 19.Jahrhundert: 1780–1914* (Berlin: de Gruyter, 1989); Jeffrey Kallberg, "Small Fairy Voices: Sex, History and Meaning in Chopin," in Rink and Samson, *Chopin Studies 2*, and *Chopin at the Boundaries: Sex, History, and Musical Genre* (Cambridge, Mass.: Harvard University Press, 1996). The earlier version of this project, my "Musical Life in Warsaw during Chopin's Youth, 1810–1830" (Ph.D. diss., City University of New York, 1997), provides a somewhat different but very detailed perspective on this subject. See also my "Chopin in Warsaw's Salons," *Polish Music Journal* 2 (summer 1999), www.usc.edu/dept/polish_music/PMJ/issues.html.

gate the particular circumstances of the salon scene in Warsaw and its impact on the young Fryderyk, subjects that have not yet received scholarly attention.

In view of these considerations, my overall purpose is to present and examine the rich musical environment of Chopin's youth, which is largely unknown to the English-speaking world, and to provide a historiographic perspective that allows a better understanding of Poland's cultural circumstances. I hope that this book will enhance our knowledge of Chopin's musical milieu in Poland, correct false impressions left by other writers, and lead to a richer understanding of his personality, his career, and, ultimately, the effect Warsaw's environment, the music he heard and learned in his hometown, had on the development of his musical style.

1

HISTORICAL AND CULTURAL BACKGROUND

But of those wounds that run so fresh with blood,
And of the tears that over Poland flood,
And of the glory that does yet resound,
The heart to think of these we never found. . . .
For in such torments even Valour stands
And gazes, and can only wring her hands. . . .

O Mother Poland, thou that in this hour
Art laid within the grave—what man hath power
To speak of thee today?

Adam Mickiewicz, Pan Tadeusz

Fryderyk Chopin, a child of a French immigrant father and a mother from an impoverished Polish noble family, was born in 1810 into a country with a thousand years of history and no name on the map of Europe. The two decades preceding his birth had witnessed the last chapter in the Polish tragedy: the ultimate loss of the nation's independence.[1]

Late eighteenth-century Poland was a stage of stormy and tragic political events. While Europe's attention was directed at the revolution and the advent of Napoleon in France, Poland's neighbors—Austria, Russia,

---

[1] For a detailed discussion of Polish history I recommend to the English speaker Norman Davies, *God's Playground: A History of Poland*, 2 vols. (New York: Columbia University Press, 1982). Much of my historical discussion is based on this book and on Stefan Kieniewicz, *Historia Polski 1795–1918* [A history of Poland 1795–1818] (Warsaw: Państwowe Wydawnictwo Naukowe, 1987).

and Prussia—dismembered and obliterated the historical and sovereign state of Poland. Poland, geographically surrounded by its political enemies, launched a series of desperate diplomatic and military efforts to uphold its sovereignty. But in spite of them, the destruction of an autonomous Poland could not be prevented. The territorial truncation of the country advanced in three stages: the first partition took place in 1772 and the second in 1793; the final partition, in 1795, erased the name of Poland from the map of Europe for more than a century.

At first, the region of Mazovia (*Mazowsze*), which includes Poland's capital, Warsaw, became a part of Prussia (fig. 1.2). The Prussian authorities imposed a new administration whereby in 1797 Poland became subject to the Prussian legislature (*Allgemeines Landrecht*). Under the new laws, lands belonging to king and clergy became the property of the Prussian treasury. The general policy of Germanization encouraged the assimilation of conquered territories; consequently, Polish landowners were not permitted to buy these lands. However, the Prussian government, in contrast with the Austrian authorities in the exploited and overtaxed Galicia (southern Poland), provided opportunities for economic growth in the form of well-functioning administration and accessible credit. These measures did not help much in the development of manufacturing halted by the fall of independent Poland, but they spurred a growth in agriculture, and aided by the favorable conditions during the 1801–1804 boom in grain export, mainly to England, they added to the wealth of Polish landowners.

The onset of the Prussian occupation caused a temporary crisis in Warsaw's cultural circles, but already by the year 1800 the city had returned to its status as a center of intellectual and artistic life. As a result of political events, Warsaw was deprived of the patronage that had been provided by the royal court during the Polish Enlightenment, and the Prussian authorities supplied neither organization nor financial support for cultural activities. The impetus and organizational framework for a cultural revival was instead provided by intellectuals, artists, and scientists. Concerned with the future of Polish national identity, they began numerous projects aimed at the preservation of Polish culture. Some wealthy aristocrats—most notably Józef Maksymilian Ossoliński, Tadeusz Czacki, and Izabela Czartoryska—started libraries and collections of Polish historical memorabilia. Scholars engaged in monumental undertakings such as Samuel Bogumił Linde's *Dictionary of the Polish Language* (*Słownik języka polskiego*). In 1800, wealthy, enlightened amateurs and professionals consolidated their forces through the foundation of the Society for the Friends of Learning (*Towarzystwo Przyjaciół Nauk*), which during its thirty years of existence gathered together pedagogues, scholars, scientists, artists, lawyers, physicians, and political activists. At the peak of its activities, the Society had nearly two hundred members. Meet-

Figure 1.1. Map of the Polish territories before 1772: the Polish-Lithuanian Commonwealth before the first partition.

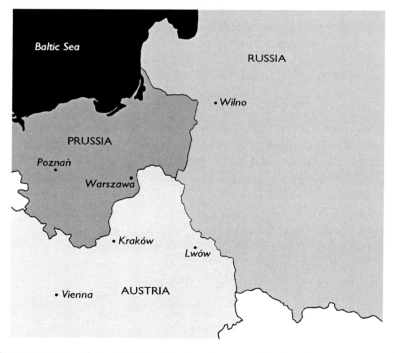

Figure 1.2. Map of the Polish territories after 1795: the Prussian occupation of Mazovia after the third partition.

ings of scientific and humanistic discussion groups took place several times in a month. The Society facilitated contact and discussion between its members and supported many cultural endeavors.

Through the initiative of Polish artists, intellectuals, aristocracy, middle class, and Prussian administration officials stationed in Warsaw, new forms of musical organization and patronage developed. In 1799, the father of the Polish theater, Wojciech Bogusławski, returned to Warsaw and energetically began reinstating the National Theater. He was soon joined by the young Józef Elsner, who was to become one of the foremost opera composers of the generation and the teacher of Chopin. Concerts and opera performances were often held in Warsaw theaters and in the palaces of the aristocracy. To provide a suitable venue for chamber and symphonic music, in 1801 the Harmonie-Gesellschaft was created, involving among its founders Elsner and the celebrated E. T. A. Hoffmann, who in the years 1804–1807 was stationed in Poland as a member of the Prussian administration. Jointly with another Warsaw musician, Father Izydor Cybulski, Elsner also began to revitalize music publishing by opening a music engraving shop in 1802.

This budding artistic life was again disrupted in the fall of 1806. The French forces that entered Warsaw in 1806 carried the promise of reestablishing a sovereign Polish state. This pledge, like many others made by Napoleon, was to remain unfulfilled. In the preceding years, he took advantage of Polish hopes by using the Polish Legions (an army of Polish émigrés created in 1797 in Italy by General Henryk Dąbrowski) against the Austrians in Italy and to fight his battles in places as distant as Haiti and Egypt. In 1807, Napoleon again used Polish soldiers, now recruited by Dąbrowski in Poland, in his campaign against Prussia. But instead of giving Poland independence, Napoleon bargained away its freedom during secret negotiations with his opponents. Some territories stayed with Prussia, Austria, and Russia; central Poland was to remain within the French sphere of influence. In June 1807, as a result of concessions made by Napoleon, a puppet Polish state known as the Duchy of Warsaw (*Księstwo Warszawskie*) was created (fig. 1.3). For Napoleon, the purpose of creating a Polish state was twofold: to gain financially from exploitation and taxation and to provide a steady supply of Polish soldiers needed for his future conquests. The duchy was to be governed by the Saxon king Frederick Augustus I, under Napoleon's supervision. This new hereditary duke of Poland, who ruled from Dresden and visited Warsaw only four times, had absolute power, tempered by the restricted participation of the Polish parliament (Sejm).

The period of the French occupation of Poland was characterized by economic, social, and political instability. The year 1809 brought a war with Austria; in 1812 the Russian campaign began, and by February 1813 the czar's army entered Warsaw. The war's devastation, migrations, and

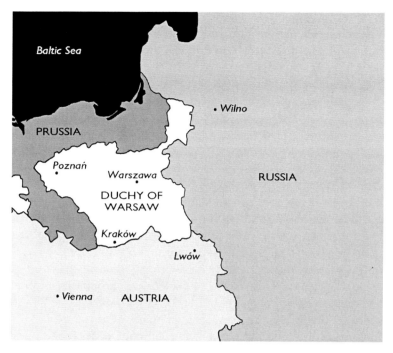

Figure 1.3. Map of the Polish Territories after 1807: the Duchy of Warsaw during the Napoleonic wars.

stagnation in industry and agriculture caused deplorable conditions in the Duchy of Warsaw. Moreover, an embargo was imposed on trade with England, affecting the export of grain and the import of colonial articles. These circumstances had a destructive effect on agriculture, but at the same time, the continental embargo and new privileges for the middle class encouraged the growth of local manufacturing and industry. Many fortunes were made and many lost.

Such economic instability did not promote cultural development. Nevertheless, the active and resolute intellectual elite in Warsaw continued their efforts to uphold Polish culture. The Society for the Friends of Learning continued its activities and in 1806 asked Julian Ursyn Niemcewicz, Poland's most cherished proto-Romantic patriotic poet, to begin work on a cycle of historical poems. During the next decade, these works, known as *Historical Chants* (*Śpiewy historyczne*), were set to music by major Polish composers and talented amateurs, becoming a formative constituent of Polish patriotic culture and providing the musical vocabulary of Polishness to the stateless Poles, starting with generation of Chopin. Steps were also taken towards the foundation of an institution of higher education in Warsaw: in 1808 the Law School was established, and a year later the Medical School followed. These institutions were the kernel of the University of Warsaw, which became the host institution for the Warsaw Conservatory, Chopin's alma mater.

The general picture of musical life did not drastically change from the preceding period, although some important developments marked these early years of Chopin's life. Kazimierz Władysław Wójcicki, a historian and an acquaintance of Chopin, reminisces that during these years Warsaw "was transforming from an ancient Mazowsze capital of sovereign Mazovian dukes into a city modeled after other larger European cities, taking on a new shape, new clothes."[2] These new trends had also an impact on Warsaw's musical scene, as Elsner reported to the *Allgemeine musikalische Zeitung*: "Since Warsaw again enjoys the splendor of a capital, we have heard more than a few of the greatest virtuosi of our time."[3] In addition to foreign virtuosi, Warsaw began to witness the influx of native talent. In 1810, the twenty-one-year-old Maria Wołowska (soon to be Szymanowska) returned from Paris. During her short-lived marriage, she seldom performed in concert, but was often heard in Warsaw's salons. She stayed in the Polish capital until 1822 and, after her separation from her husband, appeared increasingly in public performances.[4] Also in 1810, Warsaw welcomed Franciszek Lessel, who returned to Warsaw after having spent several years in Vienna studying with Haydn. He immediately began an active musical career, which involved composition, public concerts, teaching, and conducting.[5] Although a few years later he left professional musical life, he never ceased to compose and participate in musical events.

With the support of a growing bourgeois class and some backing from the authorities, Warsaw's theaters grew stronger. Bogusławski and Elsner were soon joined in their ceaseless efforts to maintain and strengthen the Polish national stage by the young Karol Kurpiński. Kurpiński, who had also arrived in Warsaw in 1810, was hired with the help of Elsner as a choir coach at the National Theater. The young, energetic musician quickly became known as a composer, pedagogue, musical activist, and writer.[6]

[2] Kazimierz Władysław Wójcicki, *Społeczność Warszawy w początkach naszego stulecia* [Warsaw's society in the beginning of our century] (Warsaw: Gebethner i Wolff, 1877), 101. All translations are mine, unless otherwise indicated.

[3] *Allgemeine musikalische Zeitung*, July 1811, 451.

[4] Igor Bełza, *Maria Szymanowska*, trans. Jadwiga Ilnicka (Kraków: Polskie Wydawnictwo Muzyczne, 1987), 36–38.

[5] Państwowa Wyższa Szkoła Muzyczna w Gdańsku, *Franciszek Lessel: W 200 rocznicę urodzin kompozytora* [Franciszek Lessel: on the 200th anniversary of the composer's birth] (Gdańsk: Państwowa Wyższa Szkoła Muzyczna, 1980), 54–55.

[6] Agnieszka Lisowska, "Karol Kurpiński jako pisarz, działacz i organizator muzyczny w Warszawie" [Karol Kurpiński as a musical writer, activist and organizer in Warsaw], in *Szkice*

At the same time, Elsner and Bogusławski were working on the initiative to create a "singing school" at the National Theater. In April 1810, their proposal was accepted in a royal decree issued by Frederick Augustus in Dresden. The Drama School, as it was called, was opened in 1811 and underwent many organizational changes, emerging in 1821 as the Institute of Music and Declamation (also known as the Conservatory or the Main School of Music). It is here that during the years 1826–1829 Chopin received his professional musical education. Thus, the years of Chopin's infancy, regardless of political and economical instability, witnessed vital developments in Warsaw's cultural life.

The "Polish problem" was settled during the Vienna Congress in 1814 with a lack of concern for Polish claims that was typical of the great European powers. After the 1813 war, most of the Polish territories were held by Russia, and Czar Alexander I would have preferred to keep these lands under his rule. The other members of the Vienna Congress were in strong opposition to the czar's plans, hoping to limit his political and territorial power. By the beginning of 1815, a compromise was reached. The territory of Poland was again divided between Austria, Prussia, and Russia. But the return of Napoleon to France created a new scenario with the possibility of a new war, and in order to assure Polish support, Poland's claims to sovereignty had to be somehow addressed. On May 3, 1815, the Congress Kingdom (*Kongresówka*) (also known as the Polish Kingdom, *Królestwo Polskie*) was created: a tiny state with an independent administration, constitution, and parliament, ruled by the czar and his viceroy. Warsaw became a part of the Congress Kingdom under Russian rule (fig. 1.4).

Theoretically, the constitution was among the most liberal in Europe. It provided voting rights to over a hundred thousand people, assured a separate Polish government and army, maintained Polish as the official language, and guaranteed citizens personal freedom, inviolability of property, and freedom of the press. The czar was to remain the ruler of Poland, with full legislative power, including the right to veto parliament's decisions and to nominate all major political and administrative dignitaries. He chose as his viceroy General Józef Zajączek, but the true power remained in the hands of two Russians: the czar's brother, Grand Duke Constantine, and a St. Petersburg reactionary named Nikola Novosil'cov. By giving his brother the unofficial rule of Poland, Alexander removed him from power in St. Petersburg. He was given the position of chief of Polish armed forces, which he used and abused to prevent any ac-

---

o kulturze muzycznej XIX wieku [Essays on the musical culture of the nineteenth century], ed. Zofia Chechlińska (Warsaw: Państwowe Wydawnictwo Muzyczne, 1973), 2:181–231.

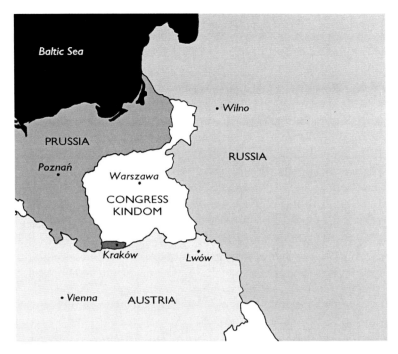

Figure 1.4. Map of the Polish territories after 1815: the Congress Kingdom after the Congress of Vienna.

tivities aimed at Poland's independence. Novosil'cov's function of "imperial plenipotentiary" (*Cesarski Pełnomocnik*) was not provided for by the constitution. He was placed in Warsaw in order to actively prepare the ground for the destruction of Polish independence. Thus, in practice the Russian authorities constantly violated the liberal Polish constitution.

The few elements of autonomy maintained in the Congress Kingdom before 1831 were eagerly used by the Poles to rebuild the country. These freedoms resulted in spirited development of the economy, improvement and increase in the number of institutions of higher education, and the strengthening of Warsaw's cultural life.

The economy of the Congress Kingdom was now recovering from the destruction of previous years. Agriculture was returning to life very slowly, although the government attempted to alleviate the crisis through financial initiatives and minor reforms. More significant changes took place in manufacturing. The development of textile and heavy industries was encouraged by the availability of credit, favorable taxes and custom duties, demand for locally produced goods, and the presence of inexpensive labor provided by recently freed peasants. As a result, cities grew in size and splendor, as did the new bourgeois class. New structures of city life created a demand for young educated people to serve in administrative positions or to enter free professions, causing a rapid increase in the ranks of the Polish intelligentsia.

Warsaw's educational system met these new needs with the creation of several important institutions. In 1816, the University of Warsaw was formed. To the already existing schools of law and medicine, three new divisions were added: sciences and fine arts, theology, and philosophy. Initially, musical education was obtainable in the School of Drama, which in 1821—renamed the Music Conservatory—became associated with the university. In addition, Warsaw had several technical schools, and in 1830 a Polytechnic Institute opened, the first such institution in Poland. The government, through the Chamber of Education, supervised a network of secular high schools and a less-developed system of elementary education. On November 1, 1810, Mikołaj Chopin, the composer's father, began his work as a teacher of French language and literature at the capital's most prestigious high school, the Warsaw Gymnasium. Given this job opportunity, he brought his family to the capital, thus placing the eight-month-old Fryderyk in the very heart of Polish intellectual and artistic life.

The intellectuals, artists, and activists who gathered in Warsaw supported the renaissance of Polish national culture. The originally small group of members of the Society for the Friends of Learning was greatly enlarged after the creation of the university. By 1830, it had fifty-seven active members, most of whom were professors at the university. In addition, there were thirty-five surrogate members, eighty-five local and foreign correspondents, and thirty-five foreign honorary members.[7] Scholarly research was now facilitated through the existence of several book collections, especially the new Public Library at the University of Warsaw and the collection of the Society for the Friends of Learning. Many local printers published Polish and foreign books, including an increasing number of musical publications. The number of newspapers grew in the years 1815–1830 from two to seven.

In May 1820, Kurpiński began the publication of a magazine devoted exclusively to music, the *Musical Weekly* (*Tygodnik Muzyczny*). It had a rather difficult existence (including a two-month interruption during November–December 1820) and survived for only slightly over a year, but it initiated several aesthetic and historical discussions, as well as professional musical criticism in Poland. Much of the discussion in the *Musical Weekly* centered around theater, especially opera—not very surprisingly, since this institution created by Bogusławski and Elsner attracted

---

[7] Wójcicki, *Społeczność Warszawy w początkach naszego stulecia*, 64–67.

the entire musical elite of Warsaw. Audience size increased and included newcomers: intelligentsia, students, merchants, even the more affluent craftsmen and servants.

The culture of Warsaw was dominated by two competing philosophical trends: rationalism and idealism. Several members of the older generation who embraced the rationalist philosophy were all overshadowed by the legendary, learned philosopher Stanisław Staszic, who embodied every idea of the Enlightenment. He was a friend of the French Encyclopedists, a naturalist, a geologist, a poet and translator, a politician, and a state minister, one of the founders of the Society for Friends of Learning and of the University of Warsaw, and an ardent supporter of the French Revolution. He was also a philanthropist, who supported the needy—who with his own savings purchased an estate and later gave it to the local people for self-governing while he himself led a very modest life. In his will he declared: "A man's main destiny on this earth is to do good unto people; to aim through the deeds of his entire life at improving the welfare of his kin, the welfare of other people; even to strive for the beneficial consequences of the deeds that he performed in his life to continue making future generations happy."[8] The philosophical concepts expressed in the treatises of Staszic, Hugo Kołłątaj and Jan Śniadecki saw reason and laws of nature as the basis of knowledge, morality, and progress. They were supported by poets and writers headed by Ludwik Osiński and Kajetan Koźmian, who strove to preserve the Classical tradition, as well as by Freemasons, who involved almost the entire Warsaw intellectual and artistic elite—Chopin's teacher, Elsner, among them.

The young intelligentsia were influenced by new trends coming from the West: the breaking away from calcified forms of art and the primacy of emotion over reason. Already the turn of the century saw translations of Dante, Lope de Vega, and Shakespeare into Polish. Soon the poetry of Goethe, Schiller, and Byron, the prose of Sir Walter Scott, and the philosophy of Herder and Schelling brought into Poland the seeds of Romanticism. Although the older generation attacked the young artists for returning to the Dark Ages and feudalism, the younger generation understood the new trends as a way of expressing their trust in common people, their defense of Polish nationality, and yearning for freedom.

The roots of Polish Romanticism can be traced as far back as the 1780s, well before the debate reached the Warsaw circles and was expressed in public forums. During the late eighteenth century, the principal proponent of the new aesthetics was Princess Izabela Czartoryska, whose

---

[8] Wielisław [Eugeniusz Skrodzki], *Wieczory piątkowe i inne gawędy* [Friday evenings and other tales], ed. M. Opałek (Warsaw: Państwowy Instytut Wydawniczy, 1962), 286.

own sensibilities made her rebel against Neoclassical attitudes. With a full awareness of opposing the prevailing aesthetics, she remodeled the splendid gardens around her Puławy residence in the Romantic English style, later explaining the conceptual and formal considerations behind this new taste in a published treatise on gardening. The Gothic House (*Dom Gotycki*), built on her estate from architectural parts gathered from all over the world and housing priceless artwork and manuscripts, was in its very concept a Romantic collection of fragments; the Temple of the Sibyl (*Świątynia Sybilli*), on the other hand, became a repository of national mementoes, crucial in the construction of a collective Polish national memory. The princess also gathered medieval poetry, recorded her own responses to reading *Werther* and Ossian, and enthusiastically defended the timeless genius of Shakespeare.

During the first years after the Vienna Congress, the Romantic tendencies became even more pronounced, with the debate moving into the public eye. The primary forum for the newest European intellectual trends, and thus the debate on Romanticism, became the *Warsaw Diary* (*Pamiętnik Warszawski*), a new periodical established in 1815 by the history professor Feliks Bentkowski, whose lectures Chopin later attended. The assessment of Shakespeare's legacy became the primary battleground. Among the most vocal proponents of the new trends, advocating the primacy of emotion over reason and contents over form, were Franciszek Wężyk, a writer, and Kazimierz Brodziński, an influential young poet and professor of literature, who later was Chopin's professor at the university. The most eloquent repudiation of Romantic irrationality was presented in 1818 by Jan Śniadecki, mathematician and philosopher at the University of Warsaw. After the publication of Adam Mickiewicz's first Romantic volume in 1822, the quiet discussions between representatives of the Classical and Romantic schools of thought transformed into an open conflict that lasted until 1830. Some more progressive members of the Society for the Friends of Learning made efforts to create a middle ground between the battling parties. Niemcewicz, whose writings and translations inspired Polish Romanticism, attempted to mediate the conflict.[9] The gentle Brodziński also did his best to calm down the bitter battles by conveying to the public the important idea that "beauty is indifferent to the cut of the clothing it is made to wear, and the poet must draw inspiration from the heavens, not from the academic pulpit."[10]

The first poems of Adam Mickiewicz, which stirred up much commotion on their publication in 1822–1823, were saturated with new Romantic aesthetic and moral values, as well as revolutionary language. The

[9] Wójcicki, *Społeczność Warszawy w początkach naszego stulecia*, 61–63.
[10] Wielisław, *Wieczory piątkowe i inne gawędy*, 100–101.

young intelligentsia responded to these works with great enthusiasm and delighted in their subtle political undertones. In private and public forums, Mickiewicz, Edward Odyniec, and Chopin's friends Stefan Witwicki and Maurycy Mochnacki defended their vision of art; the entire youth of Warsaw was captured in the whirl of new ideas: "everything that breathed of novelty and audacity was sought after and gladly accepted."[11] The most direct declaration of the new style arrived in Mickiewicz's response to Śniadecki's 1818 critique. The young bard replied with a ballad entitled "Romanticism" (*Romantyczność*), in which a woman's conversations with the invisible ghost of her dead lover are regarded as signs of madness by the wise man, while the simple folk with awe recognize her ability to see into the realm of the spirit. The poem, headed by a motto from Shakespeare's *Hamlet:* "Methinks I see . . . where? In my mind's eye," encapsulated Romantic aesthetics in the words

> Feeling and faith speak to me more strongly
> Than a wise man's looking glass and eye.

And its last line—"Have a heart and look into the heart"—became a Romantic manifesto opening and closing every conversation about Polish poetry.[12] Andrzej Koźmian, Chopin's older colleague at the gymnasium and the university, summarizes these emotions in his memoirs:

> Today, this unconditional adoration of all youths for the author of *Forefathers' Eve* [Mickiewicz] can be easily explained and understood; already then he had sung his hurrahs and apotheosis of youth. This admirer of Youth conquered all young people by indulging their tempestuous nature; prophesying that the Leyden jar was about to explode, he became their leader and worshipped bard.[13]

Chopin was right in the midst of the debate; among the gymnasium and university professors, artists, musicians, poets, and cultural activists of the older generation on the one side and the enthusiastic, fierce gymnasium, university, and conservatory students, young poets, and influential young teachers on the other. He had a deep love and respect for the great figures of the Enlightenment he was privileged to know. Although it is not known whether Fryderyk actually met the legendary Staszic, his

---

[11] Andrzej Edward Koźmian, *Wspomnienia* [Memoirs], 2 vols. (Poznań: Letgeber, 1867), 2:68.

[12] Kazimierz Władysław Wójcicki, *Warszawa, jej życie umysłowe i ruch literacki 1800–1830* [Warsaw: Its literary and intellectual life 1800–1830] (Warsaw: Gebethner i Wolff, 1880), 174–177.

[13] Koźmian, *Memoirs*, 2:47.

reverence for this great man is apparent in his report, describing the philosopher's funeral in a letter, "that out of love and enthusiasm his coffin [cover] was torn off, and that I also have as a memento a piece of pall, with which the bier was covered; finally, that twenty thousand people accompanied the remains to [its] destination.[14] His father and his older mentors, Elsner in particular, bequeathed to him the intellectual legacy of the Age of Reason. These ideals never quite left him: in his last days in Paris, he was reported to have been reading Voltaire. More significantly, the compositional principles Elsner taught him continued to shape and mediate his lifelong search for new forms of musical expression.

But the young composer also responded to the new trends. Already in 1826, at the university, he attended lectures by the two academics central to the propagation of the Romantic aesthetics: the historian Feliks Bentkowski and the very much loved literature professor Kazimierz Brodziński.[15] Another young professor, Romuald Hube—a restless, adventurous spirit—was a friend and mentor of the young Fryderyk, mentioned by him in several letters. Hube's unbridled opinions, for instance, "that a man can achieve nothing in the customary way and according to a plan devised by himself; one must leave something to chance,"[16] surely left a mark on the impressionable youth. Among his slightly older peers were Mochnacki, Zaleski, and Witwicki, who by 1825 became central to the propagation of Romanticism. The imprint left on Chopin by the multitalented Maurycy Mochnacki must have been staggering: he was one of the core conspirators of the November Uprising and a journalist who with dazzling eloquence championed Romantic poetry and new philosophies of music, while promoting most recent operas and Chopin's earliest public performances. Stefan Witwicki and Józef Bohdan Zaleski, authors of several Romantic poems set by Chopin, were among Chopin's earliest followers and lifelong friends. Their ardent Romanticism must have been an important influence on him. After the November Uprising, they all immigrated to Paris and continued to exert influence on him, as evidenced by letters in which he was reminded not to stray from the new principles of art.[17]

In the Romantic–Classical debate, Chopin declared himself through his music on the Romantic side. In 1829, he composed song settings of

[14] Fryderyk Chopin, Warsaw, to Jan Białobłocki, Biskupiec, 12 February 1826, in *Koresspondencja Fryderyka Chopina* [Fryderyk Chopin's correspondence], ed. Bronisław Edward Sydow, 2 vols. (Warsaw: Państwowy Instytut Wydawniczy, 1955), 1:63.

[15] Chopin, Warsaw, to Białobłocki, Sokołów, 2 November [October] [1926], *Korespondencja*, 1:73.

[16] Chopin, Vienna, to his family, Warsaw, 12 August 1829, *Korespondencja*, 1:94.

[17] Stefan Witwicki, Warsaw, to Fryderyk Chopin, Vienna, 6 July 1831, *Korespondencja*, 1:179–180.

Romantic poems, which very quickly traveled through the country and gained tremendous popularity.[18] Like the other young Romantics, he sought new, free forms of expression and turned to poetry, literature, and tradition for inspiration. Oskar Kolberg, younger brother of Chopin's friend Wilhelm, wrote later on in the century:

> It was a time of Romantic awakening in literature, and Music did not hesitate to pursue its sister, Poetry, which boldly hastened toward the zenith of its excellence. Nourished by such forces of nature, as inspired as the most superb bards of the time, to whose thoughts and feelings he tuned his lyre, Chopin emerged, the coryphaeus and representative of this musical epoch, though devoted exclusively to the piano.[19]

Romanticism, sweeping through all of Europe, took on specifically local features in Poland. Given the tragic political circumstances of the enslaved nation, Romanticism became both the means to recapture the heroic past and the prelude to a future armed revolt. The quintessentially Romantic notions—for instance, representations of memory and of idyllic space and time—served, above all, to construct Polishness. Often, they became conceptually intertwined with Slavophilism, most loosely defined as "the love of Slavdom," and the specifically Polish variety of political messianism—the belief that the crucified Poland will be resurrected, its sacrifice bringing about universal salvation.[20] Old noble traditions were eagerly preserved to be woven into a collective memory of an idyllic past. As part of this trend, the Romantics restored interest in Sarmatism, the belief that Polish nobility descended from the ancient Asian people of Sarmatia. The representatives of the Enlightenment vehemently rejected Sarmatism as hindering progress, but Chopin's generation viewed manifestations of the Sarmatian past with increasing nostalgia, as in Mic-

[18] Wójcicki, *Warszawa*, 168. Chopin's songs were only published posthumously by Fontana as op. 74, but Wójcicki's claim about some of them circulating and gaining popularity in Poland during Chopin's life is corroborated by other sources. For instance, his very early song "Merrymaking" (*Hulanka*) was published in Poznań with a new patriotic text by Stanisław Hernisz well before Breitkopf & Härtel's posthumous publication. Biblioteka Kórnicka Polskiej Akademii Nauk, Kórnik. Photo, Muzeum Fryderyka Chopina w Towarzystwie im. Fryderyka Chopina, Warszawa, F. 1625.

[19] Oskar Kolberg, *Dzieła wszystkie Oskara Kolberga* [The complete works of Oskar Kolberg], ed. J. Krzyżanowski, 86 vols., *Pisma muzyczne* [Music writings] part II, ed. M. Tomaszewski, O. Pawlak, and E. Miller (Wrocław: Polskie Towarzystwo Ludoznawcze; Warszawa: Ludowa Spółdzielnia Wydawnicza; Kraków: Polskie Wydawnictwo Muzyczne, 1981), 62:379.

[20] For a detailed discussion of messianic contexts for Chopin's music see Halina Goldberg, "'Remembering That Tale of Grief': The Prophetic Voice in Chopin's Music," in *The Age of Chopin: Interdisciplinary Inquiries*, ed. Goldberg (Bloomington: Indiana University Press, 2004), 54–92.

kiewicz's celebrated epic poem *Pan Tadeusz* or Wójcicki's recollections of older noblemen in the traditional Sarmatic attire of Polish nobility, *kontusz* and *żupan*, often accompanied by a sword—in particular, a memorable gathering of such characters in 1829.[21] Musical customs delineating this constructed idyllic past, the polonaise in particular, were treated with the same reverence. Wójcicki reminisces that although new fashions had entered the capital's life, every ball started with the traditional polonaise. According to him, sometimes, in the homes of old families, one could witness a polonaise danced in the old, ceremonial manner, with the men dressed in the traditional garb.[22] When Mickiewicz, in his *Pan Tadeusz*, written in his Parisian exile during the 1830s, recalls "the land of childhood! That shall aye endure as holly as a first love and as pure,"[23] it is the polonaise that embodies the idyllic and proud Poland.

> "Perhaps he is the last—you may not see, young men,
> Such leading of the polonaise again!"
> The pairs proceed in turn with merry noise,
> The ring contracts and then again deploys,
> As when the folds of a huge serpent curl,
> The varied colours of the dresses whirl
> Of ladies, soldiers, gentlemen, and gleam
> Like golden scales lit by the sunset's beam,
> Against the quilted darkness of the ground,
> On goes the dance and shouts and toasts resound![24]

The young people who barely remembered past events grew up with stories about the splendor of old Poland and the brave deeds of Polish soldiers fighting at the side of Napoleon.[25] *Pan Tadeusz* epitomizes this nostalgic reverence for the idealized past. Perhaps the most moving event of entire epic is the lengthy poetic account of Jankiel's dulcimer concert. In

[21] Wójcicki, *Społeczność Warszawy w początkach naszego stulecia*, 155. *Kontusz* and *żupan* constituted the orientalized, two-layered, brightly colored traditional attire of the Polish nobility. The *żupan* was a light under-caftan. The long outer garment, the *kontusz*, consisted of a single oblong piece of fabric with two side-panels. Slits in the inside arms were used to throw back the sleeves. This attire, in the winter lined with fur, was worn with a richly embroidered belt and often with a traditional Polish sword. On Sarmatism in Polish culture see Stanisław Grzybowski, *Sarmatyzm* (Warsaw: Krajowa Agencja Wydawnicza, 1996) and Andrzej Waśko, *Romantyczny Sarmatyzm: Tradycja szlachecka w literaturze polskiej lat 1831–1863* [Romantic Sarmatism: the noble tradition in Polish literature] (Kraków: Wydawnictwo Arcana, 2001).

[22] Wójcicki, *Społeczność Warszawy w początkach naszego stulecia*, 151.

[23] Mickiewicz, *Pan Tadeusz* [Master Thaddeus], trans. Kenneth R. Mackenzie (New York: Hippocrene Books, Inc., 1992), 582.

[24] Mickiewicz, *Pan Tadeusz*, 570.

[25] Wójcicki, *Społeczność Warszawy w początkach naszego stulecia*, 81–97.

this acclaimed and powerful scene, taking place sometime in 1811–1812, through an emotionally charged musical improvisation, the old Jewish musician retells the most recent history of Poland, starting with the loss of sovereignty and concluding with the recollection of the Napoleonic campaigns and "The Hymn of General Dąbrowski's Polish Legions":

> The Master raised his pitch and changed the strain.
> He, looking down once more, the strings surveyed,
> And, joining hands, with both the hammers played:
> Each blow was struck so deftly and so hard,
> That all the strings like brazen trumpets blared,
> And from the trumpets to the heavens sped
> That march of triumph: *Poland is not dead!*
> *Dąbrowski, march to Poland!* With one accord
> They clapped their hands, and 'March Dąbrowski!' roared.[26]

Wójcicki, who retells many tales from the past, concludes: "There came new times, new people, but the tradition of the great epic from the time of Napoleon I survived in vivid colors, passing from father to son."[27] Such stories about times gone were told in the homes of Chopin's friends and mentors, and they may also have been also recounted in the Chopin household. Out of these memories, the Romantics created a repository of patriotic culture.

The songs written on Niemcewicz's *Historical Chants* were vastly popular throughout the nineteenth century, though later their patriotic power faded; "The Hymn of General Dąbrowski's Polish Legions," however, remained among principal patriotic tunes, and after Poland regained independence it became (and continues to serve as) the national anthem. Already during Chopin's childhood, these and other patriotic songs were woven into the fabric of music heard at homes and churches, at the opera, and even in the concert hall. They remained central to Chopin's patriotic improvisations throughout his life and the national reception of his music for the succeeding generations.[28] Similarly, Mickiewicz's *Pan Tadeusz* remained at the core of the imagined national memory well into the twentieth century. This lasting influence of the Romantic patriotic impulse is borne out by images in a series of allegorical postcards issued in Kraków in 1911. The two shown here portray Mickiewicz and Chopin surrounded by national allegories of their works: the poet witnessing

[26] Mickiewicz, *Pan Tadeusz*, 568.

[27] Wójcicki, *Społeczność Warszawy w początkach naszego stulecia*, 97.

[28] On the role of patriotic tunes in Chopin's music see Mieczysław Tomaszewski, Muzyka Chopina na nowo odczytana [Chopin's music read anew] (Kraków: Akademia Muzyczna, 1996) and Goldberg, "'Remembering That Tale of Grief.'"

Figure 1.5. "Mickiewicz: Jankiel's Concert." Postcard. Ser. 95, no. 3 (Kraków: Wydawnictwo Salonu Malarzy Polskich, 1911). Author's collection.

Jankiel's improvisation as it evokes the spirits of Poland's glorious past (fig. 1.5), and the composer calling forth the memories of fallen Poland with his Funeral March from op. 35 (fig. 1.6).

The patriotic tales so cherished in the early years of the nineteenth century had a profound effect on the susceptible minds of Polish youth. The living national consciousness, impressed by increasing acts of repression and stimulated by the defiance inherent in the new cultural

Figure 1.6. "Chopin: Funeral March." Postcard. Ser. 95, no. 7 (Kraków: Wydawnictwo Salonu Malarzy Polskich, 1911). Author's collection.

trends, resulted in the escalation of covert political activities. Among the students of Warsaw, the more politically active (including Chopin's closest friends) gathered in about twenty secret organizations. Some of them consisted of a few members and existed independently; others had a wide network of groups with a definite political goal. Russian authorities, led by Novosil'cov, carefully observed these organizations, and during the 1820s arrested and severely punished many activists, among them Maurycy Mochnacki and Adam Mickiewicz, who was penalized for his political involvement with exile to Russia. Political activities were also taking place under the cover of the Masonic movement. Freemasonry was tolerated and even favored by Alexander I, but in Poland it took the shape of the National Freemasons, a military conspiracy created in 1819. The alert Russian secret police became aware of these activities, and in 1822 the authorities prohibited all secret organizations, including Masonic lodges. With the accession to the Russian throne of Czar Nicholas I in 1825, further restrictions were imposed on Poland's autonomy. These constant acts of harassment led to social unrest, culminating in the November Uprising of 1830. The repercussions were severe. After the Russian victory, Poland lost the privileges and autonomy it had enjoyed during the years 1815–1830, never to regain them until the creation of the independent Polish state in 1918.

By the time the November Uprising began, Fryderyk Chopin had already left his homeland, not knowing that he would never return. From Vienna he wrote to Jan Matuszyński:

> Write to me. You are in the army! Is she [his beloved Konstancja Gładkowska] in Radom? Did you dig barricades? Our poor parents. What are my friends doing? I live with you. I could die for you, for all of you. Why am I so abandoned today? Are you only allowed to be together in such a ghastly moment [?][29]

Living in exile, he carried with him the earnest memories of his youth, not only during the emotionally charged period of the Uprising but also for the rest of his life. He remained very closely involved with the Polish exiles in Paris, many of whom were friends and acquaintances of his youth, and he continued creating music that was born out of the traditions in which he was reared.

[29] Chopin, Vienna, to Jan Matuszyński, Warsaw, 1 January 1831, *Korespondencja*, 1:169–170.

2

INSTRUMENT PRODUCTION

"Everywhere one goes, [one finds] Leszczyński's deplorable instruments," complained Chopin in his 1828 letter to Tytus Woyciechowski.[1] This well-known comment about Polish-built instruments and Chopin's later preference for Pleyel pianos created a dismal image of instrument production in Poland. It is less well known that Chopin's statement about Leszczyński is only a part of a sentence that continues: "since I haven't seen a single one that came close in sound to your sister's pantaleon [grand piano] or to ours."[2] Here Chopin clearly states a preference for his own instruments, of which at least one was a Polish-built Buchholtz.

Contrary to negative impressions about the state of instrument making in Chopin's Poland, the Congress Kingdom had a respectable—though small by comparison with Vienna, Paris, or London—musical instrument industry. Locally produced instruments were of varied qualities: custom-built superior exemplars for the discriminating connoisseur were offered by some highly skilled local makers, several of whom had worked abroad in Germany, Belgium, France, and the United States;[3] other

[1] Fryderyk Chopin, Warsaw, to Tytus Woyciechowski, Poturzyn, 27 December 1828, in *Korespondencja Fryderyka Chopina* [Fryderyk Chopin's correspondence], ed. Bronisław Edward Sydow, 2 vols. (Warsaw: Państwowy Instytut Wydawniczy, 1955), 1:87.

[2] Chopin, Warsaw, to Woyciechowski, Poturzyn, 27 December 1828, *Korespondencja*, 1:87.

[3] An interesting case is that of a Warsaw inventor, Karl Gröl. According to Antoni Magier, it was Gröl who sold his design of a harp with the modern pedal system to Erard, who began producing such instruments in 1820; *Estetyka miasta stołecznego Warszawy* [The aesthetics of the capital city of Warsaw] (1830 manuscript), ed. Hanna Szwankowska (Wrocław: Wydawnictwo Ossolińskich, 1963), 246. These quite expensive harps were then

builders produced large quantities of mediocre instruments suitable for middle-class amateurs. The needs of the new marketplace encouraged rapid developments in instrument production: by the early nineteenth century, musical skills were considered a necessary component of a good education, not just for the aristocracy but also for the emerging middle class. A number of instruments were favored by the domestic music-making market: in the first years of the century, young women played the English guitar (a cittern with six courses of metal strings); later the harp was still favored, and at the same time the piano began its remarkable ascendancy. Men were more likely to play the violin, flute, French horn, or cello; Spanish and English guitars were also considered appropriate for men.

The forces of industrialization that shaped European economies during the nineteenth century had a profound effect on the art of instrument making. Poland, like other countries, experienced intermediate stages between craft and mass production. At the beginning of the century, the ancient system was still intact. Existing records suggest that instrument makers did not have a separate guild but most likely belonged to larger guilds. After the creation of the Congress Kingdom, favorable customs and tariffs created a new industrial market that positively influenced instrument production. To further encourage growth, the government issued several rulings pertaining to the education of a skilled work force and modernization of the old system of production. The most important ruling pertained to the creation of craftsmen's assemblies in place of the old guilds. The Assembly of Organmasters gathered together luthiers as well as organ and piano builders. Trumpet makers and builders of other wind instruments at first belonged to the Assembly of Turners but later formed their own organization; in the second part of the century, they joined the Assembly of Organmasters, which continued to exist until World War I.[4] During the period under consideration, the number of in-

---

imported to Poland from England in large quantities to satisfy the new fashion. Wielisław [Eugeniusz Skrodzki], *Wieczory piątkowe i inne gawędy* [Friday evenings and other tales], ed. M. Opałek (Warsaw: Państwowy Instytut Wydawniczy, 1962), 114.

[4] The purpose of the assemblies was to set standards for, and provide education within, the apprentice system (which included practical training and basic reading and writing skills), to provide job placement for young journeymen, and to settle disputes. Unlike the old guilds, the assemblies could not control prices of manufactured goods, bar the sale of finished products, or restrict the formations of manufactures or factories (whose owners and workers were not required to join the assembly but could not train and certify masters). The system of assemblies, which served mainly to destroy the monopoly of guilds, to facilitate new methods of production, and to encourage new industrial enterprises, remained intact until the formation of trade unions in the last part of the nineteenth century. This and much other factual information concerning instrument production is based on Beniamin

struments makers' workshops and factories (these terms were used rather loosely and interchangeably in the early industrial setting) steadily increased. By 1828, the Congress Kingdom had seventy-two factories, mostly in Warsaw, in addition to 369 certified builders working in the capital and various centers around the kingdom.[5] The factories employed about ten workers; smaller workshops consisted of a master and two to three apprentices or journeymen.[6]

Among Warsaw's instrument workshops, about ten belonged to luthiers.[7] Their production was small, and they could not compete for the popular market with its inferior yet inexpensive imports from the new centers of mass production. But the professional musician continued to require a quality that could be provided only by a master builder, and such marked the production of the Warsaw's workshops. Warsaw's luthiers, continuing a long and rich history of violin making in Poland,[8] built excellent bowed instruments and bows based on old-Italian models. However, it was the production of plucked instruments, mainly the fashionable guitar, that sustained the industry in the first part of the nineteenth century.

In the beginning of the century, when only the most affluent homes had a piano, the metal-stringed English guitar was the most popular instrument, found in almost every cultured household. After 1808, the larger and differently stringed Spanish guitar came to be preferred for accompaniment, but only for men; women continued to use the light, elegant English instrument.[9] During the second quarter of the century, the

---

Vogel, *Instrumenty muzyczne w kulturze Królestwa Polskiego: Przemysł muzyczny w latach 1815–1918* [Musical instruments in the culture of the Congress Kingdom: Music industry during the years 1815–1918] (Kraków: Polskie Wydawnictwo Muzyczne, 1980), and *Fortepian polski* [The Polish piano] (Warsaw: Sutkowski Edition, 1995). Invaluable research concerning the history of the organ in Poland is found in Jerzy Gołos, *Zarys historii budowy organów w Polsce* [A historical outline of organ building in Poland] (Bydgoszcz: Bydgoskie Towarzystwo Naukowe, 1966), *Polskie organy i muzyka organowa* [The Polish organ and organ music] (Warsaw: Pax, 1972), and *The Polish Organ,* vol. 1, *The Instrument and Its History,* trans. Barbara Dejlidko (Warsaw: Sutkowski Edition, 1993). I am indebted to both Vogel and Gołos for suggestions they made about this chapter.

[5] Archiwum Główne Akt Dawnych, Biblioteka Ordynacji Zamoyskich 97, Warsaw: *Kalendarz domowy i gospodarski 1831* [Home and farm calendar 1831] (Warsaw: 1830), 29, quoted in Vogel, *Instrumenty muzyczne,* 100.

[6] Vogel, *Fortepian polski,* 58.

[7] Vogel, *Instrumenty muzyczne,* 50.

[8] See Tyrone Greive, "A Look at the Violin in 16th- and 17th-Century Poland," *Journal of the Violin Making Society of America* 11/1 (1991): 117–142.

[9] Kazimierz Władysław Wójcicki, *Warszawa, jej życie umysłowe i ruch literacki 1800– 1830* [Warsaw: Its literary and intellectual life 1800–1830] (Warsaw: Gebethner i Wolff, 1880), 188.

two kinds of guitar continued to coexist, assuming discernibly different functions: "The quiet tones, lower tuning and lush chords of the Spanish guitar accompany singing and satisfactorily support the human voice; the English guitar plays more substantial pieces."[10]

Among the string instrument builders, the best guitar makers were Jan Baranowski and the Czech-born Antoni Weinert; Piotr Janicki was famous for bows comparable in quality to Parisian bows; but the best craftsman was Henryk Rudert I, a son and father of Warsaw's luthiers, who started his professional career in 1828. Rudert was a son of a mediocre Saxon instrument maker who settled in Warsaw before 1821. In addition to an apprenticeship in his father's shop, he studied the violin at the Conservatory with Józef Bielawski. He was also a good guitarist and violist, often participating in chamber performances in Warsaw's salons, and in the 1840s noted as a member of the National Theater's orchestra.[11] Yet he deserves most to be remembered as a builder of beautifully crafted string instruments, carved or inlaid with wood, silver, and ivory, highly praised in Poland and abroad for their beautiful and rich tone.

The gut strings for these instruments were also produced in Warsaw. A large portion of the market was supplied by Henryk Rudert's father, Johann Michael, and his other son, Johann Michael II, though the largest supplier was the Fiorentini factory.[12] The Fiorentini strings (made of gut and later also silk) were of high quality, and their production was large enough to export to the Russian Empire.

The main problem posed by the construction of wind instruments at the beginning of the nineteenth century pertained to the availability of the full chromatic scale. Several inventors experimented with mechanical systems of keys in the woodwinds and valves in brass instruments. Polish artisans were abreast of the newest inventions from abroad, and did not hesitate to experiment on their own. Gołębiowski, a historian of Warsaw contemporary with Chopin, for example, names a Jan Miller who removed the most significant faults of the clarinet by introducing thirteen comfortable keys.[13]

The production of wind instruments in the Congress Kingdom was rather small at the beginning of the century. The few Warsaw craftsmen could not sustain their businesses from instrument production only and

---

[10] Łukasz Gołębiowski, *Gry i zabawy różnych stanów* [Games and amusements of various classes] (Warsaw: Glücksberg, 1831), 234.

[11] Vogel, *Instrumenty muzyczne*, 201–203.

[12] The factory was managed by three generations of craftsmen: first by Baltasaro and his son Giuseppe Fiorentini, who arrived in Poland about 1787, and after 1826 by Franciszek Józef Fiorentini (the son of Giuseppe and Józefa Sokołowska).

[13] Gołębiowski, *Gry i zabawy różnych stanów*, 236. Sources do not mention a Jan Miller, but it is possible that Gołębiowski meant Wilhelm Müller.

offered other products and services, usually as turners. Since the quality of their products was high, several of the workshops were able to specialize when the demand for wind instruments increased. During the first quarter of the century, the initially small military bands increased in size from about ten instruments (two clarinets, two flutes, two oboes, two French horns, two bassoons, and percussion) to ensembles of fifty, eighty, or even one hundred players. These new ensembles included all kinds of trumpets, horns, and trombones incorporating new technologies; they are reported to have played with great precision, and a beautiful, organ-like sound.[14] Given such demand for their product, a few of the wind instrument workshops became large factories and continued to produce for local and foreign markets well into the twentieth century.

One such successful craftsman was Wilhelm Wernitz. At first, his workshop produced wind instruments and fine artifacts made of wood, ivory, and amber. Later he was able to limit his production to fine woodwinds and brass instruments. He was especially praised for his countless innovations and improvements (re-tuning mechanisms or new valve systems for the French horn and the bugle, just to mention some).[15] It is possible that instruments built by Wernitz were played at the bugle concert that so amazed Chopin:

> Recently I was in General Szembek's encampment. . . . Szembek is very musical, plays the violin well—he used to study with Rode and is a rabid "Paganinist," and therefore belongs to a good class of musicians. He ordered his orchestra to perform. They exerted themselves the whole morning and I heard curious things. All of this on trumpets called bugles; you would not imagine that they could execute chromatic scales as fast as possible and while descending diminuendo! It truly amazed me when I heard a cavatina from [Auber's] *La muette [de Portici]* performed on these trumpets with complete accuracy and shading.[16]

Gołębiowski credits this success to Haase, the kapellmeister general of the Infantry Regiments Orchestras, and to Czapiewski, the kapellmeister of Szembek's sixty-man orchestra, who organized the ensemble, made the witty arrangements, and brought the performance to such high level.[17]

Several other smaller workshops produced quality instruments. Józef Horalek, specializing in woodwinds, built highly praised instruments, using modern innovations and his own improvements. Antoni Weinert,

[14] Gołębiowski, *Gry i zabawy różnych stanów,* 257–258.

[15] Vogel, *Instrumenty muzyczne,* 218.

[16] Chopin, Warsaw, to Woyciechowski, Poturzyn, 31 August 1830, *Korespondencja,* I:133–134.

[17] Gołębiowski, *Gry i zabawy różnych stanów,* 258.

famous as a producer of guitars, expanded his enterprise in 1812 by hiring Ch. G. Eschenbach, a trumpet builder. In time, Wilhelm Wernitz had trained a whole generation of fine craftsmen, including his son Adolf Jan and Wilhelm Glier, both of whom started their own successful factories.[18]

The quality of organ built and maintained by local craftsmen was rather high, even if Poland's organ builders represented somewhat conservative tastes. While elsewhere in Europe new Romantic trends began to affect the sound and mechanism of the organ, in Poland the Baroque traditions of organ building were continued until the mid–nineteenth century. Occasionally, new stops were created: the most popular was the *Portunał*, invented about 1801 in Breslau (Wrocław) and characterized by a flute-like sound. The *Portunał* was frequently installed during the rebuilding and fixing of older instruments. Other more typically Romantic stops added to existing instruments were the *Vox humana*, *Vox amabilis*, *Vox coelestis*, and *Aeolina*. The last one was derived from a fashionable new invention, the harmonium.[19] Most of the organ masters abandoned the old tradition of dividing their time between piano and organ building, devoting their efforts exclusively to organs. Among the most respected were Wacław Bauer, Dominik Pilichowski, Karol Żakiewicz, Rafał Ostrowski, and Jan Ciężartowicz.[20]

Chopin started studying the organ with Václav Vilém Würfel in 1822,[21] at the same time he began informal composition instruction with Elsner. By November 1825, he was proficient enough to be given the job of Sunday organist in the Visitation Nuns' Church of the Protection of St. Joseph associated with the gymnasium: "I became the Gymnasium's organist. . . . Every week, on Sunday, I play at the Visitation Nuns' Church and the others sing."[22] The organ played by Chopin in the Visitation Nuns' church, built in the second half of the eighteenth century, was later removed to a provincial church in Nieznamierowice and subsequently perished in a fire. The present instrument was built by Antoni

[18] Vogel, *Instrumenty muzyczne*, 218.

[19] Not until the years 1837–41 did the Warsaw cathedral receive a new instrument with a typically Romantic specification: four manuals and pedal, fifty-one stops, including twelve reed stops and the new fashionable timbres: clarinet, vox humana, and melodikon. Gołos, *The Polish Organ*, 98. Such Romantic instruments were not yet common. One was more likely to encounter smaller technical improvements such as modern-compass keyboards; as elsewhere, the pneumatic action and the Venetian swell are found only at the end of the nineteenth century. Gołos, *Polskie organy i muzyka organowa*, 77.

[20] Vogel, *Instrumenty muzyczne*, 79.

[21] Václav Vilém Würfel, born in Bohemia in 1790 and educated in Prague under Tomášek, lived in Warsaw between 1815 and 1824. Later he served as conductor at the Kärntnertortheater in Vienna. Adrienne Simpson "Würfel, Vàclav Vilém," in *Grove Music Online*, ed. L. Macy (Accessed 12 October 2006), http://bert.lib.indiana.edu:2100.

[22] Chopin, Warsaw, to Jan Białobłocki, Biskupiec, [November 1825], *Korespondencja*, 1:60.

Szymański in 1909; contrary to the church's claims, it probably has no connection with Chopin.[23]

Although nothing is said about Chopin performing on the organ in the Lutheran Holy Trinity Church, it is known that he and his sister were members of the choir in this church,[24] so there is a considerable likelihood that he was familiar with its organ. The old instrument used by the Lutheran congregation was enlarged from twenty-one to twenty-three stops and given a new windchest, four bellows, and Classical architecture in 1781, when the congregation relocated to a new building. In 1817, shortly before the time when the Chopin children were known to participate in the church's musical events, the organ was again restored and enlarged: reed stops and one more bellow were added, bringing the instrument's specification to twenty-five stops.[25]

Chopin's mastery at the organ is recounted by Sikorski in the idealized description of a performance at the Visitation Nuns' church, which took place during Chopin's last year in Warsaw:

> Chopin, in the last year of his stay in Warsaw, was a frequent guest in the choir and gladly performed at the organ either fugues of various masters or his own improvisations. The difficult part of playing the organ, that is, the skillful and elaborate use of the pedal, was utterly easy for him and sometimes led him to almost showing off, which in turn led to the awakening of the keyboard's voices. It happened one time, during a break in a mass performed with an orchestra, that Chopin sat at the organ and, taking as the theme (in the manner of celebrated masters) a motive from the last passage, he began to draw out of it a wealth of ideas so immense and uninterrupted in its flow that everybody—from the oldest to the youngest crowding around the bench of the performer, lost in thought, captivated—forgot about the place and duties they came to fulfill.[26]

A little-known caricature of Chopin at the pedal piano captures the same kind of facility in using the pedal; his bare toes engage the pedals as if they were yet another set of fingers (fig. 2.1).[27] The instrument depicted

[23] Gołos, *Polskie organy i muzyka organowa*, 170.

[24] Eugeniusz Szulc, "Nieznana karta warszawskiego okresu życia Chopina" [An unknown page from the Warsaw period of Chopin's life], *Rocznik Chopinowski* 18 (1986): 125–150. See my discussion of choral performances at Holy Trinity in chapter 8.

[25] Jerzy Gołos, "Organy i muzyka w ewangielickim kościele Św. Trójcy w Warszawie" [The organ and music at the Lutheran Church of the Holy Trinity in Warsaw], *Ruch muzyczny* 34 (1990), no. 15, 3.

[26] Józef Sikorski, "Wspomnienie Chopina" [A recollection of Chopin], *Biblioteka warszawska*, 1849, no. 4, 554.

[27] I am indebted to Marta Pielech for bringing this image to my attention.

in the caricature is probably the pedal piano, since in the pseudo-organs I will discuss later, the performer's feet pumped the bellows. The pedal piano, or Pedalflugel, enjoyed some popularity at the end of the eighteenth and the first half of the nineteenth centuries. It consisted of a standard piano with a separate pedal-department of about two octaves added on—coupled with the piano's lowest register, or attached at the bottom of the main instrument to its own strings; or with the pedal-department as its own instrument in a separate case. During its heyday, the pedal piano attracted the attention of some prominent composers. There are several documented performances at the pedal piano by Mozart, who owned such an instrument. In the nineteenth century, Schumann and Alkan had a particular interest in the pedal piano. In fact, Schumann's opp. 56, 58, and 60 are specifically marked as destined for the organ or the pedal piano. The common thread connecting these composers' involvement with the pedal piano is the music of Johann Sebastian Bach. Purportedly, Mozart's interest in Pedalflugel originated with his love for J. S. Bach's fugues, as did Charles-Valentin Alkan's enthusiastic endorsement of this instrument. Schumann's op. 60 is explicitly a set of six fugues on the BACH motive.[28] In light of the importance Bach's music had in Chopin's Warsaw education and later in his career as a composer and a teacher, it is perfectly understandable that he would seize an opportunity to play an instrument of this sort and do it well. His studies at the organ would certainly have prepared him to tackle any instrument that required fine coordination between the hands and feet.

In view of Chopin's superb understanding of and proficiency at the organ, it becomes apparent that his interest in the organ, reinforced by his studies with Würfel, must have influenced his work. Chorales evoking organ-like textures appear in several of his pieces: the G Minor Nocturne op. 15, the G Minor Nocturne op. 37, the C Minor Nocturne op. 48, the C-sharp Minor Scherzo, the C Minor Prelude op. 28 no. 20, and the op. 49 Fantasy. In fact, Chopin's *Largo* in E flat (title derived from the tempo marking) is a setting of "O God, Thou who hast Graced Poland," a religious hymn Chopin would have played as a weekly conclusion of the Sunday mass during his early years as an organist at the Visitation Nuns' church, and which was central to the creation and preservation of Polish national identity.[29] Similarly, his idiosyncratic fingerings—for instance,

---

[28] Richard Maunder, "Mozart's Keyboard Instruments," *Early Music* 20/2 (May 1992): 207–219, and David E. Rowland and Richard Maunder, "Mozart's Pedal Piano," *Early Music* 23/2 (May 1995), 287–296. I am grateful to David Rowland for helping me identify the instrument in fig. 2.1 as the pedal piano.

[29] The hymn, which in our century contended for the role of the national anthem, in Chopin's youth was a praise of Czar Alexander, the king of Poland. During the subsequent century and a half, the text changed many times: for the duration of the November Upris-

Figure 2.1. Caricature of Chopin. Album of Zofia Chodkiewicz Ossolińska, Biblioteka Narodowa, Warsaw, Akc. 1861, k. 262v.

those of the A Minor Étude op. 10 no. 2—might have been influenced by Baroque organ fingerings. Much has been said about the contrapuntal underpinnings of his music, most explicitly manifested in the linear textures of his late works as stemming from his early familiarity with and continued interest in the music of Johann Sebastian Bach. Playing contrapuntal music on the organ would have intensified the young composer's conceptual, aural, and corporeal experience of independent melodic lines. Moreover, his extraordinary facility in coordinating his feet and hands, perfected at the organ, would serve him well as he later

---

ing and the painful period that followed its collapse, it became a prayer for free Poland. See Bogdan Zakrzewski, *Boże coś Polskę Alojzego Felińskiego* [Alojzy Feliński's "O God, Thou who hast Graced Poland"] (Wrocław: Ossolineum, 1983).

sought to enrich the palette of the piano's sonorities through the subtle use of pedals.

Poland had its share of the nineteenth-century craze for mechanical instruments. All kinds of music boxes, clock chimes playing favorite tunes from Polish and foreign operas, and hand organs were produced.[30] The most famous case involved a family of instruments known variously as the *eolimelodicon, melodicordion, melodipantaleon, eolipantalion, aeolopantalon, choralion, orchestrion,* and *tritonion.*[31] All of these were types of pseudo-organs, representing attempts to create household-size instruments producing an organ-like sound.[32] Two competing inventors—the taxidermist and inventor August Fidelis Brunner (with the help of the piano builder Fryderyk Buchholtz) and the piano builder and joiner Józef Długosz—constructed the most interesting of these instruments. Their instruments enjoyed short-lived but intense popularity, and at the peak of their prominence they attracted the attention of the young Chopin.

Chopin's interest in the pseudo-organs originated with his organ teacher, Václav Würfel, who gave a concert on Brunner's eolimelodicon in 1822. It was Chopin's performance on this instrument at the Lutheran Church, during the visit to Warsaw in 1825 of Czar Alexander I, that earned tokens of appreciation from the monarch in the form of a diamond ring for each, Chopin and Brunner. Among his many other documented performances on the pseudo-organs, we find the 1825 concert of Conservatory students during which the audience heard choral works by Beethoven and Elsner's cantata with Brunner's choralion, and young Fryderyk's performance of a *Fantasia for eolopantalion,* intended for Długosz's instrument.

The instruments associated with August Fidelis Brunner were the eolimelodicon, also referred to as the melodicordion, and its more sonorous adaptation, the choralion. According to Sikorski, Brunner invented the choralion together with Fryderyk Jakub Hoffman, a professor of mineralogy at the university and a friend of the Chopins.[33] The choralion and its unusual sound were thus described in 1848:

[30] Many of the producers were organ or piano builders; the most successful of them was Antoni Śpiechowski. Vogel, *Instrumenty muzyczne,* 82. Other piano builders tried their hand at the construction of newly invented, experimental instruments. Notable productions were Jordaki Kuparenko's *buzuton,* Philippe de Girard's *tremolofon,* and Roman Piotrowski's *akordometr* (a tuning device).

[31] Gołębiowski lists yet other names: *harmonichorn, panmelodion, terpodion, trombonion, eoliopantalion,* and *glaskord.* Gołębiowski, *Gry i zabawy róznych stanów,* 234.

[32] Their complex story is told in some detail by Beniamin Vogel, "Fortepiany i idiofony klawiszowe w Królestwie Polskim w latach młodości Chopina" [Pianos and keyboard idiophones in the Congress Kingdom in the years of Chopin's youth], *Rocznik Chopinowski* 9 (1975): 57–61.

[33] Sikorski, "Wspomnienie Chopina," 517.

The vibrating body in the *choralion* is the air in metal cylinders to which large brass trumpets were added, and the force of the sound produced with the help of bellows (which are pressed with the player's feet) can according to his wish increase so that it will drown out one hundred people (half of them singers). A graduated supply of air made differences in the tone color; a light blow sounded like a *melodikon*, a stronger one like a shrieking clarinet, a very strong one roared like a combined sound of trumpets, French horns and trombones. This instrument stood for some time in the choir of the Lutheran church in Warsaw, but today it lies disassembled in the church storage.[34]

Brunner's choralion and its later versions enjoyed tremendous popularity in Warsaw, and so in 1826, during funeral ceremonies for Czar Alexander I (fig. 2.2), Elsner's *Requiem* was performed at the Lutheran Church of the Holy Trinity with the accompaniment of the choralion.[35] Around the same time, Fryderyk performed on the eolimelodicon in the house of Teresa Kicka. A similar evening must have taken place in December of that year, when the press reported Chopin's splendid performance on the choralion during a gathering in a private apartment.[36] Information located by Vogel indicates that the Duchess of Łowicz, wife of Grand Duke Constantine, whose salon Chopin frequented, also owned one of Brunner's melodicordions.[37]

The instrument, impressive enough to meet the needs of the spacious Lutheran church in Warsaw, was perfectly suited for smaller churches in the provinces, especially those unable to meet the cost of the traditional organ. An effort to procure a choralion for such purpose is documented in Chopin's correspondence. An 1826 letter informs us that Antoni Wybraniecki, the stepfather of Chopin's close friend Jan Białobłocki, ordered Brunner's choralion for a parish church in his Dobrzyń-Sokołowo estate.[38] That fall, Brunner had the instrument ready, with some improvements, but in the spring of 1827 Wybraniecki had still not picked up

[34] J[ózef] S[ikorski], "Narzędzia muzyczne z klawiaturą" [Musical instruments with a keyboard], *Biblioteka Warszawska*, 1848, no. 2, 378. The disassembled choralion remained in storage until a sale of damaged and used instruments on 29 October 1860, when forty trumpets from the choralion were purchased by a Szmul Wagner. Gołos, "Organy i muzyka w ewangielickim kościele Św. Trójcy w Warszawie," 3.

[35] *Opis żałobnego obchodu po wielkopomnej pamięci nayiaśniejszym Alexandrze I* [A description of the funeral tribute to His Highness Alexander I of momentous memory] (Warsaw: Glücksberg, 1829), 82.

[36] Krystyna Kobylańska, *Chopin w kraju: Dokumenty i pamiątki* [Chopin in his own land: documents and souvenirs] (Kraków: Polskie Wydawnictwo Muzyczne, 1955), 105.

[37] Beniamin Vogel, "Jeszcze raz o dwóch nieznanych kompozycjach Chopina na eolipantalion" [Once again about two unknown compositions for eolipantalion by Chopin], *Rocznik Chopinowski* 17 (1985): 124.

[38] Chopin, Warsaw, to Jan Białobłocki, Biskupiec, 12 February 1826, *Korespondencja*, 1:63.

Figure 2.2. The Lutheran church during the funeral observance for Czar Alexander I. Lithograph by Charles Caius Renoux after Karol Liszewski, 1829, Biblioteka Narodowa, Warsaw, G. 11.159.

the choralion.[39] Unfortunately, nothing more is known about the fate of this instrument.

Długosz's eolipantalion, apparently more suited for salons than churches, enjoyed similar popularity in Chopin's time. The 1848 article

[39] Chopin, Warsaw, to Białobłocki, Sokołów, 2 November [October] [1826], *Korespondencja*, 1:73; and Chopin, Warsaw, to Białobłocki, Sokołów, 14 [12] March [1827], *Korespondencja*, 1:77.

describes it as combining "the firmness of piano touch with the advantages of continuous tone; but handling it is not easy, not only because of pedals or rather bellows, which the player himself has to press, but also because of some repetitive movements required if we want to explore the instrument's richness."[40]

Chopin's enthusiasm for the eolipantalion was equal to his fascination with Brunner's instruments; he is reported to have even composed for this instrument. The account of the two compositions for eolipantalion appears in connection with a young piano builder, Kazimierz Tarczyński, who in the 1820s worked in the workshop of Długosz and became well acquainted with Fryderyk Chopin. Tarczyński, a fluent pianist himself, was involved in the construction of the eolipantalion and received from the teenage composer manuscripts of these two compositions, which purportedly remained in Tarczyński's possession until his death.[41] Vogel traced the fate of these compositions a bit further and found that in actuality shortly before Tarczyński's death the manuscripts were borrowed by a music lover from Płock, Mrs. L., later the wife of a General D., and never returned.[42] Unfortunately, nothing more is known about these works. Zdzisław Szulc suggests that these could have been the compositions for eolipantalion performed by Chopin during the aforementioned Conservatory concerts taking place May 27 and June 10, 1825.[43] The reviewer of this concert in the *Allgemeine musikalische Zeitung*, using the terminology associated with C. P. E. Bach's *Versuch über die wahre Art das Clavier zu spielen* and his well-known fantasias, refers to Chopin's performances at the *eolipantalion* as "free fantasias" (discussed later). From this it can be inferred that the young composer either improvised on the spot or performed compositions belonging to the metrically free, rhapsodic, highly modulatory, and improvisatory fantasia genre, rather than the genre of the virtuoso fantasia based on popular themes that he preferred for his op. 13.

Chopin's performances at the eolipantalion were very successful, and the account of these events published by the *Allgemeine musikalische Zeitung* is indeed the first printed mention of Chopin's performance found outside of Poland:

> The student Chopin was heard in the first Allegro of the F Minor Piano Concerto by Moscheles and in free fantasias at the *Aeolopantalon*. This

---

[40] S[ikorski], "Narzędzia muzyczne z klawiaturą," 377.

[41] Zdzisław Szulc, "Dwie nieznane kompozycje Chopina na eolopantalion" [Two unknown compositions for eolipantalion by Chopin], *Muzyka* 1 (1955): 19–20.

[42] Vogel, "Jeszcze raz o dwóch nieznanych kompozycjach Chopina na eolipantalion," 128.

[43] Szulc, "Dwie nieznane kompozycje Chopina."

instrument, constructed by a local carpenter Długosz, combines Ae-olomelodikon with the piano in such a manner that it presents an amazing variety to a player acquainted with its features. It made a tremendous impression under the hands of the talented young Chopin, who through the wealth of musical ideas in his free fantasias showed himself a complete master of this instrument.[44]

The eolipantalion, like Brunner's instruments, found its way to Warsaw's salons. For instance, Chopin describes an evening in 1826 spent in the Zamoyski house, where the guests admired Długosz's eoliopantalion.[45] The last time we hear of Długosz and his creation in association with Chopin is in an 1835 letter from Mikołaj Chopin to his son in Paris, where he asks (on behalf of Długosz) that the composer look into selling the idea in Paris.[46] At that point any attempt to market such instruments was futile, since a new and better invention already replaced them. It was the Viennese-built *physharmonica* (an ancestor of the harmonium), which was first introduced in Warsaw in 1829 and soon superseded all other experimental instruments.

Chopin's involvement with the organ and adventures with the choralion and eolipantalion enriched his musical skills and fired his imagination, yet the instrument that played the most important role in his creative life, from the very beginning of his musical career, was the piano. Chopin's striking preference for the piano and his almost complete lack of interest in other instruments becomes perfectly understandable within the context of the piano madness that characterized his time.

The oldest records concerning the presence of pianos in Poland come from cloister inventories and archives of aristocratic and royal households. The earliest documented presence of a piano in Poland dates to 1749, when Johann Sebastian Bach was an agent in the purchase of a piano built by Gottfried Silbermann (the famous organ and piano maker) for one of Poland's most powerful magnates, Jan Klemens Branicki from Białystok.[47] The records from the court of Poland's last king, Stanisław August, indicate that in 1784 there were two pianos among the many keyboard instruments tuned at the court by J. Wierzbowski. In 1813, upon his heroic death while leading the Polish army under Napoleon, the

---

[44] *Allgemeine musikalische Zeitung,* November 1825, 764.

[45] Chopin, Warsaw, to Białobłocki, Sokołów, [15 May 1826], *Korespondencja,* 1:65.

[46] Mikołaj Chopin, Warsaw, to Fryderyk Chopin, Paris, 9 February 1835, in *Korespondencja Chopina z rodziną* [Fryderyk Chopin's correspondence with his family], ed. Krystyna Kobylańska (Warsaw: Państwowy Instytut Wydawniczy, 1972), 102.

[47] Vogel, *Fortepian polski,* 14. At first, Bach was rather skeptical toward Silbermann's pianos, but by 1745 he considered fifteen of them satisfactory, and on his recommendation Frederick the Great purchased them (21).

king's nephew Prince Józef Poniatowski left in his estate four pianos dating to the last three decades of the eighteenth century. Somewhat more detailed information is provided by the household records of the great Lithuanian *hetman* Michał Kazimierz Ogiński; paternal uncle of the famous polonaise composer Michał Kleofas Ogiński, he was not just a great music-lover but also a composer himself (both Ogińskis studied with Viotti, among others), and his court in Słonim boasted a first-rate opera theater and orchestra. In the years 1778–1801, his palace maintained over a dozen keyboard instruments, including six pianos.[48]

Pianos became widely fashionable only after the socioeconomic changes at the beginning of the nineteenth century in Poland that permitted the growth of the middle class. At first, pianos were seldom acquired for lower-class households, but homes with cultural aspirations and the financial means to satisfy them rushed to purchase imported instruments. At the beginning of the nineteenth century, *Allgemeine musikalische Zeitung* reported that in Warsaw, "in almost every home with ambitions for education, one finds a grand piano from Vienna, Dresden, Berlin, or Breslau [Wrocław], and often someone who plays it very well."[49] Soon, all boarding schools for girls provided piano lessons, and more affluent households of the aristocracy, nobility, and bourgeoisie hired piano teachers. Within the next couple of decades, piano education became commonplace in the Polish capital. In 1835, a local newspaper quoted the *Allgemeine musikalische Zeitung:* "'Musical art has spread in Poland, although we in Germany do not know about it since an artist from that country is seldom heard in Europe! It has spread, I say, because in every house you find a piano and in Warsaw pianists are swarming, and still more are arriving from Germany and Bohemia.'"[50]

The ability to play the piano became such an important element of a young woman's education (while also a very desirable skill for a young man) that even the lower classes made an effort to equip their homes with a piano and provide piano lessons for their daughters. While in 1825 the cases of two artisans (a tailor and a locksmith) who allowed their daughters to indulge in piano playing were a subject of a public debate concerning the appropriateness of allowing young women of their class such leisure pursuits, during the next decade music lessons in the homes of lower classes became routine.[51] The most significant outcome of the popularity of the piano and the emphasis on musical education was the

[48] Vogel, *Fortepian polski*, 177–188.

[49] *Allgemeine musikalische Zeitung*, January 1805, 224.

[50] *Kurier Warszawski*, 1835, no. 307, 1553–1554, quoted in Vogel, *Fortepian polski*, 180. In the 1835 *Allgemeine musikalische Zeitung*, no such passage can be found.

[51] Vogel, *Fortepian polski*, 179 and 183.

change in the social status of the musician. In light of the dramatic social changes on the one hand and the advent of Kunstreligion, granting the musician a prophetic role, on the other, the contempt for professional music making previously held by the upper classes gave way to social acceptance and admiration (to some degree even for professional women musicians). Such an atmosphere made it easier for the Chopins to encourage little Fryderyk's talents and support his professional education as a musician. The piano craze also provided opportunities for the growth of native piano production, since the local market absorbed newly built instruments with amazing speed.

The oldest Polish-made piano-like instrument still in existence was built in 1774 by Jan Skórski from Sandomierz. This instrument has a rather unusual construction: not only it is among the few square pianos in the world that uses the tangent mechanism but also it lacks dampers, which brings it closer to the concept of the pantaleon—an instrument based on the dulcimer.[52] Considering the documented earlier presence on Polish soil of foreign-built pianos, and the old, strong tradition of playing and building harpsichords and clavichords, it is likely that similar instruments were built earlier. Even if this was the case, the initially small needs of the local market were mostly fulfilled through imports. Those needs grew rapidly and unquestionably, by the 1780s, pianos were built in Gdańsk, Kraków, and Warsaw.[53]

At first, the size of production and quality of instruments was rather unimpressive. When Elsner met with Erard during his 1805 visit in Paris (in order to select and purchase a piano for Princess Sapieha), the famous piano maker questioned him about the Polish market. In his *Summary* Elsner recalls: "I told him that most often we import them [pianos], usually from Vienna, since in general our musical instrument construction and factories are at a very low level here."[54] Indeed the vigorous import of instruments continued into Chopin's times. The young pianist was well acquainted with a wide assortment of foreign instruments through these locally available imports and from his trips to Berlin, where he visited piano factories,[55] and to Vienna, where Matthäus Andreas Stein and Conrad Graf offered him pianos for his 1829 concert.[56] Without any hesi-

[52] Vogel, *Fortepian polski*, 117.

[53] See Benjamin Vogel, "Two Tangent Square Pianos in Poland," *Journal of the American Musical Instrument Society* 20 (1994): 84–89.

[54] Józef Elsner, *Sumariusz moich utworów muzycznych* [A summary of my musical works], ed. Alina Nowak-Romanowicz (Kraków: Polskie Wydawnictwo Muzyczne, 1957), 123.

[55] Chopin, Berlin, to his family, Warsaw, 16 September 1828, *Korespondencja*, Sydow ed., 1:82.

[56] Chopin, Vienna, to his family, Warsaw, 8 July 1829, *Korespondencja*, Sydow ed., 1:91–92.

tation, he chose to perform on the instrument built by Graf, whose pianos he continued to cherish even in Paris.[57] In the last years before his departure from Poland, Chopin had the opportunity to play several foreign instruments. During his 1830 visit at Tytus Woyciechowski's he played a Pleyel that resided in the salon of the neighboring estate. For the second of his spring 1830 concerts, he used a Viennese piano by an undetermined maker,[58] and in his October 11 farewell concert of the same year he played a Streicherian piano, though it is unclear whether it was a locally manufactured one using the Viennese-English action patented by Johann Baptist Streicher or an instrument of Viennese production.[59]

The local production of pianos, so meager at the beginning of the century, was growing fast with the influx of talented young builders. Many of them were foreigners who settled in Warsaw; some were Poles who had received a thorough education abroad. By the time Chopin was growing up, the kingdom had nearly twenty piano workshops (all but three in Warsaw). Among the most successful were those of Fryderyk Buchholtz, Antoni Leszczyński, Maximilian Hochhauser, Wilhelm Jansen, Wilhelm Troschel, Tomasz Max, and Antoni Śpiechowski. Most of the materials needed for piano construction were locally available. Veneers for casings were made from Polish alder, pear, birch, ash, or walnut. Spruce boards were used for sounding boards. Pins and wire used for the production of strings were imported, as were—quite obviously—ebony, mahogany, rosewood and ivory.[60] Thus, the pianos Chopin played in Warsaw were not only foreign imports but also locally made instruments not much different from European standards of the time.

The foreign and locally built pianos played by Chopin, especially during his youth, were very different from our modern instrument. They had a smaller range (five to six and a half octaves), their keys were narrower, and the resulting octave spacing was almost a centimeter smaller. The hammers were covered with leather; the strings had a lighter tension and were made from different materials from today (treble from soft steel, bass from copper and only in the lowest register overspun) resulting in sound that was singing and sustained but also more differentiated in each register. Not only was the action lighter, but the key-dip was also much shallower, thus requiring a lighter touch. Two kinds of action dominated the market in the early nineteenth century: the heavier and more complex

[57] Chopin, Paris, to his family, Warsaw, 22 December 1830, *Korespondencja*, Sydow ed., 1:161.

[58] Chopin, Warsaw, to Woyciechowski, Poturzyn, 27 March 1830, *Korespondencja*, Sydow ed., 1:115.

[59] Chopin, Warsaw, to Woyciechowski, Poturzyn, 12 March 1830, *Korespondencja*, Sydow ed., 1:146.

[60] Vogel, *Instrumenty muzyczne*, 58.

English action, with the hammer attached to a hammer rail, and the lighter and simpler Viennese action, with hammers attached directly to the key and pointing towards the keyboard. The makers of both types constantly sought new technical solutions, and the resulting continuing evolution of these types ultimately led to the creation of hybrid instruments and the blurring of the distinct characteristics of the Viennese and English instruments.

Polish piano builders implemented new inventions with only a minor delay. During the 1810s and 1820s, the influences came from both London and Vienna. Square models, typically equipped with the Viennese mechanism, were treated with little respect. The Polish builders thought of them as instruments for amateurs and seldom used them in industrial exhibitions. They preferred to show their workmanship through upright and, above all, grand pianos. In the Congress Kingdom, these could relate to either Viennese or English types (elsewhere in Poland, Viennese-type pianos dominated the market).

The square pianos built in Poland came in various sizes. The small, boudoir-size instruments had only four octaves and a retractable keyboard, and often incorporated nonmusical functions. (The one preserved in the collection of the Museum of the Jagiellonian University in Kraków doubles as a sewing table!) Needless to say, these instruments were not of high technical quality. The larger types had five octaves, and after 1820 their keyboard size increased to six octaves.[61]

The upright pianos built in Poland were of much better quality. They were based either on Viennese or on English models, both in terms of action and style of the casing. The English version of the upright piano was represented in Poland by the cabinet type, using the English sticker action and two stops (*una corda* and damper). The German and Viennese models—giraffes, pyramides, lyres, and so on—used Viennese mechanisms of the hanging or standing type, and typically included four to six mechanical stops activated with special pedals.[62]

While the less affluent customer could only afford the upright or square piano, the builders took greatest pride in the production of the grand piano. It had the best sound of them all and was the most worthy of technical improvements. The English models built in the Congress Kingdom had more massive cases, characterized by straight lines of the sides, with a partially opened bottom and a system of metal supports for the soundboard, rim, and pinblock. Sometimes they used the older-style English action with dampers above the strings. The Viennese case was lighter, with flowing curves of the sides. The lighter Viennese action em-

[61] Vogel, *Fortepian polski*, 118–119.
[62] Vogel, *Fortepian polski*, 119–120.

ployed wedge dampers. As in other types of pianos, the English models had two pedal stops, whereas the Viennese ones included additional mechanical stops. In both types, double-triple stringing was used (copper for the bass, but seldom overspun), the hammers were covered with several layers of leather (mutton or cervine), and the keyboard extended six octaves (after 1825 it could reach six and a half).[63] Polish piano makers did not hesitate to experiment with creating various combinations of the English and Viennese instruments, nor did they shy away from introducing their own improvements and technical solutions.[64] Many of them were praised for the quality of their instruments, but Warsaw's most successful piano builders during Chopin's youth were Antoni Leszczyński and Fryderyk Buchholtz.

Leszczyński spent many years as an apprentice and a builder in Vienna, Paris, and London (with Muzio Clementi). Upon returning to Poland, he settled in Warsaw and during the years 1819–1830 he was the owner of a very successful factory that produced large quantities of richly decorated but technically mediocre instruments. It is only natural that he brought to Poland the English traditions of piano building, and he was the first one to use the English action, which he presented in his pianos during the 1821, 1823, and 1828 exhibitions.[65] These did not find acceptance with Polish customers, since, as an 1823 newspaper article explains,

> its keys are a little too heavy. In England it is a custom to make strong keys, but in Poland, where (as one traveler said) young ladies do not drink porter and therefore do not have as much strength in their fingers as Englishwomen, it [the heavy action] is a noticeable fault.[66]

As a result of these preferences, most of Leszczyński's pianos utilized the Viennese mechanism, but their action was imperfect, and they were carelessly finished.

On the outside, the instruments were quite impressive; Leszczyński decorated his pianos in the Empire style popular in England and else-

---

[63] Vogel, *Fortepian polski*, 120–124.

[64] During an 1828 exhibition in Warsaw, Dominik Domagalski presented a piano "in the shape of a boat." Vogel, *Instrumenty muzyczne*, 59. Maximilian Hochhauser continued to implement innovations during his thirty-odd years as a Warsaw piano maker. In 1826, in order to create a more powerful concert instrument, he built a piano with quadruple strings. During the 1820s, he presented several instruments that combined Viennese and English characteristics (Vogel, *Fortepian polski*, 226). Similar combinations of the two mechanisms were attempted by Fryderyk Buchholtz, Wilhelm Troschel, and Tomasz Max (121–123).

[65] Vogel, *Fortepian polski*, 242 and 122.

[66] *Gazeta Warszawska*, 1823, no. 67, 888–889, quoted in Vogel, *Instrumenty muzyczne*, 61.

where, incorporating carved columns and ornaments made of brass covered with gold leaf. His grand pianos were decorated with brass encrustation in the shape of delicate floral or geometric patterns reminiscent of the English Adams style. Chopin was not alone in his dissatisfaction with Leszczyński's instruments, but these richly ornamented pianos found acceptance among less demanding amateurs. Professionals and more demanding music lovers had custom-built or imported instruments.

Locally, the best builder was Fryderyk Buchholtz, whose pianos Chopin valued very highly. The cases of his pianos were much less decorative than Leszczyński's, following the growing tendency towards simplicity. But unlike Leszczyński's, Buchholtz's instruments were of high quality, easily meeting the needs of sensitive professionals. Buchholtz's pianos were praised by Sowiński, a pianist himself, in his *Dictionary* as "excel[ing] in beauty of tone and durability" and as preferred by the piano virtuoso Aleksander Dreyschock, who "always played on a Buchholtz piano during his stay in Warsaw in 1841."[67] As a side benefit, the basement of the Buchholtz factory was always available to professional musicians, and was often used by Chopin and his friends for rehearsals of compositions for several pianos.[68] Chopin himself writes about rehearsing "the Rondo for two pantaleons" with Fontana at Buchholtz's in 1828; on another occasion he mentions rehearsing his C Major Rondo with Ernemann there.[69]

Fryderyk Buchholtz's father was a Prussian who settled in Warsaw. The young Fryderyk, trained as a carpenter, left the Polish capital for several years to gather professional experience. When he returned in 1815, he opened a piano-building shop in Warsaw (he also worked on organs, although archival materials provide information about rebuilding contracts only). At first he offered mostly vertical pianos—mainly giraffes with several mechanical stops. Mechanical stops were not very popular among Polish builders, and very soon Buchholtz refrained from including them. By 1825, he shifted his production to grands with Viennese action, but he also custom-built English type mechanisms. A perfect opportunity to learn more about English instruments presented itself in 1826, when Maria Szymanowska imported an English piano (possibly a Broadwood). The instrument was permitted a duty-free entry under the condition that

---

[67] Albert Sowiński, *Słownik muzyków polskich dawnych i nowoczesnych* [Dictionary of ancient and modern Polish musicians], 1st Polish ed. (Paris: Księgarnia Luxemburska, 1874), 44.

[68] *Echo Muzyczne, Teatralne i Artystyczne*, 1885, no. 83, 172. Quoted in Vogel, *Instrumenty muzyczne*, 61.

[69] Chopin, Warsaw, to Woyciechowski, Poturzyn, 27 December 1828, *Korespondencja*, Sydow ed., 1:86–87. Chopin is probably referring to one of the rondos published as opp. 14 or 73; and Chopin, Warsaw, to Woyciechowski, Poturzyn, 9 September 1828, *Korespondencja*, Sydow ed., 1:79.

Figure 2.3. Grand piano built by Buchholtz, 1827–30. Muzeum Fryderyka Chopina w Towarzystwie im. Fryderyka Chopina, Warsaw, M/1056. Photo by Andrzej Ring & Bartosz Tropiło.

Szymanowska make it easily available to local masters, so that they could use it as a model. Already in January 1827, Buchholtz presented his improved model, which borrowed from Szymanowska's instrument recent English innovations: iron supports for the frame and the lower portion of the body, and an open bottom of the case. The 1827 Buchholtz piano that today is housed in the Instrument Museum in Poznań and another one in the collection of the Chopin Museum in Warsaw (fig.2.3) include such improvements.[70]

The application of English solutions for the body of the piano did not preclude Buchholtz and other Polish builders from using a mechanism that would be suitable for a given customer. Thus, in the English casing one could find a Viennese, English, or combined action; Chopin himself described and perhaps even performed on such a Buchholtz combined action modeled after Streicher's patent.[71]

There were two pianos in the Chopin home: the instrument standing in the salon was a Buchholtz; of the other little is known. Chopin tells us that at the end of 1828 his parents arranged a little working-room for him

[70] Vogel, *Fortepian polski*, 121–122.
[71] Chopin, Warsaw, to Woyciechowski, Poturzyn, 4 September 1830, *Korespondencja*, Sydow ed., 1:136.

upstairs, containing just an old desk and an old piano.[72] Vogel believes this attic piano was most likely a French or an English giraffe.[73] The Buchholtz piano from the Chopins' salon was burned during the 1863 Uprising, and because reports concerning this instrument are conflicting and unreliable, they cannot provide conclusive knowledge about the instrument's construction.[74]

Much more can be learned from the information pertaining to Chopin's first public concert, for which he used his own instrument. Vogel believes that the instrument used during this concert was a giraffe, Chopin's attic piano.[75] But several objections arise in connection with this statement. First, in a letter to Tytus Woyciechowski, Chopin specifically uses the term *pantaleon* in reference to the concert instrument, saying "Elsner regretted that [the sound of] my pantaleon is dead."[76] Significantly, the term *pantaleon* or *pantalon* is reserved expressly for horizontal pianos, as affirmed in an 1850 article.[77] Second, why would Chopin want to use an inferior instrument in concert (as mentioned, an upright was not the choice of a connoisseur), and why go through the trouble of moving a mediocre instrument from the attic, if there was a superior one in the salon? If we assume that the instrument used in the first concert was not the upstairs but the downstairs piano (a Buchholtz), the debate concerning Chopin's tone during that concert would support the conclusion that it was not a Viennese but an English instrument.

The first comment concerning the sound of the piano used by Chopin in the concert that took place on March 17, 1830, comes from Chopin's letter to Tytus, in which the composer affirms that he used his own instrument and that most of the audience found his sound too "soft."[78] Among the dissatisfied was Karol Kurpiński, who jotted in his private

[72] Chopin, Warsaw, to Woyciechowski, Poturzyn, 12 December 1828, *Korespondencja*, Sydow ed., 1:86.

[73] Vogel, "Fortepiany i idiofony klawiszowe w Królestwie Polskim w latach młodości Chopina," 64.

[74] For instance, Franciszek Maciejowski, an acquaintance of Chopin, furnishes a bit of information about Chopin's instrument, but unfortunately he appears to be quite mistaken. He says that during his visit at Chopin's house, he heard the virtuoso playing excerpts of a newly composed concerto "on a piano made not of mahogany, nor of walnut, but simply of pine." Kazimierz Władysław Wójcicki, *Cmentarz powązkowski pod Warszawą* [The Powązki cemetery near Warsaw], 3 vols. (Warsaw: Gebethner i Wolff, 1855–58), 2:262.

[75] Vogel, "Fortepiany i idiofony klawiszowe w Królestwie Polskim w latach młodości Chopina," 64.

[76] Chopin, Warsaw, to Woyciechowski, Poturzyn, 27 March 1830, *Korespondencja*, Sydow ed., 1:115.

[77] E. Bohdanowicz, "Myśli o muzyce" [Reflections on music], *Atheaneum*, 1850, no. 1, 69.

[78] Chopin, Warsaw, to Woyciechowski, Poturzyn, 27 March 1830, *Korespondencja*, Sydow ed., 1:115.

journal: "it was the instrument itself that was not very suitable for such a large space."[79] Chopin's close friend Maurycy Mochnacki wrote in the review of the concert: "Mr. Chopin's touch is elegant and delicate; perhaps one should wish more energy and strength in passage work."[80] Chopin responded to this criticism, expressed by Mochnacki as "insufficient energy," by saying: "I guessed where this energy resides and I played the second concert not on mine but on a Viennese instrument."[81]

And indeed, for the second concert (on March 22) he borrowed a Viennese instrument belonging to General Diakov, which listeners liked much more and praised Chopin for "each note being thumped out like a little pearl," though Chopin would have preferred to use his own instrument.[82] In his conclusion, the reviewer of the second concert juxtaposes the Viennese instrument specifically with an English one, explaining that "the general feeling was that the tone of this [Viennese] piano was not as strong as the English one, but more distinct."[83]

In view of all these circumstances and the fact that Buchholtz did offer pianos with English action, it seems plausible that the instrument in the Chopins' salon was a Buchholtz with English mechanism and that this was the instrument used during Chopin's first 1830 concert.[84] Beyond these suppositions, the specifications of this and other pianos Chopin used in Poland must remain unknown until further evidence comes to light.

The public debate relating to the instrument he used during his spring 1830 concerts brings into focus the strong preferences Polish audiences had for the sound of Viennese instruments. In fact, the complaints expressed by Chopin's listeners were aesthetic in nature, revealing their preference for the Viennese style of pianism, even if on the surface their objections against English instruments appeared to mostly concern their heavy action. Initially, this characteristic dissuaded not only amateurs

---

[79] Tadeusz Przybylski, "Fragmenty 'Dziennika Prywatnego' Karola Kurpińskiego" [Fragments of Kurpiński's private diary], *Muzyka* 20 (1975): 106.

[80] Maurycy Mochnacki, *Pisma* [Writings], ed. Artur Śliwiński (Lwów: Połoniecki, 1910), 420.

[81] Chopin, Warsaw, to Woyciechowski, Poturzyn, 27 March 1830, *Korespondencja*, Sydow ed., 1:115.

[82] Chopin, Warsaw, to Woyciechowski, Poturzyn, 27 March 1830, *Korespondencja*, Sydow ed., 1:115.

[83] *Gazeta Warszawska*, 24 March 1830, no. 81, 747. Quoted after Vogel, "Fortepiany i idiofony klawiszowe w Królestwie Polskim w latach młodości Chopina," 182.

[84] In his most recent publication on this subject, Vogel revised his original views, agreeing that the instrument Chopin used in the concert was the Buchholtz and further supporting my belief that Chopin's Buchholtz had an English action. See Vogel, "The Young Chopin's Domestic Pianos," in *Chopin in Performance: History, Theory, Practice* (Warsaw: Narodowy Instytut Fryderyka Chopina, 2005), 57–75.

but also adepts of the pianistic art. At the beginning of the century, when the Erard selected by Elsner during his 1805 visit in Paris arrived in Warsaw, the public's response emphasized this feeling:

> The newly arrived piano was generally and exceptionally liked in terms both of its appearance and of its tone, which was big and resounding; in a word, the instrument left nothing to be desired. Only the heavy touch of the keyboard was not to the ladies' taste, and none of them wanted to perform on this instrument, even the famous Szymanowska. Only her chief rival, Miss Wołowska (today living in Paris as the wife of the attorney Franciszek Wołowski), greatly pleased the listeners when she used this piano for her performance of Steibelt's Concerto in E Major.[85]

Yet the English pianos continued to attract the musical connoisseur, and two decades later it was the same Maria Szymanowska who brought to Warsaw an English instrument featuring the latest improvements—an instrument that served as a model for Buchholtz's English-style grands. By the late 1820s, English-style instruments incorporated a host of new improvements, including solutions to counter the heavier touch. These made the pianos more attractive to artists who valued the resounding tone and more expressive touch provided by he English-type escapement action.

In its very core, the divide between the Viennese and English piano types at the beginning of the nineteenth century was intimately intertwined with two sets of pianistic and stylistic preferences. The sound cultivated by pianists associated with the *stile brillant*, most notably Hummel, was characterized by a drier, staccato touch and sparing use of the pedal. This sound, inseparable from the Viennese piano, was characterized as possessing "energy," "spirit," "strength," and "clarity." The rounder sound of the English piano invited the use of the pedal, and musicians preferring this instrument drew attention to their legato, singing touch and subtle shading.[86] The vocabulary used to describe Chopin's spring 1830 concerts clearly indicated the listeners' desire for a more "Viennese sound." After the first concert on the English-style Buchholtz, Mochnacki called specifically for "more energy and strength," and the second concert, on Diakov's Viennese instrument, left the audiences praising Chopin's "pearly" sound, while the author of the *Gazeta Warszawska* review was satisfied with the greater "clarity" of sound. This particular

---

[85] Elsner, *Sumariusz*, 124–125.

[86] This idea has been explored by David Rowland, "Chopin and Early Nineteenth-Century Piano Schools," paper presented at the fifth annual Chopin Conference, December 1–3, 2005, Warsaw.

review further underscored the association of the Viennese piano with a particular style of pianism by likening the Viennese piano Chopin used to the one Hummel used during his Warsaw concerts in the spring of 1829.[87] On the other hand, Szymanowska's 1827 concert, probably on her new English piano, was praised by the same Mochnacki, who called for more energy from Chopin, for her legato, singing, and shading:

> Mrs. Szymanowska succeeded in perfecting the nature of her instrument by making it approach the tone of the violin. . . . In her playing chords, melodies, and single tones are combined in harmonious sonority, and the continuity of whole-, half-, and quarter-notes, combined with the most diverse and gradually developed shading in passages from the highest fortissimo to piano, from piano to crescendo, from crescendo to decrescendo etc., amazes the most exacting connoisseurs. In the adagio Mrs. Szymanowska brought the illusive imitation of human singing to the highest art.[88]

One cannot help but wonder whether gender issues played a role in this acceptance of Szymanowska's pianistic style. The typically gendered reception of women performers would explain entirely different sets of expectations directed at male and female virtuosi, and a greater willingness on the part of Polish audiences to accept the less-appreciated "English sound" from the hands of a woman.[89]

Chopin first public concerts took place in a culture dominated by the Viennese piano and the associated *stile brillant* aesthetics—Warsaw had little appreciation for the English sound. Yet, because of the Warsaw piano builders' attentiveness to state-of-the-art trends, as he was searching for his own pianistic identity, he was exposed to a variety of instruments and became acquainted with the most recent technological advances in piano construction. In this sense, not having a formal piano teacher was to Chopin's advantage: he was not bound to a specific pianistic tradition but remained free in his explorations of pianism. Embarking on his pianistic career during the period when, as a result of continuous technical innovations, the distinction between the design of the Viennese and English instruments began to blur, and standing outside the two prevalent pianistic styles associated with the Viennese and English designs, Chopin was in the vanguard of change: his piano playing heralded

---

[87] *Gazeta Warszawska*, 24 March 1830, no. 81, 747.

[88] Mochnacki, *Pisma*, 377–378.

[89] Katharine Ellis, "Female Pianists and Their Male Critics in Nineteenth-Century Paris," *Journal of the American Musicological Society* 50 (1997): 353–385, is an exploration of gender issues concerning the reception of performances by female pianists, though of a later period and not particularly focused on questions of sound.

a new era of pianism, and his compositional language revealed hitherto unexplored timbral possibilities of the piano.

New advances in piano construction transformed it into a highly versatile and expressive instrument, permitting ever greater virtuosity. But Chopin's music achieved its lasting position in the canon of Western music not only by setting new standards of pianistic virtuosity in difficult bravura figurations. More remarkably, he made use of the new piano's potential for lyrical melodies and employed its rich palette of sonorities through his imaginative use of the instrument's natural registers and pedals. Furthermore, he explored the intersecting functions of harmony and instrumental color, most notably in the Prelude op. 45, or ornamentation and instrumental color, in the Berceuse op. 57. In the latter piece, the instrumental color generated through ornamentation serves as the music's structural element. His inseparable companion in these mature exploits was a Pleyel piano. For ultimately it took Pleyel's sensitive instrument to fulfill Chopin's quest for a piano that most suited his artistic temperament—begun in his youth in Warsaw.

3

MUSIC PUBLISHING

"I go to Brzezina's every day," Chopin reported in 1829 to Tytus
Woyciechowski.[1] In fact, from an 1827 letter to Jan Białobłocki one can conclude that already then Chopin visited Brzezina's store
nearly daily.[2] We first hear of Brzezina still earlier, in a letter he wrote during his summer vacation in Szafarnia when he was fourteen. Here he ac-
knowledges the receipt of musical materials from Brzezina and asks Papa
to buy him Ries's *Air Moor variée pour le pianoforte a quatre mains.*[3] Of all
the music merchants in Warsaw, Brzezina's shop had most special meaning to the young Fryderyk: not only was Brzezina the publisher of two out
of his only three works in Polish first editions (fig. 3.1), but the young
composer was also a regular guest at Brzezina's, where he spent long
hours browsing and playing through works of old masters, recently published scores, and newly arrived works from abroad.

Although nearly all of Chopin's music was published elsewhere, the
presence of a flourishing music publishing industry in Warsaw proved invaluable to the developing composer. Warsaw's music bookstores provided access to a fount of musical knowledge through the repertory
printed locally and through imported publications: the young Fryderyk
spent countless hours in their shops, which for him took on the function
of music libraries. At the same time, through the publication of fashion-

[1] Fryderyk Chopin, Warsaw, to Tytus Woyciechowski, Poturzyn, 3 October 1829, in
Korespondencja Fryderyka Chopina [Fryderyk Chopin's correspondence], ed. Bronisław Edward Sydow, 2 vols. (Warsaw: Państwowy Instytut Wydawniczy, 1955), 1:108.

[2] Chopin, Warsaw, to Jan Białobłocki, Sokołów, 8 January 1827, *Korespondencja*, 1:74.

[3] Chopin, Szafarnia, to his family, Warsaw, 10 August 1824, *Korespondencja*, 1:38.

Figure 3.1. Fryderyk Chopin, *Rondeau compose pour le pianoforte et dedié à Mme de Linde* (op. 1) (Warsaw: Brzezina, 1825), title page. Muzeum Fryderyka Chopina w Towarzystwie im. Fryderyka Chopina, Warsaw, M/2828. Photo by N. N.

able musical genres associated with opera and the salon, local printers provided Chopin with the repertory that served as the basis for the formation of his idiomatic musical vocabulary. In a more general sense, the growth of music publishing was beneficial as a function of the new socioeconomic environment that resulted in increased musical literacy, as well as greater participation in music making and musical patronage among larger segments of Polish society.

In prepartition Poland, music patronage was restricted to the very small royal, aristocratic, and ecclesiastic circles. Publishing privileges were controlled by the king and given to very few, thus preventing any competition and growth in the industry. As a result of this situation, only a very small number of musical prints were produced in eighteenth-century Poland. Gołębiowski says of the gifted composers of Poland's past: "their works disappeared, since our country had neither music printers nor permanent outlets."[4] In 1772, Jan Engel, a composer and kapellmeister at the Cathedral of Saint John in Warsaw, received permis-

---

[4] Łukasz Gołębiowski, *Gry i zabawy różnych stanów* [Games and amusements of various classes] (Warsaw: Glücksberg, 1831), 251.

sion to open a music engraving shop. To produce music he used the technique of wood-engraving.[5] Sources provide documentation of eight prints having originated from Engel's shop, though most likely he published many more of his own works and works of other composers. Unfortunately, none of the music extant today that was published by various printers in Warsaw prior to the year 1800 can be credited with certainty to Engel's shop.[6]

Notwithstanding the scarcity of local music printers, Polish musicians working for major patrons had a reasonable access to foreign music through manuscript copies and foreign prints. A testimony to the number of scores that used to exist in the royal and cathedral collections is found in Elsner's *Summary*, where he recounts one Mejnert, a former castle superintendent, as saying in 1805: "You would have been astonished, Mr. Elsner, had you seen the abundance of music we had!"[7] By the time Elsner was writing those words, there was no trace of either collection.

Already before 1795, the new social, economic, and intellectual tendencies that characterized the Enlightenment began to have noticeable impact on musical circles of Warsaw. After 1795, the radical changes caused by Poland's loss of independence only accelerated the process and effected major changes in the state of music publishing in Warsaw. Although the political instability caused temporary attrition in many other areas of the Polish economy, the music publishing industry began to develop at a rapid pace. It was the needs of the new kind of a self-reliant composer and the constant demand for new music presented by the bour-

[5] Antoni Magier, *Estetyka miasta stołecznego Warszawy* [The aesthetics of the capital city of Warsaw] (1830 manuscript), ed. Hanna Szwankowska (Wrocław: Wydawnictwo Ossolińskich, 1963), 144.

[6] Wojciech Tomaszewski, *Warszawskie edytorstwo muzyczne w latach 1772–1865* [Warsaw music publishing in the years 1772–1865] (Warsaw: Biblioteka Narodowa, 1992) 47–48. Much information concerning the history of music publishers in Warsaw comes from this source and Tomaszewski's catalogue of Warsaw publications, *Bibliografia warszawskich druków muzycznych 1801–1830* [A bibliography of Warsaw musical prints 1801–1850] (Warsaw: Biblioteka Narodowa, 1992). Also essential to my inquiry was the work of Maria Prokopowicz, especially "Musique imprimée a Varsovie en 1800–1830," in *The Book of the First International Congress Devoted to the Works of Frederick Chopin*, ed. Zofia Lissa (Warsaw: Państwowe Wydawnictwo Naukowe, 1960): 593–597, "Musique imprimée de 1800–1831 comme source de la culture musicale polonaise de l'epoque," *Fontes artis musicae* 14 (1961): 16–22, and "Z działalności warszawskich księgarzy i wydawców muzycznych w latach 1800–1831" [From the activities of the Warsaw booksellers and music publishers in the years 1800–1831], in *Szkice o kulturze muzycznej XIX wieku* [Essays on the musical culture of the nineteenth century], ed. Zofia Chechlińska, (Warsaw: Państwowe Wydawnictwo Muzyczne, 1971–84), 1: 33–50.

[7] Józef Elsner, *Sumariusz moich utworów muzycznych* [A summary of my musical works], ed. Alina Nowak-Romanowicz (Kraków: Polskie Wydawnictwo Muzyczne, 1957), 78.

geoisie that promoted growth of music printing in early nineteenth-century Warsaw.

Aware of the new market, which on the one hand was supported by wider audiences and on the other by independent, professional musicians, the ever resourceful Elsner personally ventured into the music publishing business. In 1802, in partnership with Father Izydor Józef Cybulski, Elsner opened a music engraving shop. His first print, *A Collection of Polish Songs* (*Zbiór pieśni polskich*), was received with great enthusiasm.[8] Encouraged, Elsner continued his publishing activities with a monthly publication of Polish compositions entitled *A Selection of Fine Musical Works and Polish Songs* (*Wybór pięknych Dzieł Muzycznych y Pieśni Polskich*). This publication, which lasted through the years 1803–1805, was a landmark in the history of Polish musical culture. The essential ideas of Elsner are best expressed in the press announcement soliciting subscriptions to this publication:

> It is irrefutable that artists as well as amateurs of music have long wished (following the example of other foreign cities) to have a decent music-engraving shop in the capital, the former to make their works available to the public, the latter to have an easier access to the purchase of these works.[9]

Elsner's printing shop functioned well and during the years 1802–1806 produced many important editions. Gradually, some differences emerged between Elsner and Cybulski, and eventually in 1806, when the French occupants took over the shop for the purpose of printing military maps, Elsner left the enterprise. Cybulski continued publishing music until 1818.[10] The first published composition of Chopin, the Polonaise in G Minor, dedicated to Countess Skarbek, was engraved in Cybulski's shop in November 1817 (fig. 3.2).[11]

Following the example of Elsner and Cybulski, several printers opened engraving shops. Among them was Antoni Płachecki, a relative of Father Cybulski. This young man was brought into the trade by Cybulski in 1802, and during the years 1802–1803 Elsner sponsored his apprenticeship in a printing shop of Jan Ligber, who already in the eighteenth cen-

[8] Alina Nowak-Romanowicz, *Józef Elsner* (Kraków: Polskie Wydawnictwo Muzyczne, 1957), 77.

[9] *Gazeta Korespondenta Warszawskiego i Zagranicznego*, 11 February 1803, no. 12, quoted in Nowak-Romanowicz, *Elsner*, 78.

[10] Nowak-Romanowicz, *Elsner*, 81.

[11] Józef M. Chomiński and Teresa D. Turło, *Katalog dzieł Fryderyka Chopina* [A catalogue of the works of Fryderyk Chopin] (Kraków: Polskie Wydawnictwo Muzyczne, 1990), 174–175.

Figure 3.2. Fryderyk Chopin, *Polonaise pour le pianoforte dédiée à Comtesse Victoire Skarbek* (Warsaw: Cybulski, 1817). Muzeum Fryderyka Chopina w Towarzystwie im. Fryderyka Chopina, Warsaw, M/375. Photo by Andrzej Ring & Bartosz Tropiło.

tury tried printing music to make it more easily available.[12] In the end, Libger mostly produced illustrations for books, but Płachecki learned from him the technique of copper engraving, which remained the major method of music production until the 1820s.[13] In 1814, Płachecki opened

[12] Magier, *Estetyka miasta stołecznego Warszawy*, 143.
[13] Wojciech Tomaszewski, *Warszawskie edytorstwo muzyczne*, 70–71.

Figure 3.2. *continued*

his own music engraving shop, which became the most lasting enterprise of this kind in Warsaw, active until at least 1851.

The 1820s witnessed an unprecedented flowering of music printing. The great demand for published music was conditioned by the development of the music industry, especially the production of pianos on the territory of the Congress Kingdom, which marked the unprecedented surge of interest in this instrument. The publishing industry was also sustained by the presence of musical institutions, mainly the National Theater, and the evolution of institutional musical education, evidenced by the establishment of the conservatory.

In 1819, Ludwik Letronne began printing music using lithography. During his short career, Letronne published several interesting works. Although his shop produced music prints only until 1823, other publishers took up the use this technique. One of them was Franciszek Klukowski, known in Warsaw since around 1805, first as the owner of a bookstore offering music, and from 1816 as a music publisher, a trade his family continued until 1847. Initially, Klukowski used the services of other printers to publish music, but in 1822 he began to lithograph his own musical scores. During the same year, Andrzej Brzezina's shop opened its doors to the public. By 1830, the highly successful Brzezina issued nearly 570 prints. Brzezina and later his partner Gustaw Sennenwald continued to produce musical scores until 1837. At least nine other shops printed music during the 1820s, most of them either marginally devoted to music printing or short-lived. Among them were two more enterprises with significant impact on the music market: the workshop of Karol Magnus, active in the years 1828–1839, and the Music Conservatory press, publishing scores between 1827 and 1830.[14]

Publications were in book or sheet music formats. In addition, Warsaw printers issued several periodic or multivolume publications dedicated to general or particular repertories. *Lutnia* (Brzezina), for instance, contained a variety of pieces for the piano, *Les Soirées de Famille* (Letronne) and *Terpsychora* (Letronne) were dedicated to fashionable dances, whereas *Journal de Musique Italienne* (Cybulski) or *Philoméle* (Letronne) contained vocal pieces. Music inserts in journals and nonmusical books were also common, the most notable being the musical settings to Niemcewicz's *Historical Chants* (discussed later).

The increased importance of musical education created a market for the publications of studies and methods. Prior to the publishing boom, major foreign music manuals were readily available in Poland through imports and in private circulation. Through such means, the professional musician had access to standard music-theoretical treatises of the eighteenth century; for instance, Franciszek Lessel's library contained over a dozen of such volumes, including Rousseau's *Dictionnaire de musique* and Koch's *Versuch einer Anleitung zur Composition*, as well as Marpurg's *Anleitung zur Singcomposition* and *Handbuch bey dem Generalbasse und der Composition*. We learn from letters between Lessel and his father that books of this kind routinely circulated among professional musicians. Newer works were available through the same means of distribution. But given the demands of the increasingly music-literate public and the needs of the students enrolled in the Warsaw Conservatory, particularly popular textbooks merited being reissued by local publishers. This market encouraged the Polish editions of such foreign books as *Exercises for the Fortepiano for Beginners* (*Ćwiczenia na fortepiano dla początkujących*) by August Eberhard Müller, the kapellmeister to the great prince of Weimar (part I engraved in Płachecki's shop for Klukowski in 1822; part II engraved and printed in Klukowski's own shop in 1823); the celebrated *Méthode de violon* of Rode, Baillot, and Kreuzer (*Metoda na skrzypce Rodego, Bailliota y Kreycera*), in the translation of Józef Bielawski (Klukowski, 1824); Johann Baptist Cramer's *A School for the Pianoforte* (*Szkoła na pianoforte*; Brzezina, 1826); and Henri Herz's *Exercices et preludes pour le pfte dans tous les tons majeurs et mineurs dediée à Mr. Hummel*; Brzezina, 1827.

As the needs of Warsaw's musical clientele continued to grow and the ranks of respected resident teachers increased, the market saw the emergence of didactic works by local authors. In 1818 and 1820, Płachecki published Elsner's work *The Beginnings of Music and Singing in Particular*

---

[14] Wojciech Tomaszewski, *Warszawskie edytorstwo muzyczne*, 50–54.

(*Początki muzyki a szczególnie śpiewania*). At Klukowski's request, he also printed the 1818 and 1819 editions of Kurpiński's work *A Systematic Lecture on Musical Principles for the Keyboard* (*Wykład systematyczny zasad muzyki na klawikord*) and the 1821 edition of his *Examples to the Principles of Tone Harmony* (*Przykłady do Zasad harmonii tonów*). Among Magnus's publications were Soliva's two didactic volumes *A Practical Piano School* (*Szkoła praktyczna fortepianu*) and *A School of Singing of the Music Conservatory* (*Szkoła śpiewu Konserwatorum Muzycznego*) (vol. 1, 1826; vol. 2, 1827). Such tendencies also affected other Polish cultural centers. For instance, Chopin's first theory book, the German-Polish *Kurze Einweisung die Regeln der Harmonie oder des Generalbasses*, was written and published in Poznań in 1823 by the music teacher and publisher Karol Antoni Simon (it was distributed in Warsaw by Klukowski). These trends to publish pedagogical compositions fostered such publications as *Collection of Introductions (Preludes) in All Tones for the Pianoforte* (*Zbiór przygrywek (preludiów) ze wszystkich tonów na pfte*; Letronne, 1821), by Chopin's teacher, Václav Würfel, the earliest such collection known to have been composed and published in Poland, and later the set of preludes by another professor at the Warsaw Conservatory, Heinrich Gherard Lentz (*Collection de préludes dans tous les tons usites pour le pfte*; Brzezina, 1826). Along with preludes of Szymanowska and Kessler published abroad, these sets constitute the ancestry of Chopin's preludes. Unfortunately, unlike the sets of Szymanowska and Kessler, none of the collections of preludes published in Chopin's Warsaw survived into our times.

The new patrons of music—middle class, intelligentsia, and more affluent artisans—made up a large audience of very definite tastes that provided a market for salon music. The printing of more sizable and complicated musical works was not feasible, since the small demand would not offset the costs of production, though sacred works were a notable exception, having been published on several occasions by local printers. As a result of the limited demand, only a handful of chamber compositions were published during that time—connoisseurs imported such works from Vienna, Leipzig, and Paris, and professional musicians had their own larger works published abroad as well. In 1831, Gołębiowski expressed hope that some wealthy patrons would provide the means to have large works—symphonic, sacred, operatic—copied and preserved for posterity: "Should future generations want to judge the present state of music in Poland based on printed musical works, how demeaning would their opinion of us be if they found only waltzes, mazurkas, gallopades, polonaises; and these composed mostly by amateurs."[15] There was, indeed, a great demand for small compositions for the piano or for voice accompa-

[15] Gołębiowski, *Gry i zabawy różnych stanów*, 264.

nied by the piano, mostly dances, songs, and opera arrangements. To a lesser degree, the public was interested in music for flute, guitar, harp, violin, and organ.

Dance Music

The dance element, so prominent in Chopin's music, has been the subject of much discussion, but scholars almost invariably have concentrated their attention on his indebtedness to folk music, ignoring the thriving culture of ballroom dancing into which he was born.[16] Even the most recent *New Grove Dictionary* article on "Mazurka" focuses on supposed folk sources for Chopin's pieces, sidestepping the popular tradition.[17] Such direction in research resulted from Chopin scholarship having developed against the backdrop of two folklore-promoting ideologies: nationalism, which endorsed cultural Polishness, articulated through the Herderian idea of "das Volk," as a means of resisting foreign domination; and later communism, which sanctioned folklore as the quintessential music of the common people. In actuality, Chopin's works clearly stem from urban dance culture, and direct influence of peasant music on his oeuvre was at best marginal. Elements typically cited as received by him directly from the music of the peasants—drones, modality, the lydian fourth in particular—were in reality already present in the urban dances of his youth.[18] Moreover, at times influences radiated in the other direction, originating with urban dances and migrating into peasant genres. This process was observed already in 1820 by Karol Kurpiński, who commented that in the vicinity of Warsaw, peasant dances were contaminated by the sounds of the capital.[19] Amidst the growing patriotic fervor, sustained by the rush of piano transcriptions of opera favorites and ballroom dances, Poland's musical market was inundated with folk-like dances. The brilliant Polish musicologist Tadeusz Strumiłło echoes the words of Chopin's

[16] Since the presentation of this material in my dissertation, the topic of Chopin's dances in the context of Warsaw's salon and ballroom traditions has been addressed in a couple of excellent studies: Barbara Milewski, "Chopin's Mazurkas and the Myth of the Folk," *19th-Century Music* 23 (1999): 113–135, and Eric McKee, "Dance and the Music of Chopin: The Waltz," in *The Age of Chopin: Interdisciplinary Inquiries*, ed. Halina Goldberg (Bloomington: Indiana University Press, 2004), 106–161.

[17] Stephen Downes, "Mazurka," in *Grove Music Online*, ed. L. Macy (Accessed 12 October 2006), http://bert.lib.indiana.edu:2100.

[18] Milewski, "Chopin's Mazurkas and the Myth of the Folk."

[19] Karol Kurpiński, "O pieśniach w ogólności" [On songs in general], *Tygodnik Muzyczny*, 21 and 27 June 1820.

contemporaries when he says that already during the composer's child-hood Warsaw was satiated, "fed up," with folk-inspired compositions.[20]

Native dances were adopted by the upper classes already in the seventeenth century, and by Chopin's time they were firmly entrenched in Warsaw's ballrooms and salons. Starting at the end of the eighteenth century, Polish composers, who made the creation of a Polish national musical language their chief goal, began to introduce local dance elements into operas dealing with national topics. By the early nineteenth century, the krakowiak and the mazur were recognized musical markers of ethnic nationality; the polonaise, associated with idealized traditions of Polish nobility, embodied idyllic recollections of proud and virtuous Poland before partitions.

Ironically, at the same time, Warsaw's printers frequently issued ceremonial polonaises by major local composers, dedicated to the members of the imperial Russian family on birthdays, name days, and other celebratory occasions. Such musical offerings are explained by the fact that at the end of the eighteenth century the polonaise became the imperial Russian dance: actually, until 1833, the polonaise "Thunder of Victory, Resound!"—written by a Polish composer Józef Kozłowski to commemorate Catherine the Great's 1791 victory over the Turks—served as the Russian anthem. The choice of a polonaise to celebrate festive events relating to the Romanoffs was thus consistent with the role the polonaise assumed in Russia.[21] In Warsaw, these polonaises celebrating imperial Russia existed alongside the increasingly patriotic associations of this dance (fig. 3.3).

Social dancing was pervasive in nineteenth-century Warsaw: every opportunity to dance—in private or public circles—was seized. Casual dance gatherings in salons, formal balls, and commercial dance events (*reduty*) thrived, especially during the carnival season. Since proficiency in dancing was considered a component of social education, young people of the middle and upper classes routinely received dance instruction from Warsaw's dancing masters. Dancing instructions were even included in music publications of new fashionable dances, as in the quadrille "La Duchesse de Berry" (fig. 3.4).

Given his social standing and the numerous reports of his skill on the

[20] Tadeusz Strumiłło, *Źrodła i początki romantyzmu w muzyce polskiej* [Sources and beginnings of Romanticism in Polish music] (Kraków: Polskie Wydawnictwo Muzyczne, 1956), 115.

[21] On the subject of the Russian readings of Polish dances see Halina Goldberg, "Appropriating Poland: Glinka, Polish Dance, and Russian National Identity," in *Polish Encounters, Russian Identity*, ed. David Ransel and Bożena Shallcross (Bloomington: Indiana University Press, 2005), 74–88.

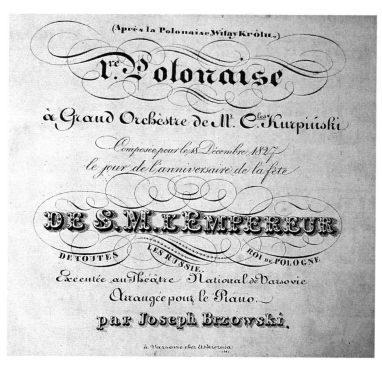

Figure 3.3. Karol Kurpiński, *1re Polonaise à Grand Orchèstre . . . Composée pour le 18 Décembre 1827 le jour de l'anniversaire de la fete de S. M. l'Empereur de toutes les Russie, Roi de Pologne . . . Arrangée pour le Piano par Joseph Brzowski (Après la polonaise "Witay Królu")* (Warsaw: Brzezina, 1827), title page. Uniwersytet Jagielloński, Biblioteka Muzykologii, Kraków, 5197.

dance floor, it is certain that Chopin, along with his sisters, took dance lessons. By all accounts, he was a rather proficient dancer who during his Warsaw years took every opportunity to participate in dance events. His experience as a dancer could not remain without impact on his compositional output, especially if one considers that dances make up almost half of his oeuvre and that in the remaining works the dance element is ubiquitous. In fact, Eric McKee has persuasively argued that the bodily rhythms and social contexts of dancing shaped the musical structure and expressive meaning of Chopin's waltzes.[22]

Dances that dominated the ballroom of Chopin's time and hence had the largest share of the publishing market were the polonaise, mazur, and waltz. The polonaise (*polonez*) had become the favorite of Polish audiences by the middle of the eighteenth century, and until 1815 this dance made up a remarkable 96 percent of the published piano dance repertory.

[22] Eric McKee, "Dance and the Music of Chopin: The Waltz," 106–161.

Figure 3.4. Quadrille "La Duchesse de Berry" from *Terpsychora, czyli zbiór nay-nowszych naybardziey ulubionych w Towarzystwach Warszawskich rozmaitych tancow na piano-forte, nr. 5* [Terpsichore, or a collection of the newest and most favored in various Warsaw societies dances for pianoforte no. 5] (Warsaw: Letronne, 1821), p. 8. Uniwersytet Jagielloński, Biblioteka Muzykologii, Kraków, 5197.

In this context, it is not surprising that all of young Fryderyk's earliest compositions are polonaises. During the years 1816–1825, the polonaise still dominated, though gradually the waltz and the mazur were conquering Warsaw. The mazur (also referred to by the diminutive mazurka [*mazurek*], a term Chopin preferred) and the related kujawiak and oberek (these genres appear in print in the 1830s and 1840s) were native dances. The German *Waltzer*, on the other hand, were brought to Warsaw during the Prussian occupation and gradually took over the Polish capital. By 1830, only a few years after Johann Strauss *pere*'s publication of his op. 1, his waltzes (and other compositions) were not only imported from Vienna but also published by local printers. Given the market's voracious appetite for waltzes, in the years 1825–1830 the ratio of published piano dances changed in favor of not only the waltz (35 percent) but also the mazur (29 percent). The polonaise was third (20 percent), followed by other fashionable dances: gallopade, cotillion, anglaise, and contredanse.[23]

[23] Wojciech Tomaszewski, *Warszawskie edytorstwo muzyczne*, 167.

All three most favored dances were in triple meter: the polonaise was majestic and moderate; the other two were very lively. Musical settings for dances were sectional and open-ended, allowing for repetitions and returns of segments in order to customize the duration of music according to the needs of the dance floor. The preferred textures were homophonic, and the accompaniments charted out simple diatonic patterns of harmonies. Rhythms and melodies were straightforward, their shapes corresponding to the movements of the dancers. Each dance had a distinct choreography: in the polonaise the chain of pairs formed elaborate geometric formations; the mazur called for foot stamping and jumps in accordance with musical accents; while in the waltz, the spinning melodies reflected the movement of the couples, who twirled in small and large circles while holding each other in direct gaze. According to Wójcicki, the waltz was danced in the Polish capital in a faster and livelier manner than elsewhere, eventually, when accompanied by the gallopade, spinning out of control in a mad whirl.[24] The direct and continuous proximity of partners that characterized the waltz was previously unheard of, making it the most flirtatious and erotic of nineteenth-century dances and causing traditionalists to view it as "scandalous."

Although the choreographies of the mazur and the waltz were dissimilar, their musical settings showed a certain degree of generic interchangeability.[25] The cause was partially in the migration of dances between taverns and ballrooms of Warsaw—while the mazurka originated with the peasants and moved to the salon, the foreign, elegant waltz was quickly adapted by the lower classes. Observing this process, Gołębiowski commented that the commoners of Warsaw danced to clumsy waltzes, while the upper classes adopted the mazurka. Naturally, the two genres could be easily differentiated when the archetypal drones, modalities, dotted rhythms, and offbeat accents of the mazurka or the twirling melodies and um-pah-pah accompaniments of the waltz did not cross over. The mazur by Count Karol Sołtyk, a competent amateur praised for his well-crafted mazurkas, is a piece observing the confines of its genre. In the same way, Świeszewski's waltz, with its typical introduction, regular accentuation, twirling and cantilena melodies, and um-pah-pah accompaniment, clearly meets the generic expectations of a waltz (see figs. 3.5, 3.6).

The generic boundaries were not so apparent when a dance employed characteristic melodic patterns common to the waltz and the mazurka.

[24] Kazimierz Władysław Wójcicki, *Społeczność Warszawy w początkach naszego stulecia* [Warsaw's society in the beginning of our century] (Warsaw: Gebethner i Wolff, 1877), 155.

[25] This problem has received attention from Edwin Kornel Stadnicki in *Walc fortepianowy w Polsce w latach 1800–1830* [The piano waltz in Poland in the years 1800–1830] (Kraków: Polskie Wydawnictwo Muzyczne, 1962), especially 112–146.

Figure 3.5. Karol Sołtyk, *Deux mazurs et une gallopade* (Warsaw: Brzezina, 1827), p. 3. Biblioteka Jagiellońska, Kraków, XVII 57.

For instance, the quicker, spinning melodies usually associated with the oberek type, were similar to waltz-like melodic lines. One unknown composer remarked on this inherent generic ambiguity by entitling his piece (a rather clear example of a waltz) "Mazur–not Mazur–but Waltz" (*Mazur–nie mazur–ale walc*).[26]

The genre of the last movement of Chopin's F Minor Concerto op. 21 likewise presents questions. The movement, marked simply "Allegro vivace," bears no generic designation, but tradition has labeled it a mazurka. Recently, this view has been challenged by Eric McKee, who argues that it has all the generic features of a waltz.[27] His theory is further supported by the association of op. 21 with Chopin's love for Konstancja Gładkowska; after all, the waltz was the ultimate dance of romance and was considered the most suitable musical gift for a woman. On the other hand, this movement's similarity to the mazurka rondo-finale of Franciszek Lessel's Piano Concerto in C Major, op. 14 (published in 1813) speaks in favor of a

[26] Biblioteka Narodowa, Warsaw, Ms. 788. Also referred to in Stadnicki, *Walc fortepianowy w Polsce w latach 1800–1830*, 124–125.

[27] McKee, "Dance and the Music of Chopin: The Waltz," 154–155.

Figure 3.6. Aleksander Świeszewski, *Valse pour le pianoforte* (Warsaw: J. Dąbrowski, 1829), p. 3. Biblioteka Jagiellońska, Kraków, XV 195.

mazurka as Chopin's model.[28] An interesting light on the question of the generic identity of the last movement of Chopin's F Minor Concerto is shed by two publications issued in 1830 by Fryderyk's conservatory friend Antoni Orłowski. Orłowski responded to Fryderyk's successful spring 1830 concerts with two brief transcriptions: *Mazur on Motives from Fryderyk Chopin's Concerto, Fantasia and Rondo* (*Mazur z motywów koncertu, fantazyi i ronda Fryderyka Chopina*) and *Waltz on Themes by Fryderyk Chopin* (*Walc z tematów Fryderyka Chopina*), about which there was much talk in letters between Chopin and Tytus Woyciechowski.[29] Orłowski's transcriptions, explored as a mode of reception through music, yield information about Chopin's contemporaries' reading of the movement in question. Naturally, as a source of generic attribution, the arrangements must be viewed with caution, since Orłowski, in a manner characteristic of his time, does not hesitate to recast melodies into new genres: the second theme of Chopin's first movement (in duple meter) becomes the

[28] The similarity between Chopin's and Lessel's works was first asserted by Hans Engel in *Die Entwicklung des deutschen Klavierkonzertes von Mozart bis Liszt* (Leipzig: Breitkopf & Härtel, 1927), 152–153.

[29] Chopin, Warsaw, to Woyciechowski, Poturzyn, 27 March 1830, *Korespondencja*, 1:116; Chopin, Warsaw, to Woyciechowski, 10 April 1830, *Korespondencja*, 1:120; Chopin, Warsaw, to Woyciechowski, 17 April 1830, *Korespondencja*, 1:121.

trio of his waltz (in triple meter); and the first theme of Chopin's krakowiak (in duple meter) is transformed into the third section of Orłowski's mazur (in triple meter). The themes Orłowski borrows from the last movement, however, are not generically altered, and apparently lend generic titles to Orłowski's arrangements: he calls the piece quoting the opening of Chopin's last movement a "waltz," and he labels "mazur" the quotation of a later episode, starting in measure 141 of Chopin's piece (in the trio of his transcription). Orłowski's reading of the last movement of the F Minor Concerto is consistent with the generic features of Chopin's two themes, and supports the thesis that Chopin designed the last movement of his F Minor Concerto as interplay of the waltz and mazur genres (see figs. 3.7, 3.8).

The celebrated amateur composer Michał Kleofas Ogiński, in one of his letters about music, written in 1828 from Florence, recognized the generic similarity between the waltz and the mazur. At the same time, he indicated that the main distinction between the two genres is in the interaction of meter and articulation during performance:

> *Mazurek*, which the French call *mazourka*, is another national dance; cheerful and lively. Its rhythm somewhat resembles the waltz: there is something, I don't know what, in the manner of playing and in the bow stroke—which must be employed to mark the meter—that causes even dilettantes, in particular if they are Polish, to easily notice the distinction between the music of these two dances.[30]

Ogiński's description suggests that some of mazurka's identity is inherent in the performative aspects of the genre and could not be captured through musical notation. His suggestion resonates with comments by other contemporaries of Chopin who associated unwritten rubato with the salon mazurka genre, Chopin's mazurkas in particular. Similar connections exist between Polish folk genres related to the mazurka and a performance style that involves tempo vacillations.[31] Not only is the mazurka's generic identity strongly associated with musical performance but also with dance execution. Indeed, one cannot intelligibly discuss the interplay of the mazur and waltz genres without considering their performative components. What on a page appears generically ambiguous in performance could be clearly defined through appropriate "marking of the meter" by musicians and through apt choreography.

[30] "The Third Letter: Florence, 1 June 1828," in Michał Kleofas Ogiński, *Listy o muzyce* [Letters about music], ed. Tadeusz Strumiłło (Kraków: Polskie Wydawnictwo Muzyczne, 1955), 57.

[31] See Anna Czekanowska, *Polish Folk Music: Slavonic Heritage—Polish Tradition—Contemporary Trends* (Cambridge: Cambridge University Press, 1990).

Figure 3.7. Antoni Orłowski, *Walc z tematów Fryderyka Chopina* [Waltz on themes by Fryderyk Chopin] (Warsaw: Brzezina, 1830). Biblioteka Jagiellońska, Kraków, 7454 II Mus.

Figure 3.7. *continued*

   The composition of dances was the domain of both the professional composer and the musical dilettante. Dances were composed by conservatory professors and students, local music mâitres, and musicians associated with Warsaw's orchestras, theaters, and ballrooms, as well as musically inclined members of the noble and middle classes. Women were no exception to this trend, and their compositions were frequently published, including pieces by several women from Chopin's circles. Apparently Chopin's sisters also tried their hands at composing dances, for in November 1825, Fryderyk wrote to Jan Białobłocki praising Ludwika's new spirited mazur for its exceptional danceability.[32] The desire to compose fashionable dances was so great that in 1828 Magnus published Franciszek Mirecki's *One Million Mazurs, Meaning a Method for Composing Millions of Mazurs Even for Those Who Do Not Know Music* (*Milion mazurów czyli sposób układania miliony [sic] mazurów dla tych nawet, którzy muzyki nie znają*). The announcement of the publication in the daily press explained that it "contains: a table with cut-up pages of music from A to Z in alphabetical order, in addition, one page with instructions in Polish and French; each packet has 12 pages of music; there are 21 packets."[33]

[32] Chopin, Warsaw, to Białobłocki, Sokołów, [November 1825], *Korespondencja*, 1:66.
[33] Tomaszewski, *Bibliografia*, 104.

Figure 3.8. Antoni Orłowski, *Mazur z motywów koncertu, fantazyi i ronda krakow-skiego Fryderyka Chopina* [Mazur on motives from Concerto, Fantasia and Cracovian Rondo by Fryderyk Chopin] (Warsaw: Brzezina, 1830). Biblioteka Warszawskiego Towarzystwa Muzycznego, Warsaw, Mus. II 30.032.

The following year, Brzezina issued a similar method for composing waltzes by a successful Warsaw theater and ballroom composer, Józef Damse. The book was apparently popular enough to have been reissued by Brzezina's partner, Sennewald, in 1832.

While these *ars combinatoria* games were intended for the amusement of musically illiterate and unskilled dilettantes, other amateurs displayed varied levels of compositional competence. Among the most talented were Aleksander Rembieliński, whose talent at the piano elicited exalted praises from Chopin in 1825, and another acquaintance of his, Count Karol Sołtyk, whose well-liked mazurs have already been mentioned. The most celebrated of the hosts of amateur composers was Prince Michał Kleofas

Figure 3.8. *continued*

Figure 3.9. Michał Kleofas Ogiński, Polonaise "Les Adieux" from *Zebranie wszelkich polonezów Hrabiego Ogińskiego, nr. 1–12* [The complete collection of Count [sic] Ogiński's polonaises, nos. 1–12] (Warsaw: Letronne, 1820), pp. 8–9. Biblioteka Narodowa, Warsaw, Mus. III.82034 Cim.

Figure 3.9. *continued*

Ogiński, much older than Chopin but still active in the 1820s. Because of his participation in the Kościuszko Insurrection of 1794, Ogiński's polonaises were received as intensely patriotic. The one titled "Les Adieux" epitomizes the genre of *polonaise triste*, characterized by minor mode, melodic lyricism, and expressiveness (see fig. 3.9). Ogiński's works, clearly destined for the salon, typify the pre-Chopin polonaise, in their sectional character, characteristic accompaniment figures, and cadential formulas, as well as simple harmonic and melodic language.

Most dances published in Chopin's Warsaw were utilitarian in character, although the boundaries between dance and listening functions were by no means firm. Fashionable orchestral compositions designated for the ballroom were instantly available in piano arrangements—to be used in the salon for dancing or for listening. Such compositions, making up a very large group of published piano dances, were melodically and harmonically uncomplicated, in accord with their original dance function. Having been originally conceived for the orchestra, they made little use of pianistically idiomatic textures and figurations, yet they were a vehicle for the introduction of thicker orchestral textures into salon repertory for the piano.

Conversely, some pieces written expressly for the piano were adopted for orchestral performance in the ballroom. Again, the suitability of the original for adaptation to the dance floor was the major criterion. Chopin's compositions were no exception. Although he explicitly told his parents that he did not design his opus 7 mazurkas for dancing,[34] his B-flat major Mazurka op. 7 no. 1 was published twice, in 1835 and again in 1842, by Klukowski as *A Favorite Mazur Composed for the Fortepiano by Fr. Chopin Played in the Variety Theater and at Dancing Soirées at Both Merchant Clubs* (*Ulubiony mazur skomponowany na fortepiano przez Fr. Chopina grywany w Teatrze Rozmaitości i na wieczorach tańcujących w obydwu ressursach*; see fig. 3.10). The reappropriation of this composition for the ballroom, from which it arose, was possible because of its relative formal, melodic, and metric directness. The dilemma arising from the conflict between the ballroom's insatiable appetite for new dances and the composer's increasing desire to place his compositions outside their utilitarian context is captured by his sister, Ludwika, in a letter written in 1835 and probably referring to the same op. 7 no. 1 mazurka:

> Your mazurka, the one that goes Bam Bum Bum in the third part (which by the way was performed by a full orchestra at the Variety Theater) was played all evening at the ball at the Zamoyskis, and Bar[ciński] who personally heard it there says that they were extremely pleased with it for dancing. What do you say about being profaned like that, since the mazurka is more properly for listening? Tymowski, who was at the ball at Zamoyskis' when many ladies showed the desire of having this Mazurka, took it from the orchestra and gave to Klukowski so he could print it, and now you can hear it everywhere: it is a favorite. What will you say about my being at the Lebruns one evening and having had to profane you? ... They had asked me if I would play your excellent

[34] Chopin, Vienna, to his family, Warsaw, [22 December 1830], *Korespondencja*, 1:161.

Figure 3.10. Fryderyk Chopin, *Ulubiony mazur skomponowany na fortepiano przez Fr. Chopina grywany w Teatrze Rozmaitości i na wieczorach tańcujących w obydwu ressursach* [A favorite mazur composed for the fortepiano by Fr. Chopin played in the Variety Theater and at dancing soirées at both Merchant Clubs] (Warsaw: Klukowski, 1835), title page. Biblioteka Jagiellońska, Kraków, 407 III Mus.

Mazurka, and thinking of you shaking your head with disapproval (I believe that you wrote it for listening), I played it for dancing with the approval of the dancers. My dear, tell me and write whether you wrote it in the spirit of a dance; perhaps we have understood you incorrectly.[35]

Unfortunately, Chopin's response to Ludwika's questions did not survive.

The desire to appropriate any musical novelties to the needs of the ballroom made way for adaptations of motives from especially loved concert and operatic performances into dances. Waltzes and polonaises, less often mazurkas and cotillions, on the motives of fashionable operas were issued in Warsaw by the dozen. As early as 1811, Elsner commented to Breitkopf & Härtel that in Warsaw "everything that is pleasing today may be converted into a polonaise."[36] This trend only intensified with time. Chopin's

[35] Ludwika Chopin, Warsaw, to Fryderyk Chopin, Paris, 9 February 1835, *Korespondencja*, 1: 252–253.

[36] Quoted after Stephen Downes, "Polonaise," in *Grove Music Online*, ed. L. Macy (Accessed 12 October 2006), http://bert.lib.indiana.edu:2100.

Polonaise in B-flat Minor, quoting from Rossini's "Vieni fra queste braccia," from act I of *La gazza ladra*, hails to such models. Incorporating melodies from concert performances were less common, though Paganini's and Lipiński's 1929 Warsaw concerts inspired such publications, and a year later Antoni Orłowski responded to Chopin's public concerts with the aforementioned waltzes and mazurkas on the motives of his compositions.

During the course of his search for new narrative compositional concepts, Chopin had to discover ways to free his dances from the confines imposed by their utilitarian function—sectionality, melodic and harmonic simplicity, and what has been called the "tyranny of the four-bar phrase."[37] Such a process would have been encouraged by the nonutilitarian compositional models available to him in Warsaw: dance compositions destined primarily for listening. Pieces of this sort were found among the works of Hummel, Weber, and Szymanowska, as well as locally published compositions stemming from a group of composers who at the time were active in Poland: Franciszek Siekierski, Ignacy Chudoba, Piotr Siegrist, Thomas Navratill,[38] and Václav Würfel.

The nonutilitarian dance-based compositions addressed the more ambitious performer, and introduced greater virtuosity and expressivity. Their titles were distinguished by such adjectives as *brillant, grand, melancolique, triste, militaire, guerriere,* and *lugubre,* indicating their *topoi* and placing them within the sentimental and brilliant styles. Beyond their interest in newer compositional styles, the composers of these pieces showed awareness of possibilities offered by the newest pianos and, in contrast to other major local composers, employed truly pianistic idiom. The single most noticeable attribute of these pieces was their expanded pianistic vocabulary: larger ranges, figurations related to vocal fioriturae, more frequent use of extreme registers, and a greater involvement of the left hand. They also make use of chromatic lines and harmonies, and occasional contrapuntal textures.

The two examples presented here of polonaises for listening that employ a grander manner are by Würfel and Siegrist (see figs. 3.11, 3.12). Like other works of this type, they are more substantial in various ways: more complex, more technically demanding, and longer. The first page of the *Trio* in Würfel's piece introduces cross-rhythms (see the quadruplets against the sextuplets in measure 2). The run starting at the end of the fourth system is typical of Würfel's chromaticized scale-based figurations. Piotr Siegrist's *Polonaise brillante* opens with an introduction that is

[37] The term used and discussed by Edward T. Cone, "The Picture Gallery: Form and Style," in *Musical Form and Musical Performance* (New York: Norton, 1968), 57–87.

[38] None of the compositions by Thomas Navratill, a musician in the service of Princess Lubomirska, were actually published in Warsaw, but his works circulated in Poland in foreign editions and manuscript copies.

Figure 3.11. Václav Vilém Würfel, *Grand polonaise pour le Piano forte*, op. 40 (Warsaw: Brzezina, 1825), p. 4. Biblioteka Jagiellońska, Kraków, 11165 III Mus.

omitted in the *da capo*. In this composition, figurations display greater variety than in Würfel's, and their operatic ancestry is apparent. The piece is notated with a specificity not often found in dance pieces published at the time in Warsaw, manifested in the profusion of pedaling and articulation detail, as well as in the frequent expressive markings.

Whereas the earliest of Chopin's polonaises—brief, diatonic, and melodically uncomplicated—follow models set by utilitarian compositions (the G Minor and B-flat Major Polonaises, both composed in 1817), polonaises he composed a few years later are more like the pieces by Würfel and Siegrist. These works, for instance, his Polonaise in G-sharp Minor op. Posthumous (see ex. 3.1), are considerably longer and more complex than the earlier ones. They are still distinctly sectional and rely on a *da capo* return (only in the E-flat Minor Polonaise op. 26 no. 2, from the mid-1830s, does he abandon the polonaise-trio-*da capo* scheme and writes out a return with a somewhat more conclusive ending). They do, however, demonstrate his penchant for chromaticism and virtuosity, as well as his understanding of the instrument. Like the works of Würfel and Siegrist, and unlike his early childhood pieces, these polonaises are written distinctly with the piano, rather than a generic keyboard instrument in mind. These works bear witness to Würfel's significance as Chopin's

Figure 3.12. Piotr Siegrist, *Polonaise brillante* (Warsaw: Brzezina, 1828), pp. 2–4. Uniwersytet Jagielloński, Biblioteka Muzykologii, Kraków, 5197.

Figure 3.12. *continued*

teacher: among his Warsaw mentors Würfel was the only one who was an accomplished pianist with concert stage experience; and his compositions represented a direct link the innovative vocabulary of his own teacher Václav Jan Křtitel Tomášek's, one of the most influential composers of proto-Romantic piano music.

Some elements of these new compositional styles also found their way into waltzes and mazurs published Warsaw. Siegrist's *Mazure* comprises many sophisticated elements (see fig. 3.13). Two pages long, it is considerably longer than typical utilitarian mazurs, which frequently are no more than a couple of lines of music. While mazur characteristics—the raised fourth and accented second beat, in particular—cannot be overlooked, the melodies of this piece are florid and rhythmically varied. The composer also seeks timbral variety by placing the melody in the left hand with a countermelody above (see the third system of the opening page.) Ignacy Chudoba's *Masure melancolique* introduces intimacy into this typically public genre (see fig. 3.14). The melancholy mood is set through the andante tempo marking and the use of minor mode. Ornamental lyric melodies, derived from vocal bel canto and its instrumental counterparts, are marked by plaintive semitones, sixth leaps, and expressive turns. Even the abundant chromaticism has expressive function.

Such instrumental dance-based pieces, which were stepping outside the confines of utilitarian functions, were important models for the young

Example 3.1. Fryderyk Chopin, Polonaise in G-sharp Minor op. post., trio, mm. 32–39.

Fryderyk. His earliest essay in the waltz genre, the B Minor Waltz of 1829, published posthumously as op. 69 no. 2, far exceeds the compositional level of the vast majority of waltzes for dancing published at the time in Warsaw; no wonder, since by the time he wrote it he was already an accomplished young composer. Although it is only a two-page work, characterized by the repetitive structure of utilitarian waltzes, it carries the marks of his extraordinary musical gift: lyrically conceived and beautifully shaped melodies, expressive chromaticism, and superb understanding of larger harmonic structures. The intimate character of this work makes it, like the pieces by Siegrist and Chudoba, less suitable for the ballroom. In the case of op. 69 no. 2, a vital reason for the intimacy is the original purpose of the piece: it was probably, like many of Chopin's

Figure 3.13. Piotr Siegrist, *Mazure* (Warsaw: Brzezina, 1829), pp. 2–3. Uniwersytet Jagielloński, Biblioteka Muzykologii Kraków, 5197.

Figure 3.14. Ignacy Chudoba, *Masure melancolique* (Warsaw: Magnus, 1828). Uniwersytet Jagielloński, Biblioteka Muzykologii Kraków, 5197.

waltzes, a private piece, conceived as a personal memento and reserved for inscriptions in albums (Wilhelm Kolberg's and Countess's Plater).

Their expressive character and compositional craft notwithstanding, Chopin's Warsaw dance compositions arose out of their functional context, at least some of them having possibly been first conceived as accompaniment to salon dancing. Various sources tell us of Chopin's willingness to accompany dancers during private gatherings, even during his later, Parisian years.[39] When in 1832 his sister Ludwika married Józef Kalasanty Jędrzejewicz, Chopin sent them a "polonaise and a mazur, so you will hop and truly enjoy yourselves, since your souls are able to cele-

[39] For instance, he is reported to have accompanied dancers during a soirée at the Wilanów Palace, hosted by Countess Potocka and Princess Czetwertyńska and attended by Prince Antoni Radziwiłł (Marceli A. Szulc, Fryderyk Chopin i utwory jego muzyczne [Fryderyk Chopin and his musical works] (1873), ed. D. Idaszek (Kraków: Polskie Wydawnictwo Muzyczne, 1986), 251–254) and during gatherings with his peers; Anna Wóycicka, "Wieczorek pożegnalny Fryderyka Chopina" [Fryderyk Chopin's farewell evening], Pion, 1934, no. 24, 1.

brate."[40] His early dance pieces retained this strong connection with the popular dance culture of his time, differing in quality but not design or aesthetic goals from the dance compositions of his contemporaries. Only gradually did Chopin move away from the formal and metric confines of dance genres and introduce melodic and harmonic complexity into his dance compositions. Metric irregularities and unexpected formal or contrapuntal devices, in particular, conflicted with the carefully mapped out choreographies of the ballroom, rendering such dances unusable on the dance floor. In later years, the presence of such elements in Chopin's dance compositions increased, and the music took on ever more narrative character, though, in his waltzes especially, the connection with the ballroom and the salon was never completely abandoned.

Nondance Piano Genres

Nondance genres of piano music are represented by over three hundred pieces published in Warsaw during the years 1810–1830. The majority of these were original piano compositions (as opposed to the large group of arrangements and transcriptions of operatic arias), mainly rondos, variations, and fantasias. Among other genres were marches, nocturnes, romances, and the études and preludes mentioned earlier. The presence of the latter group of genres signals the beginning of an interest in the piano miniature, which will intensify after 1830.

The larger compositions—rondos, variations, and fantasias—were often inspired by popular dances, songs, and thematic material from operas. Dance idiom was so pervasive that even the traditional genres of piano music could not escape its presence. Though seldom published in Warsaw, sonatas, chamber works, and concert works by local composers readily incorporated dance elements, as in the last movements of Chopin's Trio op. 8 and both of his concertos, as well as the earlier Piano Concerto in C Major op. 14 by Lessel (published in 1813).[41] Piano rondos often combined figurative episodes and dance-like refrains, as in Chopin's op. 1, in which the refrain is a krakowiak, and his op. 5, published as *Rondo à la mazur,* with the title emphasizing the dance genre of its refrain.

Operas of Mozart, Rossini, Auber, and Weber were an important source of fantasias and variations. Sets of variations on melodies loved by the public were especially marketable and thus gladly accepted for publication. Chopin composed four such sets during his Warsaw years, none of

---

[40] Chopin, Paris, to Kalasanty Jędrzejewicz, Warsaw, 9 September 1832, *Korespondencja,* 1:217.

[41] Engel, *Die Entwicklung des deutschen Klavierkonzertes von Mozart bis Liszt,* 152–153. See note 28 above.

them published during his lifetime. The earliest set (1826), the D Major Variations for four hands, used a Venetian aria arranged and published in English translation as "O Come to Me When Daylight Sets" by Thomas Moore.[42] The later E Major set, which Chopin intended to publish as op. 4, was based on the song "Steh'auf, steh'auf o du Schwetzerbub," made popular by the Tyrolese singing family Rainer. The Flute Variations on "Non più mesta" from Rossini's *La cenerentola*, dedicated to Count Józef Cichocki, are traditionally attributed to Chopin. The work is not well known, mainly because Chopin's authorship is not certain, but also because the accompaniment is so flawed. At present, the consensus is that the flute part is the work of Chopin and that the original accompaniment was either lost or the work was left incomplete by the composer. The musically clumsy and harmonically deficient accompaniment is therefore a reconstruction or realization executed by a poor composer.[43] The authenticity of the Variations in A Major, entitled *Souvenir de Paganini* and supposedly inspired by Paganini's 1829 concerts in Warsaw, is likewise questioned, though traditionally they are included in the corpus of Chopin's oeuvre. The only set of variations published during Chopin's Warsaw years, op. 2 on Mozart's "Là ci darem la mano," belongs to a somewhat different group. These are virtuoso variations intended not for the popular market but for the concertizing pianist, and are generically close to the concert pieces based on popular opera tunes (discussed later). Indeed, they were published abroad precisely because the demand for advanced virtuoso works was so limited in Warsaw.

A particularly interesting group of variations arose as result of the popularity of native operas and the drive to promote national culture. Compositionally, they were not much different from other sets of variations, but in a larger sense they contributed to the popularization of native musical culture. These sets used as their themes favorite Polish popular songs or tunes from Polish operas. Würfel's *Variations pour le piano forte sur un mazure favorite de l'opera Łokietek* (Varsovie: Fuss, 1818) are based on one of the most loved tunes, the mazur "Young Peasants from Połaniec" [*Parobcaki of Połańca*], from an opera that acquired an espe-

---

[42] In "*Wariacje D-dur na 4 ręce* w kontekście *Wariacji* F. Riesa na tematy pieśni Thomasa Moore'a" [Variations in D Major for four hands in the context of Variations by F. Ries on the theme of a song by Thomas Moore], paper presented at the fifth annual Chopin Conference, December 1–3, 2005, Warsaw. Elżbieta Zwolińska carefully traced the sources available to Chopin and asserted that his variations were based directly on the song in Moore's collection and not, as had been previously claimed, of a set of variations by F. Ries.

[43] The most exhaustive discussion of this problem is still Jan Prosnak, "Wariacje fletowe Chopina" [Chopin's flute variations], in *Studia Muzykologiczne* (1953) vol. 1: 302–307. The manuscript of this work is in Biblioteka Warszawskiego Towarzystwa Muzycznego, Warsaw, R. Ch/22.

cially strong patriotic meaning for the Poles (see fig. 3.15). Like other pieces of Würfel's, they are characterized by a solid compositional craft and rich pianistic textures, with interesting figurations, layering of sound, and challenging cross-rhythms.

The publication of numerous fantasias by Warsaw's printers is a testimony to the growing importance of the genre.[44] Born in the late Renaissance as a vehicle for purely instrumental composition, the fantasia underwent many transformations, to reemerge at the end of the eighteenth century as a genre perfectly suiting the Romantic sensibilities: it allowed for intense and intimate expression, virtuoso display, improvisation-like idiom, and experimentation with form and language.

By the middle of the century, Chopin's peer Oskar Kolberg, in his article on the fantasia for the *Orgelbrand Encyclopedia*, described the various connotations brought into the term *fantasia* by contemporary practices:

> Fantasia in musical composition is a work that has no fixed form, though in contrast to capriccio it should develop logically. In older works of this kind by Bach and Mozart [one can even find] barely altered form of song or sonata, which proves that an artist of suitable genius is able to squeeze an ingenious idea into established forms. A motive for a fantasia can be taken from anywhere, which is proven by Chopin's fantasia on Polish themes, full of freshness and imagination, or Dobrzyński's fantasia from *Don Giovanni*. Today almost every virtuoso, taking advantage of the formlessness of this sort of composition, pastes together for himself a so-called fantasia. These are often nothing but unruly collections of diverse glittery ideas, the composer's or borrowed (hence called *reminiscence*), either sewn or glued together into a whole, or else unstitched or rolled out into small bits.[45]

As Kolberg pointed out, there was more than one kind of work that could be termed fantasia. Early nineteenth-century compositions fell roughly

[44] The subject of early nineteenth-century Polish fantasias has received a cursory attention in Alina Nowak-Romanowicz, "Polskie fantazje fortepianowe doby przedchopinowskiej" [Polish piano fantasias of the pre-Chopin era], in *Studia musicologia*, ed. Elżbieta Dziębowska, Zofia Helman, Danuta Idaszek, and Adam Neuer (Kraków: Polskie Wydawnictwo Muzyczne, 1979), 349–358. See also my article "Narodowość i narracja w polskich fantazjach pierwszej połowy XIX wieku" [Nationality and narrative in Polish fantasias during the first half of the nineteenth century], in *Topos narodowy w muzyce polskiej pierwszej połowy XIX wieku* (forthcoming).

[45] Oskar Kolberg, "Fantazja," in *Encyklopedia Powszechna* [Universal Encyclopedia], 28 vols. (Warsaw: Orgelbrand, 1859–68), 8:658, after Oskar Kolberg, *Dzieła wszystkie Oskara Kolberga* [The complete works of Oskar Kolberg], ed. J. Krzyżanowski, 86 vols., *Pisma muzyczne* [Music writings] part I, ed. M. Tomaszewski, O. Pawlak, and E. Miller (Wrocław: Polskie Towarzystwo Ludoznawcze; Warszawa: Ludowa Spółdzielnia Wydawnicza; Kraków: Polskie Wydawnictwo Muzyczne, 1971), 61:110.

Figure 3.15. Václav Vilém Würfel, *Variations pour le piano forte sur un mazure favorite de l'opera Łokietek* (Warsaw: Fuss, 1818), p. 2. Biblioteka Narodowa, Warsaw, Mus. II 19209 Cim.

into two subgenres of fantasia: one defined by the presence of well-known tunes, the other comprising freely composed works.

By far the more numerous and popular with wider audiences were fantasias on favorite themes, usually from operas, a genre that emerged at the end of the eighteenth century. These pieces, typically entitled "Pot-pourri," were either strings of favorite themes or variations on such a theme or themes. In Warsaw, several such compositions for the use of un-sophisticated amateurs were published, often by the leading composer of lowbrow entertainment, Józef Damse.

A related category consisted of much more complex virtuoso concert pieces, with or without orchestra, based on the same principles. At their heart were transformations of a group of popular tunes (often all from one opera), and they typically opened with a free introduction and con-cluded with a brilliant finale. These pieces were at the core of public con-cert repertory; most nineteenth-century virtuosi wrote them for their own concert tours and later published them. Naturally, the most famous were those by Thalberg and Liszt; the latter elevated these bravura trinkets to the rank of masterpieces. Given the limited market, very few such pieces were published in Warsaw. However, works of this kind composed by virtuoso performers from Poland—for instance, the violinist Karol Lipiński's numerous such fantasies and Lessel's op. 12—were published abroad. Chopin's Grand Fantasia on Polish Airs op. 13, which the press, the concert announcement, and the composer himself originally described as a "potpourri," is a prime example of this genre. His use of Polish arias is not atypical, since native themes were used in other such pieces, including Lessel's op. 12 and Lipiński's virtuoso Fantasia on Motives from the Opera *Krakowiacy i Górale* op. 33, both composed before Chopin's op. 13.[46] Although the primary purpose of these works was a display of virtuosity, they also invoked national *topoi*, speaking to their Polish audiences through readily recognizable gestures and quotations of patriotic melodies. For instance, the dumka of Chopin's op. 13 is a quotation from Kurpiński's *Elegy on the Death of Tadeusz Kościuszko* (*Elegia na śmierć Tadeusza Kościuszki*), a composition commemorating the 1817 death of this national hero.[47]

The other subgenre of nineteenth-century fantasias was defined by freely composed works, spanning a range of possibilities between quasi improvisation and highly structured form. The eighteenth-century type of fantasia, in particular C. P. E. Bach's highly subjective pieces constructed of episodes, and featuring rhythmic freedom (the free fantasias even omitting bar lines) and daring modulations of the *empfindsamer Stil*, continued to influence nineteenth-century composers. Works such as Beethoven's op. 77 proved that the older models still offered a lot of expressive and formal potential. Polish composers of the early nineteenth century did not shy away from this type: Szymanowska, Lessel, Kurpiński all composed this older type of fantasia, though none of them were published locally.[48]

---

[46] Chopin reached for this genre one more time, soon after his arrival in Paris, composing the *Grand duo concertant sur des thèmes de* Robert le diable for his friend the cellist Auguste Franchomme. Chopin's Variations in B-flat Major, op. 2, on Mozart's "Là ci darem la mano" also belong to the genre of virtuoso concert pieces based on popular opera tunes. Compositions termed "variations" or *L'air varié* are more rigid in terms of organization than a fantasia or a potpourri and tend to be written on one theme—such is clearly the case with this piece—and the formal concepts of Chopin's op. 13 are very different. However, the terminology is not foolproof, and the virtuoso fantasia may appear under the terms *variations, caprice, reminiscence*, etc.

[47] The Polish narrative of Chopin's op. 13 has been explored by Wojciech Nowik in "*Fantazja na tematy polskie* w perspektywie intertekstualności" [Fantasia on Polish Themes in intertextual perspective], paper presented at the fifth annual Chopin Conference, December 1–3, 2005, Warsaw.

[48] The most unusual piece, roughly falling into this genre, is Kurpiński's "A Moment of a Frightful Dream" (*Chwila snu okropnego*). This exceedingly brief composition (thirty-two

While composers continued to work in the free, improvisatory idiom, fantasia also became a vehicle for expanding formal and expressive boundaries of traditional forms resulting in carefully structured large works seeking to make a bridge between C. P. E. Bach's free fantasia and the sonata cycle. Some of the most significant essays of this sort were Beethoven's sonatas *quasi fantasia,* followed by Schubert's *Wanderer-fantasie,* and later Schumann's op. 17 and Liszt's *fantasia quasi sonata* "Après une lecture du Dante." In Poland, the earliest such work is Kurpiński's *Fantaisie en Quatuor,* which, like other more substantial pieces by Warsaw's composers, was published abroad (Leipzig, 1823, in piano arrangement as op. 10). Kurpiński's *Fantaisie en Quatuor* sidesteps all formal expectations of a string quartet. The composition is constructed in the sectional manner of a keyboard fantasia, starting with a free introduction, followed by a fugue, moving into a song-like section (with passages related to the opening of the piece), and closing with a fugal presto (again recalling previously heard motives and sections). Although the language of this composition is conservative, the formal and generic ideas are innovative; no other such composition was written in Warsaw during the 1820s.

Among fantasies published in Warsaw during Chopin's youth, a large group represented a specifically Polish fantasia subgenre. These compositions used the free, episodic manner of the eighteenth-century fantasia, but they either evoked a typically Polish dance idiom or contained well-known melodies with patriotic overtones. The direct quotations or more subtle allusions to these tunes (or Polish dance idiom) determined the national narrative of these fantasies, reinforced by the evocative "funereal," "polonaise," "*ombra,*" or "military" *topoi* of the other episodes. Although these compositions, like the potpourris, used preexistent tunes, Polish composers consistently identified them as "fantasies," indicating an awareness of a specific genre of "national" or "patriotic" fantasia.

The circumstances during the years immediately following the Vienna Congress fostered in Warsaw an atmosphere of musical patriotism that was expressed in a large number of instrumental pieces on historic

---

measures), consisting of free, highly modulatory figurations, is a single rhetorical gesture: an *ombra* radiating a quintessentially Romantic affect. This piece cannot be fully understood without considering its original context, as an 1816 inscription into the musical *Stammbuch* of Maria Szymanowska. Brevity and spontaneity are characteristic of the *Stammbuch* medium, and the generic peculiarities of this piece are likely a result of Kurpiński's efforts to appropriately address the dedicatee. Moreover, the programmatic title is an afterthought: the 1816 *Stammbuch* version bears no title; only the 1820 publication in Kurpiński's periodical, the *Musical Weekly* has the title "A Moment of a Frightful Dream." The generic attribution "fantasia," typically given to this work in modern editions and commentaries, does not appear at all in the original sources.

themes. Many of these compositions commemorated events still fresh in the memory of the nation, centering around the cult of the three heroes who passed away during the second decade of the century: General Tadeusz Kościuszko (d. 1817), General Józef Dąbrowski (1818), and Marshal Józef Poniatowski (1813). The memory of Prince Poniatowski's death, still fresh, was already elevated to the rank of a national myth. In 1817, his remains were moved to the Royal Castle in Kraków, the traditional burial site of Polish monarchs, giving the Poles new reason to remember him. Among such musical commemorations were Franciszek Siekierski's *Le tombeau du Prince Joseph Poniatowski* (Płachecki, 1815) and Charles Philippe Lafont, *Le troubadour français au Tombeau de Poniatowski* (Płachecki and Glücksberg, 1818). Some of these pieces made the national narrative unequivocal through the use of well-known patriotic tunes or recognizable *topoi:* military march, funeral march, polonaise, and others. In some instances, the meaning was made explicit by the presence of the text. For instance, Kurpiński's *Elegy on the Death of Tadeusz Kościuszko* (*Elegia na śmierć Tadeusza Kościuszki*), which was originally a vocal work with the orchestra, was published as a piano piece with the text written into the music, perhaps for melodeclamation (Płachecki, 1818).

Kurpiński's Fugue on the *Dąbrowski Mazurka* (Letronne, 1821) was among the last pieces of this sort written before a long hiatus. While issuing patriotic compositions was made possible by the relative freedom from censorship in the first years of the Congress Kingdom, in May 1819 the authorities issued a new decree concerning censorship. The explosion of patriotic culture, including musical works on national topics, made the Russian rulers nervous. The popularity of operas on historic subject, in particular Elsner's *King Łokietek* and *King Jagiełło in Tenczyn,* fueled this patriotic culture. As a result, in the early 1820s the problem operas were taken off the stage, and other musical works on patriotic topics became subject to strict censorship. The period directly preceding the November Uprising saw a timid reemergence of publications hinting at the patriotic narrative, for instance, Józef Damse's *Recollections of a Pole or a Fantasia for the Pianoforte* (*Wspomnienia Polaka czyli Fantazja na pianoforte*; Klukowski, 1829, not extant). During the Uprising, however, the market exploded with publications on national tunes and addressing national topics.

Among instrumental compositions on patriotic themes, several (like Damse's piece) specifically evoked the fantasia genre. Among earliest such works were Jean Tomasini's composition *The Death of Tadeusz Kościuszko, a Fantasia for the Pianoforte* (*Śmierć Tadeusza Kościuszki, fantazja na pfte*; 1818, not extant) and Würfel's *Grande fantaisie lugubre au Souvenir de trois héros Prince Poniatowski, Kościuszko et Dąbrowski composée et dédiée à la Nation Polonaise* (Varsovie: Fuss, 1818; see fig. 3.16). Würfel's composition is an example par excellence of the "national" fantasia genre. It is

Figure 3.16. Václav Vilém Würfel, *Grande fantaisie lugubre au Souvenir de trois héros Prince Poniatowski, Kosćiuszko et Dąbrowski composée et dédiée à la Nation Polonaise par W.W. Würfel* (Warsaw: Fuss, 1818), pp. 6–7. Biblioteka Narodowa, Warsaw, Mus. II 17846 Cim.

constructed of distinct episodes whose narrative meaning is explicated through such inscriptions in the musical text as "Nuit funeste," "Les sons des cloches de trois tours," "Tristes Pressentimens," and "Vive douleur de la Nation." The piece also speaks to the audiences through the evocation of familiar national tunes associated with the three heroes: in the section marked "Souvenir de leur dévoument pour la patrie," we hear successively *Prince Poniatowki's Favorite March*, the Trio of *Kościuszko's Polonaise* "And When You Depart, Fare Well" (*A kiedy odjeżdżasz byawaj że zdrów*), and the *Dąbrowski Mazurka*.

This method of shaping a national narrative in music through familiar tunes was well known to Warsaw composers. In an 1821 article, "On Musical Expression and Mimesis," Kurpiński' asserted that music can speak to the listener by recalling tunes that have a certain meaning. That is particularly true in stage music but also can be achieved in compositions without words, by means of "arias, which—nested in everyone's memory through frequent repetitions—allow diverse allusions."[49] He stressed that "these are only reminders, but therefore they speak stronger to the heart," and gave the example of a march tune evoking in the listener the image of "national troops."[50]

The significance of the "national" fantasia genre is further underscored by the crossing of boundaries between this genre and the virtuoso "potpourri" fantasias by Polish composers. The presence of tunes with national overtones in the aforementioned op. 12 of Lessel and op. 13 of Chopin certainly problematizes their generic affiliation. Lessel's op. 12, composed after his return to Poland in 1810 and published in 1813 by Breitkopf & Härtel as *Pot-pourri pour le Pianoforte avec accomp. de l'Orchestre*, uses two Polish themes: *Kościuszko's Polonaise* and a krakowiak. Though Lessel hesitated somewhat about the genre of this work (the manuscript bears the inscription "Caprice et Variations pour le Piano"), he stayed away from the term *fantasia*. Chopin, on the other hand, called his piece at first "potpourri," but within weeks of its premiere changed the title to "fantasia" (term that was used in its later publication).[51] Chopin's vacillation about the genre of op. 13 and his ultimate choice of the term "fantasia" suggest that he was aware of this work's affinity with the "national" fantasia genre, even if its primary purpose was virtuoso display on the concert stage.

[49] Karol Kurpiński, "O expresji muzycznej i naśladowaniu" [On musical expression and mimesis], *Tygodnik Muzyczny*, 16 May 1821, no. 6.

[50] Kurpiński, "O expresji muzycznej i naśladowaniu."

[51] It is referred to as a potpourri in Chopin, Warsaw, to Woyciechowski, Poturzyn, 27 March 1830, *Korespondencja*, 1:115, and *Kurier Warszawski*, 5 March 1830, no. 62. Chopin calls it a fantasia in Chopin, Warsaw, to Woyciechowski, Poturzyn, 10 April 1830, *Korespondencja* 1:120.

The true blossoming of the "national" fantasia type, known to Chopin from these Warsaw models, came in his late works, the opp. 44, 49, and 61. The Fantasia op. 49 is a carefully structured work, pushing the limits of traditional form through means borrowed from free fantasia style. The work is distinguished by its powerful narrative features, commented on by many writers: the funereal opening, the struggle between the two keys, the victory of A-flat major over F minor, the triumphal celebration, the meditative, hymn-like character of the Lento sostenuto, and the ethereal, almost angelic conclusion.[52] Following the lead of Mieczysław Tomaszewski, I have argued elsewhere that the fantasia radiates an intensely patriotic feeling, a Polishness that resides in the echoes of patriotic and popular songs, and that it employs musical *topoi* that would have been readily understood by Chopin's compatriots—contemporary and later.[53]

The other two works, op. 44 and op. 61, explore the intersections of two genres, the fantasia and the polonaise. Chopin's vacillations concerning the genre of op. 44 are known from his letters to his friend Julian Fontana and the publisher Pietro Mechetti, in which he called it "a sort of fantasy in the form on polonaise" and "a sort of polonaise but more a fantasy."[54] In both pieces, the formal principles Chopin adopted push beyond the typical polonaise-(static) trio-polonaise scheme and show his tendency toward hybridization of forms. However, not until the Polonaise-Fantasia op. 61 did Chopin feel that the generic principles of the polonaise had been undermined sufficiently to introduce the term *fantasy* into the title.[55] Hybrid approaches of sorts were tested by older composers in Warsaw, with perhaps the most direct and compositionally most interesting ancestors of Chopin's pieces being Szymanowska's *Fantaisie* (Breitkopf & Härtel, 1919) and Franciszek Siekierski's *Polonaise quasi fantasia* (Płachecki, 1818). Szymanowska's composition contains unmistakable polonaise motives, though without any references to the polonaise in the title. Siekierski stretches the customary formal scheme of a polonaise by including an introduction that foreshadows motivic material explored later on in the piece, by weakening the articulation of subsections, and altering the return of the polonaise.

The works of Chopin's Warsaw elders in the fantasia genre were much simpler and much more timid in their exploration of new compositional

[52] For an exhaustive list of critical responses to this composition see Mieczysław Tomaszewski, "Fantazja F-Moll op. 49: Struktura dwoista i drugie dno," in *Muzyka Chopina na nowo odczytana* [Chopin's music read anew] (Kraków: Akademia Muzyczna, 1996), 73–93.

[53] Tomaszewski, "Fantazja F-Moll op. 49," and Goldberg, "'Remembering That Tale of Grief': The Prophetic Voice in Chopin's Music," in Goldberg, *The Age of Chopin*, 54–92.

[54] Chopin, Nohant, to Pietro Mechetti, Vienna, 23 August 1841, *Korespondencja*, 2:32; Chopin, Nohant, to Julian Fontana, Paris, [24 August 1841], *Korespondencja*, 2:32.

[55] On this subject see Jeffrey Kallberg, "Chopin's Last Style," *Journal of the American Musicological Society* 38 (1985): 264–315.

principles than the works of Chopin. They did, however, provide him with the initial vocabulary and narrative templates—a specifically Polish semiotic base for the national idiom he is credited with bringing into this genre.

Vocal Repertory

Vocal works published in Warsaw were nearly as important to the creation of the specifically Chopinesque musical vocabulary as compositions for the piano. The main vocal repertories found among Warsaw publications are operatic excerpts, salon romances, sacred music, as well as popular and patriotic songs. Each of these repertories made a different contribution to the growth and language of art music.

Given the tremendous popularity of musical theater, publishers were eager to quickly bring forth favorite operatic selections in the form of piano or piano-vocal transcriptions. In this large and separate group of publications, the works most often transcribed were operas, as well as the simple genres of musical theater, in Poland referred to as *komedio-opera* and *melodrama*. Ballets were a much smaller group. The most common publication format was sheet music containing a single number from a larger work. Less common were collections or multivolume publications of excerpts, transcribed for the piano or for voice with piano accompaniment. Relatively few operas received a complete publication, whether as full orchestral score or more often as a piano-vocal score.[56] These publications played an important role in the dissemination of opera repertory in the era when mechanical sound reproduction was only in its initial primitive stages.

Next to arias from operas, music bookstores in Warsaw offered large numbers of vocal pieces written directly for the salon. At the beginning of the nineteenth century, compositions of this sort were extremely popular everywhere in Europe. These songs were often strophic and were characterized by unembellished melodies and subordinate accompaniments. Among salon songs, those titled romances or nocturnes, in particular those of the Parisian type, are of particular interest as direct ancestors of piano nocturnes.[57]

In his article on the ancestry of Chopin's noctunes, James Parakilas asserts that in Parisian salon songs, the main distinction between the romance and the nocturne genres was in the number of voices: whereas the romance was destined for solo voice with piano harp or guitar accompa-

[56] Wojciech Tomaszewski, *Warszawskie edytorstwo muzyczne*, 172–173.

[57] On the vocal nocturne ancestry of Chopin's nocturnes see James Parakilas, "'Nuit plus belle qu'un beau jour': Poetry, Song, and the Voice in the Piano Nocturne," in Goldberg, *The Age of Chopin*, 203–223, and Jeffrey Kalberg, "'Voice' and the Nocturne," in *Pianist, Scholar, Connoisseur: Essays in Honor of Jacob Lateiner*, ed. Bruce Brubaker and Jane Gottlieb (Stuyvesant, N.Y.: Pendragon, 2000), 1–46.

niment, the nocturne was for two or more accompanied voices. Significantly, at least one of the singers called for in Parisian nocturnes was a woman: the most common combinations being two sopranos, or soprano and tenor.[58] Naturally, in the casual atmosphere of salon performance, the composer's specifications pertaining to the performing voices could not (or would not) always be observed. Some composers anticipated the need for some interchangeability of performing voices. In one such nocturne for two sopranos by F. Berton *fils* (presumably Henri François Berton), the composer included a note on the bottom of the first page of music explaining how to deal with such situations. The text reads: "N.B. Dans le cas ou le 2me. Soprano serait chanté par un Tenor il fault dire à l'octave au dessus tous les passages marques ainsi 8⌒⌒⌒."[59] Berton's admonition was intended to head off problems of a purely musical nature, concerning vocal ranges or voice-leading, and it attests to a widespread practice of substituting for the performing forces specified in the scores.

The Parisian romances and nocturnes, published abroad in the early part of the nineteenth century by the dozen, quickly reached Poland. The number of such compositions in the Czartoryski collection indicates a strong interest in these genres. Among the scores in the Czartoryski Library are issues of the periodicals *Journal Hebdomadaire* and *Journal d'Euterpe*, dedicated to such vocal pieces and containing numerous works by Blangini, Panséron, and Romagnesi, and a manuscript of Felix Blangini's "Romances a une, deux, trios ou quatre voix," copied in the hand of Princess Anna Czartoryska (the wife of Prince Adam Jerzy and the dedicatee of Chopin's *Rondo à la Krakowiak* op. 14).[60] Another manuscript containing "Deux Romances a deux Voix" by Blangini exists in Biblioteka Jagiellońska.[61]

Felix (Felice) Blangini was among the most significant and prolific composers of Parisian salon songs. He and another leading composer of these pieces, Auguste Panséron, seemed to have a particular connection to Poland: not only do imports of their vocal pieces appear in large numbers in Polish collections, but a few of their compositions were also published locally, some even offered to Polish dedicatees. Most notable are the four 1818 prints of Blangini's songs, in particular the two-voice nocturne issued by Klukowski (engraved by Fuss; see fig. 3.17), and Panséron's volume of French and Italian songs, dedicated to "Comtesse J—fine Ostrowska née P—sse Sanguszko" and published by Letronne in 1822.[62] Other

[58] Parakilas, "'Nuit plus belle qu'un beau jour,'" 206.

[59] F. Berton fils, "Que le jour me dure: Nocturne a deux voix" (Paris: [Ignace] Pleyel et fils, n.d.). Biblioteka XX Czartoryskich, Kraków, 100133/7.

[60] Biblioteka XX Czartoryskich, Kraków, 100150/28.

[61] Biblioteka Jagiellońska, Kraków, III 449.

[62] Biblioteka Jagiellońska, Kraków, III 207 and Biblioteka Narodowa, Warsaw, Mus. III.81458 Cim.

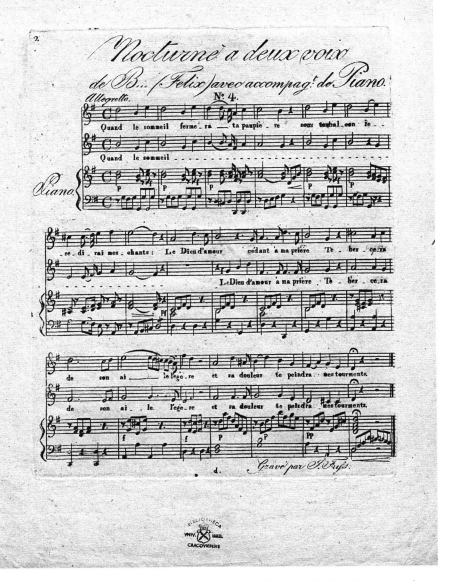

Figure 3.17. Felix B[langini], *Nocturne à deux voix* (Warsaw: Klukowski; engraved by Fuss 1818). Biblioteka Jagiellońska, Kraków, III 207.

Figure 3.17. *continued*

foreign composers of salon songs were known through publications like Glücksberg's 1818 *Recueil de trente six romances choisies*—compositions by major representatives of this genre.[63]

These vocal genres, rather than the chamber compositions of the ser-enade type also named *notturno,* were the precursors of the piano noc-

---

[63] Biblioteka Jagiellońska, Kraków, 5930 I Mus.

turne, introduced by John Field. Field's piano nocturnes were not published in Poland (though a few other works of his were), but they might have been known in Warsaw through imports. Instead, the piano nocturne (not extant) by Jean Lacoste, issued in Warsaw in the same set as his *Fantaisie polonaise*, was the earliest such publication (Fuss, 1818). A few other piano nocturnes by local composers were published in the 1820s.

Among several important features the piano nocturne adopted from the vocal compositions was the general mood indicated by their texts, since typically they were about love and the locale of their narrative was nocturnal. Instrumental nocturnes also retained their vocal counterparts' openness to the use of other genres—marches, barcaroles, or religious hymns— as *topoi* capable of conveying the imagery employed in the poems. A more specific contribution of the Parisian vocal nocturne was its use of women's voices—hence the top-dominated textures of the piano nocturnes—and its fondness for two high voices moving in parallel thirds and sixths, exchanging snippets of dialogue, engaging in brief imitation, or in passing moving in independent lines. Chopin's nocturnes in particular employ or interpolate various generic types (chorales and marches, to mention two). He also often makes use of vocal nocturnes' idiosyncratic textures, starting with his earliest nocturne, composed in Warsaw and posthumously published as op. 72 no. 1 (mm. 4–9 and 18–25), and culminating in the magnificent contrapuntal textures of his late op. 55 no. 2.[64]

Whereas Panséron, Blangini, and other leading composers of Parisian salon songs were professional composers and teachers, local composers of French salon songs were primarily amateurs.[65] One notable exception was Maria Szymanowska, especially her *Six romances* (issued by Breitkopf & Härtel around 1820). Polish professional composers concentrated on creating a genre of Polish drawing-room songs. This process was started by Elsner, and continued by Kurpiński's and Szymanowska's songs on Polish texts, especially Szymanowska's setting of Mickiewicz's ballad "The Świteź Lake Nymph" (*Świtezianka*; Moscow, 1828). Though designated for the salon, these compositions were intended to contribute to the creation of national identity in music.

Patriotic songs popular during Chopin's life could appear in the guise of various genres: funeral and military marches, mazurkas, and polonaises. The most beloved were the aforementioned *Prince Poniatowki's Favorite March*, *Kościuszko's Polonaise*, and the *Dąbrowski Mazurka*. The period before the onset of the November Uprising witnessed the growth of patriotic im-

[64] Parakilas, "'Nuit plus belle qu'un beau jour.'"

[65] This subject has been examined in Janina Cybulska, *Romans wokalny w Polsce w latach 1800–1830. Z dziejów polskiej pieśni solowej* [The vocal romance in Poland in the years 1800–1830: from the history of Polish solo song] (Kraków: Polskie Wydawnictwo Muzyczne, 1960).

portance of religious music. Brodziński, the mentor of Warsaw's restless Romantics, believed that religious chants were a primeval expression of every nation and argued for the importance of religious songs and Polish masses in encouraging national "thinking and feeling."[66] Brodziński's postulates found their realization in settings of devotional poetry in Polish by chief Warsaw composers. Kurpiński and Elsner published several such volumes during the 1820s, for instance, Kurpiński's *Pienia nabożne* (*Devotional chants*; Klukowski, 1825) and Elsner's numerous masses setting Brodziński's Polish mass text. Religious songs in Polish not only increased the role of the native language but also stood for Christianity as defining Polishness, specifically Catholicism, in contrast to Russian Orthodoxy and Prussian Protestantism. In the atmosphere of nascent political messiansm, these songs were increasingly perceived as embodying Polishness.

The largest and perhaps most influential group of patriotic songs were the *Historical Chants* (*Śpiewy historyczne*), set to poems by Julian Ursyn Niemcewicz. In 1806, as one of the endeavors aimed at maintaining and recreating Polish national identity, the Society for the Friends of Learning invited Niemcewicz to begin work on a cycle of Polish historical poems. During the next few years, these works—known as *Historical Chants*—were set to music by Polish amateurs and professional composers. Most of the songs were composed by Warsaw's best professional composers: Lessel (ten songs), Kurpiński (six songs), and Szymanowska (five songs). Among the amateurs who contributed songs to the collection were the two Czartoryski princesses Zofia Zamoyska and Maria Württemberg, and other gifted amateur musicians from the Czartoryski circle.

Several of the *Historical Chants* adopt the religious topos: for instance, Maria Szymanowska's "Jan Albrycht," with its chordal chorale-like textures, somber melody, and *Maestoso e lento* character, exemplifies this tone (see fig. 3.18). Appropriately, the poem centers on this fifteenth-century king's thwarted attempt to battle the Turks, thus dramatizing and underscoring Poland's sacrificial role in protecting Christendom from Muslims.

Another group of *Historical Chants* speak through the sounds of funeral march and lament. Among them is the last and most popular of the collection "The Funeral of Prince Józef Poniatowski," commemorating the tragic death of the idolized nephew of Poland's last king (see fig. 3.19). The death of Prince Józef is bemoaned through slow ceremonial tempo and minor mode accentuated by plaintive chromaticism. The solemn mood

<hr>

[66] Brodziński, from "Uwagi nad potrzebą wydania wyboru poezyj dla młodzieży: Zbioru pieśni duchownych i narodowych" [Remarks on the necessity of issuing a selection of poetry for the youth: A collection of religious and national songs], lecture delivered at the meeting of the Society for the Friends of Learning, 12 March 1821, in Brodziński, *Pisma Estetyczno-Krytyczne* [The aesthetic-critical writings], 2 vols., ed. Aleksander Łucki (Warsaw: Z Zasiłku Funduszu Kultury Narodowej, 1934), 1:222–229.

Figure 3.18. Maria Szymanowska, "Jan Albrycht," in Julian Ursyn Niemcewicz, *Śpiewy historyczne: Z muzyką, rycinami i krótkim dodatkiem zbioru historyi polskiéj* [Historical chants with music, engravings, and a brief supplement of the collection of Polish history], 5th ed. (Lwów: Kajetan Jabłoński, 1849), music insert after p. 82.

of mourning is further emphasized by the presence of falling melodic motives and elegiac rhythms—in Poland particularly associated with the genre referred to as duma, dumka, or Polish elegy.

Military marches are numerous among settings of Niemcewicz's poems. The heroic type can be illustrated by a song in which the brisk tempo, reso-

Figure 3.19. Franciszek Lessel, "The Funeral of Prince Józef Poniatowski," in Julian Ursyn Niemcewicz, *Śpiewy historyczne: Z muzyką, rycinami i krótkim dodatkiem zbioru historyi polskiéj* [Historical chants with music, engravings, and a brief supplement of the collection of Polish history], 5th ed. (Lwów: Kajetan Jabłoński, 1849), music insert after p. 292.

lute rhythms, and bright diatonic sonorities depict the great deeds of the fearless, victorious fifteenth-century knight Zawisza Czarny (see fig. 3.20).

Historical Chants with music was first published in 1816 and almost instantly become the pillar of national patriotic culture. Right away the chants took on the role of a vehicle through which Polish history was

Figure 3.20. Franciszek Lessel, "Zawisza Czarny," in Julian Ursyn Niemcewicz, *Śpiewy historyczne: Z muzyką, rycinami i krótkim dodatkiem zbioru historyi polskiéj* [Historical chants with music, engravings, and a brief supplement of the collection of Polish history], 5th ed. (Lwów: Kajetan Jabłoński, 1849), music insert after p. 62.

taught to children (as originally intended), and remained so for most of the nineteenth century. They were published several times in Warsaw and in other Polish cities, in spite of the censor's efforts to limit their availability. Within a decade, their political power became such that during 1827, a year characterized by harassment, repressions, and arrests, Russian authorities forbade teaching them in schools, for they "awoke patriotic feelings."[67] By 1842, shortly after Niemcewicz's death, their success as national music was held as a model for the national status Chopin's music was to attain in the future. In a review of Chopin's opp. 42–49, his later biographer Marceli Antoni Szulc wrote: "As someone once said to a foreigner, that there is no Pole that would not know a few *Historical Chants* by heart, so a time will come when Chopin's masterpieces will permeate the nation, for they are native, immaculate, and purely Polish."[68]

Chopin was a child of the first generation raised on *Historical Chants*: he would have sung these songs at home, with his friends, and later, in Paris, through them he would remember Poland. Liszt tells us that when Chopin improvised on *Historical Chants* in the presence of Niemcewicz, his music captured "crash of arms, the chant of vanquishers, festive hymns, complaints of the illustrious prisoners, and ballads over dead heroes."[69] According to another report, on December 24, 1836, Chopin played, sang, and improvised, while Niemcewicz was recounting for the children the time of the Four-Year Sejm.[70] The most common *topoi* found in the musical settings of the *Historical Chants*—the hymn, the lament, the military march—became important elements of the narrative fabric of Chopin's music, and through them his audiences heard Poland.

Imported Music

While it is clear that the output of Warsaw's publishers reflected primarily the popular taste, scores required by connoisseurs and larger works such as concertos and symphonies often existed in manuscript only or were imported from abroad. There was enough local demand to justify publications of select foreign works. For instance, composers of piano music especially popular in Warsaw—Kalkbrenner, Dussek, Gelinek, Hummel, Steibelt, Weber, Ries, Moscheles, and Field—merited some local publication, typically of dances, rondos, and variations. But the vast majority of foreign works was available through imports. In a letter written in 1825, Chopin lists some authors of scores in his possession: "how many hundreds of scores await me lying in disorder on the piano like a mishmash (indeed with an insult to the Hummels, Rieses, Kalkbrenners, whom fate has probably placed in this immense expanse next to Pleyel, Hemer-

---

[67] Fryderyk Skarbek, *Pamiętniki* [Memoirs] (Poznań: Żupański, 1878), 136.

[68] Marceli Antoni Szulc, "Przegląd ostatnich dzieł Chopina" [A review of Chopin's latest works], in *Tygodnik Literacki*, 14 March 1842, no. 11, 83.

[69] Franz Liszt, *Chopin*, trans. Nicole Priollaud (Paris: Liana Levi, 1990), 93.

[70] Report by Januszkiewicz in Krystyna Kobylańska, "Improwizacje Fryderyka Chopina" [Fryderyk Chopin's improvisations], *Rocznik Chopinowski* 19 (1987): 90.

lein, Hoffmeister)!"[71] The scores he refers to were probably local issues and imports purchased in Warsaw.

Nearly all Warsaw's music publishers imported music from abroad, mostly from Vienna, Paris, Leipzig, and Offenbach am Main. Warsaw during Chopin's youth had access to all works popular elsewhere in Europe—announcements in the daily press regularly brought news of import arrivals. For instance, in 1823 one could purchase all the works of Field, Ries (including his symphony), Dussek, Steibelt, Hartknoch, Klengel, Kalkbrenner, and Spohr. In 1827, Klukowski imported from Vienna the works of Onslow, Weber, Horzalka, Randhartinger, and Schoberluhner and several books of Czerny's piano études. During the next year, the same store brought from Vienna new compositions by Moscheles, Czerny, Kalkbrenner, Herz, Ries, Pixis, Beriot, Rode, and especially Paganini. Hummel's new *Piano School*, published in Vienna in the end of 1828, arrived in Warsaw in July 1829. Brzezina also imported scores from other Polish and foreign publishers. In 1825 he received from Paris the complete works of Hummel (twenty-two books) and the following year the newly published piano method by Cramer. The shop of Magnus advertised in 1830 a new *Piano School* by Pleyel, revised by Czerny, and the very popular "Là ci darem la mano" variations of Mr. Chopin, published by Haslinger.[72]

The shop of Natan (Mikołaj) Glücksberg, though only marginally involved in music publishing, was a major importer of music. As the official typographer of the University of Warsaw, Glücksberg had an immense significance for the cultural and musical circles of Warsaw: he published most important new Romantic works, many translations of new and significant books, and *monumenta* of Polish culture. Glücksberg was listed as music merchant in the 1826 *Warsaw Guide* because his bookstore had an ample assortment of scores.[73] Chopin often shopped at Glücksberg's store, and what he reports to have found there was an assortment typically offered by music bookstores:

There are only *Eutherpe*, that is, a collection of arias and other pieces by Rossini, arranged in Vienna at Diabelli's for the piano alone (this work is an equivalent of *Philomela* for singing) and a Polonaise by

[71] Chopin, Warsaw, to Białobłocki, Sokołów, 8 September 1825, *Korespondencja*, 1:56.

[72] Jan Prosnak, "Środowisko warszawskie w życiu Fryderyka Chopina" [The Warsaw circle in the life of Fryderyk Chopin], *Kwartalnik muzyczny* 28 (October–December 1949): 54–55 and *Kurier Warszawski*, 11 June 1825, no. 137; after Krystyna Kobylańska, *Chopin w kraju: Dokumenty i pamiątki* [Chopin in his own land: documents and souvenirs] (Kraków: Polskie Wydawnictwo Muzyczne, 1955), 105.

[73] *Przewodnik warszawski 1826* [Warsaw guide 1826] (Warsaw: Glücksberg, 1826), appendix, 18.

Kaczkowski—very good, beautiful, in a word, for listening and taking delight in.[74]

The thriving local enterprises provided publishing opportunities for area musicians, even if professional composers, including the young Chopin, published their larger works abroad, to be imported for the use of musicians and highly educated amateurs (like Chopin's' op. 2 offered by Magnus in 1830). Young composers, who did not yet have the international recognition required by foreign publishers, were able hone their skills and build a local following through publications of their youthful works. In addition to the printing of Chopin's rondos opp. 1 and 5 by Brzezina, Warsaw publishers also encouraged the talents of other gifted Conservatory students by issuing their works. Among the large group of Chopin's friends and colleagues whose works appeared in print were Napoleon Tomasz Nidecki, later the kapellmeister of the Leopoldstadt Theater in Vienna and the director of the National Theater in Warsaw; Antoni Orłowski, who conducted the orchestra of Théâtre des Arts in Rouen; Ignacy Feliks Dobrzyński, the most important Polish composer of symphonic and chamber music belonging to the Chopin generation; and one of the most successful pianists of the era, Antoni Kątski. The presence of local publishers also permitted the printing of music that was of no interest abroad: Polish songs, sacred works with Polish texts, national operas and ballets, popular Polish dances, and instrumental works with patriotic narratives. From this perspective, the contribution of Warsaw's printing industry to the creation of a national musical language was incalculable.

Each one of the occupying Warsaw governments—Prussian, French and Russian—imposed some form of censorship. With the exception of a few instances, though, most censorship restrictions pertained to theatrical works and had a limited effect on musical works until the collapse of the November Uprising in 1831. Already during the Uprising, the czar imposed strict constraints on music publishing, realizing that patriotic songs were important in the building of nationalistic feeling. After the fall of the Uprising, as one of the measures of the final loss of independence, Poland became a subject to decades of severe censorship. The crisis caused by the November Uprising closed the doors of several printers, and the recession that followed resulted in a decline of production by over 30 percent.[75] It took the Warsaw printing industry decades to return to the prosperity it had enjoyed in the years between 1810 and 1830.

[74] Chopin, Warsaw, to Białobłocki, Sokołów, [15 May 1826], *Korespondencja*, 1:64–65.
[75] Wojciech Tomaszewski, *Warszawskie edytorstwo muzyczne*, 93.

4

MUSICAL EDUCATION

"**Y**ou can't make a silk purse out of a sow's ear" read a comment on Elsner's pedagogical skill by an anonymous (and doubtlessly, envious) writer when, in light of Chopin's amazing musical achievements, the press was extolling Elsner's teaching.[1] Although it is true that the ultimate credit for Chopin's extraordinary pianistic and compositional accomplishments must go to Chopin's own musical genius, there was nevertheless much merit in having fine teachers who shaped his musical and aesthetic ideas and nourished his extraordinary innate talent. For instance, while Wojciech Żywny (really a violinist, and by all accounts, a quite ineffectual teacher) cannot be credited with Fryderyk's amazing dexterity at the piano, Żywny's almost daily presence at the Chopin household assured a continual proximity of an experienced musician, who, if nothing else, bequeathed the love of Bach's music to his pupil.

Despite the disparaging remark just mentioned, there is much less skepticism about the merit of Elsner as Chopin's composition teacher. Józef Elsner (see fig. 4.1) kept his eye on the young genius from as early as 1817, and some form of private tutelage must have begun in the ensuing years. Under Elsner's recommendation, it was decided that beginning in the fall of 1826, the sixteen-year-old Fryderyk would continue his education at the Warsaw Conservatory. Chopin attended the Conservatory while it enjoyed a short-lived period of remarkable prosperity, soon to be disrupted by the November Uprising and its political and cultural aftermath. The preceding years (between 1810 and 1821) had been dedicated to the establishment of the Conservatory—Poland's first institution of higher musical learning.[2]

[1] *Gazeta warszawska*, 4 April 1830, no. 91, 858–861. The two writers involved were probably Cichocki and Kurpiński. (The literal translation of the original Polish proverb is "Not even the devil can make a whip out of sand.")

[2] My discussion of the history of the Conservatory is largely indebted to Marta Sankowska, "Studia Fryderyka Chopina w Szkole Głównej Muzyki Królewskiego Uniwer-

The Creation of the Warsaw Conservatory

Prior to 1810, the possibilities of obtaining advanced musical education in Warsaw had been rather meager. Although several attempts were made to create a higher institution of musical learning, none of them was successful, and there was only some rudimentary music instruction in Warsaw's schools, supplied by private lessons.[3] During his 1805 visit in Paris, Elsner became acquainted with the Conservatory. At the time, the Parisian Conservatoire National de Musique was the only institution of this kind in existence; other major cities of Europe became home to modern institutions of musical education considerably later (Prague, 1811, Vienna, 1817, Leipzig, 1843, and Berlin, 1850). Immediately on his return to Warsaw, Elsner began to pursue possibilities of creating a similar institution in Poland. Together with Wojciech Bogusławski, he launched a campaign to create a specialized educational institution, primarily to train professional singers for the National Theater. In 1810, they received an official approval and a promise of a yearly grant from the Saxon king then ruling Poland, thus succeeding in opening the doors of the School of Drama (*Szkoła Dramatyczna*). Elsner, however, was initially not hired to teach in the school; he joined the faculty only in 1815.[4]

After Bogusławski's resignation, Elsner became seriously involved in

---

sytetu Warszawskiego" [Fryderyk Chopin's studies at the Main School of Music of the Royal University of Warsaw] (master's thesis, University of Wrocław, 1994). An important source is also Alina Nowak-Romanowicz, *Józef Elsner* (Kraków: Polskie Wydawnictwo Muzyczne, 1957), 168–192.

[3] In 1783 the Commission for National Education included music in the curriculum of all types of schools, but since music was to serve as a didactic tool, it was taught on a very basic level. The Commission also suggested the need for a higher institution of musical learning, and again in 1792 Father Wacław Sierakowski (an organizer of Kraków's musical life, who created a music school at the Wawel Castle) presented the Sejm with a specific plan for a professional music school created under the state's patronage. After the loss of Poland's independence, several fleeting attempts were made to remedy the lack of a professional music school. During the years 1805–1807, the Music Society, organized by Józef Elsner and E. T. A. Hoffmann, sponsored a Singakademie. The free education of the Singakademie consisted of lessons in solo and choral singing. The teachers of the Society also led master classes for amateurs, including lectures in music theory and history, and discussions referring to events of musical life. Magdalena Kwiatkowska, "Kultura muzyczna Warszawy w latach 1795–1806" [Musical culture of Warsaw in the years 1795–1806] (master's thesis, University of Warsaw, 1981), 67–68. In 1809, Father Izydor J. Cybulski organized an Organists' School (Szkoła Organistów), but its fate is unknown. Some sources also mention the existence of a music institute organized by Elsner at the Piarist church in order to improve religious music. Maurycy Karasowski, *Rys historyczny opery polskiej* [An historical outline of Polish opera] (Warsaw: Glücksberg, 1859), 309.

[4] There is some confusion in literature as to whether the school was opened in 1810 or 1811. Sankowska clears up the confusion by providing information which shows that the

Figure 4.1. Józef Elsner. Lithograph by Maksymilian Fajans, *Wizerunki Polskie* [Polish images], c. 1850 (Warsaw: Fajans, 1851–63). Biblioteka Uniwersytecka, Warsaw, Inw. dz. 1, tabl. 2.

reshaping the curriculum, extending the musical requirements and making the institution more effective. As a result, on February 15, 1817, the school was officially inaugurated as the Elementary School of Music and

king's decision was dated 14 April 1810, and although the press described the school's official opening on 4 June 1811, already in September 1810 weekly sessions, devoted chiefly to creating curriculum, took place. Sankowska, "Studia Fryderyka Chopina," 25. Further proof of some kind of an experimental program having existed already during this first year comes from a letter written in the spring of 1811, in which Princess Maria Würtemberg described the pupils of the school. The princess and her sister Countess Zofia Zamoyska were very impressed during an April 27 visit to the budding drama school. They met six young

Dramatic Art (*Szkoła Elementarna Muzyki i Sztuki Dramatycznej*). In the four-year course of studies, future actors were required to attend all classes in music (singing and piano) and drama (diction, fencing, acting), while students specializing in music did not have to participate in drama subjects. In order to teach basic musical skills to students lacking fundamental musical knowledge, a two-year preparatory institution called the Public School of Elementary Music (*Szkoła Publiczna Muzyki Elementarnej*) was opened on December 14, 1818. This freed the teachers to increase the level of expectations in the School of Music and Dramatic Art, now officially divided into two separated departments, drama and music.

Tireless in his efforts to improve musical education in Warsaw, Elsner made attempts to expand his music school as part of the newly formed University of Warsaw in 1818. He suggested the creation of a department of music at the university (devoted to the teaching of figured bass, composition, and theory), and a separate Conservatory providing practical instruction (vocal and instrumental). The realization of his plans was not immediate, though first steps were taken rather quickly. In November 1819, the government provided the school with buildings that had once belonged to the convent and church of the Bernardine Sisters, along with the money needed for renovations. Classrooms and the rector's living quarters were placed in the refurbished nunnery, and the church was converted to a concert hall. University professors felt that although the instruction in music theory could, in proper time, be accepted at the Department of Sciences and Fine Arts (*Oddział Nauk i Sztuk Pięknych*), the "mechanical practicing of music" would be highly inappropriate in the university context. Against these objections, in April 1821, the school, now known as the Institute of Music and Declamation (*Instytut Muzyki i Deklamacji*), including the Main School of Music (*Szkoła Główna Muzyki*) and the Conservatory, became a part of the Department of Sciences and Fine Arts at the University of Warsaw (see fig. 4.2).[5]

---

ladies and six young men, who after a year of studies showed considerable progress in acting, reciting, singing, foreign languages, and dancing. Bogusławski himself provided two gold medals as rewards to the best student of each gender. Ludwik Dębicki, *Puławy (1762–1830): Monografia z życia towarzyskiego, politycznego i literackiego na podstawie archiwum ks. Czartoryskich w Krakowie* [Puławy (1762–1830): A monograph on social, political and literary life based on the Princes' Czartoryski Archives in Kraków], 4 vols. (Lwów: Gubrynowicz i Schmidt, 1888), 1:180.

[5] The very intricate organization of the new school can be clarified as follows. There were three branches: the two-year Public School of Elementary Music, the Conservatory (music and drama departments), and the department of theory and composition, called the Main School of Music. The second and third branches constituted the Music Division of the Department of Sciences and Fine Arts and the University of Warsaw, but, to sooth conflicts with the university's administration, the Conservatory classes were held in the Bernardine convent buildings. There was further division, resulting mainly from disagreements be-

Figure 4.2. View of Krakowskie Przedmieście; the building of the Conservatory is on the left. Aquatint by Fryderyk Krzysztof Dietrich, from *12 widoków* [Twelve vistas], c.1820 (Warsaw: Dal Trozzo, 1827–29) Biblioteka Uniwersytecka, Warsaw, nr. 1032, tabl. 12.

Elsner maintained a high level of education at the Conservatory by hiring very able and respected faculty recruited from among local musicians and from abroad. Among the teachers who most influenced Chopin were composer-pianists: Václav Würfel, with whom Chopin studied thoroughbass and the organ; Józef Jawurek, an accomplished pianist and popular teacher, whose advice Chopin gladly accepted;[6] and Henryk Lentz, who took over organ and thoroughbass instruction after Würfel left Warsaw.[7] Chopin also greatly benefited from the presence of the young

---

tween Elsner and Soliva: the Music Department of the Conservatory and the Theory Department were directed by Elsner and as part of the university were supervised by the Commission of Public Education (*Komisja Oświecenia Publicznego*); the Drama Department was directed by Soliva and, along with the elementary school, was overseen by the Commission of the Interior (*Komisja Spraw Wewnętrznych*). Sankowska, "Studia Fryderyka Chopina," 34–35.

[6] Oskar Kolberg, "Chopin," in *Encyklopedia Powszechna* [Universal Encyclopedia] (Warsaw: Orgelbrand, 1861), 5:459. Jawurek (Javůrek), born in Bohemia in 1756 and educated in Prague, established himself permanently in Poland after 1792. Irena Poniatowska, "Jawurek [Javůrek], Józef," in *Grove Music Online*, ed. L. Macy (Accessed 12 October 2006), http://bert.lib.indiana.edu:2100.

[7] Heinrich (Henryk) Gerhard Lentz lived in Warsaw for forty years, after having taught in Paris and London. Among his compositions the most highly praised are his preludes and symphonies. Oskar Kolberg, *Dzieła wszystkie Oskara Kolberga* [The complete works of Oskar Kolberg], ed. J. Krzyżanowski, 86 vols., *Pisma muzyczne* [Music writings] part II, ed. M. Toma-

violin professor Józef Bielawski, with whom he performed on numerous occasions;[8] and the voice teacher and conductor Carlo Soliva, whose teaching skill and musical opinions were usually endorsed by Chopin in spite of the conflict between him and Elsner.[9] Although there was much competition and quarreling, Chopin was able to maintain good relationships with everyone, and he took mischievous pleasure in inviting all the feuding musicians to the rehearsal that took place before his October 11, 1830 performance: "Never before was there an instance when all these gentlemen came together. I am able to accomplish it and I do it for [my] pleasure."[10]

Chopin's Studies at the Conservatory

Chopin first entered the university as a student at the Main School of Music in September of 1826. He had already completed the required curriculum of the gymnasium, but would need to stay there a year longer in order to receive his *maturitas* (certificate of completing gymnasium education, typically required for university admission). Chopin himself explained his decision not to stay to his friend Jan:

> Know . . . that I don't attend the Gymnasium. It would be foolish to sit six hours a day perforce, when German and German-Polish doctors ordered me to walk as much as possible; it would be foolish to listen the second time to the same [material], when during that year one can learn something new.[11]

---

szewski, O. Pawlak, and E. Miller (Wrocław: Polskie Towarzystwo Ludoznawcze; Warszawa: Ludowa Spółdzielnia Wydawnicza; Kraków: Polskie Wydawnictwo Muzyczne, 1981), 62:379.

[8] Bielawski was also the first violinist of the National Theater orchestra and was often heard in concert and in private gatherings. His playing was characterized by solidity and clarity. Kazimierz Władysław Wójcicki, *Cmentarz powązkowski pod Warszawą* [The Powązki cemetery near Warsaw] (Warsaw: Gebethner i Wolff, 1855), 2:87.

[9] The Italian-born Soliva studied in Milan with Asioli and Federici, and later conducted and had his operas performed at La Scala. Zofia Chechlińska, "Soliva, Carlo Evasio," in *Grove Music Online*, ed. L. Macy (Accessed 12 October 2006), http://bert.lib.indiana .edu:2100. There are numerous mentions of Soliva in Chopin's correspondence, especially during the last year in Warsaw. Soliva conducted Chopin's final Polish concert, and the young pianist described his conducting in the highest terms. Fryderyk Chopin, Warsaw, to Tytus Woyciechowski, Poturzyn, 12 October 1830, in *Korespondencja Fryderyka Chopina* [Fryderyk Chopin's correspondence, ed. Bronisław Edward Sydow, 2 vols. (Warsaw: Państwowy Instytut Wydawniczy, 1955), 1:146–147.

[10] Chopin, Warsaw, to Woyciechowski, Poturzyn, 9 September 1830, *Korespondencja*, 1:141. At times the professional rivalry between Elsner, Kurpiński, and Soliva became exceedingly hostile. The resentment caused injurious plotting and even gave rise to an ugly smear campaign aimed at Elsner's ethnicity, although it must be conveyed that Elsner's "Polishness" was attacked only by a few and was defended by many. Nowak-Romanowicz, *Elsner*, 174–179.

[11] Chopin, Warsaw, to Jan Białobłocki, Sokołów, 2 November [October 1826], *Korespondencja*, 1:73.

This option was available and was described by the university's rector, Wojciech Szweykowski, in his speech inaugurating the 1820–21 academic year:

> The youth who are not accepted as permanent students, unless they present the *maturitas* certificate, still can attend subjects for which they have inclination. However, they will be required to complete all classes for each year of a full course of studies in accordance with the profession they have selected for their future in society.[12]

It appears that initially Chopin had the intention of taking the *maturitas* exam a year later, but since the Department of Sciences and Fine Arts permitted him to continue his studies without the certificate, he gave up the idea and concentrated his efforts on university education.

Past attempts to reconstruct Chopin's education at the Main School of Music have not been very fruitful.[13] It is known that the curriculum of the Conservatory involved instrumental instruction, singing, theory, practical composition, and counterpoint. The course of studies anticipated two years for instrumentalists and three years for composers; these were often extended because of the demanding program. Composers were expected to attend theory lectures at the university, in addition to the practical classes at the Conservatory. The practical topics might have possibly included instrumental lessons, but the two subjects considered most essential for composition students were thoroughbass, given by Würfel and later Lentz, and counterpoint, taught by Elsner.[14] Relating this information to Chopin's studies at the Main School, however, presents a number of problems.

The first question concerns Chopin's studies of thoroughbass. Since Václav Würfel left Warsaw for Vienna in 1824 and his place was taken by Henryk Lentz, one could surmise that Lentz was Chopin's thoroughbass teacher. Such conclusion is complicated by the fact that Chopin had taken organ with Würfel since 1822, and by 1825 his organ skills were sharp enough to land him the position of gymnasium organist.[15] Furthermore, on the basis of his Conservatory course being described as "organ playing coupled with instruction in thoroughbass," one can infer that Würfel's private organ instruction of Fryderyk also included thor-

---

[12] *Posiedzenie Publiczne Królewsko-Warszawskiego Uniwersytetu odbyte 2 października 1820 roku* [A public meeting of the Royal University of Warsaw on 2 October 1820] (Warsaw: Glücksberg, 1820), 1–2.

[13] Tadeusz Frączyk, *Warszawa młodości Chopina* [Warsaw of Chopin's youth] (Kraków: Polskie Wydawnictwo Muzyczne, 1961), 208–220; and Sankowska, "Studia Fryderyka Chopina," 47–54.

[14] Karasowski, *Rys historyczny opery polskiej*, 309.

[15] Chopin, Warsaw, to Białobłocki, Biskupiec, [November 1825], *Korespondencja*, 1:60.

oughbass.[16] It is, therefore, plausible that Fryderyk did not need to study thoroughbass with Lentz at the Conservatory.

The second confusion pertains to Chopin's participation in Elsner's practical classes. On Fryderyk's own testimony, we know that he took regular lessons with his teacher: "I go to Elsner six hours a week for strict counterpoint; I listen to Bentkowski, Brodziński and other subjects that are in any way associated with music."[17] However, since the lectures of both professors Bentkowski and Brodziński conflicted with the schedule of Elsner's practical classes, this statement has introduced much confusion. Scholars have argued at length over how to reconcile the apparent problem.[18] The issue may be resolved, however, by considering Elsner's teaching schedule and the unusual musical qualifications of the young genius. Elsner's theoretical classes were divided between the university and the Conservatory: "Józef Elsner, Professor *Ordinarius*, will explicate the theory of musical composition every other week, on Thursday, 12 to 1. However, he will teach practical musical composition at the Music Conservatory, on Monday, Wednesday and Friday, 2 to 4."[19]

According to the official schedule, Chopin was able to attend the theoretical-aesthetic lecture, which took place on Thursdays at the university and did not conflict with lessons given by the other professors. It is the scheduled practical instruction at the Conservatory that conflicted with Bentkowski's and Brodziński's lectures. In solving the dilemma, one must remember that Fryderyk's preparation as a performer far exceeded the Main School's requirements: not only was he already a virtuoso pianist and an excellent organist who had mastered the techniques of thoroughbass but he is believed to have also studied the violin, cello, and the flute.[20] Taking into consideration that Chopin had been receiving theoretical instruction from Elsner in the years preceding his studies at the university, that Elsner's teaching style presumed much attention given to each student's individual needs, and that Chopin was the single composition student entering the Conservatory that year, it is plausible that Elsner met with Chopin individually, perhaps at his private quarters in the Conservatory building, at a mutually suitable time, leaving Fryderyk free to attend other lectures.[21]

[16] *Allgemeine musikalische Zeitung*, August 1821, 570.

[17] Chopin, Warsaw, to Białobłocki, Sokołów, 2 November [October 1826], *Korespondencja*, 1:73.

[18] The most careful discussions of this problem are found in Sankowska, "Studia Fryderyka Chopina," 51–53, and Frączyk, *Warszawa młodości Chopina*, 208–220.

[19] *Index Praelectionum in Universitate Literarum Regia Varsaviensi, September 15, 1826– Juli 15, 1827* (Warsaw: Glückberg, 1826), 9.

[20] Chopin writes about playing the violin and the cello during his summer visit to Szafarnia. Chopin, Szafarnia, to his family, Warsaw, 26 August 1825, *Korespondencja*, 1:54.

[21] The position that Chopin and a few other outstanding students received individual lessons seems to be supported by Sankowska ("Studia Fryderyka Chopina," 47–48). Given

The studies of counterpoint and composition took three years: for the first two years, the students attended theoretical lectures and practical training; the last year was devoted only to practical training. During the first year, students were expected to write counterpoint assignments, and compose polonaises, marches, variations, rondos, and, ultimately, sonatas. Most of Chopin's early works, including his Sonata in C Minor, op. 4, were probably composed as a part of this program of studies. During the second year, Elsner wanted to familiarize his pupils with choral and orchestral textures, so he required them to write cantatas and masses. No such works by Chopin are known, but his early works with the orchestra, the Variations, op. 2, the Fantasia in A Major, op. 13, and the Rondo in F Major, op. 14, date from this period. In the last year of schooling, Elsner encouraged the cultivation of student's individual talents and inclinations. Chopin's natural preference was to continue writing for the piano and among the many works from that period are the two piano concertos opp. 21 and 11.

Composition Studies with Elsner

Józef Elsner, a respected composer himself, was firmly rooted in the Germanic musical tradition. Most of his musical instruction came from local teachers in the musically rich German university town of Breslau (today Wrocław), but he also spent some of his formative years in Vienna (1789–1791), gaining direct exposure to the music of Mozart, Haydn, and their contemporaries. Acquainted with current pedagogical trends, Elsner also had the rare attributes of an excellent mentor: the ability to foster both creative discipline and freedom. He gave his students solid grounding in thoroughbass, counterpoint, aesthetics, and compositional theory, thus exposing them to a variety of musical concepts and genres. At the same time, each student also received much individual attention and was permitted a great deal of creative freedom. This approach was in accordance with new trends in education, initiated by the Swiss education reformer Johann Heinrich Pestalozzi, whose work Elsner highly respected. Inspired by Jean-Jacques Rousseau's concepts, Pestalozzi's new approach revolutionized education. It influenced musical traditions as disparate as Hans Georg Nägli's Liedertafel gatherings in Zurich (and their offshoots elsewhere), Friedrich Wieck's piano instruction in Leipzig, Rev. Curwen's Tonic Sol-fa method in England, Lowell Mason's teachers' training at the Boston Academy of Music, and Adolph Bernhard Marx's theoretical writ-

that, her statement (54) that because of the scheduling Chopin could not have attended Bentkowski's and Brodziński's lectures appears contradictory.

ings in Berlin.[22] Marx's organicist views of music were rooted in the Pestalozzian view of human development as inherently organic: starting from a seed, germinating and maturing into a harmonious whole—given Chopin's exposure to Pestalozzian concepts, it is perhaps more than a coincidence that his music lends itself well to the organicist approach. Pestalozzi also advocated a move away from mechanical instruction, as well as respect for the pupil's individuality and caring as basis for the relationship between the student and the teacher. Accordingly, it was Elsner's belief that "in the teaching of composition one should not dictate rules, especially to students whose talents are apparent; let them search alone, so they can surpass themselves; let them have the means of finding that which is still unknown."[23]

An approach to teaching that allowed the pupil's individuality to blossom was ideal for the cultivation of Chopin's raw talent. By the time he entered the Conservatory, he already surpassed some of his teachers' skills, but in other areas he was an absolute greenhorn. He had no experience in working with bigger forms that require a sense of large-scale harmonic direction, structural and tonal organization, and motivic coherence; he had no knowledge of orchestration; he did not understand counterpoint; and his metric organization was rigid and unimaginative. On the other hand, his innate melodic gift, even in those early years, outshined that every other Warsaw composer. Through his pianistic experience he also mastered the newest variation techniques and challenging passagework—his figurations held much more melodic interest and challenge than almost anything else composed in the Polish capital; and his daring use of harmony was unrivaled.

His teachers' conservative instruction in harmony was probably of very little use to Chopin. At first, he studied Karol Antoni Simon's Polish-German theory textbook, *Nauka harmonii—Anweisung zum General Baß* (full title, *Kurze Einweisung die Regeln der Harmonie oder des Generalbasses auf eine leicht fassliche Art gründlich zu erlernen*) (fig. 4.3), published in Poznań in 1823. Simon's textbook was recommended by Elsner and Kurpiński as a competent introduction to the fundamentals: from scales, intervals, and chords to principles of figured bass and voice-leading. A basic manual of this sort would have prepared Chopin for admission into the Conservatory and perhaps was used during his lessons with Würfel. Similar level of instruction is represented by the only theory manual of Elsner that has come down to us: an 1807 half-autograph of a handbook dedicated to his pupil Anna Łubieńska, entitled *A Brief Course of Thorough-*

---

[22] In 1821, the twelve-year-old Felix Mendelssohn composed an opera entitled *Die beiden Pädagogen*, which satirized the debate concerning the educational methods of Pestalozzi and Basedow.

[23] Elsner, Warsaw, to Chopin, Paris, 27 November 1831, *Korespondencja*, 1:197.

Figure 4.3. Karol Antoni Simon, *Nauka harmonii—Anweisung zum General Baß* (Poznań: Simon, 1823), title page with Chopin's signature. Not extant; until 1942 in the collection of the Warsaw Music Society; photograph from reproduction in Leopold Binental, *Chopin. W 120-tą rocznicę urodzin. Dokumenty i pamiątki* [Chopin: on hundred-and-twentieth anniversary of birth. Documents and memorabilia] (Warsaw: W. Łazarski, 1930). Muzeum Fryderyka Chopina w Towarzystwie im. Fryderyka, Warsaw, F. 4131. Photo by Franciszek Myszkowski.

bass.[24] Since this manuscript contains signatures of a few Conservatory students, one can infer that it might have circulated among them, but the scope of this manual is rather limited, and it cannot be viewed as representative of Conservatory instruction. However, on the basis of its organization and contents, we can place Elsner's lessons within the tradition of Albrechtsberger and Kirnberger.[25] The actual texts of Albrechtsberger's *Gründliche Anweisung zur Komposition* (1790) and Kirnberger's

[24] Józef Elsner, *Krótko zebrana nauka generałbasu* [A brief course of thoroughbass], or *Przykłady z harmonii* [Examples in harmony], with manuscript dedication to Countess Łubieńska (autograph, from p. 21), Warszawskie Towarzystwo Muzyczne (Library of the Warsaw Music Society), Warsaw, sygn. 940. Although his *Summary* lists also two manuscripts containing lecture notes, "Rozprawa o muzyce i harmonii" [Treatise on music and harmony] and "Listy o muzyce i harmonii" [Letters on music and harmony], neither work survived. Józef Elsner, *Sumariusz moich utworów muzycznych* [A summary of my musical works], ed. Alina Nowak-Romanowicz (Kraków: Polskie Wydawnictwo Muzyczne, 1957), nos. 14 and 63.

[25] Maciej Gołąb, *Chromatyka i tonalność w muzyce Chopina* [Chromaticism and tonality in Chopin's music] (Kraków: Polskie Wydawnictwo Muzyczne, 1991), 31–33.

Die Kunst des reinen Satzes in der Musik (1774–79) might also have been studied, as well as Kurpiński's harmony book.[26]

Karol Kurpiński's *A Systematic Lecture on Musical Principles for the Keyboard* (*Wykład systematyczny zasad muzyki na klawikord*) and *Examples to the Principles of Tone Harmony* (*Przykłady do Zasad harmonii tonów*), published 1818–1821, followed a different theoretical tradition. Kurpiński praised progress and supported the harmonists, in response to the conservatism of Villoteau's *Recherches sur l'analogie de la musique avec les arts*. He was also the first to introduce Polish words for several harmonic terms and concepts: tonic, dominant, root position, and inversion, to mention a few. Among Kurpiński's influences were Johann Gottfried Schicht's *Grundlagen der Harmonie nach Verwechslungssystem* and Gustav Schilling's *Polyphonomos oder die Kunst zur Erwerbung einer vollständigen Kenntniss der Harmonie in 36 Stunden;* and out of the 182 examples, the thirteen pertaining to thoroughbass came from Emmanuel Aloise Förster's *Praktische Beyspiele als Fortsetzung zu seiner Anleitung des Generalbasses.* Most notably, the outline and contents of this work bear close similarities with Anton Reicha's *Cours de composition musicale, ou Traité complet et raisonné d'Harmonie pratique* (1818), from which Kurpiński already quoted extensively in the *Musical Weekly.*[27] Reicha—a professor at the Parisian Conservatoire and the teacher of Onslow, Liszt, Berlioz, among others—was well known to both Elsner and Chopin.[28] The young Chopin admired Reicha and was disappointed to learn upon his arrival in Paris that Reicha "does not like music: he doesn't even attend Conservatory concerts; he does not want to discuss music with anyone; during his lessons he just keeps glancing at his watch, etc."[29] Notwithstanding this disillusionment with Reicha the man, the impact of Reicha's approach to music theory was lasting: in the years to come, Chopin recommended that his pupils study theory with Henri Reber, whom he respected very highly and who had been Reicha's student.[30]

None of the harmony texts available in Warsaw or for that matter anywhere else in Europe could have taught Chopin his chromatic melodic and harmonic invention: it came directly from pre-Romantic compositional models, and matured through his genius and gradually acquired experience. In his Warsaw-period pieces, the audacious chromaticism often over-

---

[26] When Franciszek Sołtyk studied composition with Elsner, he used Kurpiński's 1821 harmony manual. *Ruch muzyczny,* 1861, no. 7, 103.

[27] Jan Prosnak, "Karol Kurpiński jako teoretyk" [Karol Kurpiński as a theorist], *Kwartalnik Muzyczny* 25 (January–March 1949): 141–152.

[28] Ludwika Chopin, Warsaw, to Fryderyk Chopin, Paris, 27 November 1831, *Korespondencja,* 1:193.

[29] Chopin, Paris, to Józef Elsner, Warsaw, 14 December 1831, *Korespondencja,* 1:206.

[30] Jean-Jacques Eigeldinger, *Chopin: Pianist and Teacher as Seen by His Pupils,* trans. N. Shohet with K. Osostowicz and R. Howat (Cambridge: Cambridge University Press, 1986), 59.

lays very straightforward tonal progressions. The compositional success of his Variations in B-flat Major, op. 2 on Mozart's "Là ci darem la mano," for instance, hinges on his familiarity with the pianistic and generic idiom of variations: he can dazzle with devilishly difficult chromatic diminutions, but Mozart's tonal structure lends coherence to each variation. Most inventive harmonically are the freely composed introduction and the fifth (minor) variation of op. 2—both essentially piano nocturnes modeled after slow movements of concerti *brillant* by Chopin's virtuoso predecessors. Elsner's instruction is mainly audible in Chopin's attempts at creating motivic coherence within this piece: the opening motive binds together the introduction and returns frequently in the orchestral parts throughout the work. The orchestral writing, a new task for Chopin, is appropriate for the genre of virtuoso variations *brillant*. Some minor but consistent corrections of string voicings are evident in the working autograph score of this composition, probably indicative of Elsner's guidance and possibly even in Elsner's hand (fig. 4.4). Replacing the very opening of the piece with a new imitative version was also very likely suggested by Elsner, who at the time was broadening his student's understanding of counterpoint (fig. 4.5). Moreover, the reason for the second version (ultimately chosen for Stichvorlage and publication) may have been orchestrational: knowing the realities of the contemporary concert stage, Elsner might have advised Chopin not to open with solo winds, in case a chamber string ensemble had to be used in place of the full orchestra.[31] The op. 2 Variations were a milestone for Chopin, but he needed to work on large cyclic forms to learn how to incorporate principles vital to Elsner's teaching of composition.

Elsner's views about the process of creating musical artwork followed time-honored rhetorical procedure outlined by Heinrich Christoph Koch, based in turn on the writings of Johann Georg Sulzer, Johann Mattheson, and Charles Batteux. Yet his views also clearly resonate with the Pestolozzian organicist principles, later expounded by Adolf Bernhard Marx. In Elsner's own words, the process consisted of

1. The germination—planning of the thoughts and feelings that are to be evoked in the listener.
2. The shaping of the musical material.
3. Parenthetical beautification of the work (details).[32]

The shaping of the musical material into a logically satisfactory architectural whole was essential. In his "Treatise on Melody and Chant" Elsner explained: "Everything should advance toward one goal, so to speak, that

[31] Halina Goldberg, "Chamber Arrangements of Chopin's Concert Works," *Journal of Musicology* 19 (2002): 39–84, especially 65.
[32] *Gazeta Korespondenta Warszawskiego i Zagranicznego*, 23 March 1813, no. 24/01: 321–322.

Figure 4.4. Fryderyk Chopin, Variations in B-flat Major, op. 2 on Mozart's "Là ci darem la mano," autograph manuscript, corrections of string voicings. Pierpont Morgan Library, New York, R. O. Lehman Deposit.

is why each component must appear as belonging to such totality or else attention would be disrupted and the artwork could not please, for all beauty lies in the union of totality and multiplicity."[33] This aesthetic belief was at the heart of his disapproval of Kalkbrenner, who, without hearing the full work, suggested that Chopin eliminate a section of his concerto:

> had he given you the advice, that in your next work you should make a shorter allegro, it would be different, but to cross out from a completed work cannot be forgiven. [Elsner] compared it to an erected house that stands finished, and to someone presuming that there is one pillar too many, who wants to change the entity by removing it, thus destroying what appears to him unsatisfactory.[34]

Similarly, Elsner was disturbed by Maria Szymanowska's willingness to eliminate passages from Hummel's Concerto in B Minor and to incorporate Field's Andante in another composer's variations. In a letter to

[33] "Rozprawa o melodyi i śpiewie" [Treatise on Melody and Chant], Biblioteka XX Czartoryskich, Kraków, Ms. 2276.

[34] Ludwika Chopin, Warsaw, to Fryderyk Chopin, Paris, 27 November 1831, *Korespondencja*, 1:193.

Figure 4.5. Fryderyk Chopin, Variations in B-flat Major, op. 2 on Mozart's "Là ci darem la mano," autograph manuscript, original discarded opening. Pierpont Morgan Library, New York, R. O. Lehman Deposit.

Chopin describing these aesthetic concerns, Elsner summed up: "the sense of unity in a work is a mark of a true artist; [in contrast, a simple] artisan sets stone on a stone, places beam on a beam."[35] On numerous occasions, Elsner expressed his dissatisfaction with fashionable compositions in which sheer virtuosity replaced musical architecture. For instance, in an article published by the *Allgemeine musikalische Zeitung*, Elsner complained that in Steibelt's piano compositions "one hears all too clearly that what they lack in fundamentals is replaced by fashionable passages, spectacular runs, etc."[36] and said of a double concerto by the Bohrer brothers from Munich that "in general, it does not lack effective ideas, but rather their congruity, internal connection and harmonic contents."[37] For Elsner good music required equilibrium among logic, emotional expression, and technical skill. Such was the ideal of the Enlightenment advocated by Rousseau, and in the same vein Pestalozzi's pedagogical principles endorsed maintaining a balance between the hands, the heart, and the head.

[35] Elsner, Warsaw, to Chopin, Paris, 27 November 1831, *Korespondencja*, 1:198.

[36] *Allgemeine musikalische Zeitung*, July 1811, 454.

[37] *Allgemeine musikalische Zeitung*, July 1811, 458.

There is no doubt that such guidance was invaluable to the young Chopin; the process of maturation under Elsner's tutelage is apparent in works he composed at the time. The C Minor Sonata op. 4, dated to perhaps as early as 1827 and dedicated to Elsner, was Chopin's earliest attempt to work within a multimovement instrumental genre, preparing way for the later Warsaw works of this type: the Trio op. 8 and the two piano concerti.[38] The four-movement outline of op. 4, with the slow moment shifted to the penultimate position, sets the model for all of Chopin's later works in the sonata genre. Not surprisingly, the last two movements are most successful. Chopin is quite comfortable with the nocturne style of the larghetto, and in the final rondo the principles and language—modulatory episodes of passagework anchored by tonally stable returns of thematic material—are also familiar to him. The minuet of the C Minor Sonata follows Classical models and incorporates traits favored by Elsner, including imitative passages and internal connections, yet the melody struggles to break out from the confines of a language that is not natural to Chopin; eventually the trio is taken over by waltz idiom and *stile brillant* figurations.

The first movement most bluntly reveals the young composer's lack of experience. Chopin's preoccupation with technical matters considered vital by his teacher is apparent: much of his effort goes into incorporating contrapuntal writing, establishing motivic cohesiveness, and creating a larger sense of balance. The movement neatly falls into three almost perfectly equal sections. Such a plan is advocated for the *grand coupe binaire* by Anton Reicha in his *Traité de haute composition musicale,* which Warsaw's musical circles, well acquainted with Reicha's earlier writings and cultivating a direct connection with the Parisian musical scene, might have known very soon after its publication (1824–1826). Chopin takes every opportunity to reiterate the main motive introduced in the opening theme and to include counterpoint, imitation in particular. Monothematicism, pervasive motivic integration, and frequent use of imitation are markers of Elsner's instrumental style, and no doubt his young student was encouraged to incorporate them. But Chopin fails to reconcile the Hummelesque chromatic passagework with the compositional principles just acquired from Elsner. He is at his weakest with skills he could not have learnt from composing sectional and harmonically static polonaises, rondos, and variations but which are needed in large narrative forms: channeling foreground chromaticism into long-range harmonic goals and creating a sense of dramatic momentum. Thus, for all the surface chromaticism of the first section (or perhaps because of it), he fails to establish a secondary key area. Similarly, the second section, in spite of incessant key changes (or

[38] Chopin intended to publish the Sonata as op. 3, together with the Variations op. 2, but this plan was never realized, and the piece was only published posthumously, as op. 4.

perhaps because of them), seems purposeless. When the primary thematic idea returns, it does so in B-flat Minor rather than the expected C Minor tonic. Forestalling a tonic recap in itself was not such an unusual procedure, and it is found, for instance, in Elsner's Piano Sonata in D Major. Chopin, though, continues to modulate for most of the last section as well, not returning to the original key until the very last page of the movement.

It is incorrect and simplistic to outright dismiss these idiosyncrasies by claiming that the principles of sonata composition were not known in Warsaw.[39] Judging from Elsner's own sonata movements, which adhered to the expected tonal schemes, and his reliance on Koch's theoretical writings, Chopin would have learned about the customary harmonic plan in his composition lessons. As I show later on (chapters 6 and 8), Chopin also had a considerable exposure to multimovement genres in the Classical tradition through his own playing, as well as public and private concerts he attended, and it is precisely the variety of schemes available in actual compositions that would have inspired him. Learning from the living compositional practice, rather than abstract and antiquated theoretical principles, was advocated by Reicha in *Traité de haute composition musicale*—a view that offended the French musical establishment. But Elsner, in his openness to individualized learning process, would likely have endorsed Reicha's controversial opinion.

Such educational background and Chopin's later avoidance of conventional tonal schemes throughout his oeuvre suggest an explanation for the rambling harmonic design of this movement: a search for an individual manner of articulating larger musical structure that would better suit his complex harmonic vocabulary. Interestingly, Chopin does not work with the initial motive of the theme, which—as remarked by many authors—is obviously derived from Bach's two-voice invention in C Minor. Instead, he uses a chromatic idea heard in the second measure of the theme. In this way, he provides himself with opportunities to build chromatic melodic lines as well as generating chromatic contrapuntal structures that result in audacious harmonies. For all its lack of direction and motivic tedium, the piece anticipates some of the characteristically Chopinesque harmonic concepts of his later works—startling tonal and modal shifts, and departures from established modulatory schemes. In fact, in his later large-scale works, Chopin continues to defy traditional key relationships, instead exploring mediant and modal associations, often achieved through contrapuntal means.

The lessons learned from Elsner were not lost on Chopin. In the years to come, he discovered ways of shaping the musical narrative through motivic and harmonic procedures that were distinctively his, transform-

[39] Charles Rosen, *Sonata Forms* (New York: Norton, 1980), 392.

ing glittery virtuoso passagework and audacious harmonies to serve his carefully thought-out narrative and expressive plan. He also explained to his own students how form worked in the compositions of others and in his own works. By instructing them to begin work on every selected musical composition by examining its plan, as well as the feelings and psychological processes it evoked, Chopin made his students highly aware of musical structure and its role in shaping the musical narrative.[40]

Elsner's Views on Musical Rhetoric and Grammar

Chopin's students repeatedly said that their master thought of music in rhetorical terms; for him it was a language following the rules of punctuation and elocution.[41] He expressed just such an idea in his sketch for a piano method by saying: "We use sounds to make music just as we use words to make a language."[42] This was in accord with Elsner's views of music, which he called the "language of emotions."[43] Elsner's lectures on the aesthetic and theoretical aspects of composition relied closely on the music-rhetorical tradition. They were described as "lectures on composition, its grammatical as well as rhetorical part."[44] In them, Elsner preserved much of the original thought of Johann Nikolaus Forkel, who carefully described the oratorical qualities of music and whose theories Elsner propagated with great ardor.[45] He gave much attention to Polish prosody, using his own publication *On Meter and Rhythm of the Polish Language* (*Rozprawa o metryczności i rytmiczności języka polskiego*) as a textbook.[46] Considering affinities between language and music, Elsner addressed not only meter, rhythm, and accent but also the musical implications of grammar and syntax. He devoted much attention to the need for dissimilar musical approaches to grammatical accent, dictated by the internal structure of the language, and oratorical accent, aimed at achieving psychological objectives.

[40] Eigeldinger, *Chopin*, 59; according to Carl Mikuli's account.

[41] Eigeldinger, *Chopin*, 42–44.

[42] Eigeldinger, *Chopin*, 42.

[43] Elsner, Warsaw, to Chopin, Paris, 27 November 1831, *Korespondencja*, 1:197.

[44] *Allgemeine musikalische Zeitung*, August 1821, 570.

[45] In fact, there was so much interest in Forkel's work in Poland that during the years 1818–1819, at the request of the Society for the Friends of Religious and National Music, Kazimierz Brodziński translated the practical sections of Forkel's *Allgemeine Geschichte der Musik* (1788). He presented the Society with his translation in 1822, but unfortunately the Society could not publish it due to shortage of funds. Kazimierz Brodziński, *Wspomnienia mojej młodości* [Memories of my youth] (Kraków: Spółka Wydawnicza Polska, 1901), 87.

[46] Józef Elsner, *O metryczności i rytmiczności języka polskiego* [On meter and rhythm in the Polish language] (Warsaw: S. Dąbrowski, 1818). In 1823, Brodziński prepared the practical part for this work and selected songs for the use in churches. Brodziński, *Wspomnienia mojej młodości*, 87.

The companion volume to Elsner's book on prosody was his "Treatise on Melody and Chant" (*Rozprawa o melodyi i śpiewie*), preserved in manuscript only.[47] The treatise, which Elsner intended to publish, presumably contains the essence of his lectures on logical and aesthetic principles of composing vocal and instrumental melodies. Elsner's simple melodic examples could not have served as models for Chopin's exquisite melodies, but Chopin's newly found attentiveness to the potentials of melodic ideas clearly dates to the period of his studies with Elsner. Naturally, he was stimulated by exposure to a broader musical repertory, opera in particular. Such manner of learning was also encouraged by his teacher, who even proposed that musical artists and amateurs collaborate in gathering examples of "characteristic and passionate ideas" from Classical compositions into a "Music Dictionary" for the edification of budding composers.[48] Though this project was never carried out, Chopin had other means of learning "characteristic and passionate ideas," and I discuss the venues and repertories through which he became directly acquainted with the compositional models of his eminent elders and peers at length in the chapters that follow. His knowledge of the masterworks notwithstanding, a thorough study of the principles of melodic structure with Elsner would have had profound impact on him.

Expression was central to Elsner's understanding of music, and he cautioned young composers against using "fashionable turns of melody which today will be accepted with applause but tomorrow will be forgotten."[49] To Chopin, who in his earlier works blindly followed the conventional melodic language of salon dances and *stile brillant* showpieces, developing such an awareness of the expressive powers of melody was crucial. In his instruction, Elsner considered tonal and harmonic contexts for melodies, as well as temporal organization on the level of individual tones, measures, and phrases. Thus, the selection of appropriate melodic intervals merited an in-depth discussion for Elsner, who was first and foremost an opera composer, concerned with crafting recitatives. For instance, he advised the student that

> diatonic movement has something light and pleasant, while chromatic one something painful and sometimes frightening. Consonant intervals moving upwards are appropriate for lively feelings; less consonant or dissonant for sad and gloomy ones. One can also mention that smaller intervals are calm, whereas large ones can express restless and vigorous emotions.[50]

[47] "Rozprawa o melodyi i śpiewie;" *śpiew* is translated as "chant" in the sense of the Italian *canto*.

[48] "Rozprawa o melodyi i śpiewie." This plan was never accomplished.

[49] "Rozprawa o melodyi i śpiewie."

[50] "Rozprawa o melodyi i śpiewie."

Example 4.1a. Józef Elsner, "Rozprawa o melodyi i śpiewie" [Treatise on melody and chant], Biblioteka XX Czartoryskich, Kraków, Ms 2276; simple period.

Example 4.1b. Józef Elsner, "Rozprawa o melodyi i śpiewie" [Treatise on melody and chant], Biblioteka XX Czartoryskich, Kraków, Ms 2276; expanded period.

Similarly, the composer was to use tempo, meter, and rhythm that best express an appropriate affect. To clarify his point, Elsner provided examples of the same melodic pattern set in different rhythms appropriate for the affects of contentment, cheerfulness, humor, gravity, amplification, and religious chant, respectively.

Having selected a suitable intervalic and rhythmic character for the melody, the composer would concern himself with musical syntax, skillfully articulating simple and extended musical sentences.[51] Since extending the musical sentence through melodic means requires changing syntactic punctuation, Elsner detailed the potential of the successive degrees of the scale to take on the various syntactic functions, generating a comma, a colon, or a semicolon. To illustrate his point, he presented a straightforward eight-bar period, which he likened to the sentence "[He] who loves his homeland is a good citizen" (ex. 4.1a) and then showed the

[51] The subject of lengthening phrases is treated briefly by Kirnberger in *Die Kunst des reinen Satzes in der Musik* and extensively by Koch, *Versuch einer Anleitung zur Composition,* both of which formed the basis of Elsner's instruction in other areas. Reicha's discussion of this subject in *Traité de mélodie* of 1814 appears also to have been known to Elsner, since his treatise shows a number of very clear connections to Reicha's.

various means of extending it, by avoiding closure on a perfect authentic cadence. Ultimately he arrived at a musical phrase that he understood as a double or triple period and compared to the sentence "[He] who loves his homeland, is a good and virtuous citizen, does not spare [his] fortune, nor health, nor life" (ex. 4.1b).

Elsner was also keenly aware of achieving such extensions by means other than modifications of melody, such as altering the underlying harmony while preserving the original melody, whereby the tone changes its syntactic meaning because of a different harmonic context. To demonstrate such harmonic reinterpretations of a melodic pattern, Elsner provided musical illustrations, one of which is shown (exs. 4.2a, b, c).

In his Variations in E Major on "Steh'auf, steh'auf o du Schweizerbub," Chopin used such harmonic reinterpretation to evade closure and bridge into the coda (ex. 4.3b, m. 140). The Variations are an early work, sometimes erroneously claimed to be Chopin's earliest effort in genre other than the polonaise.[52] Bound to the ubiquitous four-bar phrase

---

[52] The Variations in E Major are dated to 1824 in the Breitkopf & Härtel 1880–85 edition and in Niecks, *Frederick Chopin as a Man and Musician*, 2 vols. (1888; reprint, New York: Cooper Square, 1973); several modern sources, including Józef M. Chomiński and Teresa D. Turło. *Katalog dzieł Fryderyka Chopina* [A catalogue of the works of Fryderyk Chopin] (Kraków: Polskie Wydawnictwo Muzyczne, 1990) and the *Grove Music Online* article on "Chopin," repeat this dating without scrutinizing it. On the basis of Chopin's correspondence (1 December 1930 and 11 September 1841), however, we can infer that the autograph Stichvorlage (Vienna, H. Wertitsch, listed in Chomiński and Turło but not in Krystyna Kobylańska, *Rękopisy utworów Chopina: katalog* [The manuscripts of Chopin's works: a catalogue], 2 vols. (Kraków: Polskie Wydawnictwo Muzyczne, 1977), bearing the inscription "op. 4," was sent to Haslinger in 1829, to be published with Variations op. 2 and Sonata op. 3. The Sonata and the E Major Variations were only published posthumously, the earlier as op. 4 and the latter without opus. These dating discrepancies cannot be reconciled unless we follow Niecks in presuming the existence of some earlier version of the "Schweizerbub" Variations. Furthermore, even accepting the later date does not erase the discrepancy between the dating of the Stichvorlage to 1829 and the alleged direct inspiration by concerts of Henriette Sontag, which took place only in 1830. The "Schweizerbub" was made famous by the singing Tyrolese family Rainer during their extensive European tours. In particular, their astonishingly successful 1827 London debut made an impression on Moscheles, who immediately published transcriptions of their songs and wrote several pieces based on them. See Hans Nathan, "The Tyrolese Family Rainer, and the Vogue of Singing Mountain-Troupes in Europe and America," *Musical Quarterly* 32/1 (January 1946): 63–79. These publications could easily be available in Warsaw shortly after they were issued in London. In addition, by his own admission, Chopin intended to hear performances of Tyrolese singers in Warsaw in 1830 and implied having heard them in 1828 (letter dated 4 September 1830). Thus there is no reason to assume that Chopin did not know the song before Sonntag's visit in Poland. Ultimately, the account involving Henrietta Sonntag, passed on by tradition and in a manuscript that does not stem from Chopin (Polska Akademia Nauk, Kraków, Ms. 1439), needs to be reexamined or dismissed as inaccurate, and the dating to 1824 abandoned in favor of the 1829 indicated in the correspondence.

Example 4.2a, b, c. Józef Elsner, "Rozprawa o melodyi i śpiewie" [Treatise on melody and chant], Biblioteka XX Czartoryskich, Kraków, Ms 2276; harmonic reinterpretations of a melodic pattern, Elsner's examples 2a, b, and c.

structure of salon dances on which he modeled his own dance composi-tions, Chopin did not dare to disturb the metric regularity within his ear-liest works. This piece, too, features perfectly symmetrical four-bar phrases throughout, echoing the original groupings of the theme. However, in the concluding *tempo di valse*, Chopin disrupts the established symmetry. The final statement of the opening section of the *tempo di valse*, the sec-ond phrase is expanded from eight to nineteen measures (exs. 4.3a and b). The delayed arrival on the tonic and the ensuing coda create a strong sense of closure providing an appropriate conclusion.

Sent for publication to Haslinger in Vienna alongside the other works (op. 2 and op. 4), completed under his teacher's watchful eye, the E Major Variations bear an imprint of Elsner's tutelage in the structure of its con-clusion. In the "Treatise on Melody and Chant," in the section entitled "Musical Considerations Regarding Higher or Greater Rhythm" (sect. 9 of chap. 4), Elsner discusses higher or greater rhythm (hypermeter), which he defines as the grouping of measures containing stressed and light (ac-cented and unaccented) constituent measures. In fact, he specifically ad-vises abandoning phrase symmetry at the conclusion of a composition in order to create closure:

> The lengthening of the final or the penultimate measure [here: phrase or hypermeasure], or the repetition of the last idea, heard several times straightforward within a period, does not contradict the above indi-cated principles of symmetry, but rather, for logic-aesthetic reasons, helps and in some ways is necessary for the concluding punctuation in symphonies, arias, etc.[53]

These kinds of concluding expansions become a common feature of Chopin's mature style.[54] He used them in his larger works, but already during his early years in Paris, even in his miniatures, mazurkas, and waltzes in particular, concluding expansions and extensions became the

[53] "Rozprawa o melodyi i śpiewie."
[54] Charles Burkhart, "Chopin's Concluding Expansions," in *Nineteenth-Century Piano Music: Essays in Performance and Analysis*, ed. David Witten (New York: Garland, 1997), 95–116.

Example 4.3a. Fryderyk Chopin, Variations in E Major on "Steh'auf, steh'auf o du Schweizerbub" op. posth.; the original phrase as appearing in mm. 89–96 and 113–120.

Example 4.3b. Fryderyk Chopin, Variations in E Major on "Steh'auf, steh'auf o du Schweizerbub" op. posth.; the expanded phrase, mm. 137–155.

preferred means of creating closure.[55] Elsner also encouraged this method of preparation for conclusion, explaining that "sometimes even in smaller pieces—ariettas, duettinos, and songs—such lengthening can enliven a period consisting of only two or four measures."[56]

The example he provided to support his point was none other than a two-phrase period from the celebrated duet from Mozart's *Don Giovanni* "Là ci darem la mano" (see ex. 4.4). This example also appears in the analogous context in Reicha's *Traité de mélodie* (Paris, 1814), which along with other similarities between the two treatises points to Reicha's work as one of Elsner's models. The example includes a symmetrical second phrase and an alternate version with a two-measure expansion of the conclusion. It is odd that Elsner did not credit this well-known piece to Mozart (as he does with other examples taken from recognizable sources) and that he uses Reicha's modification of the ending, rather than reproducing Mozart's more musically convincing original. Nor is their variant stemming from compositional clumsiness. Rather, it has a pedagogical intent: by equipping their expansion with an ending identical with the model phrase, Elsner and Reicha simplify and underscore the relationship between the two.

Reicha's and Elsner's choice of "Là ci darem la mano" for their demonstration was not arbitrary: the duet, containing several expansions and extensions, is a masterpiece of rhythmic manipulations.[57] Elsner idolized Mozart, and to the widely held belief that he imparted this love of the Viennese composer to his pupil, one can add the likelihood that he made him aware of Mozart's rhythmic ingenuity. It has been suggested elsewhere on a stylistic basis that Mozart's sonatas were the source of Chopin's concluding expansions.[58] This influence may have been more extensive, stemming not just from the sonatas but other genres, chamber music, symphonies, and operas which, as I demonstrate in the chapters that follow, would have been known to Chopin during his Warsaw years.

Considering the metric subtleties of "Là ci darem la mano" and the fact that Elsner and therefore probably also Chopin were keenly aware of them, it is very telling that when the young composer used this duet as a variation theme in op. 2, he purged it of all metric irregularities. The normalization of Mozart's eloquent asymmetries was presumably dictated by the nature of variation form, in which their expressive power would wane through repeated use. Instead, Chopin deferred metric irregulari-

[55] Jeffrey Kallberg, "The Problem of Repetition and Return in Chopin's Mazurkas," in *Chopin Studies*, ed. Jim Samson (Cambridge: Cambridge University Press, 1988), 1–23.

[56] "Rozprawa o melodyi i śpiewie."

[57] The topic has been treated extensively in Charles Burkhart, "How Rhythm Tells the Story in 'Là ci darem la mano,'" *Theory and Practice* 16 (1991): 21–38.

[58] Burkhart, "Chopin's Concluding Expansions."

Example 4.4. Józef Elsner, "Rozprawa o melodyi i śpiewie" [Treatise on melody and chant], Biblioteka XX Czartoryskich, Kraków, Ms 2276; Mozart, "Là ci darem la mano," with Elsner's ending.

ties until the end of the piece, cascading through witty asymmetries, elisions, expansions, and extensions in the concluding *Alla polacca*.

Over time, Chopin learned to use similar disturbances of periodic symmetry as a means of fashioning closure in smaller compositions. The mazurkas were especially suited for such treatment because of their generic segmentation, iterations, and open-endedness.[59] Already in his early mazurkas, he became dissatisfied with the conventional *da capo* endings and sought to lengthen the returning section in a manner recommended by Elsner. The conclusion of Mazurka op. 7 no. 3 is among the earliest examples of such treatment. In his later mazurkas, op. 59 no. 2, for instance, the manipulation of expansions and extensions to achieve closure reached a remarkable degree of sophistication.

Elsner's views concerning asymmetrical measure groupings were not limited to conclusions of compositions. He said plainly that although maintaining symmetry in the structure of the higher rhythm assures more refined and more expressive musical art, the smoothness should not be exaggerated, because "although every work of art through symmetry becomes lucid, easier to comprehend (resulting in musical art which is fluent and easily falls into the ear), sometimes because of the same it can be monotonous, and ultimately tiresome, inappropriate and tedious."[60] For that reason, he claimed, in longer compositions it is necessary to combine symmetrical groupings (two, four, and eight) with longer and irregular ideas, in particular groupings of five, seven, or more measures. In his later works, Chopin became a master of metric asymmetries, setting them against the regular four-bar groupings of mazurkas, etudes, and nocturnes.[61] But even during the Warsaw period he ventured to attain

[59] On Chopin's efforts to evade these generic confines see Kallberg, "The Problem of Repetition and Return," 1–23.

[60] "Rozprawa o melodyi i śpiewie."

[61] William Rothstein, *Phrase Rhythm in Tonal Music* (New York: Schirmer Books, 1989), 214–428, and "Phrase Rhythm in Chopin's Nocturnes and Mazurkas," in Samson, *Chopin Studies*, 115–141; Carl Schachter, "Idiosyncracies of Phrase Rhythm in Chopin's Mazurkas,"

rhythmic and metric variety and elasticity, most notably in the Trio op. 8 (discussed in chapter 6).

Even Elsner's discussion of symmetrical measure groupings contains passages of interest, for he discusses possibilities of regular phrases of three or even five or six bars. His two examples of "ritmo di tre battute" are native to eastern Europe. The first one, identified as a "Russian Song," is a tune that is earlier found in the manuscript collection of folk tunes compiled by or for Prince Adam Kazimierz Czartoryski, and that later makes several appearances in Russian music, most notably in the last movement of Tchaikovsky's Fourth Symphony (see ex. 4.5a). This example is also used to illustrate three-bar groupings by Reicha in his *Traité de mélodie*. Elsner's second example is a mazurka from Jan Stefani's opera *Cracovians and Highlanders* (see ex. 4.5b).

Perhaps it is in Elsner's endorsement of atypical but regular hypermeters, including the groupings of five, that Chopin found the inspiration to set the slow movement of his Sonata op. 4 as a nocturne in the unusual 5/4 meter.

Other aesthetic considerations of Elsner's lectures included the influence of music and the other arts on mind and emotions; its role in everyday life; and ancient and medieval theories on musical perception.[62] Inspired by the writings of Forkel and Gerber, he recognized the importance of historical documentation and lectured on history of music, giving special attention to the history of harmony.[63] Among other sources of historic knowledge Elsner used, the most vital were Grétry's *Memoires ou Essais sur la musique* and Rousseau's *Dictionnaire de musique*, both also extensively quoted in the *Musical Weekly*.

Elsner's instruction might have been further expanded through the inclusion of other sources available in translation in Kurpiński's short-lived journal, the *Musical Weekly* (1820–1821). The contents of the periodical reveal the scope of musical interests in early nineteenth-century Warsaw: articles on aesthetics (music and words, music and emotions, the nature of national music), biographical sketches, series on musical instruments and musical genres, historic essays about the Western tradition (opera, medieval music) and non-Western musical cultures (Turkey, South America, China, ancient and contemporary Egypt; music of the

---

in *The Age of Chopin: Interdisciplinary Inquiries*, ed. Halina Goldberg (Bloomington: Indiana University Press, 2004), 95–105.

[62] Nowak-Romanowicz, *Elsner*, 181.

[63] Since his early years in Warsaw, he had carefully collected materials pertaining to history of Polish music: old manuscripts, folk songs, biographical documentation. His intention was to use these materials for a history of Polish music. His plans were never realized, although some fragments were published as longer articles in the *Allgemeine musikalische Zeitung*. The *Music Lexicon* (*Leksykon muzyczny*) remained in manuscript and was destroyed in World War II. Nowak-Romanowicz, *Elsner*, 169–170.

Example 4.5a. Józef Elsner, "Rozprawa o melodyi i śpiewie" [Treatise on melody and chant], Biblioteka XX Czartoryskich, Kraków, Ms 2276; "Piosnka ruska" [A Russian song].

Example 4.5b. Józef Elsner, "Rozprawa o melodyi i śpiewie" [Treatise on melody and chant], Biblioteka XX Czartoryskich, Kraków, Ms 2276; Mazurka from Jan Stefani's opera *Cracovians and Highlanders*.

ancient Greeks, Romans, and Hebrews)—all next to musical news.[64] The texts of feature articles were frequently taken from Forkel, Grétry, and Rousseau, but in many instances other sources were consulted: for instance, Drieberg's *Die musikalischen Wissenschaften der Griecher, Costumes des Othomans* by A. L. Castellan, and a fragment entitled "De l'Opera en France" from François-Henri-Joseph Castil-Blaze's *Essai sur la musique*. The range of articles in the *Musical Weekly* makes apparent that Warsaw's musical circles had considerable exposure to established musical knowledge, and kept abreast of new scholarship and musical news.

Studies at the University

The Conservatory students were also encouraged to attend lectures outside of their specialty. We know that Chopin attended singing classes with

[64] These included news from other countries of Europe and America: information about premieres and special concerts, postings of interesting publications on music, and death notices. Local musical events were given due consideration: announcements of opera performances, postings of newly published musical works, reviews of new compositions and performances. In addition, each issue contained a musical annex.

Walenty Kratzer, required of all university students,[65] and that in anticipation of an international career, Chopin's parents and teachers encouraged him to study foreign languages. Thus, in addition to his earlier
schooling in French, German, ancient Greek, and Latin, he received instruction in Italian and English. Italian lessons with Stanisław Rinaldi
were provided in the Conservatory curriculum, though required of
singers only.[66] Consequently, Chopin's Italian lessons with Rinaldi took
place at the Chopins' apartment.[67] At the same time, he also studied English with a well-liked teacher named McCartney.[68] Given Fryderyk's en-
joyment of and aptitude for drawing (see fig. 4.6), it is conceivable that he
had interest in architecture, sculpture, and painting classes offered by the
Fine Arts Department, but no proof of his participation exists.[69]

On his own testimony, Chopin attended lectures given by the dean of the
Department of Sciences and Fine Arts, the historian Feliks Bentkowski.
Bentkowski's history course was required of almost all students, so his
classes enjoyed the greatest audience. Although as a lecturer he lacked fire
and brilliance, Bentkowski presented the material in a systematic and ordered manner, giving his students solid and honest knowledge of ancient
and modern history supported by traditional and contemporary historical
research.[70] As a founder and editor of *Pamiętnik Warszawski* (a periodical
associated with the Society for the Friends of Learning), Bentkowski provided a public forum for the aesthetic debate and for increasing awareness
about the new Romantic ideas. This receptiveness was characteristic of Enlightenment concepts of learning, and Bentkowski, though concerned
about maintaining "good taste," urged openness to all knowledge:

> Let us guard ourselves against contempt towards any useful knowl-
> edge; let us support all scholarly endeavors; let us not talk about the

[65] Chopin, Warsaw, to Woyciechowski, Poturzyn, 9 September 1828, *Korespondencja*,
1:78–79. Walenty Kratzer was one of the Conservatory's singing teachers (the vocal department, headed by Soliva, consisted of Kratzer, Wejnert, and Żyliński). Kratzer was a
renowned opera tenor (and a composer of some fifty vaudevilles and operettas), who retired
form the stage in 1821. In addition to the Conservatory, he taught voice at several other institutions (including the general classes at the university, attended by Chopin) and coached
the opera chorus. Ferdynand Hoesick, "Luminarze warszawscy w roli przyjaciół i znajomych F. Chopina" [Warsaw luminaries as Chopin's friends and acquaintances], in
Hoesick, *Warszawa: Luźne kartki z przeszłości syreniego grodu* [Warsaw: Loose leaves from the
past of the "mermaid city"] (Poznań: Księgarnia Św. Wojciecha, 1920), 259.

[66] Karasowski, *Rys historyczny opery polskiej*, 309.

[67] Chopin, Warsaw, to Białobłocki, Sokołów, 14 [12] March [1827], *Korespondencja*,
1:76. According to Frączyk, Chopin attended Italian lessons with Rinaldi in the company of
his friends Weltz and Woyciechowski. Frączyk, *Warszawa młodości Chopina*, 220.

[68] Frączyk, *Warszawa młodości Chopina*, 220. After Oskar Kolberg.

[69] These classes are listed in the *Index Praelectionum*, 9.

[70] Franciszek Salezy Dmochowski, *Wspomnienia* [Memoirs] (Warsaw: Jaworski, 1858),
127–129.

Figure 4.6. Landscape with a bridge. Drawing by Fryderyk Chopin. Muzeum Fryderyka Chopina w Towarzystwie im. Fryderyka Chopina, Warsaw, M/334. Photo by Franciszek Myszkowski.

harmfulness of sciences and fine arts; let us not mock good taste. Even in the darkest ages, there were theologians with the vast erudition of a lawmaker, profound philosophers. But only when all skills started to be cultivated, when good taste was added to exactitude, when valuable studies began to extend to all classes; only then, I am saying, the light of civilization ascended on our horizon.[71]

Bentkowski also demonstrated distinct concern for the reaffirmation of the Polish identity through the Polish language. He believed that "it is a great barrier for the improvement of skill, when a language used for teaching is foreign to the populace. . . . The entire system of thinking and reasoning must lack clarity, vitality, strength and shadings, when it takes on the clothes of a foreign language."[72]

---

[71] *Posiedzenie Publiczne Królewsko-Warszawskiego Uniwersytetu odbyte 5 października 1818 roku* [Public meeting of the Royal University of Warsaw on 5 October 1818] (Warsaw: Glücksberg, 1818), 44.

[72] *Posiedzenie Publiczne Królewsko-Warszawskiego Uniwersytetu odbyte 5 października 1818 roku,* 40.

The propagation of the Polish language was central to the lectures of the two literature professors: Ludwik Osiński and Kazimierz Brodziński.

> During this time, the University of Warsaw had two professorial chairs of literature, which attracted great attention from the university's youth and the entire public. The one devoted to comparative literature was taken by Osiński, the other, dedicated to the national literary tradition, belonged to Brodziński. The first brought pleasant diversion, but no adequately versatile learning; the timid and modest voice rising from the other directed young minds to the path of national feelings, ideas and images.[73]

Osiński, who directed the National Theater, was a poet, translator of Corneille and Voltaire, and authority on ancient, especially Roman, and modern French literatures. His lectures, based on the writings of Jean-François La Harpe and Hugh Blair, dealt with the ancients (Homer, Virgil, ancient Greek drama) as well as poetry and theater in modern France.[74] Appointed to his university position in response to popular demand, he was a splendid lecturer, who with the musical magic of his voice could cast a spell on his listeners; there was always a crowd of enthusiastic students attending his classes.[75]

> The hour of Osiński's lecture was a feast, an eagerly sought after banquet. People rushed to his lecture hall as if to a concert, not to a literary talk. Nobody read like him, nobody recited poems so exquisitely, nobody had such a sonorous voice. This voice was like the most perfect instrument, which he commanded like the most excellent artist. He knew how to roar, he knew how to bring forth sweet and tender tones. Paganini's fiddle was in his voice.[76]

Brodziński's Proto-Romanticism

Kazimierz Brodziński's oratory skill was not of the same caliber as Osiński's, but his classes lured the youth with an offer of brotherly guidance, which was kind and wise, and with his concern for subject matters close to the hearts of young Romantics. His essays, which added up to a substantial and influential opus of critical-aesthetic writings, referred directly to the concepts of Jean Paul, Herder, Schelling, and Kant.[77] In fact, his 1825

---

[73] Andrzej Edward Koźmian, "Wizerunki osób towarzystwa warszawskiego" [Images of Warsaw's socialites], *Przegląd Poznański* 24 (1857): 3.

[74] Koźmian, "Wizerunki osób towarzystwa warszawskiego," 14.

[75] Wójcicki, *Cmentarz powązkowski*, 1:222.

[76] Koźmian, "Wizerunki osób towarzystwa warszawskiego," 14–15.

[77] Kazimierz Brodziński, *Pisma Estetyczno-Krytyczne* [The aesthetic-critical writings], 2 vols., ed. Aleksander Łucki (Warsaw: Z Zasiłku Funduszu Kultury Narodowej, 1934).

translation of the essay on the beautiful and the sublime, "Beobachtungen über das Gefühl des Schönen und Erhabenen," was among the earliest Polish translations of Kant, although Kantian idealism, especially the concepts of the beautiful and the sublime and their role in the expression of the infinite, was discussed in earlier articles.[78]

A proto-Romantic poet, Brodziński was one of the first and the most resounding voices in the debate on Polish Romanticism; his essential views were contained in the famous 1818 article "On Classicism and Romanticism, as well as on the Spirit of Polish Poetry," published in Bentkowski's *Pamiętnik Warszawski*. As expected of a literature professor, he was conversant in classical antiquity, freely referring to Horace, Aristotle, Homer, and Virgil. He was likewise at ease with medieval sagas, Dante, Petrarch, Ariosto, Tasso, and Shakespeare. Given such broad background, Brodziński was able to fluently articulate his views on how Corneille, Racine, and La Harpe compared to the traditions of classical antiquity, while relating Byron, Scott, Schiller, and Goethe to Nordic legends and early modern Christian writings. For Brodziński, the battle between the Classical and Romantic camps held in its core the conflict between modern French and German aesthetics, and although he acknowledged the merits of the foremost masterpieces of the both schools, he also found fault with each. The real classical writers were the poets of Greek antiquity whose craft was true because it stayed close to nature and spoke to the whole people, not just a selected class. He accused French poets of artifice, superficiality, rigidity, and formality: for them courtly *bon gôut* was of utmost importance, to the detriment of the poetic substance. The Germans, on the other hand, though able to reach into emotions and convey the sense of the infinite, sought gratuitous thrills in gloomy visions of ghosts, death, and passionate suffering. He also scorned their unconditional acceptance of the Middle Ages as harmful. In Brodziński's view, Hebrew poetry, Nordic myths, and early Christian writings, which embodied the Arcadian age of innocence, were better suited for inspiration. It is these works, along with the songs of the people, that he considered most important for modern poets, whose mission was to promote the Christian and national spirit though the veneration of innocence: poetry was not to simply seek beauty, but to serve moral and patriotic causes.

Each nation had to find a style of poetry that suited its national spirit. A Pole could not fully comprehend the aesthetics that arose from a different soil. For that reason, blindly following the French, the Germans, or the English, no matter how excellent their works might be, was detrimental. He proposed that the solution for Polish poets was to return to native

---

[78] Kł . . . , "O idei i uczuciu nieskończoności" [On the idea and the feeling of the infinite], *Pamiętnik Naukowy* 2 (1819): 5–30.

models of expression provided by the preceding generations of Polish writers and by the songs of the people:

> As for the spirit of our poetry, we see in it the love of the fatherland reigning everywhere, zeal in the reverence for noble citizenly deeds, moderation in exaltation, liberal rather than frightful imagination without fantastic visions, with gentle tenderness, simplicity—which is the attribute of too few modern foreign writers—country pictures of rusticity and family life, the morality of practical philosophy, nonviolent passions, and modesty of customs.[79]

To realize this goal, he gave much attention to Polish literary heritage, attempting to create a "Polish classical tradition." Thus, in his critical writings, he devoted increasingly more space to the works of Polish writers of the past and the present, as well as the Polish language as the primary vehicle for nationality. On another front, he encouraged writers to become familiar with native folk poetry. His repeated extolments of the simplicity and beauty of the unadulterated folk song resonate years later in Chopin's description of Oskar Kolberg's folk song arrangements as "beauties with tagged-on noses, tinted cheeks, with clipped legs or on stilts."[80] Perhaps in this respect for the untainted music of the land lies the reason for Chopin's reluctance to use direct folk models: the composer stayed away from arranging Polish folk songs, and no strong case has ever been made for specific quotations from folklore in his mazurkas.[81]

Driven by the belief that the customs and taste of the Slaves resembled the purity of the ancient Greeks, Brodziński extended his interests to the folklore of Poland's Slavic neighbors:

> The Slavic people—in general agricultural and brave, but neither savage nor spoiled by civilization, attached to its rituals, and above all respecting family virtues—who by and large have not yet become differentiated into classes, and for whom the dialect of the people is not, as in other nations, the dialect of the masses: these people, like the ancient Greeks, hold abundance of true poetry.[82]

In this veneration of spiritually united Slavdom as the repository of Europe's innocence, to which the overcivilized West would have to turn for

---

[79] Brodziński, "O klasyczności i romantyczności tudzież o duchu poezji polskiej" [On Classicism and Romanticism as well as the spirit of Polish poetry], *Pisma Estetyczno-Krytyczne*, 1:89.

[80] Chopin, Paris, to his family, Warsaw, started a week before Easter [28 March], completed 19 April [1847], *Korespondencja*, 2:193.

[81] Barbara Milewski, "Chopin's Mazurkas and the Myth of the Folk," *19th-Century Music* 23 (1999): 113–135.

[82] Brodziński, 1826 letter to *Dziennik warszawski*, in *Pisma Estetyczno-Krytyczne*, 2:53.

moral guidance, Brodziński (alongside Staszic) initiated the articulation of the Slavophile doctrine that was to become central to the art and politics of the region.[83]

Brodziński's Slavophile ideas were clearly familiar to Chopin when, during his 1829 visit in Prague, he and his traveling companions met Václav Hanka, acclaimed Slavist, scholar of Czech antiquities, and curator of the Prague museum. Honored by a request for an album inscription, Chopin wrote to his family:

> We had to inscribe his book devoted to those among the visitors of the Prague Museum whom he deemed particularly worthy. Brodziński, Morawski, etc., are already there. Every one of us, therefore, fired up his brain: one through rhyme, other in prose. Szwejkowski wrote in a *perora*. What can a musician do? Fortunately, Maciejowski came up with the idea of writing four stanzas of a mazurka; I made music to them and inscribed myself together with my poet, as one could most originally. Hanka was glad, because it was a mazur for him, directed to his achievement in the field of Slavdom.[84]

The result was a little poetic tribute by Ignacy Maciejowski, two stanzas of which I translate here, accompanied by a musical tribute to the famous Slavophile: Chopin's mazurka set to Maciejowski's text and inscribed below on the same page.

> What flowers, what wreaths
> Can I in honor of Hanka weave,
> Who from oblivion's mould
> Snatched brotherly nation's songs.
>
> Hence a song of Polish meadow
> From our hand he will get,
> For it is known in all the world
> That Czech of old the brother is of Lech.[85]

It was not difficult for Chopin to apply his teacher's ideas to music, since Brodziński himself extended his aesthetic concerns to the union of music and poetry and to music in general. Already his 1818 essay included fundamental Romantic thoughts on music, echoing the aesthetics

---

[83] On the impact of Polish Slavophilism on the formation of Russian musical identity see Halina Goldberg, "Appropriating Poland: Glinka, Polish Dance, and Russian National Identity," in *Polish Encounters, Russian Identity*, ed. David Ransel and Bożena Shallcross (Bloomington: Indiana University Press, 2005), 74–88.

[84] Chopin, Dresden, to his family, Warsaw, 26 August, 1829, *Korespondencja*, 1:99.

[85] Chopin's inscription in Vaclav Hanka's album, Prague, 23 August 1829, Národní muzeum, Prague, IX. H. 25; photo in Muzeum Fryderyka Chopina w Towarzystwie im. Fryderyka Chopina, Warsaw, F. 812.

of Kant and Jean Paul. In this seminal article, Brodziński defines Romantic German poetry and music as "metaphysics of feeling."[86] Originally, he says, music, the "divine language," accompanied poetry, but later poets separated "the two sisters," allowing each to become more beautiful. The time has arrived for them to join their forces again so they can speak to the feeling and thoughts of the listener, as is being done in German songs and ballads, which are adorned and popularized through music: "Music— like poetry reaching for infinity, awakening hazy imaginings, and in Germany perfected in the same spirit as poetry—must have important influence on the current Romanticism."[87] These concepts would be most definitely known to Elsner even before Brodziński's essay was published, either directly from the eighteenth-century German philosophical discourse or through E. T. A. Hoffmann, with whom he enjoyed close acquaintance and collaboration during Hoffmann's Warsaw days (chapter 8).

As a close friend of Elsner, Brodziński not only translated, on Elsner's advice, fragments of Forkel's *Allgemeine Geschichte der Musik* but also provided poetic illustrations for Elsner's 1818 treatise *On Meter and Rhythm of the Polish Language*—the earliest study considering the prosody of the Polish language in the context of music. In these songs, Brodziński expressed his proto-Romantic ideal of simple idyllic poetry intended to join forces with folk-inspired music for the purpose of upholding nationality among the people. One of the six songs set to music by Elsner, "The Rustic Muse" (*Muza wiejska*), portrays a carefree girl from a peaceful village (see ex. 4.6). Its undemanding vocal style, typical of Elsner's songs, is suitable for the intended performances by untrained singers in an average Polish home. Despite its unpretentiousness, the song demonstrates Elsner's mastery of musico-poetic prosody. Fashioned as a spirited polonaise, it is much more vigorous than the poetic text would suggest. Yet the setting is very skillful, following the rules of prosody by aligning stressed syllables with metric accent and allowing grammatical accent to determine placement of more important words with longer and higher notes. Moreover, the very crafty phrase structure contains irregular groupings, elisions, and creative phrase-linkage (a topic Elsner also discussed in his "Treatise on Melody and Chant"). These can be observed in the very opening of the piece: the piano introduction and the interlude are linked with the first vocal section in ingenious ways. The last measure of the five-bar introduction concurrently initiates a two-bar group in the piano that overlaps into the opening of the vocal section, and the closing bar of the vocal section overlaps into the three-bar piano interlude. Within the texted section, the seemingly simple subdivision of the period into four two-bar

---

[86] Brodziński, "O klasyczności i romantyczności," 1:36.
[87] Brodziński, "O klasyczności i romantyczności," 1:41.

Example 4.6. Józef Elsner, "Muza wiejska" [The rustic muse], with brackets marking phrase groupings, mm. 1–15.

groups, each corresponding to a single line of the poem, has some features of interest: bar groups 3 and 4 are linked together by hastening the start of the fourth verse, which enters already in the middle of the preceding bar. The accelerated recitation and shift in the placement of grammatical accent in group 3, as well as the premature entry of group 4 and the resulting continuity of rhythmic motion, build a sense of momentum toward a cadence within the last four measures of the vocal section. This ingenious structure concealed under the naïve exterior of "Muza wiejska" shows Elsner to be a practitioner of the theories he taught to his students, under whose guidance Chopin would become aware of prosodic possibilities of music.

Chopin's songs were composed on the aesthetic models established by Brodziński and Elsner. Brodziński's proto-Romantic idyllic style found continuation in the poetry of Józef Bohdan Zaleski and Stefan Witwicki, Chopin's closest poet friends. In Poland and during his early years abroad, Chopin turned mostly to Witwicki's poetry, setting his songs even before they appeared in print in the volume *Idyllic Songs* (*Piosnki sielskie*, 1830). Seven songs can be dated with certainty to the Warsaw period: those written by Chopin into the *Stammbuch* (no longer extant) of Elsner's daughter, Emilia, who collected new compositions written by young conservatory composers under her father's tutelage. Six of these songs are settings of Witwicki's poems; one sets a text by Mickiewicz. The setting of Mickiewicz's poem, "Out of My Sight" (*Precz z moich oczu*), although striving for harmonically expressive language to match the text, is not very successful; in contrast, the unassuming songs to Witwicki's poems meet their proto-Romantic aesthetic goals. In keeping with the principles mapped out by his teachers, Chopin responded to Witwicki's pastoral texts with folklike music—their musical simplicity made them suitable for promoting nationality with the general populace. Although most are in strophic form, Chopin—following the course set by Elsner— took great pains to capture each poem's meaning and mood though the appropriate use of musical elements. "What She Likes" (*Gdzie lubi*) (see ex. 4.7), the only one of the early songs set in ternary form, has also other features pointing to Elsner's tutelage. Here Chopin goes even further in his attentiveness to the text.

> The stream likes the gorge,
> The doe likes the grove,
> The bird likes the thatch,
> The girl, with delight
> Likes blue eyes,
> Likes dark eyes,
> Likes joyful songs,
> Likes sad songs.
> She knows not what she likes;
> Everywhere she loses her heart.

The pastoral mood of the first section is prepared in the open fifths, drones, and 6/8 rhythms of the brief piano introduction. The serene description of nature's favorite places is contrasted with a witty mazurka, starting in measure 12, representing the fickle girl: the genre change provides for the shift from the realm of the natural to the realm of the human. Although the mazurka is clearly in 3/8, the notated meter remains the 6/8. The generic and metric change for the middle section stem from the text meaning as much as from the shift in poetic meter: for lines 5–8, Witwicki switches from three to four accents per line. Chopin accommodates this metric change, and also successfully deals with the enjambment found in lines 4–5. To do so, he condenses the recitation of line 3 to one and a half measures, in place of the two given to each previous verse, begins line 4 half a measure sooner, and repeats "the girl," so that "with delight" already serves as a pick-up to the mazurka section. The transitional character of the start of line 4 is further underscored by a detour to C-sharp Major, which is especially pronounced coming after the static A drone in the bass. For the last two lines of the text, the pastoral music returns—Chopin sets the text of the two concluding lines twice for balance, but through alterations avoids literal repetition. The piece concludes with the return of a mazurka with metric groups displaced by half-measures, as a postlude—this time, through the absence of dotted rhythms and the preference for arched melodies, hinting at the more amorous waltz, and thus underscoring the girl's fickleness.

Chopin's teachers' concern for Polishness extended beyond composing suitable parlor songs. In 1821, in alliance with Elsner and Kurpiński, Brodziński presented the Society for the Friends of Learning with a rationale for a volume of Polish religious songs.[88] He argued for the importance of religious songs in encouraging national feeling and thinking, because they would enhance the Polish language used by the people and propagate the proper national and Christian moral values. Such a volume

> would be used in all the provinces of the nation, and would nourish one taste and one spirit in the youth, who without that could descend into the same indifference and unconsciousness about national dignity, of which sad examples we observe in the many Slavic lands under the rule of the Germans.[89]

According to the proposal, Brodziński was to select the poetry from the finest ancient and modern Polish poets. Elsner and Kurpiński, both of whom already were heading societies devoted to national religious music, expressed their readiness to furnish preexisting folk melodies or compose new ones in the national-religious spirit. The plan was never realized, though individual religious songs in Polish were composed and quickly became part of the Polish national culture. It was during that period that Brodziński provided Elsner with the Polish text for a "Folk Mass" (*Msza ludowa*), intended for use by the simple people in parish churches. The text was set by Elsner as op. 15 and reused by him, with small changes, for several later Polish masses. With the support of some clergymen eager to increase the quality of music in the provincial churches, within a couple of decades, these "Folk Masses" became familiar even in distant villages of the country.

The devotion with which these two artists engaged in the propagation

[88] Brodziński, "Uwagi nad potrzebą wydania wyboru poezyj dla młodzieży: Zbioru pieśni duchownych i narodowych" [Remarks on the necessity of issuing a selection of poetry for the youth: A collection of religious and national songs], lecture delivered at the meeting of the Society for the Friends of Learning, 12 March 1821, in *Pisma Estetyczno-Krytyczne*, 1:222–229.

[89] Brodziński, "Uwagi nad potrzebą wydania wyboru poezyj dla młodzieży," 1:224.

Example 4.7. Fryderyk Chopin, "Gdzie lubi" [What she likes], with brackets marking phrase groupings.

of Polish religious songs was a manifestation of the evolving modern concept of nationhood based on the Polish language and traditions and on Catholic Christianity as fundamental determinants of Polishness. In this context, religious songs became vital in articulating musical Polishness, a concept that did not escape Chopin's attention. Although modern scholarship has concentrated on Chopin's use of dances to denote Polish identity, the religious *topos* played an important role in his music (for instance, op. 15 no. 3, op. 48 no. 1, op. 28 no. 20, and op. 49, to mention some) and was read as quintessentially Polish by his contemporaries.[90]

90 Chopin's use of the religious *topos* is discussed extensively by Kallberg, "Rhetoric of a Genre: Chopin's Nocturne in G Minor," in Kallberg, *Chopin at the Boundaries; Sex, History, and Musical Genre* (Cambridge: Harvard University Press, 1996), 3–29, and Goldberg, "'Remembering That Tale of Grief': The Prophetic Voice in Chopin's Music," in Goldberg, *The Age*

Example 4.7. *continued*

In view of the affinities of their national-aesthetic principles, it is not surprising that Elsner enthusiastically recommended Brodziński's lectures to his students. In the foreword to his treatise *On Meter and Rhythm of the Polish Language*, Elsner echoed Brodziński's views on the union of music and poetry from the article "On Classicism and Romanticism" published the same year: "The influence of music on poetry and poetry on music is so significant, that one of them viewed as an art cannot be accurately and thoroughly explained without the help of the other."[91] Although the overall tone of Brodziński's tentative endorsement of selected Romantic concepts pales in comparison with the zealous Romanticism of the 1820s, represented by Mickiewicz and Chopin's older friends Mochnacki and Witwicki, Chopin's proximity to Brodziński's tutelage and exposure to his ideas were important. Undeniably he made an impact on the development of Chopin's views concerning the relationship between language and music and the patriotic role of art, as well as the larger philosophical concepts framing the Romantic ideal of expression.

It has been suggested that Chopin's education was largely private and had little to do with the Conservatory.[92] Although it is true that the young genius's schooling entailed much individual instruction, one cannot neglect the significance of his access to a broad scope of subjects and philosophies, or the pertinence of his total immersion in music making. Elsner made the school an active center of musical life through public concerts at the Conservatory and in other halls, participation in religious and charity events, and performances of students' compositions. The daily press showered its praises on the high level of pupils in this institution. Maybe the loudest voice is Chopin's, who responded with his usual modesty to the harsh words that were quoted at the opening of this chapter: "[H]ad I not learned from Elsner, who knew how to speak to my reason, I would know even less than I know today."[93]

---

of Chopin, 54–92. See also Jan Węcowski, "Religious Folklore in Chopin's Music," *Polish Music Journal* 2 (1999): www.usc.edu/dept/polish_music/PMJ/issue/2.1.99/wecowski.html.

[91] Elsner, *O metryczności i rytmiczności języka polskiego*, introduction.

[92] Frączyk, *Warszawa młodości Chopina*, 201–202.

[93] Chopin, Warsaw, to Woyciechowski, Poturzyn, 10 April 1830, *Korespondencja*, 1:118.

5

SALONS

Background and Intellectual Trends

Chopin's involvement in the musical world of fashionable salons is a well-known aspect of his life, as is his lifelong reluctance to participate in public concert performances. In fact, the great
pianist's preference for the salon has been somewhat of an embarrass-
ment to scholars, who attempted to reconcile the "frivolous" environment of the salon with the profound music of the Polish genius. A case
in point is Hugo Riemann's dismissal of the relevance of salon style to
Chopin's oeuvre:

> When some ... number Chopin among salon composers, they are
> guilty of a dreadful terminological muddle; it is much more correct to
> put Chopin's music in strict opposition to salon music, which is charac-
> terized by the illusion of virtuosity, whereas Chopin's music often
> seems easy but in fact requires advanced technical skill.[1]

The nineteenth-century salon has been stigmatized as light-minded,
effeminate, a playground for high society, in contrast to the eighteenth-
century "chamber." Whereas the Classical structures and contrapuntal
underpinnings of chamber music have been viewed as representing a
conceptual art, the improvisatory nature of salon music caused it to be
perceived as superficial, sensuous, and simply inferior. Only in recent
years have scholars considered the nineteenth-century salon in a more
constructive manner. Some have addressed the complex question of what

---

[1] Hugo Riemann, *Geschichte der Musik seit Beethoven (1800–1900)* (Berlin: 1901), 318,
quoted in Andreas Ballstaedt, "Chopin as Salon Composer," in *Chopin Studies 2*, ed. John
Rink and Jim Samson (Cambridge: Cambridge University Press, 1994), 33.

salon music is, recognizing its entertainment function, and the preference for the piano and instrumental miniatures, while drawing attention to the inclusion of chamber works or Beethoven's piano sonatas as an integral part of the salon tradition. Others have dealt with the assessment of salon culture as effeminate, examining the language of gender ambiguity and the cultural roles of the otherworldly metaphors. Still others have elucidated the nationalist clash between the French and German traditions, pointing out that the German scholars included Chopin in "the great tradition" only reluctantly because of the French and Italian contexts for his music as well as his Polish origin.[2] These and other preconceptions relating to Chopin as a salon composer, created by generations of writers, biographers, and scholars going back to Robert Schumann and Franz Liszt, tainted the reception of his music, obscuring his contribution, even to salon music itself. As Andreas Ballstaedt notes in his essay on Chopin in the salon, "only when Chopin is freed from the stigma of the salon can one do justice to him in the salon."[3]

Although much has been said about Chopin's participation in Parisian salon life, the salons frequented by Chopin in Warsaw are at best given marginal mention. This void is partially a result of political circumstances: in the late nineteenth- and early twentieth-century Polish biographers, eager to "nationalize" Chopin, emphasized the grounding of his music in the Herderian *Volksgeist*, stemming from the inhabitants of the countryside rather than urban culture;[4] in post–Word War II Poland, salon culture in general was disparaged by the communist establishment as typifying capitalist self-indulgence. In addition, the Chopin literature abroad almost invariably marginalized Polish culture as a whole. Yet it was in Warsaw's salons that the young Fryderyk received his social grooming and it was there that he met many of his future Parisian hosts or made connections that opened the doors to the most respected house-

---

[2] Most notable are the extensive studies of the German salon tradition by Andreas Ballstaedt and Tobias Widmaier, *Salonmusik: Zur Geschichte und Funktion einer bürgerlichen Musikpraxis* (Stuttgart: Steiner Verlag Wiesbaden, 1989); Peter Gradenwitz, *Literatur und Musik im geselligem Kreise: Geschmacksbildung, Gesprächsstoff und musikalische Unterhaltung in der bürgerlichen Salongesellschaft* (Stuttgart: Steiner Verlag, 1991); and Petra Wilhelmy, *Der Berliner Salon im 19. Jahrhundert: 1780–1914* (Berlin: de Gruyter, 1989). Issues pertaining to Chopin and the salon context have been addressed by Ballstaedt, "Chopin as Salon Composer"; Jeffrey Kallberg, "Small Fairy Voices: Sex, History and Meaning in Chopin," in Rink and Samson, *Chopin Studies 2*, and *Chopin at the Boundaries; Sex, History, and Musical Genre* (Cambridge, Mass.: Harvard University Press, 1996); Halina Goldberg, "Chopin in Warsaw's Salons," *Polish Music Journal* 2 (summer 1999): www.usc.edu/dept/polish_music/PMJ/issues.html.

[3] Ballstaedt, "Chopin as Salon Composer," 34.

[4] Maja Trochimczyk, "Chopin and the 'Polish Race': On National Ideologies and the Chopin Reception," in *The Age of Chopin: Interdisciplinary Inquiries*, ed. Halina Goldberg (Bloomington: Indiana University Press, 2004), 278–313.

holds of European capitals. But more significantly, he was fortunate enough to mature amid the intellectual discussions of his elders, the aesthetic battles of his artistic peers, and musical experiences unattainable in public concert—stimuli for his mind and senses beyond and above the already excellent education he had received at the gymnasium and the Conservatory.

The Emergence of the Salon Tradition in Poland

The tradition of salon gatherings in Poland goes back to close association with French salon circles in the eighteenth century. In 1753, before he even dreamed of becoming king of Poland, the young Stanisław Poniatowski was sent to study in Paris and while there became a protégé of Marie Thérèse Rodet Geoffrin, who hosted a famous Parisian salon. Her celebrated salon dinners were frequented by Parisian luminaries, native and foreign alike: among the artists and men of letters, the Encyclopedists held a particular place of honor. Geoffrin adopted a motherly pose toward all her illustrious guests, but a particular closeness developed between her and the young Polish aristocrat, attested to by voluminous correspondence.[5] Their friendship continued beyond Poniatowski's stay in Paris, and in 1766, Madame Geoffrin—who rarely left Paris otherwise—made a trip to Warsaw to visit her "adopted son," now Stanisław August, the last king of Poland.

Under the influence of Geoffrin's salon, King Stanisław August instituted Thursday Dinners in his palace, social gatherings to which he invited distinguished scholars and artists. An invitation to a Thursday Dinner was a reward and an acknowledgement of mastery in scholarship, poetry, or the fine arts. The king was not just blindly copying the Parisian model of a salon, but instead—being a man of vast knowledge—he saw it as a means of encouraging the advancement of learning and arts in his country. He himself was a proud owner of a priceless library and an outstanding collection of pictures (engravings, drawings, architectural projects, etc.). He also had a fine orchestra at his court, and he greatly influenced the growth and improvement of music in Poland. Musical performances were customary at Thursday Dinners, and discussions frequently concentrated on music, opera in particular.[6]

Following the king's example, several of the capital's aristocrats gath-

[5] *Correspondence inédite du roi Stanislas-Auguste Poniatowski et de Madame Geoffrin,* ed. Charles de Mouÿ (Paris: E. Plon, 1875).

[6] Aleksander Kraushar, *Salony i zebrania literackie w Warszawie* [Salons and literary gatherings in Warsaw] (Warsaw: Towarzystwo Miłośników Historyi, 1916), 4–7; Łukasz

ered interesting guests together in salon meetings. The two most famous places of such gatherings were the palace of Polish-born Princess de Nassau and the "Palace under a Tin Roof" (*Pałac pod blachą*) belonging to the king's nephew, Prince Józef Poniatowski. In these homes, the guests would amuse themselves with the typical drawing-room pastimes, conversation, music, and readings, but occasionally they would undertake more ambitious projects. Thus, in the house of Princess de Nassau, the aristocratic amateurs prepared performances of operas (Paisiello's *Nina* and *La serva padrona*) and plays (the Polish premiere of Beaumarchais's *Marriage of Figaro*). A theater for similar amateur performances of foreign plays was built later (1800) in the Palace under a Tin Roof.[7] There were also other kinds of amusements: during the first decade of the nineteenth century, it was fashionable to perform *tableaux vivants*, a still pantomime involving people dressed in appropriate costumes and posing against an elaborate stage set as a life painting, often to a musical background.[8]

After the fall of sovereign Poland in 1795 and the disappearance of all official cultural institutions, the need to maintain Polish culture through gatherings in private salons of the aristocracy became more pronounced. The two most impressive of Warsaw's earliest intellectual salons, which also fostered the creation of the Society for the Friends of Learning, belonged to Stanisław Sołtyk and Stanisław Potocki. These two eminent men had been present on the Polish political and cultural scene since the time of King Stanisław August, and their activities were essential to the rebirth of learning in occupied Poland. Their salons were established in order to provide a specifically Polish venue for artistic and intellectual endeavors, in opposition to the homes of Princess de Nassau and Prince Józef Poniatowski, which catered to foreign customs (ironically, it was the

---

Gołębiowski, *Gry i zabawy różnych stanów* [Games and amusements of various classes] (Warsaw: Glücksberg, 1831), 254 and Klementyna Hoffman, *Obiad czwartkowy: Opis wyjęty z nieznanych dotąd pamiętników* [A Thursday Dinner: a description taken from heretofore unknown memoirs] (Warsaw: Gebethner i Wolff, 1917), 31.

[7] Kraushar, *Salony i zebrania literackie w Warszawie*, 10 and Antoni Magier, *Estetyka miasta stołecznego Warszawy* [The aesthetics of the capital city of Warsaw] (Manuscript of 1830), ed. Hanna Szwankowska (Wrocław: Wydawnictwo Ossolińskich, 1963), 152–153.

[8] During one of the earliest concerts sponsored by the Benevolent Society [Towarzystwo Dobroczynności], on 1 May 1814, a *tableau vivant* accompanied a performance of the Priestesses' chorus from Spontini's *La vestale*. *Allgemeine musikalische Zeitung*, September 1814, 655. This tradition must have still been well alive in 1820, when a benefit performance of historical and other pictures was organized. It involved dramatic and musical artists from both the National and the French theaters, as well as the painters Zygmunt Vogel and Antoni Brodowski. *Gazeta warszawska*, 18 March 1820, no. 23, 581. Incidentally, Mendelssohn's Italian and Scottish symphonies were associated with a similar tradition of *tableaux vivants* in Berlin. See Thomas S. Grey, "Tableaux Vivants: Landscape, History Painting, and the Visual Imagination in Mendelssohn's Orchestral Music," *19th-Century Music* 21 (1997): 38–76.

same Prince Poniatowski whose death in 1813 was instantly mythologized as the ultimate Polish heroic narrative). Distinctively Polish traditions were maintained in varying degrees by other aristocratic salons active during the time of the Duchy of Warsaw: these included the Badenis, the Gutakowskis, Maria Lanckorońska, Princess Würtemberg, and Anna Nakwaska.[9] Several of these continued their hospitality into the 1820s and even later, and some were attended by the young Chopin.

During the 1820s, the Potocki and Sołtyk salons were no longer the major forces of intellectual progress, but Chopin still might have met the elderly Sołtyk, who continued to participate in literary meetings. Most likely he also had the honor of meeting Potocki when as a child he performed in his distinguished home, and he certainly continued to attend soirées organized after Potocki's death by his wife, Aleksandra. A particularly eloquent testimony of Chopin's relationship with Warsaw's intellectual elders exists in the Czartoryski Museum in Kraków: a copy of *On Articulation and Style* (*O wymowie i stylu*), the celebrated 1815 treatise on rhetoric by Potocki, inscribed with Fryderyk Chopin's name in the adolescent composer's own hand (see fig. 5.1). Potocki's treatise, written at the request of the Society for the Friends of Learning, was based on the work of ancient as well as modern rhetoricians. Its aim, however, was to translate their ideas into Polish and to facilitate learning by "making the art of rhetoric national."[10] Predictably for the staunchly conservative Potocki, the treatise endorsed Classical aesthetic concepts, yet he allowed some merit to literary fiction and modern romances. While claiming that most of these do not survive the test of time, he acknowledged the good points of Rousseau's *Julie, or the New Heloise* (in spite of its "propensity toward passion") and Goethe's epistolary novel *The Sorrows of Young Werther*. He even reluctantly lent credence to Shakespeare.[11] Potocki's publication was especially influential in reclaiming the dignity of the Polish language, so the signed volume in Kraków connects Fryderyk with the most crucial intellectual endeavors of Warsaw's salons during the first decade of the nineteenth century.

Chopin in Middle-Class and Aristocratic Salons

The trend to host salon meetings, initially limited to the highest elite, quickly spread among the bourgeoisie, who under the new political and

[9] Kraushar, *Salony i zebrania literackie w Warszawie*, 17–18.

[10] Stanisław Potocki, *O wymowie i stylu* [On articulation and style], 4 vols. (Warsaw: Zawadzki i Węcki, 1815), 1:x.

[11] Potocki, *O wymowie i stylu*, 4:211–213.

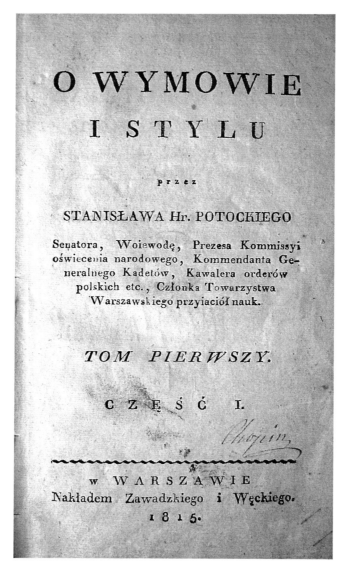

Figure 5.1. Stanisław Potocki, *O wymowie i stylu* [On articulation and style], 4 vols. (Warsaw: Zawadzki i Węcki, 1815), vol. 1, title page with Fryderyk Chopin's signature. Biblioteka XX Czartoryskich, Kraków, saf. 1294 I.

economic circumstances grew in size and strength. By the second decade of the nineteenth century, both social groups displayed equal proclivity for salon meetings. Typically, class divisions were very pronounced notwithstanding the impending social changes, and the aristocratic and bourgeois circles did not mingle; however, social class considerations were overlooked in salons with a particularly strong interest in culture, learning, and the arts. Chopin was invited to salons from both circles. His talent earned the admiration of the aristocracy, initially as a *Wunderkind* and later as a mature artist. His own affiliation by birth and profession was with the middle-class intelligentsia, and the style of salon gatherings at the Chopins was typical of the middle-class, although privileged by the attendance of academics who were Mikołaj Chopin's professional associates and by musicians who were attracted by Fryderyk's uncommon musical gifts.

The continuous contacts with foreign salons, as educated Poles who traveled abroad visited social gatherings elsewhere, caused the salons of the Polish capital to resemble the salons of other European cities, except for the much more intense political and national atmosphere.[12] There were games (especially whist), conversations, dancing, reading aloud, and discussions of new books. Music making most frequently involved fashionable songs with piano accompaniment. Most of the salons attended by Chopin during his childhood and adolescence had some cultural aspirations, their profile varying according to the hosts' intellectual or artistic interests, entertainment preferences, financial situation, and social status.

Middle-class Warsaw society was centered around family circles, which included relatives and friends. Each such circle would select a particular day of the week on which a score of families would gather for an evening together. The Chopins hosted regular salon meetings on Thursdays. Through Mikołaj Chopin's professional connections, they had close associations with academic circles; thus from his earliest childhood, Fryderyk mingled with gymnasium and university professors, many of whom also hosted their own salons—usually devoted to lively intellectual debates. Moreover, the Chopins resided in the Kazimierz Palace (see fig. 5.2), together with the families of other gymnasium and university professors (later, they moved across the street to the Krasiński Palace; see fig. 5.3).[13] One of Fryderyk's childhood friends describes this elite intellectual company:

---

[12] For example, in 1829, the young Andrzej Edward Koźmian—with whom Chopin was well acquainted—was a guest in the famous salon of Madame Apponyi, the wife of the Austrian ambassador in Paris. A few years later, Chopin himself frequented her salon, and he dedicated the Nocturnes op. 27 to her. Koźmian's description is full of admiration for the performances by the virtuoso pianist Friedrich Kalkbrenner and the acclaimed singer Henriette Sontag that took place in Madame Apponyi's salon, and he found that salons of Warsaw and Paris did not differ much. Andrzej E. Koźmian, Paris, to his parents, Warsaw, 5 November 1829, in *Listy 1829–1864* [Letters 1829–1864], 4 vols. (Lwów: Gubrynowicz i Schmidt, 1894), 1:24–25.

[13] The building is today known as the Czapski Palace (*Pałac Czapskich*). The Chopins' salon in the Czapski Palace is today open to the public as a museum.

Figure 5.2. Kazimierz Palace, home of the University of Warsaw and the Warsaw Gymnasium; the Chopins' apartment was in the right wing. Two-tone lithograph by Jan Feliks Piwarski (Berlin: Lassalle, 1824). Muzeum Fryderyka Chopina w Towarzystwie im. Fryderyka Chopina, Warsaw, M/575. Photo by Andrzej Ring & Bartosz Tropiło.

> We lived on the second floor in the wing on the right, next to the Gymnasium, which was downstairs in a building called "Cadets Quarters," where the public library is today. On the first floor of the same wing lived Samuel Bogumił Linde, the rector of the Gymnasium, and Father Wojciech Szwejkowski, the rector of the University of Warsaw. Downstairs were university professors [Juliusz] Kolberg, Kazimierz Brodziński, and many others.[14]

Thus the gatherings at the Chopins included the neighbors just mentioned, and often present were professors Hoffman (mineralogist), Jarocki (zoologist), Maciejowski (historian), Brodowski (art professor and a painter), and Count Skarbek (the pianist's godfather and a renowned political economist). Fryderyk's musical talent brought in the Conservatory professors Elsner, Jawurek, and Würfel, as well as his first piano teacher, Żywny, who was like a family member in the Chopin household. As elsewhere, the guests at the Chopin salon gatherings loved card

[14] Ferdynand Hoesick, "Z pamiętników Marylskiego" [From Marylski's memoirs], in Hoesick, *Pisma zbiorowe* [Collected works], vol. 1, *Słowacki i Chopin Chopin. Z zagadnień twórczości* [Słowacki and Chopin: on issues regarding oeuvre], 2 vols (Warsaw: Trzaska, Evert i Michalski), 1932, 1:90.

Figure 5.3. Salon at the Chopins' apartment in the Krasiński Palace. Pen drawing in India ink, with a few details lightly indicated in watercolor, by Antoni Kolberg, 1832. According to the inscription on the drawing, Kolberg sent an original of this picture to Chopin in Paris. Not extant; until 1942 in the collection of the Warsaw Music Society; photograph from reproduction in.Leopold Binental, *Chopin. W 120-tą rocznicę urodzin. Dokumenty i pamiątki* [Chopin: on hundred-and-twentieth anniversary of birth. Documents and memorabilia] (Warsaw: W. Łazarski, 1930). Muzeum Fryderyka Chopina w Towarzystwie im. Fryderyka Chopina, Warsaw, F. 3335. Photo by Franciszek Myszkowski.

games. Music, though, had a special place here. It was often the subject of discussions—in particular Cherubini, who was everybody's favorite. There were also many occasions for musical performances, which were of a much higher quality than in typical middle-class salons, giving Fryderyk the opportunity to learn from all of the musicians present.[15]

The traditional celebration of a name-day presented a special opportunity for musical performances. This Polish observance took on a particularly festive aspect on the patriarch's name-day, frequently with offerings or performances from his progeny: handmade crafts, Latin recitations, essays written, poetry recitations, poetry composed, and other products of talent and intellect. Typically, the celebration involved a family concert that included fashionable favorites and compositions by family members, created especially to salute the guest of honor.[16] Mikołaj Chopin's name-

[15] Ferdynand Hoesick, *Chopin: Życie i twórczość* [Chopin: life and works], 2 vols. (Warsaw: Hoesick, 1927), 1:65–67.

[16] *Gazeta warszawska*, 9 September 1820, no. 117: 1936.

day celebrations were always solemn and joyful occasions of this kind for the gathering of friends and acquaintances. During one such event, when Chopin was in the fifth or sixth grade in the gymnasium, among the many guests were the professors Elsner, Hoffman, and Count Skarbek. First, Żywny conducted a chamber performance by artists and amateurs, including Molsdorf (a cellist), and the violinists Kaczkowski and Ledoux. A performance by Fryderyk and his sisters followed.[17] Another guest commented: "Every year, on [his] father's holiday he gave a concert with the accompaniment of other instruments; I was always invited to such celebration and every year one could observe astounding advancement of the young artist [Chopin]."[18] Indeed, Fryderyk's performances in the salon of his parents became known in Warsaw, and soon he began to receive invitations from the aristocracy.

The salons of the highest aristocracy were held in grand palaces, which often housed magnificent galleries of paintings and impressive libraries. A typical upper-class salon would have luxurious furnishings. The piano was the required instrument, but the more affluent homes also kept other instruments. A full description of an evening in an unnamed salon was provided by the historian Antoni Magier in his stylized "letter of 1826," which made an insightful comparison between past and then-present life in Warsaw. First, Magier described the salon, saying with pride that the lavish furnishings of the room, which included a pantaleon, were all of local production. He also saw a couple of violins, a harp, and a cello in the study. The guests, a dozen or so, were first invited to dinner, accompanied by liberal quantities of good wine. The conversation at the table dealt with political and administrative issues, since several guests were members of the administration; among other topics, the director of the National Theater, Ludwik Osiński, complained about the theater's financial problems. After dinner, the company busied themselves with various occupations; Magier found the musical production of the host's daughter especially pleasing. She sat at the pantaleon and sang with a very pretty voice. To Magier's amazement, she had a Polish teacher (Faustyn Żyliński, a teacher at the Conservatory), unlike "in the olden times [when] to learn singing, one always had to take an Italian teacher."[19]

Chopin's participation in the world of aristocratic salons can be arranged into two stages. The first stage officially began with the charity

[17] Wielisław [Eugeniusz Skrodzki], "Kilka Wspomnień o Chopinie" [A few recollections of Chopin], *Bluszcz*, 1882, no. 33, 258.

[18] Andrzej E. Koźmian, *Wspomnienia* [Memoirs], 2 vols. (Poznań: Letgeber, 1867), I:210.

[19] Magier, *Estetyka miasta stołecznego Warszawy*, 56–57.

concert organized by Countess Zamoyska in February 1818. It stands to reason, however, that the aristocracy had become acquainted with Fryderyk's pianistic skill beforehand. Once the young virtuoso grew to be known in the fashionable aristocratic world of Warsaw, featuring a performance by him during a musical soirée became chic. Some of the many patrician names mentioned in connection with young Fryderyk's salon performances were Czartoryski, Sapieha, Czetwertyński, Lubecki, Radziwiłł, Zamoyski, Potocki, Mostowski, Skarbek, Zajączek, Wolicki, and Łempicki. There is also plenty of information concerning Chopin's performances in the Russian aristocratic spheres during his childhood. While Chopin mingled in the patriotic circles and during his last years in Poland was close to the November Uprising conspirators, it would be amiss to overlook associations between Poland's "greatest national composer" and the Russian residents of Warsaw. Even in the years directly preceding the Uprising, Chopin continued his social and musical contacts with Russians and their affiliates. The most apparent is his friendship, or maybe even a youthful infatuation, as a teenager, with the daughter of the private tutor to Grand Duke Constantine's son, Aleksandryna de Moriolles, to whom he dedicated his Rondo *à la mazur* op. 5. Sources also indicate that at the time Chopin associated with other courtiers and administrators: Colonel Teodor Friedrich Philippeus, Prince Aleksander Galitsin, Petr Diakov, and, most regrettably, Jerzy Okołów, perhaps the most hated agent of Russia in Warsaw.[20] During his earlier years, in particular, he was a regular guest at Belweder (see fig. 5.4), the Warsaw residence of Grand Duke Constantine, the younger brother of Czar Alexander I of Russia.

Chopin's relationship with the Russian imperial family had begun already in September 1818, when during a visit paid by the Czar's mother to the university and the gymnasium, the young composer presented her with "two Polish dances of his own making."[21] During his celebrated visit to Poland in 1825, Czar Alexander I himself heard the young Polish genius perform on the eolimelodicon. On this occasion the monarch, impressed, bestowed diamond rings on both Chopin and Brunner (the creator of this new instrument). However, Fryderyk was best acquainted with the czar's younger brother, Constantine.

Grand Duke Constantine lived in Warsaw as chief commander of the Polish forces. In 1820, he married a Polish noblewoman Joanna Grudzińska, after having given up his rights to the Russian throne in exchange

---

[20] For detailed discussion of Chopin's contacts with individual salons see Halina Goldberg, "Musical Life in Warsaw during Chopin's Youth, 1810–1830" (Ph.D. diss., City University of New York, 1997).

[21] *Gazeta Korespondenta*, 6 October 1818, no. 80.

Figure 5.4. Grand Duke Constantine's residence at Belweder. Aquatint and aquafort by Fryderyk Krzysztof Dietrich, c. 1827. Muzeum Fryderyka Chopina w Towarzystwie im. Fryderyka Chopina, Warsaw, M/1119. Photo by Janina Mierzecka.

for his brother's permission to divorce Duchess Anna. From an earlier mistress, the duke had an out-of-wedlock son, Paweł, whom he loved dearly and kept with him in the palace. He often invited young, talented boys to keep his young son company, and since Paweł took a special liking to Fryderyk, the young pianist was a frequent guest in Belweder. Sometimes Paweł, accompanied by his tutor, Count de Moriolles, would personally fetch Fryderyk from his home in order to take him for a walk or to Belweder.[22]

Constantine's morganatic marriage to Countess Grudzińska turned out to be an unhappy one, and Belweder was a wearisome and gloomy place: evenings were long and empty, the duchess was always sick, and

[22] Józef Krasiński, *Pamiętniki* [Memoirs] (Poznań: Kraszewski, 1877), 120; Napoleon Sierawski, *Pamiętnik Napoleona Sierawskiego oficera konnego pułku gwardyi za czasów W. Ks. Konstantego* [A memoir of Napoleon Sierawski, officer of the cavalry regiment of the guard during the times of Great Prince Constantine], foreword by Stanisław Smołka (Lwów: Gubrynowicz i Schmidt, 1907), 7; and a letter from Antoni Eustachy Marylski to Ferdynand Hoesick written in 1900, quoting from his father's memoir (a collection of notes). Biblioteka Narodowa, Warsaw, II 7125 k 51–63.

the duke increasingly escaped into solitude. Even evenings spent together passed often in silence, which seemed better than uncomfortable conversation. This monotony was only sometimes interrupted by visits, and then Belweder took on some life.[23] Chopin's visits were welcomed not just by Paweł but also by the duke for his own musical pleasure: purportedly Chopin's playing was a sure method to sooth Constantine's violent temper.[24] It was during these early years that Fryderyk composed a march and dedicated it to Duke Constantine, possibly the unidentified march published without the author's name between 1818 and the Variations op. 2.[25] The reclusive duke's interest in Chopin's music must have continued beyond Fryderyk's childhood, since Mikołaj Chopin uses him as a reference in an 1829 letter: "His Imperial Highness Grand Duke Chief Commander most graciously often deigned to allow [Fryderyk] to demonstrate his developing talent in his presence."[26] The nature of Polish-Russian social contacts changed in the period directly preceding the November Uprising, and Chopin's associations with the young revolutionaries had an impact on his relationships with Russian officials. Yet we learn from Fryderyk himself that when he was leaving Warsaw, in the eve of the November Uprising, the grand duke still supported his art by providing him with a letter of recommendation to the Russian ambassador in Vienna.[27]

Soon, Chopin's parents and teachers became concerned with the constant intrusions into the boy's education and emotional welfare and for a period of time forbade his salon performances. Not until 1826 or 1827 did his participation in Warsaw's salon life resume, when as a result of special pleas by Miss Teresa Kicka, the hostess of prominent social gatherings, the young virtuoso was introduced into her salon.[28] The performance in Kicka's house must have been one of the first in a new phase of Chopin's participation in the salon milieu.

The second stage of his participation in Warsaw's social life spanned

[23] Count de Moriolles, *Pamiętniki* [Memoirs], trans. Z. Przyborowska (Warsaw: Biblioteka Dzieł Wyborowych, 1902),102–105; and Natalia Kicka, *Pamiętniki* [Memoirs], ed. T. Szafrański and J. Dutkiewicz (Warsaw: Pax, 1972), 185.

[24] Hoesick, *Chopin*, 1:61

[25] Oskar Kolberg, "Chopin," in *Encyklopedia Powszechna* [Universal Encyclopedia] (Warsaw: Orgelbrand, 1861), 5:458.

[26] Mikołaj Chopin, Warsaw, to Stanisław Grabowski, Warsaw, 13 April 1829, in *Korespondencja Fryderyka Chopina* [Fryderyk Chopin's correspondence], ed. Bronisław Edward Sydow, 2 vols. (Warsaw: Państwowy Instytut Wydawniczy, 1955), 1:88.

[27] Fryderyk Chopin, Vienna, to his family, Warsaw, 1 December 1830, *Korespondencja*, 1:157.

[28] Antoni Edward Odyniec, *Wspomnienia z przeszłości opowiadane Deotyemie* [Recollections from the past recounted for Deotyma] (Warsaw: Gebethner i Wolff, 1884), 325.

the years 1827–1830. He was no longer regarded as a *Wunderkind* but as a budding professional whose art embodied the newest aesthetic trends. He was welcomed not only for his musical gifts but also for his charm, wit, and intellect. Having been exposed to the salon atmosphere since his earliest years, he felt at ease in the company of aristocrats, political leaders, and the intellectual and artistic avant-garde of Warsaw: "He was the embodiment of grace, subtlety, [and] refinement. When he wanted to be liked by someone, nobody could resist his charm. In normal situations cheerful, witty, giddy, only at the piano did he become serious."[29] No wonder his elegant presence and astounding performances were highly sought after. At times Chopin complained that he was so busy socially that he could not find time for composition. Some evenings he visited more than one salon—everywhere they expected him to play and improvise. Exhausted by these demands, he complained: "You know how pleasant it is when you are sleepy and they ask you to improvise. Try to satisfy everybody!—Seldom do I happen upon an idea similar to those that so easily got into my fingers some mornings at your piano."[30]

Complaints aside, it is apparent that Chopin thrived among people, in the salon environment, and that he did not enjoy solitude: "He disliked being without company—something that seldom occurred. In the morning he liked to spend an hour by himself at the piano; but even when he practiced—or how should I describe it?—when he stayed at home to play in the evenings, he needed to have at least one of his friends close at hand."[31] In his letters we find information about numerous salon concerts he attended. Apparently, the late 1820s was a period of extreme animation in the musical world of Warsaw. It was particularly during Lent, when more profane entertainment was considered improper, that Warsaw's salons would present private concerts.[32] Chopin marveled at this phenomenon in his letters: "I will have you know that our world has become terribly involved in music making, not even Holy Week was spared."[33] The main reasons for this abundance of musical events were certainly the presence of a large and active circle of musicians and music lovers and the prosperity and quiet Warsaw enjoyed between political disasters. But

[29] Reported by Mrs. Józefa Kościeliska, the younger sister of Chopin's beloved Maria Wodzińska, in Hoesick, *Słowacki i Chopin*, 2:295.

[30] Chopin, Warsaw, to Tytus Woyciechowski, Poturzyn, 27 December 1828, *Korespondencja*, 1:87.

[31] Ferdinand Hiller, quoted in Jean-Jacques Eigeldinger, *Chopin: Pianist and Teacher as Seen by his Pupils*, trans. N. Shohet, K. Osostowicz, and R. Howat (Cambridge: Cambridge University Press, 1986), 270.

[32] Antoni Wieniarski, *Warszawa i warszawianie. Szkice towarzyskie i obyczajowe* [Warsaw and its residents: essays on the society and customs], 2 vols. (Warsaw: Bernstejn, 1857), 2: 35.

[33] Chopin, Warsaw, to Woyciechowski, Poturzyn, 30 April 1830, *Korespondencja*, 1:117.

most significantly it is the political circumstances that created the particular need for the salon to become the main outlet for Polish culture.

Intellectual Trends in Salons Attended by Chopin

The Vienna Congress provided a new context for the intellectual life in Warsaw's salons: the administrative autonomy under Russian rule permitted a renaissance of Polish culture that fostered historical and national awareness. While new public institutions intended to support research and writing were being established, every opportunity to create a forum for an exchange—intellectual or artistic—was seized on: a private meeting, a café, or a salon gathering.

The unequivocal leaders of the aristocratic intelligentsia were the intermarried princely families of the Czartoryskis and the Zamoyskis. In their salons, the social boundaries between the aristocracy and the intelligentsia were frequently traversed:

> Both homes . . . were models of fine manners, national aspirations and strict preservation of social dignity. In the attempt to bring closer people of learning and people of the world, these hospitable abodes received all people distinguished in literature and fine arts and no less those endowed with higher talents, even though both groups lacked the refinement that is usually dictated by worldly elegance.[34]

Izabela Czartoryska's Proto-Romanticism

The Czartoryski family was long famous for art patronage, but Izabela Czartoryska, née Fleming, was a woman of extraordinary intellect and artistic taste. As the matriarch of the Czartoryski-Zamoyski clan, it was she who set the tone of her children's intellectual and artistic interests. Born in 1746, she was two generations older than Warsaw's young Romantics. Yet already in the eighteenth century, she wholeheartedly embraced the new aesthetics and promoted it with all the force of her keen intellect and the vast financial resources at her disposal.

After 1784, when the Czartoryskis acquired a country estate in Puławy, Izabela's forward-looking tastes became apparent. She set out to implement the new aesthetic principles, at first by renovating the garden at Puławy in the English style. In the treatise on gardening she published

[34] Fryderyk Skarbek, *Pamiętniki* [Memoirs] (Poznań: Żupański, 1878), 125.

in 1805, she directly opposed the French pseudoclassicism by saying that "for the last hundred or more years, everybody planted at a great expense ugly gardens."[35] Her intentions of breaking away from this older style were equally clearly articulated:

> Unnatural things cannot please—only things in which nature seems at its most perfect are pleasing; to me forced shapes in trees seem to be disgusting: shaped into columns or knobs, or opened into fans they are no adornment for any site. Trimmed spruce trees, tormented hornbeams, cut linden trees always offend, never enhance.[36]

She emphasized that in creating such natural-looking gardens, the work of the gardener should be invisible—the arrangement should not betray the gardener's plan underlying the apparently naturally flowing space. This approach to composition epitomized the essential formal principles of Romantic aesthetics: the seemingly spontaneous, improvisatory surface overlaying a meticulously conceived but concealed design. Chopin structured his pieces in this manner, as he laboriously crafted his effortless improvisations into carefully designed finished artifacts.

The larger aesthetic objectives were equally clear to Princess Izabela when she freely admitted that she did not have the knowledge of a gardener; that her goal was to develop new taste rather than to give specific gardening advice.[37] Obviously, the source of this aesthetics was in the Enlightenment's advocacy of harmony between man and nature; however, Izabela's project went further. Not only was she endorsing Kantian concepts concerning the beautiful and the interaction between art and nature decades before the debate on Romanticism in Poland became public but also she was referring to the new aesthetics as "romantic": "we must give priority to trees—their stature, the abundance of branches, [and] solemnity—as far as that glorious beauty (meaning the romantic beauty); beauty cherished by the painter or the poet, which one should aspire to imitate as closely as possible."[38] This connection between nature and art was repeatedly made explicit. Thus her description of each tree included references to artifacts possessing the same essence as that tree. She employed highly poetic language, often quoting famous poets' thoughts on specific trees or plants. In this vein, for Czartoryska, the ash tree embodied Ossianic imagery, and her narrative concerning the ash tree referenced Ossian, Scotland, and old rites

[35] I[zabela] C[zartoryska], *Myśli różne o sposobie zakładania ogrodów* [Various thoughts on the method of setting up gardens] (Wrocław: Wilhelm Bogumil Korn, 1805), iv.

[36] I. C., *Myśli różne o sposobie zakładania ogrodów*, 3.

[37] I. C., *Myśli różne o sposobie zakładania ogrodów*, v–vi.

[38] I. C., *Myśli różne o sposobie zakładania ogrodów*, 1.

throughout.[39] Oak trees added gravity to ruins: "An oak in [its] wild and natural realm, as in the one fashioned by art, is always splendid. Stretching its moss-overgrown limbs onto walls lined with vines, it adds weightiness to Gothic or other architecture, a devastated ancient tower, [or] age-old ruins."[40] Dried-out trees (see fig. 5.5), likewise, helped to accentuate the sense of timelessness:

> Dry or even split trees can sometimes be of use. On a distant hill, in places which are supposed to be left somewhat wild or next to ancient ruins, they do not disturb the eye among freshly and lavishly blooming trees. At times like this they appear to be contemporaries of these ancient walls; it seems even that the same hand set them and the buildings.[41]

These and other descriptions time and again conveyed quintessentially Romantic notions. For Czartoryska, the seemingly untamed nature of the English garden embodied formal spontaneity while concealing a precise artistic plan. Nature contained and conveyed the essence of emotional states, and it was a vessel enfolding memories of the past.

The cult of memory and the veneration of a constructed past became the basis for shaping historical awareness, essential for the articulation of national identity. These were epitomized by the two edifices built for Izabela's park. These structures—the Temple of the Sibyl (*Świątynia Sybilli*) and the Gothic House (*Dom Gotycki*)—made Puławy famous. The Temple of the Sibyl was older; it dated to 1800. Here, in gloomy half-shade, the visitor was taken through the thousand years of Polish history; one could see shields with coats of arms belonging to the most distinguished families, spoils taken in distant wars, and the arms and armor of Polish knights and kings. It was in essence the first Polish historical museum. The Gothic House (see fig. 5.6) opened in 1809, and by 1828 it contained over fifteen hundred items from around the world. They ranged from manuscripts (including some musical ones) and paintings (works by Raphael, Rembrandt, and da Vinci among them) to objects enshrining memory and history—a twig from the site of Troy, or a blade of grass from the site of Agricola's encampment in England. Perhaps most impressive was the collection of hundreds of letters written by celebrities (Ariosto, Beethoven, Mozart, Pope, Hume, Hummel, Cherubini, Blangini, Weber, Metastasio, Gluck, Jefferson, Franklin, and Washington, to mention some). Although the objects collected in the Gothic House came from all over the world, the building itself was a lapidarium, assembled of frag-

[39] I. C., *Myśli różne o sposobie zakładania ogrodów*, 7–8.
[40] I. C., *Myśli różne o sposobie zakładania ogrodów*, 5.
[41] I. C., *Myśli różne o sposobie zakładania ogrodów*, 8–9.

Figure 5.5. "Suche drzewo" [A dried-out tree]. In I[zabela] C[zartoryska], *Myśli różne o sposobie zakładania ogrodów* [Various thoughts on the method of setting up gardens] (Wrocław: Wilhelm Bogumil Korn, 1805), before p. 8. Biblioteka XX Czartoryskich, Kraków, 104166 III.

ments that came mostly from historical sites and structures around Poland—stones, bricks, gates, coats of arms, tombstones, pillars, and fragments of funereal sculptures. In her account of the mementoes, Czartoryska explained:

The Temple of the Sybil was designated exclusively for national memorabilia. The Gothic House was supposed to contain foreign antiquities; thus it gathered everything contributed through frequent trips, parcels, and gifts. It already held souvenirs of France, Italy, Germany, England, mementoes of the ancient age, the knightly age, and later eras; added were mementoes of Egypt, Asia, [and] America. For some time, though, the Gothic House appeared incomplete, lacking something. Indeed, it lacked the most tender and meaningful mementoes—the Polish ones. . . . For that reason our antiquities are not just in the Temple of the Sybil—a large number of them are placed inside and on the external walls [of the Gothic House].[42]

The motto above the entrance of the Temple of the Sybil read "From the Past to the Future" (*Przeszłość-Przyszłości*). Indeed, this connection between past and future was central to Czartoryska's design: the collection of memorabilia was the basis for creating a history of Poland, and the historical awareness that was thus achieved served as a foundation on which a future was to be built: "May God grant it! that to these mementoes of our fame, valor and patriotism, and, unfortunately all national sorrows, God grant that to these mementoes, in the future ages, our grandchildren may add memorials of glory and happiness![43]

A three-volume commonplace-book of poetic and literary excerpts written in her own hand reflects some of these and other interests of Princess Izabela.[44] She copied excerpts from manuscripts and rare prints held in the Gothic House and from books in Puławy's library (holding some sixty thousand tomes) into volumes 1 and 3. In volume 1, she started with French translations of Arab poetry and Provençal songs. She then continued on to chivalric epics, including fragments of "Song of the Cid" and "Song of Roland," and other items, among which were excerpts from the letters of Eloise and Abelard. Volume 3 was dedicated to medieval history from Charlemagne to the fifteenth century.

The nature of volume 2, written between the 1780s and 1804, was different, confirming a growing interest in the new trends. Although she still used French, much of that volume was written in Polish, in accord with the patriotic and national identity she now propagated. The entries were also more personal and spontaneous, including recollections of her life as well as her own observations on history, various cultures, and poetry. Her responses to reading Goethe's *Werther,* Ossian, and Shakespeare are particularly indicative of her aesthetic concerns. In an essay headed "A Praise of Shakespeare" (*Pochwała Shakespeara*) she acknowledged that

---

[42] Elżbieta [Izabela] Czartoryska, foreword to *Poczet pamiątek zachowanych w Domu Gotyckim w Puławach* [Account of mementoes preserved in the Gothic House in Puławy] (Warsaw: Drukarnia Banku Polskiego, 1828).

[43] Czartoryska, foreword to *Poczet pamiątek zachowanych w Domu Gotyckim w Puławach.*

[44] Biblioteka Czartoryskich, Ms. 6069 (vol. 1); Ms. 6070 (vol. 2); Ms. 6070a (vol. 3).

Figure 5.6. Dom Gotycki. In [Izabela Czartoryska], *Poczet pamiątek zachowanych w Domu Gotyckim w Puławach* [Account of mementoes preserved in the Gothic House in Puławy] (Warsaw: Drukarnia Banku Polskiego, 1828), *verso* before the title page. Biblioteka XX Czartoryskich, Kraków, 105577 II.

his works possessed beauty independent of time and place, unlike other glitzy works that soon become old:

> Shakespeare had unique, rare, and natural genius; full of fervor and abundance. Never knowing the boundaries, in the heat of his imagination, he often offended taste and long-accepted rules. His works are miracles, which are sometimes spoiled by indecent imagery—belonging more to the times in which he wrote than to him—which was in the taste of the audiences that he had to indulge. These are grave errors, which are perhaps characteristic of unenlightened ignorance. Yet, the same works contain ideas that are completely new, powerful, fitting, and showing the highest knowledge of the human heart, in its most detailed and most secret shades. His imagination—spirited, fresh and ardent—renews itself constantly in thousands of images that only he knew how to sketch.[45]

Izabela surrounded her five children, Adam Jerzy, Maria, Zofia, Konstanty, and Teressa Anna, with the best tutors, mentors, role models, and young people—rich or poor, but always exceptionally inspiring. Thus Puławy developed into a whole colony: an intellectual and artistic nest. It also became a place of pilgrimage for Poles, especially the fiery, young, emotional Romantics. Although Chopin never visited Puławy, he was affected, like his Romantic peers, by the intensely patriotic aura emanating from Izabela's estate, and he refers to Puławy, the Temple of the Sybil specifically, in a letter.[46] He had lifelong direct contact with the Czartoryskis, including his later association with the Hôtel Lambert, the Parisian home of Prince Adam Jerzy, the most prominent of Izabela's children, who was exiled after the November Uprising by the Russian authorities. Chopin was invited to Czartoryskis' Warsaw salon numerous times and dedicated a number of compositions to the members of the family.

In the capital, social gatherings organized by Izabela, her husband, Prince Adam Kazimierz Czartoryski, and their children took place in the family's residence known as the Azure Palace (*Błękitny Pałac*). By the time Chopin began frequenting salons, the Azure Palace belonged to Izabela's daughter, Zofia, who was married to Count Stanisław Kostka Zamoyski. Under the Zamoyskis, the Azure Palace housed an outstanding library and several cultural establishments. Their salon, though catering to the highest social strata, was open to guests of great merit, including literati and musicians. Particularly celebrated were the Literary Fridays during the winter of 1827, which were held in honor of Prince

---

[45] Biblioteka Czartoryskich, Ms. 6070, 109–110.
[46] Chopin, Szafarnia, to Jan Matuszyński, Warsaw, [beginning of August 1825], *Korespondencja*, 1:51.

Adam Jerzy Czartoryski, imprisoned for his strong patriotic stand.[47] Talented young artists were invited to live in the Azure Palace: the writer Józef Korzeniowski, the Italian painter Luigi Rubio, the poet Antoni Edward Odyniec, and the writer Klementyna Tańska, who hosted her own literary salon.

Klementyna Tańska and the Restoration of the Polish Language

The writings of Klementyna Tańska were a direct source of inspiration for the Chopin children. In fact, the enthusiasm with which Chopin, in a letter to his family, recounts lodging in Ojców in a room once used by Tańska implies his sisters' admiration for the acclaimed writer: "He gave us a room under the rock, in a house built expressly for tourists. Izabela! . . . there where Miss Tańska has lodged!"[48] Tańska was one of the first Polish women for whom writing was not a leisurely pursuit but the primary source of income.[49] Inspired by Brodziński's call for the restoration of the Polish language, she began her professional writing career in 1817. She wrote for adults and for children, books and articles, but the purity of the Polish language remained of utmost importance to her. Children knew her best for her publication of *Diversions for Children* (*Rozrywki dla dzieci*), a magazine well known in the Chopin household. Little Emilia Chopin, a youngster with uncommon literary talents, especially loved the magazine, which was intended to propagate the Polish language among children and to encourage them to write in that tongue.

Fryderyk and his sisters were well familiar with Tańska's celebrated description of Ojców near Kraków, which helped to construct Ojców as a destination of patriotic pilgrimages. Indeed, Chopin's own account of his visit to Ojców abides by Tańska's model. For the Romantics, the alluring valley of the Prądnik stream around Ojców, with its medieval castles and ruins, picturesque rocks and mysterious caves, became the locale of legends and historical tales; the dwelling place of noble knights, distressed

---

[47] Odyniec, *Wspomnienia z przeszłości opowiadane Deotyemie*, 322.

[48] Chopin, Vienna, to his family, Warsaw, 1 August 1829, *Korespondencja*, 1:89.

[49] No other sources of income were available to her until at the age of thirty (1829) she married Karol Hoffman, also a writer. The impoverished Tański family was brought to Warsaw by Prince Adam Czartoryski, who hired Klementyna's father; young Klementyna joined her family in Warsaw in 1805. Czesław Pieniążek, *O autorkach polskich a w szczególności o Sewerynie Duchińskiej* [On Polish female writers, especially Seweryna Duchińska] (Poznań: Merzbach, 1872), 12. Prince Adam continued helping the family, and in 1822 the sisters and their sick, widowed mother moved to a wing of the Azure Palace. Klementyna Hoffman, *Pamiętniki* [Memoirs], 3 vols. (Berlin: Behr, 1849), 1:97–98.

maidens, and highway robbers; inhabited by witches, devils, and good spirits (fig. 5.7). The strongholds summoned up key historical moments. The caves hid and protected the inhabitants in moments of greatest distress. The legend had it that when the local people hid from the attacking Tatars in the Dark Cave (*Jaskinia Ciemna*), the very hand of the Creator sealed the entrance; hence the hand-shaped rock at the opening of the cave. The Łokietek Cave (*Jaskinia Łokietka*) was the legendary shelter of King Władysław Łokietek, who while leading the battle for the unification of Poland in the thirteenth century found support and haven among the people of the Prądnik Valley.

The emergence of destinations like Ojców was part and parcel of the making of national memory. Ojców became a locus, a tangible physical site that brought together threads of historical narratives and folk tales— a convergence of the historical and the supernatural. The divine intervention of the Dark Cave legend in which God was a willing participant and Poles were his chosen people was paradigmatic of Polish political messianism. As a type of patriotism that fashioned itself in religious models, political messianism required the creation of places of worship and pilgrimage destinations. For Chopin, raised in this intensely patriotic atmosphere and surrounded by the early proponents of political messianism, the visit to Ojców had certainly the aura of a pilgrimage, even more so since it was the locale of Elsner's opera *King Łokietek*, beloved of Poles and forbidden by the Russian authorities. That aura and the natural beauty of Prądnik Valley captured his Romantic imagination, fired in his childhood by Tańska's vibrant description.

Starting in the winter of 1823, the three Tański sisters hosted regular salon meetings at their homes. Klementyna invited guests every Tuesday, her older sister Aleksandra Tarczewska had Sunday and Wednesday evening gatherings, and their younger sister Maria Hermann was a hostess to Thursday meetings. Among the young writers, poets, and philosophers was also the elderly Sołtyk, who participated in the weekly literary sessions at Klementyna's salon in a wing of the Azure Palace.[50] As could be expected, the meetings had an intensely patriotic profile, and the Polish language was given particular attention. In fact, Tańska had the custom of penalizing her salon guests for using a French word instead of a Polish equivalent by asking them to place money in a collection box she kept expressly for that purpose.[51]

Of the three sisters, Aleksandra had the greatest love for music. It was she who described their first meeting with the young pianist named

[50] Hoffman, *Pamiętniki*, 1:106–107.

[51] Kazimierz Wójcicki, *Warszawa: Jej życie umysłowe i ruch literacki 1800–1830* [Warsaw: its literary and intellectual life 1800–1830] (Warsaw: Gebethner i Wolff, 1880), 144.

Swallet de David d'après le dessin de J.N. Głowacki.　　　　　　　*Lith. de Engelmann.*

Świątiska Zamku Ojcowa　　　　*Ruines du Château d'Ojcow.*

Figure 5.7. The castle in Ojców. Lithograph by Engelman after a drawing by J.N. Głowacki, *24 widoki miasta Krakowa i jego okolic zdjętych podług natury* [Twenty-four vistas of the city of Kraków and its surroundings taken from nature] (Kraków: Daniel Edward Friedlein, 1836). Biblioteka Uniwersytecka, Warsaw, [4.7.1.1], tabl. 20.

Chopin during an evening in the house of Olimpia and Tomasz Grabowski (the director of the Commission for the Religions): "During the course of the evening young Chopin, a child of eight years, played the clavichord. He promises, connoisseurs maintain, to replace Mozart, so soon is he starting to compose."[52] This meeting must have initiated a rather close association, for in volume 7 of her journal, Klementyna Tańska wrote about the Chopins with affection, and when Emilia died, she published a lengthy eulogy. Exiled after her brave involvement with the November Uprising, she maintained contacts with Chopin in Paris, where she was a part of the Polish artistic and political circle gathering in Prince Czartoryski's Hôtel Lambert.

The Guardians of the Classical Tradition

The Zamoyskis and the Czartoryskis belonged to a large circle of aristocrats who considered matters of literary and theater criticism of utmost

[52] Aleksandra Tarczewska (Tańska), *Historia mojego życia* [The history of my life], ed. I. Kaniowska-Lewańska (Wrocław: Ossolineum, 1967), 50.

importance. In fact, these highborn literati were organized into a group of critics who in the years 1815–1819 wrote theater reviews signed X— hence were known as the Society of Exes. The principal members were the founder of the society, Tadeusz Mostowski, Prince Adam Czartoryski, General Krasiński, Julian Ursyn Niemcewicz, the Plater brothers, Maksymilian Fredro, and Kajetan Koźmian, as well as women versed in literary matters—Róża Mostowska and two of Izabela Czartoryska's daughters, Princess Maria Würtemberg (the author of the acclaimed romance *Malwina*) and Zofia Zamoyska.[53] During the Society of Exes meetings, members read their literary works and took turns preparing theater reviews. The program of the Society was to shape the tastes of the audiences in the spirit of "post-Stanislavian Classicism" (*klasycyzm poststanisławowski;* referring to the era following the reign of King Stanisław August, as opposed to "Stanislavian Classicism," which coincided with the French Enlightenment and Stanisław August's reign). The participants in these meetings upheld the traditions of the Enlightenment, including a strong liberal and anticlerical stand and an emphasis on moral and social order. They also continued to follow French Classical models of the seventeenth and eighteenth century with their highly formalized poetic tradition. However, the supporters of this distinctly Polish late variety of Classicism shifted the subject matter to Polish history, especially the veneration of the heroic past, and aimed at establishing national tragedy as the leading theatrical genre. Some members of the Society of Exes wrote in the newer proto-Romantic and sentimental styles (Niemcewicz and Princess Würtemberg) and were open to the new German and English Romantic ideas; others staunchly defended Classical values. Thus the gatherings of the Society's members provided a forum for lively debates on current literary issues. The resulting regularly published theatrical reviews were Poland's first consistent attempt at expert theatrical criticism.

Chopin knew well the members of this literary circle and performed in many of these homes. In the future years, the daughters of Mostowski and Plater were to become his pupils. As a matter of fact, Chopin's dedications of Mazurkas op. 33 to Róża Mostowska and Mazurkas op. 6 to Paulina Plater confirm his continuing relationship with the Mostowskis and acknowledge the help he received in Paris from the Platers. Through Koźmian's sons—Jan, Andrzej, and Stanisław, with whom the young virtuoso studied at the gymnasium—he was often invited to the Koźmians' salon, where "he amazed everybody with his extraordinary gift and through his politeness and good heart won approbation."[54] He also asso-

[53] For more detailed discussion of the individual members of the Society of Exes see Goldberg, "Musical Life in Warsaw during Chopin's Youth, 1810–1830."

[54] Koźmian, *Wspomnienia*, 1:210.

ciated with the circle gathering at the home of General Voivod Count Wincenty Krasiński.

The homes of Koźmian and Krasiński readily extended their hospitality to the younger generation. Although the patriarchs of these salons were loyal Classicists, their sons had keen interest in the new ideas. Therefore, in these homes, the works of Mickiewicz and other young Romantics were read, and the older writers, poets, and scholars, who sturdily guarded the traditional values, were confronted by the young Romantics in an atmosphere of aesthetic debate.

During the years 1820–1827, the meetings at Krasiński's salon were considered among the most influential of Warsaw's literary gatherings. They were also considered the most pleasant and cheerful salon meetings in Warsaw. There one would find the older generation of writers and poets, in the previous decade associated with the Society of Exes: Niemcewicz, Osiński, Koźmian, and Fredro. The scholars and university professors Linde, Lelewel, Bentkowski, Brodziński, Ciampi, and Szubert were equally welcomed. As for the young literati—especially Korzeniowski, Odyniec, and Grzymała, who was destined to become Chopin's closest Parisian friend—not only were they invited, but the general even provided patronage for some aspiring artists.

> From the time when Osiński began his literature class in the University building and every Saturday gave lectures between 3 and 4, straight after the lecture, the society—including Osiński —gathered in the house of General Krasiński for dinner. How much learning, amusement and cheer accompanied these gatherings, for the host—an enthusiast of learning and literature—was gracious, generous, cheerful and witty; he encouraged and permitted good humor.[55]

Since during the years 1826–1828 Chopin attended Osiński's lectures, many of his close acquaintances were regular guests at Krasiński's soirées, and since from 1827 the Chopins lived in the apartment in the Krasiński Palace, it is likely he also visited the general's salon. There, he would have certainly met the general's son, Zygmunt, whom the literature professor Kazimierz Brodziński considered his best student.[56]

Count Zygmunt Krasiński, Chopin's peer, already as a child had amazed Warsaw with his improvised poetry; in fact Chopin's 1818 childhood public debut was also little Zygmunt's first open performance. He was later to become one of the three leading Polish Romantic poets. Like Fryderyk,

[55] Andrzej E. Koźmian, "Wizerunki osób towarzystwa warszawskiego" [Images of Warsaw's socialites], *Przegląd poznański* 24 (1857): 21.

[56] Natalia Kicka, *Pamiętniki* [Memoirs], ed. T. Szafrański and J. Dutkiewicz (Warsaw: Pax, 1972), 127.

Zygmunt was destined to spend most of his adult life away from Poland. The main cause of his travels away from home was the ideological conflict he had with his much-loved father. General Krasiński represented quite controversial political tendencies, and his ostensibly most embarrassing and enraging political act, which made him an outcast in public opinion, took place in 1828, when he was the only senator to condemn Polish patriotic organizations. This action conclusively distanced Zygmunt from his father (though it did not free him from his influence) and led him to spend years roaming aimlessly around Europe. At the end of 1838, in Naples, Zygmunt met Countess Delfina Potocka, who for the remainder of his life remained the object of his ardent love. Delfina was also a student and a close friend of Chopin; he dedicated his Concerto in F Minor, op. 21 and Waltz op. 64 no. 1 to her. It was in her *Stammbuch* that he wrote his last song, known as "Melody," setting Krasiński's intensely messianic text.[57] In "Melody," both Krasiński's poem and Chopin's musical setting provide mature and bleak commentaries on the quintessentially Romantic messianic ideology that found its roots in concepts the two artists first eagerly explored and embraced in their early years in Warsaw, in the company of their Romantic peers.

The Young Romantics

The young Romantics typically gathered in the homes of Chopin, Mochnacki, Reinschmidt, or Magnuszewski. Each of these salons draw together a slightly different circle; for instance, the group frequenting Chopin's home included several young musicians and some of his gymnasium and university friends, many of whom were soon to join the ranks of Poland's leading intellectuals and artists. By the late 1820s, Chopin was among the core participants in all the salons that catered to the young people who were passionate about the new Romantic ideas. The works of the younger ones were to take Polish Romanticism into full maturity in the ensuing decades. Dominik Magnuszewski (1810–1845) became a writer—a translator of Hugo and the main representative of Romantic expressionism in Polish literature. Konstanty Gaszyński (1809–1866) and Zygmunt Krasiński (1812–1859) already started publishing their poetic writings in the late 1820s. However, the intellectual tone for these meetings was set by their somewhat older colleagues—the generation born around the turn of the century.

---

[57] For a detailed discussion of Chopin's "Melody" see Halina Goldberg, "'Remembering That Tale of Grief': The Prophetic Voice in Chopin's Music," in *The Age of Chopin: Interdisciplinary Inquiries*, ed. Goldberg (Bloomington: Indiana University Press, 2004), 79–82.

Several of Chopin's older peers transferred the vigorous debates that took place in their private gatherings into the public eye already in the mid-1820s. They were the spokesmen for Romantic ideology and aesthetics and the authors of poetic works that sought to embrace the Romantic ideal. Not only did they use the new idiom in their works but also they advanced the Romantic cause by translating major foreign works, such as those of Byron, into Polish. Their direct inspiration came from Adam Mickiewicz and the 1822 publication of his *Ballads and Romances* (*Ballady i romanse*). Mickiewicz towered intellectually over the Warsaw Romantics, but he was connected with the Vilnius rather than Warsaw intellectual circles, and by 1825 was already exiled in Russia for his patriotic activities. In Warsaw his vision was carried on by Antoni Edward Odyniec; the poets of most of Chopin's songs, Józef Bohdan Zaleski and Stefan Witwicki; and the multitalented Maurycy Mochnacki.

Maurycy Mochnacki is today most remembered as a revolutionary and a historian of the November Uprising. He was also a gifted pianist and a fiery literary critic. After the initial public outburst in the years immediately following the Vienna Congress, the discussion about Romanticism receded into the salons and was conducted in the polite atmosphere of discourse. It was Mochnacki, the most outspoken of the Romantics, who took it back into the open; by 1825, through his printed essays, he gave the public debate renewed intensity. He eloquently defended Polish Romantic poets, drawing on his vast knowledge of aesthetics, metaphysics, and literary and cultural history. Restless, uncompromising, and rebellious, he was no longer willing to mediate with the traditionalists, calling for a radical break with the past. Thus his writings are a categorical rejection of rationalism and empiricism, and a total acceptance of transcendentalism and idealism. In his articles he refers to Schiller, Madame de Staël, Novalis, Jean Paul, and the Schlegels, making inspiration, spirit, and imagination the sine qua non of poetry. For him, the skill of rhyming and versifying, the ability to follow rules and retrieve readily available imagery, were the mark of a mere rhymester, not a poet. As the means of communicating the metaphysical, poetry could not be in the service of the mundane, nor could it be trapped in the present: it mediated the connection between our reality and the timeless and the infinite.[58]

Much of the debate was taken up with the question of national character, as well as the role of old poetry and myth in the shaping of individual national qualities in poetry. Here the Romantics continued addressing questions first articulated in the Polish context by Brodziński and put

---

[58] Mochnacki's writings have been published as *Rozprawy literackie* [Literary treatises], ed. Mirosław Strzyżewski (Wrocław: Zakład Narodowy Imienia Ossolińskich, 2000) and *Pisma* [Writings], ed. Artur Śliwiński (Lwów: Połoniecki, 1910).

in a more radical light by Mickiewicz in the foreword to his 1822 *Ballady i romanse*.[59] What clearly emerged from these debates were a preference for German and English models and a search for native, Polish sources to inspire most Romantic genres. The ballad was such a quintessentially Romantic genre, and Mickiewicz's ballads not only stirred commotion but also invited many immediate followers; in fact, by 1825, both Odyniec and Witwicki published ballads. In this manner, the genre of the ballad became an important battleground for the new aesthetics, treated in prefaces to each of the published sets, in theoretical essays on Romanticism, and in press reviews of the published works (Witwicki's ballads, in particular, were attacked with harsh criticism). In order to define the Romantic ballad, these writers surveyed its history, which they believed to be traceable back to medieval and folk models, as well as the immediate British (English, Scottish, Irish) and German ancestry of their own works. Odyniec, in the introduction to his *Ballads and Legends* (*Ballady i legendy*) emphasized the generic mixture inherent in the modern ballad and rooted in its ancestry: the epic narrative elements of the medieval romance; the lyrical and dance-like characteristics of the ballad; the subject matter based on folklore and historical legends, allowing the poet to draw on supernatural imagination.[60] Mickiewicz, Odyniec, and Mochnacki emphasized that for ballads to be effective in articulating national character, they had to rely on native rather than foreign myths and legends. They sought specifically local tales and praised the efforts of early collectors of folklore and scholars of Slavic antiquities, but Mochnacki, in particular, also invented "Polish mythology" by adopting foreign myths and giving them local color.

In the transcendental sense, "the poetic" was the expression of "the infinite," which for Mochnacki in the late 1820s took on the sense of "the divine." Therefore, the artist, who was an intermediary between the two realms, human and spiritual, acquired priestly characteristics. The specifically Polish incarnation of this role was the folk prophet-poet-musician, the *guślarz* or *wieszcz*, most convincingly presented by Mickiewicz in his Romantic drama of 1823, *Forefathers' Eve*, parts 2 and 4. This expressly Polish rendering of *Kunstreligion*, after the catastrophe of the November Uprising, developed into political messianism. The spiritual dimension became historiosophic: Poland's Christ-like sacrifice was to offer expia-

---

[59] Adam Mickiewicz, *Ballady i romanse* [Ballads and romances] (Wilno: Józef Zawadzki, 1822); the foreword entitled "O poezji romantycznej" [On Romantic poetry] is reprinted in *Idee programowe romantyków polskich: Antologia* [Program ideas of Polish Romantics: an anthology], ed. Alina Kowalczykowa, 2nd ed. (Wrocław: Zakład Narodowy Imienia Ossolińskich, 2000), 43–65.

[60] Antoni Edward Odyniec, *Poezye* [Poems], vol. 1, *Ballady i legendy* [Ballads and legends] (Wilno: [s.n.], 1825), xv–xxx.

tion for the world's sins. The selflessness expected of a Romantic artist was now understood as a patriotic sacrifice.

Mochnacki equated "poetic" with "Romantic," hence poetry encompassed all philosophical and aesthetic phenomena, including theater, music, and the other arts. As a result, his interests extended to theatrical and musical criticism. In his writings, he attempted to establish criteria for aesthetic criticism applicable to all arts, and he authored scores of theater and concert reviews (including the articles quoted in chapters on concert and opera in Warsaw), thus establishing musical criticism in Poland. Music was often mentioned in his critical writings on literature as well. For instance, when claiming that beauty in art must be in accord with nature, Mochnacki cited Haydn's representation of the creation of light in *The Creation* and its relationship to actually experiencing a sunrise.[61]

The inclusion of music in "the poetic" allowed for the prophet-poet to be construed also as a musician and initiated a search for a composer who was capable of fulfilling such a mission. Initially, Karol Lipiński was proposed as a suitable candidate.[62] But once Chopin's talent became known, the hopes of the Romantics turned to him. Chopin was at the heart of their meetings, his presence recognized as pivotal in the articulation of Polish musical Romanticism and rewarded with utter admiration for his genius. While Chopin learned from salon debates on the intellectual topics occupying his Romantic peers, and his emerging compositional style was nourished by the new artistic tendencies surrounding him, it cannot be overlooked that by then his innovative musical genius had already made him an active agent in the creation of Polish Romanticism.

[61] Maurycy Mochnacki, "Artykuł do którego powodem był 'Zamek kaniowski' Goszczyńskiego" [Article instigated by "The Castle of Kaniów" of Goszczyński], *Gazeta Polska*, 1829, nos. 15–30, quoted in Mochnacki, *Rozprawy literackie*, 150.

[62] Jan Ludwik Żukowski, "O sztuce" [On art], dated 1826 and published in *Gazeta Polska*, 1828 nos. 96, 98, 100–102; quoted in *Idee programowe romantyków polskich: Antologia*, 183.

6

MUSIC IN SALONS

Musical Entertainment in the Social
and Intellectual Salons

The Musical Training and Contribution
of Amateurs

Most of Warsaw's salons invited some kind of musical entertainment,
and, naturally, the extent and the quality of musical performances reflected the tastes and the musical skills of the hosts. Along with other es-
sentials of education, some level of musical training was expected of all
members of the middle and upper classes. It was no secret that by learning to play the piano a young man provided himself with the opportunity
to court his lady while making music with her, or that by nurturing artistic talents a young woman could show her social standing and attract a
suitor. In 1833 the Polish press reprinted the following description of
Warsaw's social life from an unidentified Berlin periodical.

> Warsaw represents all the elements of educated, attractive and glam-
> orous society. Some local women are writers, and though their works
> can be considered literary experiments, they are not without wit and
> originality; and since they received a much better education than
> women in southern countries, their conversations are more reasoned
> and full of life and wit. . . . In general, everybody here dances charm-
> ingly, ladies play the piano splendidly, and draw some (though until
> now only one true piano talent [Szymanowska?] has been produced

who is recognized in Europe); they also paint flowers and landscapes, but all these stop with marriage.[1]

Obviously, musical training was not limited to women, nor did everybody abandon interest in music on reaching adulthood—in homes with intellectual aspirations, in particular, music was an essential component of salon meetings.

> During the first half of this century, we had not a few people who scorned the loud and uproarious life within the circles to which they belonged by birth, habit, and financial standing; they preferred domestic entertainments and sought nourishment for the intellect among a selected circle of friends. Not infrequently, they themselves were the souls of such gatherings, animating them with joyful and witty chat, or music and dance.[2]

Many hosts and guests of the prominent salons had good musical training; some had considerable musical talent. They were trained by local and foreign teachers residing in Polish cities. Mochnacki, for instance, was considered a fine pianist, praised particularly for his execution of Mozart, Beethoven, and Weber.[3] Since his parents considered music an important component of their sons' comprehensive education, Maurycy received theory, piano, and violin lessons in Lwów.[4] Some other amateur musicians had illustrious foreign teachers. Thus, Count Franciszek Sołtyk studied violin with Lafont and Kreutzer in Paris,[5] and his relative, Count Karol Sołtyk, studied the violin with Mayseder in Vienna.[6] Amateur musicians participated in private music making and sometimes even public concerts, typically associated with philanthropic projects—for instance, the female amateurs who in 1820 performed for the Society for the Friends of Religious and National Music, winning the admiration of their

[1] *Gazeta warszawska*, 14 June 1833, no. 157: 1356.

[2] Oskar Kolberg, manuscript, Biblioteka Narodowa, Warsaw, III. 8893.

[3] Józef Bohdan Zaleski, *Pisma zbiorowe* [Collected works], 4 vols. (Lwów: Gubrynowicz i Schmidt, 1877), 4:86. In 1832, during his last years, already in exile in Metz, he gave a public concert that was later mythologized by poets.

[4] Maurycy Mochnacki, *Rozprawy literackie* [Literary treatises], ed. Mirosław Strzyżewski (Wrocław: Zakład Narodowy Imienia Ossolińskich, 2000), viii.

[5] Albert Sowiński, *Słownik muzyków polskich dawnych i nowoczesnych* [Dictionary of ancient and modern Polish musicians], 1st Polish ed. (Paris: Księgarnia Luxemburska, 1874), 344–345.

[6] Karol Sołtyk went to Vienna as a young man, after inheriting a large sum of money. In short time, his luxurious lifestyle made him a pauper, but, thanks to the help of his teacher, Mayseder, he got a job as a second violinist in the imperial court orchestra. Soon after, his family paid up his debts, and he was able to return to Poland. In 1827 he moved to Warsaw and was in Chopin's closest musical circle. *Tygodnik Ilustrowany*, 1869, 492–493.

audience: "Among the members of this Society are four . . . outstanding female pianists, one of whom—still a very young lady—performs the most difficult compositions by Beethoven, Field, Ries, and Dussek with admirable proficiency."[7]

Princess Izabela Czartoryska made sure that her children's musical skills were cultivated and that there was good music at her residence in Puławy and in the local parish church. For this purpose, she hired Wincenty Lessel, a Bohemian who had previously served as a violinist at the court orchestra in Dresden. Izabela herself had an interest in music (fig. 6.1), and her husband, Prince Adam Kazimierz, was a patron and a music historian of sorts—he left a detailed description of forty-five musical instruments (published posthumously in 1828 as "A Dictionary of Old Musical Instruments in Poland").[8]

Wincenty Lessel was a competent and knowledgeable teacher—not only was he acquainted with Dresden musical circles but also, because of his association with the Czartoryskis, he had lived in Vienna and Warsaw for periods of time. He instructed all of Izabela's children. Many years later, Zofia recalled: "I had a good piano maître, who hit me sometimes and I cried very much, but he taught well and I would have been a good musician would I have not already then neglected my talent."[9] Still, Izabela's children did not squander the musical education she provided for them. Her eldest daughter, Princess Maria Würtemberg, to whom Chopin dedicated his Mazurkas op. 30, continued to play the piano in private, and she is reported to have comforted her dying father with her keyboard playing in 1823.[10] She also joined professionals in music making; for instance, in 1809 she took part in a sung mass with Miss Naimska, Szczurowski, and Kratzer (renowned professional singers).[11]

Maria and her siblings participated in a number of important musical endeavors. The musical circle associated with the Czartoryskis contributed many settings for Niemcewicz's *Historic Chants*; indeed, Maria and Zofia each composed a song. Maria and Zofia were involved with the founding of what later became the Warsaw Conservatory and the estab-

[7] *Allgemeine musikalische Zeitung*, August 1820, 534.

[8] Biblioteka Ossolińskich, Wrocław, Ms. 496.

[9] Ludwik Dębicki, *Puławy (1762–1830): Monografia z życia towarzyskiego, politycznego i literackiego na podstawie archiwum ks. Czartoryskich w Krakowie* [Puławy (1762–1830): A monograph on social, political and literary life based on the Princes' Czartoryski Archives in Kraków]. 4 vols. (Lwów: Gubrynowicz i Schmidt, 1888), 4:288. As the Czartoryskis' fortunes tumbled, Lessel's employment conditions deteriorated. His last destitute years with the Czartoryski family were full of disappointment and bitterness. See letters collected in Hanna Rudnicka-Kruszewska, *Wincenty Lessel* (Kraków: Polskie Wydawnictwo Muzyczne, 1968).

[10] Klementyna Hoffman, *Pamiętniki* [Memoirs], 3 vols. (Berlin: Behr, 1849), 1:109.

[11] Maria Würtemberg, letter to her mother, Izabela Czartoryska, 1809, quoted in Dębicki, *Puławy*, 4:173.

Figure 6.1. Izabela Czartoryska at a clavichord. Mezzotint by G[iuseppe Filippo Liberati] Marchi, 1777. Biblioteka Uniwersytecka, Warsaw, Zb. Król. T. 33 nr. 69.

lishment of the Society for Religious and National Music at the Piarist church; their brother, Adam Jerzy, who presided over the Society, mandated Lessel with the creation of its chapter in Puławy. In a letter of 1813, he wrote about encouraging members of his musical circle in Puławy to collect folk melodies so national music would be given proper attention and protected from dying out (the project took place decades before Polish folklorists undertook such projects).[12] A couple of manuscript collections today in the Czartoryski Library may be the result of this initiative: one is an anthology of one-line monophonic mazurkas and krakowiaks, apparently of folk origin. The other one, headed "Adam Czartoryski's Music for Flute from Sieniawa" [Muzyka na flecik Adama Czartoryskiego w

[12] Rudnicka-Kruszewska, *Wincenty Lessel*, 61–62.

Sieniawie; referring to the Czartoryskis' other country estate], contains, among other short pieces, mazurs, krakowiaks, dumas, and polonaises; it might have been a record of the same undertaking or a collection associated with Adam Jerzy's father.[13] Konstanty Czartoryski, who sponsored a first-rate military band, had a particular taste for chamber music, and after he settled in Vienna in 1829, his salon became well known in artistic circles. In the 1840s, Konstanty held Quartet Thursdays, which were attended by Berlioz, Meyerbeer, Thalberg, Vieuxtemps, Dreischock, Servais, Mayseder, and Liszt. In this salon, Chopin's music was presented by Konstanty's daughter-in-law, Marcelina Czartoryska, who was reputedly one of Chopin's finest students.[14]

Invited Performances by Professionals

Warsaw had plenty of local musicians, who could be invited to give guest performances in salons. There were the older generation of musicians and the young professionals—students and new graduates of the Warsaw Conservatory. Some musicians forged ongoing formal or informal relationships with particular families. For instance, Franciszek Lessel, on his return from studies with Haydn in Vienna, continued his relationship with his father's employers, the Czartoryskis, most closely with Princess Maria Würtemberg. Although he left music as a profession, he never ceased to compose and to participate in musical performances. In addition to local talent, visits of renowned Polish artists in between European engagements, performances of foreign virtuosi, and appearances of *Wunderkinder* added zest to private concerts.

Child virtuosi were frequent guests in salons; indeed, Chopin's career was launched by his appearances as a *Wunderkind*. Around the time of his first public performance, the 1818 concert for the Benevolent Association, organized by Julian Ursyn Niemcewicz and Zofia Zamoyska, it became fashionable to invite the young virtuoso to a musical evening—his early biographers list some fifteen aristocratic homes that hosted young Fryderyk's performances.[15] But Chopin was just one of many performing

[13] Biblioteka XX Czartoryskich, Kraków, 100601 and 100033/1.

[14] The Viennese branch of the Czartoryski clan was very involved with the Gesellschaft der Musikfreunde. *Ruch muzyczny*, 1860, no. 24, 392, and Dębicki, *Puławy*, 4:345–348.

[15] Czartoryski, Sapieha, Czetwertyński, Lubecki, Radziwiłł, Skarbek, Pruszak, Lempicki, and the home of Constantine at Belweder. Maurycy Karasowski, *Fryderyk Chopin.*, 2 vols. 1st Polish ed., (Warsaw: Gebethner i Wolff, 1882), 29. Oskar Kolberg expands the list with the names of Zajączek, Wolicki, Okołow; Kolberg, "Chopin," in *Encyklopedia Powszechna* [Universal Encyclopedia]. 28 vols. (Warsaw: Orgelbrand, 1859–68), 5:459. Ferdynand Hoesick adds Zamoyski, Potocki, Mostowski; *Chopin: Życie i twórczość* [Chopin: life and works], 2 vols. (Warsaw: Hoesick, 1927), 1:52.

in Warsaw in the early decades of the nineteenth century. Warsaw's other favorite young musicians were the Kaczyński brothers and the Kątski brothers. The Kaczyńskis, a violinist and a cellist, were first heard in Warsaw in 1814.[16] The Kątskis were introduced into the capital's homes in the early 1820s. The oldest brother, Karol (b. 1813) played the violin; the middle brothers, Antoni (b. 1817) and Stanisław (b. 1820), were pianists; and the little Apolinary (b. 1824) was later admired for his virtuosity on the violin.[17] Chopin knew these two families of musicians quite well, and they continued to cross musical paths well beyond their childhood. At times, one would hear angry voices criticizing the exploitative nature of the *Wunderkind* business; this was clearly the position of Chopin's parents and teachers, who, concerned with the constant intrusions into the boy's education and emotional welfare, forbade his salon performances.

Performances in the most influential households and the more reputable musical salons would frequently precede public appearances; in fact, for some, the reputation gained in a private setting could open the doors to a public concert. Thus it was common for an artist first to be heard in salons and to make many more private than public appearances. Naturally, salons welcomed artists of great acclaim who needed no endorsement. Ferdinand Paër, Pierre J. Rode, Daniel Steibelt, Luigi Cherubini, August Klengel, Franz Xavier Wolfgang Mozart (the son of Wolfgang Amadeus), Gasparo Spontini, Jan Ladislav Dussek, Angelica Catalani, and many others are reported to have performed in Warsaw's salons. When Catalani, a famous soprano, visited Warsaw during 1819–1820, Chopin met her in the salon of her relative, Konstanty Wolicki. It is here that the diva heard the young virtuoso perform; highly impressed, she awarded him a gold watch adorned by an engraved dedication that read:

> Mme Catalani
> à Fréderic Chopin
> agé de 10 Ans
> à Varsovie
> le 3 Janvier 1820.

[16] Their 1814 performance, like the one Chopin gave in 1818, was associated with a charity concert organized by Countess Zamoyska: the violinist played a Rode concerto, and the cellist performed a potpourri by Romberg. Ultimately, the brothers settled in St. Petersburg, invited by the patron and musician Count Wielhorski. Sowiński, *Słownik muzyków polskich dawnych i nowoczesnych,* 170.

[17] On the occasion of their 1823 performances in Warsaw, the press extolled their extraordinary talents. *Kurier warszawski,* 1 February 1823, no. 27, 1. Following concert tours in Poland, they tried performing in various European cities and met with much success. In the aftermath of the November Uprising they relocated to Paris, where they were held in high esteem in musical circles. Sowiński, *Słownik muzyków polskich dawnych i nowoczesnych,* 180–182.

In the late 1820s, the most memorable were the private appearances of Nicolò Paganini, the world-famous Polish violinist Karol Lipiński, Anna Caroline de Belleville (a successful German concert pianist), and the celebrated soprano Henriette Sontag.

The Musical Salons

The Hosts

In about a dozen Warsaw salons, making music was the main purpose of meetings. We are told by a contemporary of Chopin that "some private homes also hosted musical soirées, during which string quartets and other works—for the solo or accompanied piano—were performed."[18] The most acclaimed were the gatherings in the homes of Kessler, the Lindes, the Cichockis, the Jabłonowskis, the Sauvans, the Wolffs, and the Wołowskis. In some musical salons, meetings were regular: Kessler hosted Friday soirées, and the Cichockis kept Musical Mondays at their salon. In other homes, musical soirées were intermittent. The social standing of these homes varied: the Jabłonowskis were of the highest aristocracy, the Cichockis were of lesser nobility, Sauvan and Wolff were medical doctors, Linde was the rector of the Gymnasium, Kessler was a pianist, and the Wołowskis (parents of Maria Szymanowska) were wealthy brewers of Frankist descent.[19] What they shared was the aspiration to experience fine music.

Typically, the hosts of musical salons not only were passionate about music but also had some musical proficiency. The highest level of musicianship was represented by Joseph Christoph Kessler, of whom Robert Schumann said "Mann von Geist und sogar poetischen Geist," and who was admired by his professional contemporaries everywhere in Europe as a concert pianist and composer.[20] Some other hosts of musical soirées were quite good amateur musicians. For instance, Józef Cichocki was a good flutist, and his wife Anna was a pianist and a singer. Eleonora Wolff (born Oesterreicher) in her youth was designated one of Warsaw's best amateur pianists.[21] Mrs. Linde (born Ludwika Nussbaum in Eislingen), being a daughter of a conductor of an army orchestra, received system-

---

[18] Kolberg, manuscript, Biblioteka Narodowa, Warsaw, III. 8893.

[19] In the mid–eighteenth century, a Jewish pseudo-messiah, Jakub Lejbowicz Frank, founded an anti-Talmudist sect following a philosophy that led his supporters to mass conversions to Catholicism. Among Frank's followers was Maria Szymanowska's ancestor Solomon ben Elias, who converted about 1759 and took on the name Wołowski.

[20] Hugo Riemann, *Musik-Lexikon*, 6 vols. (Leipzig: Verlag des Bibliographischen Instituts, 1882), 1:917; and F. Pyllemann, *Allgemeine musikalische Zeitung*, 1872, no. 12.

[21] *Allgemeine musikalische Zeitung*, September 1812, 612.

atic piano training. Mrs. Sauvan, an able singer, was the daughter of Ludwik Dmuszewski, a prominent comic actor and director of the National Theater, and Konstancja Pięknowska, an operatic singer—she would have been brought up almost literarily "on the operatic stage." Not much is known about the Jabłonowskis' particular skills, but they would have had access to the best musical education, given the broad musical interests of their families: the prince's mother, Tekla Jabłonowska, participated in the performances of Elsner's Lwów Musikakademie,[22] and in Vienna she took lessons with Wolfgang Amadeus Mozart;[23] the princess, born Lubomirska, came from a family equally well known for music patronage. On the other hand, the Wołowskis are not known to have received musical training. However, the concerts in their home were intended to nourish the talents of the two talented young pianists: their daughter Maria and her cousin, Tekla Wołowska. Maria and Tekla, as well as the children of the Wolffs, received excellent musical training, and one child from each family went on to become a music professional: Maria Wołowska (later Szymanowska) and Edward Wolff both had impressive international careers as concert pianists. To boot, the Wolffs' grandsons, Józef and Henryk Wieniawski, became world-famous virtuosi.[24]

Many of the hosts of musical salons made lasting contributions to Warsaw's musical life through broadly conceived musical patronage. Some of these music lovers were instrumental in the organization of musical life in Warsaw. Most notably, Count Cichocki, after the fall of the November Uprising, when most public musical institutions were dissolved, established weekly chamber concerts, engaged a permanent string quartet, and established a choir to make possible the performances of large choral works, like Haydn's oratorios *The Creation* and *The Seasons* at the Merchant Club.[25] His interest in the musical repertories of the past inspired him to collect old manuscripts and to spearhead the 1838 publica-

[22] Józef Elsner, *Sumariusz moich utworów muzycznych* [A summary of my musical works], ed. Alina Nowak-Romanowicz (Kraków: Polskie Wydawnictwo Muzyczne, 1957), 101.

[23] Oskar Kolberg, *Dzieła wszystkie Oskara Kolberga* [The complete works of Oskar Kolberg], ed. J. Krzyżanowski, 66 vols., *Pisma muzyczne* [Music writings], part II, ed. M. Tomaszewski, O. Pawlak, and E. Miller (Wrocław: Polskie Towarzystwo Ludoznawcze, 1981) 62:286.

[24] They were the sons of the Wolffs' daughter, Regina. Another son of the Wolffs, Maksymilian, who graduated from the gymnasium in 1825 and received medical training at Warsaw University, participated in the musical life of Warsaw as a dedicated amateur. Eugeniusz Szulc and Jadwiga Szulc, *Cmentarz Ewangielicko-Reformowany w Warszawie* [The Calvinist cemetery in Warsaw] (Warsaw: Państwowy Instytut Wydawniczy, 1989), 280. The Wolffs were Jewish. Regina's family and Maksymilian converted to Christianity; Edward kept the Jewish faith.

[25] Bronisław Dobrzyński, *Ignacy Dobrzyński w zakresie działalności dążącej do postępu muzyki współczesnej jemu epoce* [Ignacy Dobrzyński in the arena of activities aiming at musical progress during his time] (Warsaw: Felicyia Krokoszyńska, 1893), 29, 45–46, 63.

Figure. 6.2. *Śpiewy kościelne na kilka głosów dawnych kompozytorów polskich zebrane i wydane przez Józefa Cichockiego* [Church chants for several voices by ancient Polish composers collected and published by Józef Cichocki] (Warsaw: Sennewald, 1838), title page. Biblioteka Narodowa, Warsaw, Mus. II 19184 Cim.

tion of Polish Renaissance and Baroque compositions in modern transcription, the earliest such effort (see fig. 6.2). Cichocki was a dedicated patron of musicians, and his efforts were crucial to the creation and operations of the Society for the Assistance for Destitute Musicians and Their Widows and Orphans.[26] He also took interest in many talented young musicians from Chopin's circle, especially by providing support to the Turowski family of young singers.[27] In his capacity as an amateur

[26] Sowiński, *Słownik muzyków polskich dawnych i nowoczesnych,* 425.

[27] The Turowski family—three sisters and a brother—made up a vocal quartet: Marya (1820–1885), whose married name was Stolpe, was a soprano; Józefa (1819–1884), who

musical critic—he wrote about music for *Powszechny Dziennik Krajowy,* *Kurier Warszawski,* and *Pamiętnik Muzyczny Warszawski* (in the years 1835–1836 he was even the editor of the third publication)—Cichocki championed young artists' performing careers. In his well-known article for *Powszechny Dziennik Krajowy,* written after Chopin's concert of March 22, 1830, Cichocki, a great admirer of Chopin's talent, compared him to Mozart and called for more performances by the young virtuoso.[28]

Through salon associations, musicians were able to obtain introductions to prominent or musically connected individuals and families abroad. For Chopin, the association with the well-respected Kessler was valuable in entering musical circles abroad; more personal connections were also helpful. For instance, during his stay in Vienna, he was a frequent guest in the musical home of Mrs. Weberheim, the sister of Eleonora Wolff of Warsaw.[29]

The patronage associated with Warsaw's musical salons occasioned a litany of compositions conceived expressly for their hosts and dedicated to them. Scores of such pieces were published by local printers; Chopin's Rondo in C Minor, op. 1, dedicated to Mrs. Linde, among them. More significantly, there were chamber works, not published in Warsaw because of the limited demand for such compositions. Elsner's Septet in D Major for flute, clarinet, violin, viola, cello, double bass, and piano (fig. 6.3);[30] the Quintet in E-flat Major, op. 1, no. 2 for flute, violin, viola, cello, and bass by the French composer Georges Onslow;[31] and Chopin's little-known Flute Variations on Rossini's *La cenerentola* (discussed in chapter 3)— all works dedicated to Cichocki—were inspired by the count's love for chamber music and proficiency as a flutist. Ignacy Dobrzyński honored

---

married Leśkiewicz, was an alto; Waleria (later Bonfis) sang tenor; the brother, Seweryn, was an excellent bass. Dobrzyński, *Ignacy Dobrzyński w zakresie działalności dążącej do postępu muzyki współczesnej jemu epoce,* 53. Later, two of the Turowski sisters (Marya and Józefa) joined the Warsaw Theatre, and Józefa Leśkiewicz became one of the finest altos the capital knew. "Antoni Orłowski," *Pamiętnik Muzyczny i Teatralny,* 1862, no. 24, 375, and *Kurier warszawski,* 1849, no. 337.

[28] *Powszechny Dziennik Krajowy,* 25 March 1830, no. 83.

[29] Fryderyk Chopin, Vienna, to his family, Warsaw, 1 December 1830, in *Korespondencja Fryderyka Chopina* [Fryderyk Chopin's correspondence], ed. Bronisław Edward Sydow, 2 vols. (Warsaw: Państwowy Instytut Wydawniczy, 1955), 1:156; Chopin, Vienna, to his family, Warsaw, [22 December 1830], *Korespondencja* 1:158.

[30] Elsner, *Sumariusz,* 57. Elsner erred in his description of this piece as a septet for viola, flute, clarinet, French horn, cello, and piano. Partial autograph score, Biblioteka Warszawskiego Towarzystwa Muzycznego, Warsaw, R. 942.

[31] Jerzy Habela, "Cichocki, Józef," in *Encyclopedia Muzyczna* [Music encyclopedia], ed. Elżbieta Dziębowska (Kraków: Polskie Wydawnictwo Muzyczne, 1981–), 2:201. The published version of this quintet, dedicated to his friend Hippolyte de Murat, is scored for two violins, viola, and two cellos; perhaps Onslow provided a transcription with a flute substituted for a violin part for Cichocki.

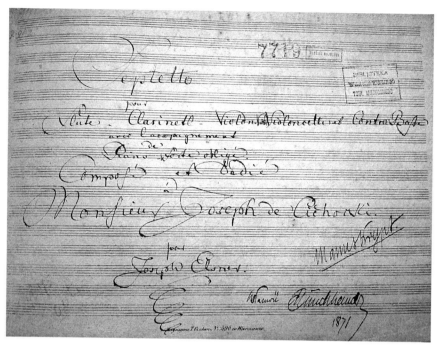

Figure 6.3. Józef Elsner, *Septetto* in D Major, for flute, clarinet, violin, viola, cello, double bass, and piano, dedicated to Józef Cichocki, autograph manuscript, title page and the opening of the first movement. Biblioteka Warszawskiego Towarzystwa Muzycznego, Warsaw, R 942.

Cichocki's name-day with the composition of a cantata, which was performed by a solo quartet made up of the Turowski family and a mixed choir.[32] Mrs. Wolff's pianistic skill was the reason for Elsner's dedication of his Piano Quartet in F Major to her.[33] Chopin' Piano Trio in G Minor op. 8 was conceived in analogous context and dedicated to Prince Antoni Radziwiłł, an avid cellist, who was only a sporadic quest in Warsaw's musical salons but hosted regular chamber concerts in his salon in Berlin and his Antonin estate outside Poznań. Perhaps the greatest acknowledgment of the inspiration Chopin found in musical salons of his youth came nearly a decade after Chopin's departure from Warsaw. It was the dedication to Kessler of the autograph manuscript and the first German edition of his *Préludes* op. 28.

The Performers

Visiting performers of international renown, as pointed out previously, were sought after by the hosts of fashionable salons, but their preference was for music making in the company of true music lovers and professional peers. The Wolffs often invited foreign virtuosi; the Wołowski salon was visited by nearly every prominent musician who traveled through Warsaw during the first quarter of the nineteenth century; Musical Mondays at the Cichockis

> gathered not only local but also foreign artists. There, visiting guests gave their first performances; there was formed the opinion about the abilities and talents of musical artists—opinion gained in this artistic circle was a guarantee of public success. Visiting celebrities: Henselt, Servais, Perelli, Nicolai, and many others, also performed in this home. It was, I would say, the musical heart of all Warsaw, and the famous Mondays gathered and united nearly all talents—literary and scholastic luminaries and generally people of distinction in the fields of the arts and sciences or of other personal merits.[34]

The local performers of concerts in the homes of musical connoisseurs were Warsaw's best musicians, professionals, and amateurs, including some of the hosts. Mrs. Wolff clearly had the necessary skill and did not shy away from playing chamber music; she even did so in public, for

[32] Dobrzyński, *Ignacy Dobrzyński w zakresie działalności dążącej do postępu muzyki współczesnej jemu epoce*, 30.

[33] Elsner, *Sumariusz*, 58. Biblioteka Narodowa, Warsaw, Ms. 6216 might be the violin part of this piece.

[34] Dobrzyński, *Ignacy Dobrzyński w zakresie działalności dążącej do postępu muzyki współczesnej jemu epoce*, 29–30.

instance, when she played the piano part in Mozart's Piano Quartet in E-flat Major at a concert in 1800.[35] Count Cichocki took part in performances at the Piarist church alongside his protégés the Turowskis,[36] and presumably routinely played the flute part in chamber concerts at his home, including the performance of Spohr's Quintet for piano, clarinet, bassoon, French horn, and flute reported by Chopin.[37] Ludwika Linde— the wife of Samuel Bogumił Linde, the rector of the Gymnasium and the author of the epochal *Dictionary of the Polish Language*—was Chopin's next-door neighbor and loved to play four-hand piano pieces with him during her musical soirées.[38] Among other amateurs often performing in musical homes and closely associated with Chopin were the aforementioned Sołtyks, both first-rate violinists. Chopin also frequently writes about playing with two government employees who were good amateur musicians—the cellist Józef Molsdorf and the violinist Franciszek Ledoux. The viola part was typically taken by Colonel Teodor Friedrich Philippeus, first aide-de-camp to Duke Constantine and court administrator, whom Chopin sometimes cordially addressed by the nickname Filip. Another Russian, Prince Aleksander Galitsin, member of a family famous for musical patronage in St. Petersburg and in Vienna, who made his home in Warsaw after marrying a Polish noblewoman, often took part in chamber performances as a pianist. Naturally, the level of expertise varied, though the extraordinary talent of one amateur, Aleksander Rembieliński, elicited Chopin's utter admiration upon hearing Rembieliński after his return from a six-year sojourn in Paris:

> he plays the piano like nobody else that I have heard. You can well imagine what joy it is for us, who never hear anything of perfection here. He does not consider himself an artist, but an amateur. I will not expand the description of his fast, smooth and round playing, but I will tell you only that his left hand is as strong as the right one, which is unusual in one person. An entire sheet of paper would not suffice, if I wanted to describe his most exquisite talent.[39]

In addition to the professionals hosting their own musical salons— Maria Szymanowska in her parents' home and Joseph Christoph Kessler—

[35] Alina Nowak–Romanowicz, *Józef Elsner* (Kraków: Polskie Wydawnictwo Muzyczne, 1957), 315.

[36] Dobrzyński, *Ignacy Dobrzyński w zakresie działalności dążącej do postępu muzyki współczesnej jemu epoce*, 53.

[37] Chopin, Warsaw, to Tytus Woyciechowski, Poturzyn, 18 September, 1830, *Korespondencja*, 1:139.

[38] Eugeniusz Szulc and Jadwiga Szulc, *Cmentarz Ewangielicko-Reformowany w Warszawie*, 130–131.

[39] Chopin, Warsaw, to Woyciechowski, Poturzyn, 30 October 1825, *Korespondencja*, 1:59.

other professional musicians of older and younger generations joined in private music making in Warsaw's homes. The older conservatory professors often took part in salon concerts; among the younger professionals, Antoni Teichmann, an orchestra cellist and a performing singer who also taught voice, and Józef Bielawski, a young violin professor at the conservatory, most often participated in chamber performances with Chopin. As for Chopin's own peers, we often hear of the Kaczyński brothers, the cellist in particular, and of his conservatory colleagues Maurycy Ernemann and Józef Brzowski, as well as two classmates with whom Chopin's friendship continued into the years of exile, Julian Fontana and Antoni Orłowski. An excellent pianist, Fontana became one of Chopin's closest friends in Paris and the editor of his works. Orłowski, who studied composition with Elsner and the violin with Bielawski, took the position of the theatre orchestra's conductor in Rouen, and in 1834 Chopin gave concerts in Rouen while visiting Orłowski. Orłowski was a child of another musical family: his father Walenty was a well-known amateur bassoonist, and his little sister Joanna studied singing and piano at the Conservatory.[40] His stepbrother, Józef Szabliński, a cellist and a French horn player working for the theater orchestra who in 1829 became a wind instrument professor at the Conservatory, also regularly took part in salon chamber concerts.[41]

Musical Repertory

The repertory of music performed in salons spanned a wide range of genres and styles. A case can be made for two distinct repertories—a menu of typical parlor entertainment consisting of easy vocal and instrumental pieces, and a weightier repertory of chamber and transcribed orchestral works performed in soirées for music devotees. The boundaries between the two types of salon concerts, however, must be understood as fluid: popular entertainment was sometimes heard in the company of connoisseurs, and more demanding compositions were on occasion performed in dilettantes' homes.

Vocal Music

Compositions for voice and piano, typically vocal romances and operatic arias, made up a large portion of private concert repertory. Hundreds of

[40] Joanna was a fine pianist and an excellent sight-reader. After 1835 (when she was already known by her married name, Naimska), she often participated as a chamber pianist in the famous musical Wednesdays she held at her home, which were attended by such celebrities as Vieuxtemps, Paganini, Servais, Dreyschok, and Liszt. Dobrzyński, *Ignacy Dobrzyński w zakresie działalności dążącej do postępu muzyki współczesnej jemu epoce*, 51, and Eugeniusz Szulc and Jadwiga Szulc, *Cmentarz Ewangielicko-Reformowany w Warszawie* 162–163.

[41] Sowiński, *Słownik muzyków polskich dawnych i nowoczesnych*, 373.

such compositions published in Poland, further supplemented by ample imports from abroad, were available for the use of professional and amateur performers. By the time Chopin took part in salon gatherings, the piano replaced older keyboard instruments in accompanying singers, its richer timbres and larger range allowing a more satisfactory transcription of orchestral accompaniment for operatic arias:

> The piano does not present itself favorably in spacious dwellings, among a flock of instruments, but gains esteem in the salon, where it alone becomes a small orchestra, whether a fluent hand performs musical works or accompanies a singing voice. The piano is the treasure of the harmonist and the singer. In the city, in the village, how much boredom chased away, how many evenings beautified. When it is difficult to put together a quartet, a piano, two or three voices and a score of Mozart, Paër or Rossini will suffice to create a splendid concert.[42]

This piano-vocal repertory constituted the core of dilettante parlor performances, but even music lovers did not shy away from arranging a private concert around such works. In 1830 the press reported that the Jabłonowskis held "a musical soirée, in which amateurs and artists performed various songs."[43] Chopin gave an account of a similar performance at the home of Philippeus: "this Monday there was a major soirée at 'Filipeus,' where Mrs. Sauvan pleasantly sang the duet [sic] from *Semiramide;* the duet *buffo* from the *Turk,* sung by Soliva and Gresser, had to be accompanied again on demand."[44]

The standard piano repertory of dances, rondos, potpourris, and variations was also popular with Warsaw's publishers and consumers. Destined for the parlor, it was also played in the homes of music lovers. In his Warsaw days, Fryderyk did not think it beneath him to partake in bourgeois entertainment by playing four-hand pieces with Mrs. Linde or taking turns with Julian Fontana at Magnuszewski's to provide cheerful mazurs, polkas, and waltzes for the young Romantics and their companions to dance to.[45] Chopin's familiarity with this repertory (discussed in chapter 3), was crucial to his achievement in elevating genres of popular music, romances and dances in particular, to the rank of masterpieces of the salon tradition.

---

[42] Łukasz Gołębiowski, *Gry i zabawy różnych stanów* [Games and amusements of various classes] (Warsaw: Glücksberg, 1831), 234–235.

[43] *Kurier Warszawski,* 16 March 1830, no. 73, 365.

[44] Chopin, Warsaw, to Woyciechowski, Poturzyn, 10 April 1830, *Korespondencja,* 1:117.

[45] Anna Wóycicka, "Wieczorek pożegnalny Fryderyka Chopina" [Fryderyk Chopin's farewell evening], *Pion,* 1934, 24, 1.

Piano Music

Salon piano-repertory extended beyond uncomplicated popular compositions. Private concerts, those in musical salons in particular, included a wide range of works, Classical sonatas and virtuoso pieces among them. Mozart, Beethoven, and Weber were part of Mochnacki's piano repertory. Chopin reportedly played sonatas of Beethoven, Hummel, and Mozart for two and four hands in a salon concert in 1828.[46] Naturally, he also played his own compositions, especially admired by the young Romantics, for whom his music embodied the Romantic ideal: "Chopin—then cheerful and young—whom we all called Szopenek [diminutive of Szopen], played for us his marvelous pieces. Equipped with a genius mind—quick, witty and sensitive—he frolicked with the art, mastered it and captivated listeners with the natural abundance of his Polish rhythm."[47]

Such performances by Chopin, as well as the concerts at the Wołowskis featuring Maria's and Tekla's expert performances, and other salon appearances of virtuosi exemplified a sort of private piano recital, anticipating the public piano recital established by Liszt decades later.

Because of the limited consumer market, the more demanding works typically were not published in Poland, but a steady flow of publications from abroad made the masterpieces of piano repertory accessible and known to Polish professionals and music lovers. A glimpse at the piano compositions available in Warsaw through imports or even through handwritten copies can be gotten from documentation concerning the Czartoryskis' musical circle. The letters from Wincenty Lessel to his son, Franciszek, often comment on music purchased by and borrowed between the two Lessels and other musicians.[48] Franciszek Lessel's musical library, probably including some scores inherited from his father, is known to us from his estate inventory recorded by a notary shortly after his death in 1838.[49] And finally, the collection of manuscripts and early prints today in the holdings of the Czartoryski Library in Kraków reveals the musical interests of a refined, wealthy family—pieces taught to the Czartoryski children, played by the adults for home use, and performed by the musicians associated with them. It includes items from various sources, some of them perhaps originating with the Lessels' libraries, others acquired and copied by the various family members, most notably

[46] At the house of Prince Radziwiłł with the house maître, Kapelmeister Klingohr. Marceli Antoni Szulc, *Fryderyk Chopin i utwory jego muzyczne* [Fryderyk Chopin and his musical works] (1873), ed. D. Idaszek (Kraków: Polskie Wydawnictwo Muzyczne, 1986), 56.

[47] Zaleski, *Pisma,* iv: 86.

[48] Rudnicka-Kruszewska, *Wincenty Lessel.*

[49] Czesław Erber, "Inwentarz notarialny Lessla" [Notarized inventory of Lessel's estate], *Muzyka* 34 (1989): 37–57.

Anna Czartoryska. Anna, the wife of Prince Adam Jerzy from 1817, to whom Chopin dedicated his Rondo á la Krakowiak in F Major, op. 14 (of which the autograph is still held in the Czartoryski Library) was drawn to music, and much of the library's *musicalia*, many pieces copied in her hand included, are from her collection. The sources allow us to ascertain that a wide range of more ambitious piano solo literature circulated in Warsaw during Chopin's time. They show familiarity with piano sonatas by Clementi, Dussek, Haydn, Mozart, and Beethoven. In fact, Franciszek Lessel had a sizable collection of Beethoven's piano works, mostly dating to the period before 1810, when Lessel permanently relocated from Vienna to Warsaw, but including Beethoven's Fantasia op. 77 (among these were opp. 2, 10, 13, 14, 26, and 28).[50] Moreover, keyboard works by Johann Sebastian and Carl Phillip Emanuel Bach, as well as Handel and Froberger, were also known to musicians and connoisseurs: Franciszek's estate inventory lists several compositions by the Bachs, and his father speaks in his letters of purchasing scores by all four composers, and of the particular admiration he had for Bach's *Die Kunst der Fuge*.

The piano virtuosi active in Warsaw's salons also made considerable contributions as composers to the piano repertory performed in private concerts. Aleksander Rembieliński's waltzes and mazurkas, mentioned earlier, outshined most contemporary pieces in these genres. Franciszek Lessel's numerous piano works, mostly published abroad or remaining in manuscript, included fantasias, sonatas, variations, and rondos. Lessel's solo piano compositions are superbly crafted but mostly conservative, and thus contributed little to the new musical language. Among Maria Szymanowska's piano compositions, *Vingt Exercices et Préludes* published in 1820 by Breitkopf & Härtel, had the greatest impact on Chopin. These pieces, alongside Kessler's *Études* op. 20 and *24 Préludes* op. 31, make up an important ancestry of Chopin's etudes and preludes.

Trained in Vienna, Joseph Christoph Kessler arrived in Warsaw in 1829 after almost a decade in Lwów, hoping to settle in the Polish capital as a piano teacher. After giving numerous concerts, he quickly became well known in local musical circles. He grew especially fond of Chopin, who was only ten years his junior, and they often met, played together, and spoke much about art and music. The younger musician learnt a great deal from Kessler, who was already an accomplished composer. His famous *Études* op. 20, reissued many times throughout the nineteenth cen-

---

[50] Elsner must have shown some interest in Beethoven as well, since after settling in Paris, Chopin sent him François-Joseph Fétis's *Études de Beethoven: traité d'harmonie et de composition* (Paris: Schlesinger, 1833), actually an annotated translation of Ignaz Ritter von Seyfried's *Ludwig van Beethoven's Studien im Generalbasse, Contrapuncte und in der Compositions-Lehre* (1832). The volume with inscription from Chopin to Elsner, dated 24 August 1833, is in Muzeum Fryderyka Chopina w Towarzystwie im. Fryderyka Chopina, Warsaw.

tury, were highly valued by his contemporaries, including Kalkbrenner, Fétis, and Moscheles; Liszt even performed them in recitals. Since these pieces, published in 1825, are technically quite complex and stylistically precede Chopin, one must consider their relationship to Chopin's oeuvre, especially the earlier etudes of op. 10, which Fyderyk began composing while he kept company with Kessler. The relationship between the preludes of the two composers is underscored by the dedications of two sets: Kessler's *Préludes* op. 31 were published in 1835 by Ricordi in Milan with a dedication to Chopin, well after the two composers left Warsaw, and Chopin responded with his *Préludes* op. 28, published in 1839 with a dedication to Kessler (replaced by a dedication to Pleyel in the French edition).

Much has been said about the antecedents of Chopin's preludes and etudes, but the names of Kessler and Szymanowska are conspicuously absent from most accounts.[51] Whereas the etudes of Cramer and Moscheles, typically invoked, are important models for Chopin's op. 10, the early nineteenth-century preludes usually cited, for instance those by Hummel or Kalkbrenner, are no more than brief figurations, open-ended cadenzas of a few bars establishing a key, hardly justifying any claims to the ancestry of Chopin's op. 28. Perhaps the most important contribution of Hummel's collection to Chopin's set is its ordering: major keys moving in circle of fifths, each major key followed by its relative minor. In contrast, Szymanowska's collection and Kessler's *Préludes* present random tonal organization: Kessler employing all twenty-four major and minor keys in an unordered manner; Szymanowska drawing on an assortment of major and minor tonalities with clear preference for certain keys (for instance, setting four pieces in E-flat major and four in B-flat major). Their pieces are, however, more substantial than other contemporary works in the prelude genre, in particular Szymanowska's works, which, crossing the generic boundaries of the prelude and the etude, range between one and six pages in length. None of the pieces in Szymanowska's collection have the cadenza-like character of other contemporary preludes; instead she consistently designs them on the monothematic principle, which also becomes the rule for Chopin's op. 28. Kessler's op. 31 is more stylistically varied—some of the preludes (the first five, for instance), are typical few-

[51] Charles Rosen, *The Romantic Generation* (Cambridge, Mass.: Harvard University Press 1995), Jim Samson, *The Music of Chopin* (London: Routledge & Kegan Paul, 1985), and Samson, *Chopin* (New York: Schirmer Books, 1997) do not mention them at all; Eigeldinger, "Twenty-Four Preludes Op. 28: Genre, Structure, Significance," in *Chopin Studies 2*, ed. John Rink and Samson (Cambridge: Cambridge University Press, 1994), and Simon Finlow, "The Twenty-Seven Etudes and Their Antecedents," in *The Cambridge Companion to Chopin*, ed. Samson (Cambridge: Cambridge University Press, 1992), bring them up in passing. Finlow conflates Kessler's preludes and etudes into a nonexistent "*24 études*, op. 20, 1835," misplacing the chronology of Kessler's op. 20 in relationship to Chopin's op. 10; "The Twenty-Seven Etudes," 53.

measures cadenzas; others (among them nos. 22 and 23) are longer and more appropriately described as monothematic miniature studies. In this sense they are close precursors of Chopin's preludes, which freely cross various generic boundaries, particularly those of the prelude and the etude. Both Kessler's and Szymanowska's collections present an advanced level of technical demands, making them suitable for an ambitious amateur or an aspiring professional. Kessler's Prelude no. 9, for instance, in addition to quick repetition with the same finger, demands that the pianist's hand opens to a tenth (ex. 6.1). This kind of open position is typical of Kessler's pianistic technique and appears in other preludes and his *Études* op. 20. The etudes, in particular, demand considerable technical skills of the performer. They feature such challenges as large leaps in fast tempi, layering of melodic planes, and fast double-octave arpeggios and scales (ex. 6.2).

Kessler's and Szymanowska's compositions often employ foreground chromaticism. More notable, however, is the large-scale tonal language of their works. Szymanowska frequently makes use of bold modulations, exploring chromatic mediant relationships, as in the Prelude in D major no. 3, where the middle section is in F major, or Prelude no. 5 in B-flat Major, which moves to G major, and later to D-flat major. She also often favors modal shifts, the clearest example being the Prelude in G Minor no. 4, which actually oscillates throughout between major and minor tonic. In some works, Szymanowska shows preference for large-scale Neapolitan motions (see no. 15 in E-flat Major, where the middle section is in E major, or no. 18 in E major with a modulation to F major). The brevity of Kessler's preludes precludes bolder tonal excursions, but in the etudes he is as daring as Szymanowska. The G Major Etude no. 23, for instance, modulates to G minor, E-flat minor, and E-flat major before returning to the tonic.

Textures and figurations found in these etudes and preludes demonstrate attentiveness to the technical potential of newly constructed pianos. Some of the challenging figurations, Kessler's in particular, would not be possible on the earlier pianoforte; nor would an earlier instrument provide the extreme registers or wide dynamic range he used. Similarly, some of the textures employed in these compositions are idiomatic to the contem-

Example 6.1. Joseph Christoph Kessler, Prelude in D Major no. 9 op. 31, mm. 1–2.

Example 6.2. Joseph Christoph Kessler, Etude in C Minor no. 8 op. 20, mm. 1–4.

porary instrument. For instance, by layering sonorities—requiring that the melodic line, the bass, and the inner voices be provided with different tone qualities—the composers made use of the inherently distinct registers of their instrument. In order to bring forth these sonorities, performers had to explore the contemporary piano's natural singing tone and sensitive pedals. In some compositions, the sound layers are given further rhythmic vitality through the introduction of cross rhythms and accents.

Models established by Szymanowska and Kessler resonate in Chopin's oeuvre. Chopin's no. 14 from op. 28 echoes Kessler's no. 23 op. 31 (see exs. 6.3 and 6.4), and one can hear the textures of Szymanowska's no. 15 and Kessler's no. 9 from op. 20 in Chopin's first etude of op. 25, the A-flat Major (see exs. 6.5–7). The last one of Chopin's op. 10 etudes (no. 12 in A Minor) is foreshadowed in several fiery minor mode pieces from Kessler's op. 20, designed as right-hand chords over left-hand figurations, most notably the Etude in F sharp Minor no. 20 (see ex. 6.8). There are other direct anticipations of figurations and textures found in Chopin's preludes and etudes. Some of the most conspicuous are a section of Kessler's Prelude no. 21 foreshadowing Chopin's op. 28 no. 12 (see exs. 6.9 and 6.10), or Szymanowska's opening piece that resonates in two of Chopin's compositions: the prelude in F major and the F major etude from op. 10 (see exs. 6.11–13), the last one not only by emulating Szymanowska's figurations but also by echoing her return to the tonic via a chromatic shift from C sharp to C natural.[52] These specific features as well as the modu-

<hr />

[52] Some of these similarities have been previously pointed out by George Golos, "Some Slavic Predecessors of Chopin," *Musical Quarterly* 46 (1960): 443; Finlow, "The Twenty-Seven Etudes," 67, and Ferdynand Gajewski, preface to Joseph Christoph Kessler, 24 *Préludes* op. 31 (Kraków: Polskie Wydawnictwo Muzyczne, 1994).

Example 6.3. Joseph Christoph Kessler, Prelude in B-flat Minor no. 23 op. 31, mm. 1–4.

Example 6.4. Fryderyk Chopin, Prelude in E-flat Minor no. 14 op. 28, mm. 1–2.

latory paths these composers favored left an imprint on Chopin's style. He also adopted and expanded their approach to the sonorous potential of the nineteenth-century piano, the exploration and layering of tone colors through the use of registers and pedals, thus making way for the emancipation of sonority as a formal element.

Part and parcel of salon concerts were improvisations. Performances by outstanding improvisers were particularly sought after, and Chopin's exceptional reputation in this sphere emerged very quickly. Although he was expected to include extemporizations in his public concerts, his unrehearsed improvisations were not dazzling enough for his audiences, accustomed to the more polished "extemporizations" prepared in advance by lesser improvisers. The salon, however, was a perfect home for Chopin's spontaneous, highly poetic extemporizations, and he continued to improvise in Parisian salons even after he abandoned public career. In his earlier years in Warsaw's salons, he was often asked to extemporize. At Magnuszewski's, in the company of his Romantic peers, he did so gladly and often asked Klara, Magnuszewski's sister, to sing him a song from which he would draw hours of improvisation.[53] During 1826, at the height of

[53] Wóycicka, "Wieczorek pożegnalny Fryderyka Chopina," 1.

Example 6.5. Joseph Christoph Kessler, Etude in A-flat Major no. 9 op. 20, mm. 1–4.

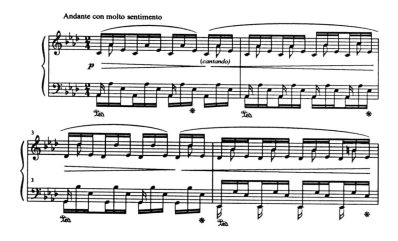

Example 6.6. Maria Szymanowska, Prelude in C Major no. 15, mm. 52–55.

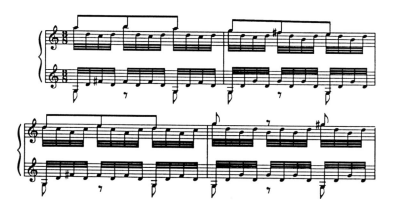

Example 6.7. Fryderyk Chopin, Etude in A-flat Major no. 1 op. 25, mm. 1–2.

Example 6.8. Joseph Christoph Kessler, Etude in F-sharp Minor no. 20 op. 20, mm. 1–4.

Example 6.9. Joseph Christoph Kessler, Prelude in E-flat Minor no. 21 op. 31, mm. 17–25.

Example 6.10. Fryderyk Chopin, Prelude in G-sharp Minor no. 12 op. 28, mm. 1–4 (top) and 19–20 (bottom).

the craze for pseudo-organs, Fryderyk was often asked to showcase newly acquired instruments. Several locally constructed eolipantalions appeared to have been purchased by the members of the Czartoryski circle: one was owned by Princess Izabela's foster daughter Zofia Kicka (née Matuszewska); another one was reported by Chopin after attending a soirée "at the Zamoyskis, where almost the entire evening they marvelled at Długosz's eolipantalion."[54] His improvisation on Kicka's eolipantalion was described many years later by Odyniec:

> After playing two or three works of other composers, he began to improvise on the last one. The mournful and solemn tones of the little organ apparently influenced the atmosphere of inspiration, which seemed to engulf him. There was universal admiration. No one was judging any more, but listening. He played and played farther on, ever more suggestively and mournfully, and he would have continued no one knew how long, had not the venerable Juljan Ursyn [Niemcewicz], noticing an unusual change and pallor of his countenance, taken pity on him. Therefore he approached him, and silently sitting by him, he took him by the hand, saying: "Enough already, enough, young man! it is time that you rest." Only then he was surrounded by everybody. Nobody dared to loudly praise him; the hostess and the guests only clasped his hands in appreciation.[55]

Odyniec's poetic account was written down more than half a century after the actual event took place, and like other posthumous texts relating to Chopin, it transmits an image of the composer already enshrined as Poland's musical prophet, the *wieszcz*. These portrayals epitomize the particularly Polish perception of Chopin as the nation's spiritual guide, whose music carried the weight of prophecy. But in a larger cultural context, these idealized narratives frame the particular role of improvisation in the construction of the specifically Romantic, related notions of genius, the artist, the poetic, and *Kunstreligion*. For the Romantics, an improvisation, as a moment of spontaneous outpouring, took on the function of a mystic revelation. In the manner of a priest or a prophet channeling the divine to the faithful, the artist served as a spiritual medium through whose agency the listeners were allowed to partake in the realm of the spirit.

Chamber Music

While the piano reigned supreme, chamber performances were also welcomed in private music-making. In 1831 we are told that "the so-called

---

[54] Chopin, Warsaw, to Białobłocki, Sokołów, [15 May 1826], *Korespondencja*, 1:65.

[55] Antoni Edward Odyniec, *Poezye* [Poems], vol. 1, *Ballady i legendy* [Ballads and legends] (Wilno: [s.n.], 1825), 325–326.

Example 6.11. Maria Szymanowska, Prelude in F Major no. 1, mm. 1–4.

Example 6.12. Fryderyk Chopin, Prelude in F Major no. 23 op. 28, mm. 1–2.

Example 6.13. Fryderyk Chopin, Etude in F Major no. 8 op. 10, mm. 1–2.

quartets are the most pleasant chamber music. In a short time the taste for this kind of music became so popular in Poland, and especially Galicia, that in every significant household one would be entertained by quartets."[56]

Chamber repertory of Warsaw's private concerts was made up of pieces by local composers as well as works composed elsewhere in Europe. Kurpiński, Elsner, and Franciszek Lessel composed a considerable amount of chamber music, often with a dedication to a specific local patron. The ensembles employed by these composers range from duos to a septet, en-

[56] Gołębiowski, *Gry i zabawy różnych stanów.*

compassing the standard forces of a string quartet or piano trio, as well as then common combinations stemming from the divertimento tradition, such as Lessel's Trio for two clarinets and a bassoon, *Parthiae,* for two clarinets, two bassoons, and two French horns, or Kurpiński's *Nocturne* op. 18 for French horn, bassoon, and viola. The language of these works is unequivocally Classical, though one finds innovative formal solutions, for instance in Kurpiński's *Fantaise en Quatuor* (discussed in chapter 3).

Some of these compositions, Lessel's in particular, are very well constructed. Even early works of Lessel, a musician of exceptional talent, demonstrate a mastery of harmony and counterpoint, and their design shows Lessel's thorough understanding of musical architecture. Their melodic style is expressive and lyrical, and their rhythms compelling and vibrant, as exemplified in the Flute Quartet op. 3, composed in 1806 and dedicated to Prince Fryderyk Lubomirski (exs. 6.14 and 6.15). But rather than exploring new trends, Lessel upheld the musical idiom of his teacher,

Example 6.14. Franciszek Lessel, Flute Quartet in G Major op. 3, Allegro, mm. 1–5 and 30–37.

Example 6.14. *continued*, mm. 30–37

Joseph Haydn. In fact, Lessel's earlier chamber works were crafted in his early years in Vienna under Haydn's watchful eye. Lessel's greatest misfortune was his failure to secure a niche as a professional musician on his return to Warsaw. Although he continued to compose first-rate chamber music, he never attained his full potential as a composer, nor did he receive recognition worthy of his talent.

The repertory of foreign chamber works available in Warsaw can be glimpsed from Wincenty Lessel's correspondence, Franciszek Lessel's estate inventory, and the early nineteenth-century holdings in the Czartoryski Library. These interrelated collections contained at one time large quantities of chamber music. Numerous early prints and manuscript copies of compositions for various ensembles by Haydn, Mozart, Dussek, Ignaz Pleyel, and Daniel Steibelt are still preserved in the Czartoryski Library. Wincenty Lessel's letters contain references to quartets by Albrechtsberger and Romberg, and quintets by Michael Haydn and Mozart.

Some of these works must have found their way to his son's impressive music collection. The music of Franciszek's teacher, Joseph Haydn, is most abundantly represented, with dozens of scores, including many chamber works. Among these, String Quartets op. 76 and op. 71/74 (dedicated to Count Anton Georg Apponyi) can be identified. Mozart's chamber compositions in Lessel's possession included several unnamed string quartets and piano trios. Among Beethoven's works in his collection we find the Violin Sonatas opp. 12, 23, 24, and 30 and a String Quintet (op. 4 or op. 29). As for chamber works with winds, Lessel's library contained Beethoven's Sonata op. 17 for piano and cello or horn; Mozart's Trio in E-flat Major K. 498 for piano, clarinet, and viola; and the two E-flat Major Wind Quintets (oboe, clarinet, horn, bassoon, and piano)—Mozart's K. 452 and Beethoven's op. 16.

From Chopin's letters we can surmise how much of his musical education came in the guise of salon chamber concerts. Performances of this sort gave him the opportunity to become acquainted with repertory not heard in concert (by listening to or participating in performances). They also provided him with a venue through which he could test and customize his own compositions. For instance, he writes about an upcoming evening at Michał Lewicki's, the commandant of Warsaw, where Hummel's *Sentinella* ["La sentinelle," song for voice, violin, guitar or cello, cello and double bass ad lib., op. 71] will be performed: Prince Galitsin will play Rodin's quartet [*sic*], and "my polonaise with the cello, to which I added an Adagio introduction especially for Kaczyński. We tried it and it will do."[57]

Particularly engaging were the musical soirées at the Cichockis, who had great fondness for chamber music. Count Józef took part in the chamber performances at his home as a flutist. Not only did he inspire the dedications of several chamber compositions, but also he himself transcribed Onslow's Eighth String Quintet in D Minor, op. 24 for flute, violin, viola, cello, and bass (the transcription was published by Breitkopf & Härtel in 1833 and was favorably received by reviewers).[58] Chopin, who frequented his salon, tells of a performance in which he participated:

> Yesterday I was at Cichocki's, the heavy fellow's, for his name-day celebration. I played in Spohr's Quintetto for piano, clarinet, bassoon, French horn and flute [C Major, op. 52]. Most beautiful. But terribly uncomfortable for the hand; everything that he deliberately wanted to write as a display for the piano is insurmountably difficult and often it is impossible to find fingerings.[59]

Chopin learned the most at Kessler's Friday soirées, where Warsaw's best musicians, professionals and amateurs, gathered for "quartets" and made music ad lib—without a prearranged program.[60] It is at Kessler's that Chopin heard Spohr's Otteto (E Major, op. 32), which he thought incredibly beautiful.[61] On other occasion, in October 1829, he witnessed performances of Ries's Concerto in C-sharp Minor (in "quartet" version), Hummel's Trio in E Major (probably op. 83), Prince Ferdinand's Quatuor (which contemporaries incorrectly suspected to be the work of Dussek) and Beethoven's last trio (the *Archduke*, B-flat Major, op. 97), which left Chopin dumbfounded: "it's a long time since I heard something equally great; there Beethoven mocks the whole world."[62] At the time Chopin became first acquainted with the *Archduke*, he was completing his own Piano Trio, perhaps the most successful of his early compositions.

[57] Chopin, Warsaw, to Woyciechowski, 10 April 1830, *Korespondencja*, 1:117–118.

[58] *Allgemeine musikalische Zeitung*, December 1833, 824.

[59] Chopin, Warsaw, to Woyciechowski, Poturzyn, 18 September, 1830, *Korespondencja*, 1:139.

[60] Chopin, Warsaw, to Woyciechowski, Poturzyn, 20 October 1829, *Korespondencja*, 1:110.

[61] Chopin, Warsaw, to Woyciechowski, Poturzyn, 3 October [1]829, *Korespondencja*, 1:108.

[62] Chopin, Warsaw, to Woyciechowski, Poturzyn, 20 October 1829, *Korespondencja*, 1:110.

The Trio in G Minor, op. 8 was composed for Prince Antoni Radziwiłł, a great music lover, an accomplished cellist, and a fairly successful composer. Radziwiłł, married to the Hohenzollern princess Friederike Dorothea Luise (the niece of Frederick II the Great) and holding the post of plenipotentiary to the Prussian king, was one of the most powerful men in Poland. He mingled in the highest musical circles in Europe and was the dedicatee of major works, including Beethoven's Overture *Zur Namensfeier* op. 115 from and Mendelssohn's Piano Quartet in C Minor, op. 1. In the late 1820s, the paths of Radziwiłł and Chopin frequently intersected— the young composer visited the prince's musical salons in his residences in Berlin and in Antonin near Poznań; they would meet during Radziwiłł's periodic visits in Warsaw; and there are even unconfirmed rumors of the prince contributing financially to Chopin's education.[63] Chopin thought the prince a very good cellist and a talented composer; he especially praised his music to Goethe's *Faust*, which he found unexpectedly inventive, with traces of genius:

> Among others, there is one scene in which Mephistopheles tempts Gröthen [Gretchen] [while] playing the guitar and singing at her window, and at the same time choral chants are heard from the nearby church. This contrast makes a great effect in performance; on paper one sees artificially put together chant, more [like] a diabolic accompaniment to very somber chant. From this you can get the sense of his manner of understanding music; in addition [he is] a rabid Gluckist. Theater music is significant to him only in its capacity to paint situations and emotions—that is why even the overture has no ending, but continues directly into the introduction, and the orchestra is always offstage, so that the movement of the bows, exertion, and blowing would not be seen.[64]

[63] The statements concerning Radziwiłł's financial support for Chopin's studies are highly debatable. The earliest assertion of help from Radziwiłł comes from the perennially unreliable Liszt. Marceli A. Szulc later admitted that his claim is entirely based on Liszt, and that he had no other evidence to support it. Marceli A. Szulc, *Fryderyk Chopin i utwory jego muzyczne*, 278–279. Sowiński also reports that Radziwiłł was paying for Chopin's education, but his account of the events is similarly contestable. Sowiński, *Słownik muzyków polskich dawnych i nowoczesnych*, 54. Given the undependability of these claims, the only report stemming from a source close to the Chopins is Oskar Kolberg's clear declaration that Radziwiłł "much contributed to Chopin's education." Kolberg, "Chopin," 459. Liszt's, Szulc's, Sowiński's, and Kolberg's claims are vehemently opposed by other writers. Karasowski, writing on the authority of Chopin's sisters and mother, firmly denies any help from Radziwiłł. Karasowski, *Chopin*, 62–66. A similar position is taken by Julian Fontana, who firmly believes that Radziwiłł did not support Chopin in, he says, the gymnasium; Krystyna Kobylańska, *Chopin w kraju: Dokumenty i pamiątki* [Chopin in his own land: documents and souvenirs] (Kraków: Polskie Wydawnictwo Muzyczne, 1955), 193.

[64] Chopin, Warsaw, to Woyciechowski, Poturzyn, 14 [November] 1829, *Korespondencja*, 1:112–114.

During that one-week stay in Antonin, in November of 1829, when Chopin's gave piano instruction to Radziwiłł's musically gifted seventeen-year-old daughter Wanda, he composed his Polonaise op. 3 for the pleasure of the princess and her father. As the composer himself acknowledged, op. 3 is pure glitter.[65] In contrast, the Piano Trio, inscribed with a dedication to Prince Radziwiłł and delivered shortly before his sojourn in Antonin, is an early masterpiece in which the composer's own voice is heard.

Chopin began work on his Trio already in late summer of 1828, and by September the first Allegro was ready for rehearsal.[66] A year later, the work was still not completed, perhaps because the recognition that the Trio was destined for publication abroad and that it needed to impress a potential patron weighed heavily on the young composer.[67] When it was finally completed, the composer found it entirely satisfactory, so much so that he continued to perform it in private as late as 1847 and gave it to his pupils to play.

The progressive character of this work has been obscured by presumptions concerning the history of the piano trio genre. Opus 8 has been criticized for the brilliant piano score, incompetent writing for the strings, and formal shortcomings. These criticisms do not hold up under closer scrutiny when the chronology of the piano trio genre is considered. Both Schubert trios are late works, not even published at the time Chopin began working on his trio; Mendelssohn's trios were still far off in the future; and Beethoven's later trios were new and known to few—most composers of the time followed Mozartian models. Mozart's ancestry is clearly recognizable in Chopin's work, especially in the notation of the manuscript where the piano part is placed between the violin and cello parts (the first editions are in parts only; the scores issued much later place both string instruments above the piano part). The virtuoso piano texture is also Mozartian.

In other respects, however, Chopin is closer to Beethoven's model.[68] Op. 8 is in four movements, with Adagio as third and Scherzo as second movements. The much-criticized tonal plan of the first movement, where the second theme remains in the tonic in the exposition, but modulates in the recap, results in a shifting of the dramatic focal point to the second part of the moment. Such tonal plan, evading strong movement closure, works better in achieving cyclic continuity. The brilliant writing for the piano is not an anomaly—it persisted throughout the nineteenth cen-

[65] Chopin, Warsaw, to Woyciechowski, Poturzyn, 14 [November] 1829, *Korespondencja*, 1:112.

[66] Chopin, Warsaw, to Woyciechowski, Poturzyn, 9 September 1828, *Korespondencja*, 1:79.

[67] Chopin mentions the plans for publication in his letter to Tytus; Chopin, Warsaw, to Woyciechowski, Poturzyn, 9 September 1828, *Korespondencja*, 1: 79.

[68] Several of my points have been made before by others, most lucidly in Andrzej Chodkowski, "Notes on Chopin's *Piano Trio*," *Chopin Studies* 2 (1987): 55–63.

tury, the imbalance of the instrumental texture in favor of the piano being typical of the piano trio genre. In fact, Chopin is more attentive to the role of the strings than most of his contemporaries: the violin and cello parts, though not as virtuosic as the piano, contain all the important melodic and thematic material, and the lush piano figurations are often intended as accompaniment to the strings—such textural relationship would have been facilitated by the more natural balance between instruments used in Chopin's time.

The importance of the strings' lyrical role is most apparent in the Adagio sostenuto, one of the most exquisite and expressive movements composed by the young Chopin. This and the first movements, in their intense lyricism, emulate early Romantic chamber works, Onslow's, Weber's and Spohr's in particular. As for the charges of incompetent writing for the violin by almost completely excluding the E string, it is clear that Chopin simply sought the darker timbre of the violin's low register and a better balance between the higher string instrument and the cello. He made several references to replacing the violin with a viola, "because in the violin the fifth resonates the most and therefore is used the least; the viola is going to be stronger against the cello, which is written in its normal range; and this [would be for use] in print."[69] Indeed when he first submitted the work for publication to Farrenc, the work was described as "Trio en sol min., pour Piano, Violon ou Alto & Violoncelle."[70] Composing with substitute instrumentation in mind was common during the nineteenth century: for instance, all of Onslow's string quintets were published with substitute parts, allowing the lower cello part to be taken by a double bass or the higher one by a viola. Perhaps the ultimate choice of violin over the viola for the printed version reflects the publisher's marketing choice rather than Chopin's aesthetic preference.

Chopin's contemporaries appreciated his novel approach to the trio genre. In recognition of the new role of the strings as principal carriers of the melodic and thematic material, the first English edition (1833) hailed Chopin's op. 8 as the "First Grand Trio for Piano Forte, Violin and Violoncello Concertant," "Book 1" of "Wessel & Co.'s Series of Modern Trios" (fig. 6.4) For them it was evident that the way the piano part often took backstage to the lyrical melodies of the strings was unlike in the majority of older trios.

The Scherzo movement of the Trio is a tour de force of rhythmic ingenuity and elasticity, heralding some features of Chopin's mature style. Al-

[69] Chopin, Warsaw, to Woyciechowski, Poturzyn, 31 August [18]30, *Korespondencja*, 1:132.

[70] Aristide Farrenc, Paris, to Friedrich Kistner, Leipzig, 17 April 1832, in Zofia Lissa, "Chopin w świetle korespondencji współczesnych mu wydawców" [Chopin in light of the correspondence of his contemporary publishers], *Muzyka* 5 (1960): 7. Ultimately, his works were published in Paris by Schlesinger rather than Farrenc.

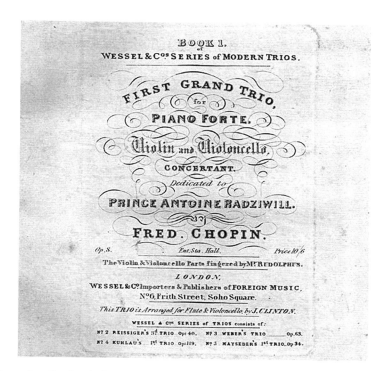

Figure 6.4. Fryderyk Chopin, Piano Trio in G Minor op. 8 (London: Wessel & Co., [1833]), title page. University of Chicago Library, Special Collections Research Center, ff M312.C54T83 c.1.

though the first section is organized in regular four-bar phrases, from the very first note, the composer undermines regular metric organization, by shifting the perception of bar lines in the piano part through the use of ties and accents on weak beats. A similar effect is accomplished in measures 13–16, with the strings carrying the offbeat groupings and the piano's top line further destabilizing the sense of metric organization with eighth-note syncopations. In the second section, starting with measure 26, Chopin intensifies the disturbances of metric symmetry by obscuring or even abandoning the regular four-bar phrases that underlie bar line shifts and syncopations. In combination with the pervasive chromaticism, the effect is almost dizzying (ex. 6.16). The Scherzo's trio, in contrast, is direct and unmarred by any appearances of disorder, its naiveté underscored by the diatonicism, as well as the *sotto voce* and *dolce* markings. This contrast reinforces the impact of the Scherzo's rhythmic complexity, bringing to the fore Chopin's extraordinary compositional skill.

Chopin learned about phrase structure from Elsner, who considered it an important element of compositional craft and gave it much attention in his instruction (see chapter 4). In this work, however, Chopin went be-

Example 6.16. Fryderyk Chopin, Piano Trio in G Minor op. 8, Scherzo, mm. 26–45.

yond models provided in his teacher's lessons, searching for inspiration in the works of other composers. Elsner stressed to his students the limits of instruction and encouraged them to learn from the masters and then follow their own musical intuition:

One cannot teach invention. Theory and skill provide true preparation only for those who were not denied talent by nature. Yet it is an unquestionable truth that one cannot attain great talent without some work and diligence. That is why the advice for a music devotee, composer in particular, is—while assiduously exercising singing and playing—to listen to good works of singers and virtuosos as much as possible in order to obtain various distinct musical thoughts of true and beautiful expression. Not only to exploit them in his inspiration, but mostly so that through the diverse rhythmic and metric variants he can discover their effects, in particular noticing of what sets and changes expression, and whether this or another temporal form enhances or spoils the melody.[71]

[71] "Rozprawa o melodyi i śpiewie" [Treatise on melody and chant], Biblioteka XX Czartoryskich, Ms. 2276.

Example 6.16. *continued*

Specifically concerning irregular groupings of measures, Elsner advised the young composer not to count the measures in a group but rather follow a gut feeling. This feeling, however, had to be formed through "hearing, playing and analysis of musical works, or at least by the means of certain inner conviction, easily found through simply understood structure of ideas and periods in dances by anybody whom nature did not deny a sense of meter."[72]

Chopin would have been exposed to plenty of inspiring models in honing his compositional intuition. Some of the most interesting models for metric irregularities in minuet/scherzo movements would be found in the works of Haydn, which were often performed in Warsaw. Other examples of the Haydnesque tradition were available to him through the works of George Onslow, whose minuet movements (for instance in op. 9 no. 1) feature complex rhythms and who frequently shifts the minuet (often really a scherzo) movement to the second position. A local representative of this tradition was Haydn's pupil Franciszek Lessel, whose minuet of the Flute

[72] "Rozprawa o melodyi i śpiewie."

Example 6.17. Franciszek Lessel, Flute Quartet in G Major op. 3, Minuetto Allegro, mm. 15–22.

Quartet op. 3 contains numerous examples of procedures shifting the sense of the bar line by the means of accented offbeats (ex. 6.17).

The innovative rhythmic features of Chopin's work force a comparison with the *Archduke* Trio. His remark about Beethoven mocking the whole world hints at the character of the *Archduke*'s Scherzo: Beethoven begins with a naïve, almost insipid tune, and by the trio section, through bar line shifts and syncopations, and pervasive chromaticism, he reaches the same dizzying effect as Chopin's Scherzo from op. 8. In light of Radziwiłł's admiration for Beethoven, whom he knew personally and whose quartets were regularly performed at Radziwiłł's soirées, it is only natural that Chopin would reach for Beethoven's compositions as a model for his trio. Given the short time interval between the completion of op. 8 and Chopin's first hearing (judging from the tone of his comments) of the *Archduke,* one would be hard pressed to make a conclusive case for direct influence of this particular work. The correspondences, however, are remarkable and underscore the proximity between Beethoven's models and Chopin's first youthful masterpiece.

Transcriptions of Orchestral Works

In addition to music specifically designated for private performing spaces, the salon invited performances of public music—operatic, concert, and symphonic—in transcription. The most informal of these transcriptions were for the piano (two or four hands) or, in the case of operatic works, voice accompanied by the piano. Some of these, mostly operatic works, were published in Poland; others were imported from abroad, for instance William Crotch's transcriptions of Mozart's symphonies, overtures by Mozart and Beethoven published in London, Handel's oratorios issued by Haslinger in Vienna, and *The Creation* and *Die Sieben letzten Worte unseres Erlösers am Kreuze* of Haydn—all found in the Czartoryski Library. Obviously, piano arrangements were used by amateurs as a means of disseminating favorite and fashionable compositions.[73] But they also served the serious musician and music lover in becoming more intimately acquainted with orchestral works. Their importance did not escape the attention of Elsner, who argued that studying piano arrangements was more advantageous to a young composer than studying full scores. In his unrealized plan for a music dictionary, an anthology of musical examples for aspiring young composers, he envisioned a selection of "classical compositions arranged in piano-vocal score." He explained that "full score would not be needed, because employing the resources provided by contemporary progress in music, for instance instrumental color, would not be the young composer's main objective, and because working from the full score would encourage slavish copying instead of disguising borrowed concepts through various means."[74] This conclusion is consistent with his instruction, which stressed structure and expression, attained through melodic, rhythmic, and harmonic ideas. Instrumental color was to him of secondary importance.

Transcriptions for chamber groups, on the other hand, allowed for the approximation of the composition's original sonorities. Such arrangements, often referred to as "quartets," were frequently used in Warsaw salons. The term "quartets" [*kwartety*] was used in Poland not just to denote an ensemble of four instruments but to designate a variety of chamber groups. It referred to chamber music in general, and it also described salon-size ensembles performing orchestral music. All evidence suggests that, while chamber performances of orchestral works (or works with orchestra) were very much a part of the early nineteenth-century tradition, the ensemble size was by no means fixed: on occasion, quartet in-

---

[73] Thomas Christensen, "Four-Hand Piano Transcriptions and Geographies of Nineteenth-Century Musical Reception," *Journal of the American Musicological Society* 52 (1999): 255–298.

[74] "Rozprawa o melodyi i śpiewie."

struments were doubled, and a double bass was added, resulting in a nonet performance; in other instances, obbligato or ad libitum winds would be included in the transcription. Another apparently popular option was a chamber orchestra of some thirteen members (typically four violins, viola, cello, double bass, flute, two oboes or clarinets, two French horns, and a bassoon). This group, perfect for salons, was deemed inappropriate for large performing spaces; a sound that was marvelous in a salon would get lost in the vast space of a theater.[75]

Whereas the chamber orchestra would simply read from the existing orchestral parts, the other ensembles required appropriate transcriptions. Indeed, arranging symphonic compositions for chamber groups was remarkably popular during the nineteenth century, as is readily shown by a glance at the never-ending lists of concertos and flashy virtuoso works, overtures, symphonies, and even dramatic works in publishers' catalogues. Everywhere in Europe, hundreds of chamber arrangements were published: pieces by contemporaries and masters of past eras; works by minor composers and Beethoven's symphonies; compositions featuring the piano and other solo instruments; arrangements labeled quartet or quintet, and sometimes calling for additional instruments.[76]

It is apparent that this manner of performance was common in Poland, since there are many reports of such performances and many scores of this sort have survived in Poland. The Czartoryski Library contains several such chamber versions of symphonies and concerti, for instance Dussek's concerti for "clavecin ou forté piano, deux violins, alto, basse, deux hautbois et deux cors."[77] Arrangements were also provided by local musicians. For instance, Count Cichocki's Monday gatherings directly inspired Chopin's peer and a talented amateur composer, Konstanty Wolicki, to make arrangements of orchestral works for chamber performances. Some years after Chopin's departure from Warsaw, Wolicki arranged several symphonies and overtures by Beethoven, Mendelssohn, Onslow, and Dobrzyński for a double string quartet plus a bass.[78]

The tradition of private performances of orchestral works by chamber ensembles was of great consequence to Chopin.[79] He had numerous opportunities to hear such performances, and he participated in several. For instance, he reports a "quartet" performance of Ries's Concerto in

[75] *Tygodnik muzyczny i dramatyczny*, 23 May 1821, 26.
[76] See for instance Carl Friedrich Whistling and Adolph Moritz Hofmeister, *Handbuch der musikalischen Literatur 1829* (1829; reprint, Hildesheim: Olms, 1975).
[77] Biblioteka Czartoryskich, Kraków, 99561/III.
[78] *Ruch muzyczny*, 1857, no. 4, 28.
[79] For an in-depth study of this topic see Halina Goldberg, "Chamber Arrangements of Chopin's Concert Works," *Journal of Musicology* 19 (2002): 39–84.

C-sharp Minor in 1829 at Kessler's salon.[80] The public performances of his own concerti, in 1830, were preceded by a number of rehearsals at the Chopins' salon in the Krasiński Palace. On August 31, Chopin informed his friend Tytus Woyciechowski of a planned rehearsal of the entire concerto "in quartet."[81] Some two weeks later, Tytus was told that the rehearsal actually occurred (with considerable delay), that the performance left Chopin moderately content, and that another practice with "quartet" was planned before an orchestral rehearsal.[82] Fryderyk himself explained the purpose of "quartet" rehearsal, saying: "already this week I am to rehearse the entire Concerto [E Minor] in quartet, so that at first this quartet can communicate with me—get accustomed a bit—without which, says Elsner, an orchestral rehearsal would not proceed smoothly."[83] The benefits of such rehearsal to the performer and the conductor are apparent, but Chopin says clearly that the intention is for the orchestra to become acquainted with the work. If we keep in mind that the term "quartet" denotes more than the customary four string instruments, it makes perfect sense that, when the leaders of each orchestral section have an opportunity to first familiarize themselves with the ensemble sound of the composition, it makes for a more efficient rehearsal with the full orchestra.

Because of the trend of hosting musical soirées, Chopin was able to reap the benefits of participating in daily music-making sessions with experienced elders and peers. There he could master the skills and enjoy the pleasures of a chamber musician, play intimate and lyrical music in an environment free of the public concert spectacle. Perhaps nothing captures the intimate, unpretentious atmosphere of a connoisseur's salon better than an article sent to a Warsaw newspaper during Paganini's visit to the Polish capital in 1829. It describes this acrobat of the concert stage in the stunningly unexpected role of a lyrical chamber musician during a private performance:

> Whereas in public concerts this great virtuoso amazes with fluency, overcoming extraordinary difficulties and bringing heretofore unknown sounds out of the instrument, in quartets a new [experience], almost ecstasy, intoxicates the senses of the listener. The cause is in the very

[80] Chopin, Warsaw, to Woyciechowski, Poturzyn, 20 October 1829, *Korespondencja*, I:110.

[81] Chopin, Warsaw, to Woyciechowski, Poturzyn, 31 August 1830, *Korespondencja*, I:132.

[82] Chopin, Warsaw, to Woyciechowski, Poturzyn, 18 September 1830, *Korespondencja*, I:138.

[83] Chopin, Warsaw, to Woyciechowski, Poturzyn, 31 August 1830, *Korespondencja*, I:132.

difference in the compositions themselves; furthermore (unlike in concert), he does not try to impress the general audience with the use of means known to him only, but plays without additions, with a moving simplicity and ease typical of himself, yet he amazes and touches.[84]

Such a description and others like it indicate that the nineteenth-century connoisseur salon should be viewed as a continuation of the eighteenth-century chamber. While the concert stage presented the public persona—the artist for the broader audience—the salon was a home of the private artist performing with and for other musicians and educated amateurs. A contemporary of Chopin who heard him play on many occasions maintained:

> Fryderyk Chopin did not like to perform in public. Although he could bring forth from the piano a powerful and ringing sound, his playing was too learned and did not make an impression in a big room. Since he deeply felt the music and liked tender melodies, he was better understood in a small circle.[85]

In the same vein, Chopin was reported to have instructed a student: "concerts are never real music; you have to give up the idea of hearing in them the most beautiful things of art."[86] In fact, there is plenty of evidence to suggest that Chopin espoused the aesthetic of a chamber musician and that he did not train his students to be concert musicians. With all that in mind, we must come finally to realize that Chopin chose the salon over the concert stage precisely because it was the better forum for a serious musician and for sophisticated compositions, a place that nurtured him into his intellectual and musical maturity.

[84] *Kurier warszawski*, 18 July 1829, no. 189, 848.

[85] Sowiński, *Słownik muzyków polskich dawnych i nowoczesnych*, 53.

[86] Jean-Jacques Eigeldinger, *Chopin: Pianist and Teacher as Seen by his Pupils*, trans. N. Shohet with K. Osostowicz and R. Howat (Cambridge: Cambridge University Press, 1986), 5.

7

MUSICAL THEATER

It was a great hope of Chopin's family, teachers, and friends that one day he would become the great Polish national opera composer. His friend the poet Stefan Witwicki said it clearest in a letter to Fryderyk during the November Uprising from the besieged Warsaw:

> You absolutely must be the creator of Polish opera; I am deeply con-
> vinced that you are capable of becoming one, and as a Polish national
> composer you will open for your talent a new, immensely rich domain,
> in which you will achieve exceptional fame. . . . I am certain, that
> Slavic opera, brought to life by true talent, by a feeling and thinking
> composer, will one day shine in the world like a new sun—maybe it
> will even surpass all others—and it will have as much melodiousness
> as Italian opera, much more tenderness and incomparably more
> thought. . . . You will be the first one who knows how to draw on the
> rich treasures of Slavic melody.[1]

[1] Stefan Witwicki, Warsaw, to Fryderyk Chopin, Vienna, 6 July 1831, in *Korespondencja Fryderyka Chopina* [Fryderyk Chopin's correspondence], ed. Bronisław Edward Sydow, 2 vols. (Warsaw: Państwowy Instytut Wydawniczy, 1955), 1:179. The history of musical culture of Warsaw, concentrating on concert and opera stage, has been studied in a handful of articles and three master's theses of varied quality: Magdalena Kwiatkowska, "Kultura muzyczna Warszawy w latach 1795–1806" [Musical culture of Warsaw in the years 1795–1806] (master's thesis, University of Warsaw, 1981); Anna Bućko, "Kultura muzyczna Warszawy w latach 1807–1815" [Musical culture of Warsaw in the years 1807–1815] (master's thesis, University of Warsaw, 1982); and Halina Sieradz, "Kultura muzyczna Warszawy w latach 1815–1830" [Musical culture of Warsaw in the years 1815–1830] (master's thesis, University of Warsaw, 1983). Also pertinent is Alina Nowak-Romanowicz, chapter entitled "Opera," in *Klasycyzm 1750–1830* [Classicism 1750–1830], vol. 4 of *Historia muzyki polskiej*, ed. S. Sutkowski (Warsaw: S. Sutkowski, 1995).

After the collapse of the Uprising, Chopin's sister Ludwika and Józef Elsner both wrote to Fryderyk on the subject of opera. Ludwika said:

> Mr. Elsner does not want to see you only as concertizer, piano composer and a famous performer, because this is easier and means less than the composition of operas, but he wants to see you follow your nature as it predisposes and compels you. You have your [illegible word] place between Rossini, Mozart, etc. Your genius may not rest with the piano and concerts; you must immortalize yourself through operas.[2]

Even as late as 1834, Elsner still expressed hope of one day hearing an opera composed by his most talented pupil: "While I am still walking in this vale of tears, I would like to live to see an opera composed by you—not only for the augmentation of your fame, but also for the general advancement of the musical art brought by your composition of this kind (in particular, if the subject of the opera is from Polish history)."[3] Initially these hopes were shared by Fryderyk, who loved opera and who embraced the ideology that placed national opera at the top of musical hierarchy, both politically and aesthetically. It is no wonder that Chopin felt this way, growing up in a city saturated with the sounds of opera.

History of Opera Theater in Warsaw

Poland had a long tradition of court theaters, not only at the royal palace but also in the residences of the aristocracy. In 1724, a theater open to the public was constructed at the initiative of King August II, who with great pleasure attended the new theater and liberally endowed it from his own treasury. Since the king enjoyed a full-house performance, the people of Warsaw were invited to attend foreign ballets and operas free of charge. After the monarch's death, the theater lost its splendor, and it had to be demolished for safety reasons in 1772.[4]

In the meantime, the first Polish public theater was opened in Warsaw in 1765. It moved several times and frequently changed owners until 1779, when under the auspices of King Stanisław August, the national stage known as the National Theater (*Teatr Narodowy*) was founded.[5] The National Theater was housed at Krasiński Plaza, in a building belonging

[2] Ludwika Chopin, Warsaw, to Fryderyk Chopin, Paris, 27 November 1831, *Korespondencja*, 1:192.

[3] Elsner, Warsaw, to Chopin, Paris, 14 September 1834, *Korespondencja*, 1:246.

[4] Antoni Magier, *Estetyka miasta stołecznego Warszawy* [The aesthetics of the capital city of Warsaw] (1830 manuscript), ed. Hanna Szwankowska (Wrocław: Wydawnictwo Ossolińskich, 1963), 255–57.

[5] Magier, *Estetyka miasta stołecznego Warszawy*, 257–258.

to Countess Tyszkiewicz (the sister of Prince Józef Poniatowski). Originally the building was capable of holding an audience of 800, but in 1791 it was rebuilt to accommodate about 1200 people.[6] The theater's first director was the celebrated actor and writer Wojciech Bogusławski, the man who established the Polish national stage and led it for the first few decades of its existence. The new theater was not destined to flourish freely: already by 1794 its existence was disrupted by the Kościuszko Insurrection. Because of his political affiliations, Bogusławski left for Lwów, but he returned to Warsaw in 1799, bringing along the young Józef Elsner, an energetic, skillful musician who would take on the responsibilities of a musical director. Elsner's duties as the musical director of the National Theater included casting, vocal coaching, preparation of the chorus, soloists, and orchestra, and selection of the music to be performed during intermissions. He was also expected to compose new operas and music for special events.[7] Bogusławski's and Elsner's work was repeatedly intruded on by censorship, political intrigue, or disastrous historic events. Yet, in spite of difficulties, they persisted and succeeded in establishing the institution of a public theater staging plays and operas.

In addition to the National Theater's cast, Warsaw audiences were entertained by other theatrical troupes, which usually performed at the Radziwiłł Theater. Among foreign troupes working in Warsaw were Vincenzo Chiavacci's Italian theater ensemble, performing in the Polish capital in the years 1801–1803; François Gabriel Ledoux's ballet ensemble working in collaboration with French actors (1803–1805), later replaced by a French group of Fourès (1805–1806); and a German ensemble under Carl Döbbelin, which arrived in Warsaw in 1804, but encountered competition of a local German group that was directed by Bogusławski during the 1804–1806 seasons.[8]

The audiences of opera spectacles included nobility, landowners, and intelligentsia, and some craftsmen and better paid servants frequented theaters.[9] Members of the German administration and military were actively involved in theater life, the most active of them being E. T. A. Hoffmann, who was stationed in Warsaw during the years 1804–1807 (see chapter 8). During this period, the National Theater, unlike the foreign institutions in Warsaw, had neither benches nor chairs. The parterre was a great hall in which the audience constantly moved to greet each other, pay visits to ladies' boxes, converse, comment, and eat. This movement ceased only if there was an unusual crowd or particularly interesting

[6] Wielisław [Eugeniusz Skrodzki], *Wieczory piątkowe i inne gawędy* [Friday evenings and other tales], ed. M. Opałek (Warsaw: Państwowy Instytut Wydawniczy, 1962), 65.

[7] Kwiatkowska, "Kultura muzyczna Warszawy w latach 1795–1806," 27.

[8] Kwiatkowska, "Kultura muzyczna Warszawy w latach 1795–1806," 50–54.

[9] Kwiatkowska, "Kultura muzyczna Warszawy w latach 1795–1806," 24.

events on the stage seized the attention of the audience. Yet this atmosphere was integral to the national stage, and should the administration have decided to put in chairs and introduce order, the theater would have lost much of its audience. The higher echelon of theater-goers called *la société* belittled the use of the Polish language, and showed contempt for the actors, the memories of the historical past, and the sentimental patriotism. They preferred the private French theater of Mme. Vauban or Chiavacci's Italian opera.[10]

The repertory of the National Theater consisted of various types of spoken and musical plays, as well as ballet. The musical performances run a full range of genres—Liederspiel, Singspiel, vaudeville, opéra comique, tragedie lyrique, opera seria and buffa, and grand opera. The opera repertory at the turn of the century included foreign as well as Polish operas. It was dominated by Italian works, mainly by Cimarosa, Paisiello, Anfossi, Salieri's *Axur* and *Palmira*, and Mozart's *Don Giovanni*. Polish works followed; the most interest was given to Stefani's *Cracovians and Highlanders* and Kamieński's *Misery Made Happy*. Some German operas were introduced, most notably *Die Zauberflöte* and *Die Entführung aus dem Serail* of Mozart, and *Das unterbrochene Opferfest* of Winter. Among the few French operas performed in Warsaw at the turn of the century were compositions by Méhul, Dalayrac, Grétry, and *Les Deux Journees* and *Lodoïska* of Cherubini.[11]

In spite of financial losses caused by the Napoleonic wars, the popularity of the National Theater increased. In 1809, the administration of the theater initiated season tickets for loges, attempting to raise its revenue by eliminating unauthorized free admissions:

> in the last few years the number of persons entering the Theater free of charge became so large that one can count up to a hundred people . . . so many squeeze into the Theater under various pretenses and neither their persons nor names are known to the Theater's management.[12]

In the economically unstable climate and the political disasters of the Napoleonic period, the theater was able to survive and flourish, partly due to the support of King Frederick August, the Saxon ruler of Poland, who represented Napoleon's administration.

Much artistic momentum during the Duchy of Warsaw and the ensuing Congress Kingdom periods was generated by the talented, young

[10] Skarbek, *Pamiętniki Seglasa* [Seglas's memoirs], ed. K. Bartoszyński [Warsaw: Państwowy Instytut Wydawniczy, 1959], 150–151.

[11] Kwiatkowska, "Kultura muzyczna Warszawy w latach 1795–1806," chart following p. 39.

[12] The public announcement for a performance of *Ciche Wody Brzegi Rwą*, a comedy translated from German, 15 October 1809, specifies the new ticketing policy. Zakład Dokumentacji Życia Społecznego, Biblioteka Narodowa, Warsaw.

Karol Kurpiński. In 1810 Kurpiński joined Elsner as music director of the National Theater. Initially Elsner and Kurpiński worked well together, but growing disagreements led Elsner to resign in 1824, leaving Kurpiński as the musical director. Bogusławski also retired and left Ludwik Osiński, the critic, poet, and professor of literature at the University of Warsaw, who was also his son-in-law, in charge of the National Theater. Kurpiński continued in this capacity until 1840, conducting most of the performances and selecting repertory.

During the first years of Kurpiński's tenure—partially because of the changing taste of the audiences and the new political environment, but also due to Kurpiński's own preferences—Polish works led the repertory, with French operas following (Paër, Gaveaux, Dalayrac, Mayr, Isouard, Cherubini, Méhul); Italian and German productions were least favored.[13] In the 1820s, after Kurpiński's European trip, the presence of Italian operas increased. This change was conditioned both by Kurpiński's admiration for Rossini and by the intrusion of Russian censorship in reaction to the proliferation of Polish operas. There were many fewer historical Polish operas, since the authorities carefully scrutinized them for political content. Instead of politico-historical subject matter, Polishness was now manifested through the use of folk-inspired music, and thus the Polish operas of the 1820s were increasingly saturated with tunes that evoked real or imagined folklore. The foreign composers most often premiered at the National Theater during the 1820s were Rossini and Boieldieu. At the same time, audiences adored works as dissimilar as *Der Freischütz* of Weber, *La vestale* of Spontini, and *Der Bauer als Millionär* of Drechsler, the latter staged by the newly established Variety Theater (*Teatr Rozmaitości*).

The Variety Theater was the most important among other theatrical institutions active in Warsaw during the period of the Congress Kingdom.[14] It was created by the artists of the National Theater in 1829, in response to the Russian authorities' attempts to censor and control the theater repertory.[15] The goal was to provide a more popular stage and to

[13] Bućko, "Kultura muzyczna Warszawy w latach 1807–1815," 59–60.

[14] The French Theater, which was brought to Warsaw mainly for the pleasure of Grand Duke Constantine, produced many notable stagings of Molière, Destouches, and Beaumarchais, but due to the lack of good singers, it could not compete with the National Theater in opera production. Wielisław, *Wieczory piątkowe i inne gawędy*, 65. The institution, however, was active until the period of the November Uprising and was well known to Chopin. See Fryderyk Chopin, Warsaw, to Tytus Woyciechowski, Poturzyn, 9 September 1828, *Korespondencja*, 1:86; and Chopin, Warsaw, to Woyciechowski, Poturzyn, 27 December 1828, *Korespondencja*, 1:78.

[15] The Russian authorities, in the person of Novosil'cov, reacted with fear to the increasingly national character of Polish operas. To counterbalance this patriotic mood, Rożaniecki and Novosil'cov initiated the creation of an alternative Polish stage devoted to a lighter, apolitical repertory: *Teatr Polski* (the Polish Theater).

make the plays accessible to everyone, but at the same time include moral values for the common people.[16] The National Theater stayed with the more ambitious repertory of opera, and the new venue provided a lighter repertory of vaudevilles, farces and comic operas. The Variety Theater functioned side by side with the National Theater until the November Uprising; the two theaters shared the same staff, singers, and orchestra, and performed on alternate days.

Józef Damse's adaptation of the vaudeville *Mädchen aus der Feenwelt, oder Der Bauer als Millionär* (*Chłop milionowy, czyli Dziewczyna ze świata czarownego*), written by Ferdinand Raimund and set to music by Josef Drechsler, was staged by the Variety Theater at the end of 1829 and won unrivaled popularity. Conceived in the Viennese magic opera tradition typical of the Theater in der Leopoldstadt, *Der Bauer* was a nonsensical play with splendid decorations and machinery: Chopin thought the play foolish and infantile.[17] Mochnacki described it as

> comic-satiric-harlequin Romantic fantasy that amazes to the highest degree a certain class of theater goers. . . . Every minute something new: here fairies in a floating palace, there ghosts, elsewhere a sorcerer with a gun loaded with talismans. . . . one can find here everything but logic in the conception, about which writers of such works do not care and have no reason to care, since the audiences do not require it.[18]

As a measure of the play's commercial success, many of its tunes immediately became subjects of transcriptions, improvisations, and variations. Especially popular was the "Broom Song," in some degree due to Jan Nowakowski's marvelous rendition, which was deemed "a triumph of art."[19] Chopin did not escape the *Chłop milionowy* craze and during the concert of December 19, 1829, at the Merchant Club he greatly pleased his audience by improvising on their favorite "Broom Song."

The standard of performances at the National Theater in the 1820s was very good, mostly as a result of Kurpiński's efforts. He was instrumental in organizing a professional chorus necessary for the newer opera repertory. Kurpiński's chorus was a welcomed addition to the theater, though its performances often left much to be desired.[20] Under Kurpiń-

[16] Fryderyk Skarbek, *Pamiętniki* [Memoirs] (Poznań: Żupański, 1878), 157.

[17] Chopin, Warsaw, to Woyciechowski, Poturzyn, 14 January 1829 [1830], *Korespondencja*, 1:114.

[18] Maurycy Mochnacki, *Pisma* [Writings], ed. Artur Śliwiński (Lwów: Połoniecki, 1910), 340.

[19] Mochnacki, *Pisma*, 342.

[20] In 1821 performances of *La vestale*, the chorus was the least competent element of the spectacle: not quite together and seldom precise. *Tygodnik muzyczny i dramatyczny*, 18 April 1821, no. 2, 8.

ski's direction, the performance the level of the orchestra improved. The theater orchestra was rather small (in 1821 it had only eight violins) and some felt that the balance was not quite right, especially because of the poor quality of the string playing and the unwillingness of the wind players to hold back.[21] On occasion, like the performance of Spontini's *La vestale*, the orchestra was enlarged, and in such instances no fault could be found.[22] In the late 1820s, opera-goers appeared rather pleased with the orchestra. Chopin's older friend Andrzej Koźmian, who visited many European capitals, had a very good opinion of the theater's orchestra, though he felt that the singing could be better.[23] At the end of the nineteenth century, Eugeniusz Skrodzki, a younger neighbor of Fryderyk, praised not only the orchestra but also the opera's singers:

As far as voices, our opera was perhaps on a higher level than today. Without borrowing from abroad, we had beautiful basses, tenors, and not bad sopranos. The orchestra, though half the size of today's, even nowadays would not embarrass itself playing in front of our audience, which is much more discerning than the old audiences. The orchestra's precision was a credit to the untiring fervor of its director, Kurpiński, a famous composer and even a member of the Society for the Friends of Learning.[24]

Initially, the National Theater had very few decent singers, though there was a good number of first-rate dramatic and comic actors. Some comic actors, like Zdanowicz, Damse, and Dmuszewski, often doubled as singers in smaller parts.[25] Józef Zdanowicz, in particular, was Warsaw's most revered comic actor. There was honesty in his performance of comedies and operas, and even in buffo parts he was funny without resorting to exaggeration. His voice, although small, was sonorous and pleasant; among his best was the part of Don Basilio in *Il barbiere di Siviglia* of Rossini.[26] Chopin highly admired Zdanowicz, and his sympathy was later supported by Soliva's approval of Zdanowicz as "non plus ultra."[27]

With time, Kurpiński increased the number of actor-singers and introduced the idea of double casting. As a result of new hires, by the mid-1820s, in addition to several outstanding dramatic actors, the National

[21] *Tygodnik muzyczny i dramatyczny*, 23 May 1821, no. 7, 26.

[22] *Tygodnik muzyczny i dramatyczny*, 18 April 1821, no. 2, 8.

[23] Andrzej E. Koźmian, *Wspomnienia* [Memoirs], 2 vols. (Poznań: Letgeber, 1867), 1:151.

[24] Wielisław, *Wieczory piątkowe i inne gawędy*, 113.

[25] Franciszek Salezy Dmochowski, *Wspomnienia* [Memoirs] (Warsaw: Jaworski, 1858), 188.

[26] Kazimierz Władysław Wójcicki, *Cmentarz powązkowski w Warszawie* [The Powązki cemetery in Warsaw]. Warsaw: Gebethner i Wolff, 1855), 2:80–81.

[27] Chopin, Warsaw, to Woyciechowski, Poturzyn, 21 August 1830, *Korespondencja*, 1:130.

Theater had a larger group of very good singers. The first voice of the opera was the bass Jan Nepomucen Szczurowski (fig. 7.1). Chopin as a regular at the opera heard Szczurowski repeatedly and expressed strong, albeit shifting, opinions about his singing. At first he was impressed with his singing and commended the strength and clarity of his voice, in particular given the singer's age (Szczurowski was already in his mid-fifties). In later years, Chopin was much more critical and thought him dreadful in Paër's *Agnese*. This harsh criticism notwithstanding, his view seems to have changed when, after having heard the new bass, Mr. Bondasiewicz, in *La gazza ladra* of Rossini, Chopin expressed the hope that the indisposed Szczurowski will be well in time to perform with Chopin's darling Konstancja Gładkowska.[28]

The leading tenors at the opera were Walenty Kratzer, Filip Wejnert, and Józef Polkowski. By the time Chopin began to frequent the opera, Kratzer, his singing teacher at the conservatory, was no longer in the public eye. His place was taken by the two younger singers, Wejnert and Polkowski, both some ten years Chopin's senior. Filip Wejnert, the son of a conservatory voice professor, Antoni Wejnert, debuted in 1819, as Lindoro in *L'italiana in Algeri* of Rossini. Later he performed in Kurpiński's *Kalmor*, as well as *La vestale, Le petit chaperon rouge, Das unterbrochene Opferfest, Le calife de Bagdad, Don Giovanni*, and others.[29] Two years after Wejnert's debut, Polkowski was introduced to the public in *L'inganno felice* of Rossini. His performance was received as a success, and his voice was hailed as pleasing, strong, and skilled.[30] As a result of this performance, Polkowski quickly became Wejnert's competitor; parts in *Jean de Paris, Freischütz*, and *Il barbiere di Siviglia* were given to him. Although his performance as Figaro in *Il barbiere* of Rossini was received as inferior to Wejnert's, his magnificent rendition of Masaniello in the 1831 production of *La muette de Portici* of Auber made him the crowd's favorite.[31]

The best female voice during the first decades of the nineteenth century was Karolina Elsner, the wife of Józef Elsner. When Mrs. Elsner sang the part of the High Priestess in Spontini's opera *La vestale*, her voice was saluted as perfectly suited for Italian opera, and her vocal, dramatic, and lyrical skills as excellent.[32] Her early retirement in 1824 was a result of

[28] Chopin, Warsaw, to Jan Białobłocki, Biskupiec, 30 October 1825, *Korespondencja*, 1:59; Chopin, Warsaw, to Woyciechowski, Poturzyn, 21 August 1830, *Korespondencja*, 1:130; and Chopin, Warsaw, to Woyciechowski, Poturzyn, 22 September 1830, *Korespondencja*, 1:141–142.

[29] Wójcicki, *Cmentarz powązkowski*, 2:82–84. Wójcicki mistakenly refers to Lindoro as Linion.

[30] *Tygodnik muzyczny i dramatyczny*, 13 June 1821, no. 10, 40.

[31] Wójcicki, *Cmentarz powązkowski*, 2:85.

[32] *Tygodnik muzyczny i dramatyczny*, 18 April 1821, no. 2:7.

Figure 7.1. Jan Nepomucen Szczurowski as High Priest Selim in Spontini's *La vestale*. Lithograph, from Ludwik Dmuszewski, *Dzieła Dramatyczne*, vol. 9. (Warszawa: 1823). Biblioteka Uniwersytecka, Warsaw, 117043(9).

her failing health: at first, Elsner worrying about his wife's health discouraged her from frequently performing at the opera, but when during the 1820s she suffered a progressive loss of hearing, she was forced to completely abandon her career.[33] The spotlight then focused on Katarzyna Aszperger, Barbara Mejer, and, to a certain extent, Konstancja Dmuszewska, the wife of Ludwik Dmuszewski. Aszperger, whose skill

[33] Alina Nowak-Romanowicz, *Józef Elsner* (Kraków: Polskie Wydawnictwo Muzyczne, 1957), 160.

Chopin admired and acknowledged, gained the position of one of the chief singers of the National Theater with her beautiful soprano voice and excellent acting. Especially memorable were her performances as Rosa in Boieldieu's opera *Le petit chaperon rouge* and the part of Youth in Drechsler's *Der Bauer als Millionär.*[34] Dmuszewska, in contrast, although her voice was considered very beautiful, lacked vocal control and the ability to place her dramatic performance in service of the vocal and musical requirements of her role, though her performance in the title role of *Jadwiga, the Polish Queen* (*Jadwiga królowa polska*) was hailed as excellent and dramatically persuasive.[35]

By the mid-1820s, the quality of operatic performances at Warsaw's National Theater was quite good. In addition to a reputable orchestra and a decent chorus, the theater now had professional dancers again. For some years before, Warsaw's opera had had only a few dancers, kept for rudimentary dancing scenes, since the professional dancers and students of the Ledoux's Ballet School who provided the ballet at the beginning of the century had been dismissed in 1805. However, later Bogusławski hired a group of skilled dancers who were capable of performing complete ballets, an arrangement that continued into the 1820s.[36] Stage sets and costumes for National Theater's productions received particular praises from the viewers, as Bogusławski's successor, Osiński, always provided ample funds to give the audiences the spectacle they expected. Most important, in the late 1820s much young vocal talent was introduced into the theater as a result of the educational activities of the conservatory.

German Romantic Opera in Warsaw:
Mozart and Weber

Starting in 1825, Chopin's letters contain increasingly numerous references to operas. He welcomed every opportunity to listen to opera in Warsaw or while traveling abroad. For instance, during his 1829 visit to Vienna, attending opera performances was one of his top priorities. He reported to his parents: "I saw three operas: *La dame blanche, La ceneren-*

---

[34] Wójcicki, *Cmentarz powązkowski,* 3:250.

[35] *Gazeta Korespondenta Warszawskiego,* 1817, no. 6, after Małgorzata Chachaj, "*Jadwiga, królowa polska* Juliana Ursyna Niemcewicza w ocenie warszawskiej publiczności teatralnej" [Julian Ursyn Niemcewicz's *Jadwiga, the Polish Queen* in the assessment of Warsaw theater audiences], *Annales universitatis Mariae Curie-Skłodowska Lublin-Polonia* 20/21 (2002/2003): 7.

[36] *Tygodnik muzyczny i dramatyczny,* 18 April 1821, no. 2, 8; and Maurycy Karasowski, *Rys historyczny opery polskiej* [A historical outline of Polish opera] (Warsaw: Glücksberg, 1859), 275.

tola, and Meyerbeer's *Il crociato [in Egitto].* The orchestra and choruses were magnificent. Today [Mehul's] *Joseph in Aegypten.*"[37] In Warsaw he was almost a daily guest in the theater; in fact, he visited the National Theater for the last time on November 1, 1830, the night before he left Poland.[38] Frequenting opera was natural for a young man of his standing: the opera house was the hub of social activities in every major European city, the place to see others and be seen. In Chopin's case, it was more than entertainment—he was a musician, one being groomed to become an opera composer to boot. Having Elsner, who personally built the institution of national opera in Warsaw, as his composition teacher and mingling in the professional theatrical circles brought him very close to the affairs of the national stage. Moreover, his own peers showed avid interest in opera. Among his fellow conservatory students, several were training to enter the professional world of the opera; his friends the singers Anna Wołkow and Konstancja Gładkowska were just beginning their operatic careers. The young Romanic writers and poets, so closely associated with Chopin, also had keen interest in opera: its fantastic world fueled their imagination, the union between text and music fulfilled the fundamental aesthetic principles of Romanticism, and most important, they considered opera central to the construction of Polish national identity. Maurycy Mochnacki displayed a particular concern for opera; his eloquent reviews of opera performances make up the foundations of Polish musical criticism.

The young opera enthusiasts crowded eagerly into performances, regardless of the inadequate conditions at the theater. Even as late as the 1820s, the theater was lit with too few oil lamps, which left it rather dark, and the tile-stove located in the center did not provide adequate heat, but the audiences did not seem to mind. Whereas opinions about the play and the acting came from the professionals gathered around the parterre stove, the musical evaluations came from the *paradyz* (literally paradise, ironic Polish slang for gallery; also in French and German). There, near the ceiling, the acoustically superior space attracted all the music lovers.[39]

The opera-going Romantics sought manifestation of the Romantic spirit through diverse means: articulation of national identity (musically and in the choice of the subject); certain themes (they were enamored with qualities as disparate as hazy melancholy, playful magic fantasy, and torrid human passion); emotional intensity; and new musical features (gracious melodic lines, innovative orchestration, or startling harmonic complexities).

[37] Chopin, Vienna, to his family, Warsaw, 8 August 1829, *Korespondencja,* 1:91.
[38] Kazimierz Władysław Wójcicki, *Kawa literacka w Warszawie* (1829–1830) [Literary coffee in Warsaw] (Warsaw: Gebethner i Wolff, 1873), 23.
[39] Wielisław, *Wieczory piątkowe i inne gawędy,* 65.

At the heart of the Romantic veneration for opera stood Mozart's *Don Giovanni*. E. T. A. Hoffmann thought Mozart to be the father of Romantic opera, writing: "Fiery imagination, deeply felt humor, and extravagant abundance of ideas, pointed this Shakespeare of music in the direction he had to follow: Mozart broke new ground, and became the incomparable creator of romantic opera."[40] *Don Giovanni* was known in Poland already in the eighteenth century and in the years 1804–1806 was performed in Warsaw by the German troupe under Bogusławski's leadership. A new production premiered in the National Theater in 1817 and remained in the theater's repertory through the 1820s. Chopin undoubtedly heard Mozart's masterpiece on stage, even though no record of his presence at a specific performance exists. His familiarity with Mozart's opera is confirmed by the choice of Don Giovanni's and Zerlina's duet, "Là ci darem la mano," for the theme of his first concert work, the Variations in B-flat Major, op. 2, composed in 1827. During his later years in France, when the musical public's reverence for *Don Giovanni* intensified, the opera continued to inspire members of Chopin's inner circle. Among his closest friends was the singer Pauline Viardot, famous during the 1840s for her roles of Zerlina and later Dona Anna. In fact, it was Viardot who contributed greatly to the growth of the cult of Mozart by purchasing the autograph of *Don Giovanni* in 1855 and elevating it to the rank of a sacred relic.[41] Judging from the writings of Chopin's companion, George Sand, the family puppet theater performances that Chopin, Sand, her children, and visiting friends liked to stage during their summers in Nohant included motives from *Don Giovanni*. Ultimately Sand explored these motives in her *Le Château des Désertes*.[42]

In 1821, Weber's opera *Der Freischütz* premiered in Berlin and immediately was considered the ultimate embodiment of Romantic opera. Within the following years, Warsaw's publishers began to be issue piano arrangements of excerpts from this work, familiarizing the city's inhabitants with the opera's music. Five years later, Chopin, already well acquainted with the music of *Der Freischütz*, awaited the first Warsaw performance of Weber's masterpiece with youthful eagerness.[43] As the Warsaw premiere of *Der Freischütz* neared, Chopin expressed doubts about the ability of the Warsaw audience to appreciate the work truly:

---

[40] David Charlton, ed., *E. T. A. Hoffmann's Musical Writings: Kreisleriana, The Poet and the Composer, Music Criticisms* (Cambridge: Cambridge University Press, 1989), 440.

[41] Mark Everist, "Enshrining Mozart: *Don Giovanni* and the Viardot Circle," *19th-Century Music* 25 (2001): 165–189.

[42] Béatrice Didier, "George Sand et *Don Giovanni*," *Revue des Sciences Humaines* 226 (1992): 37–53; and Clara van den Broek, "Le Château des Désertes de George Sand, cours de jeu dramatique: Don Giovanni en prose," *Revue belge de philologie et d'histoire* 76/3 (1998): 687–708.

[43] Chopin, Warsaw, to Białobłocki, Biskupiec, [November 1825], *Korespondencja*, 1:60.

The rumor is getting louder, that in two or three weeks *Freischütz* will be performed; I suspect that *Freischütz* will create much commotion in Warsaw. Probably there will be many commendations and rightly so, since it means a lot that our opera can stage Weber's famous work. However, taking into consideration the goal that Weber tried to achieve in *Freischütz*—its German plot, the bizarre Romanticism, unusually intricate harmonies (which suit the Germans' taste)—one can assume that after the first performance, the Warsaw audience (accustomed to Rossini's light songs) will praise the opera not because of conviction, but because of the opinion of experts: because Weber is praised everywhere.[44]

Chopin was completely mistaken in his projections—the audiences truly loved the opera. The premiere took place on July 4, 1826, and *Der Freischütz* became an instant success: with fifty-three performances between 1826 and 1830, it was one of the most frequently played operas of the time.[45] To meet the public's demand for music from the opera, the local publishers immediately stepped up the production of excerpts and arrangements from it, some of which Fryderyk forwarded to his dear friend Jan Białobłocki.[46] According to contemporaries, the performance level of *Der Freischütz* was very high; the young Juliusz Słowacki, later one of Poland's foremost Romantic poets, had special praises for this performance of Weber's opera.[47] Unfortunately, Chopin's opinion about the Warsaw production has not come down to us, although we know that his experience of the opera in Warsaw in 1826 made him eager to see the Berlin production two years later.[48]

As a model for Romantic vernacular opera, *Der Freischütz* stirred Polish poets and composers, who for some years had been attempting to create Romantic opera that would suit the specifically Polish context. Weber had selected a libretto that appealed to the Romantics' thirst for the supernatural and their veneration of folklore as a vehicle for conveying moral lessons. These principles were no different from those embodied in the ballads of Mickiewicz that were published just four years before the opera's Polish premiere caused such uproar. The young artists admired Weber's ability to use various elements—the motives, harmony, orchestration, and tonality—to build a musical drama, and his effective use of musical language while making it accessible to audiences. Coming out of and elevating the Singspiel tradition, the opera was a superb example of musical drama set successfully to the vernacular language.

[44] Chopin, Warsaw, to Białobłocki, Sokołów, [between 15 and 22 June 1826], *Korespondencja*, 1:67.

[45] Sieradz, "Kultura muzyczna Warszawy w latach 1815–1830," 226.

[46] Chopin, Warsaw, to Białobłocki, Sokołów, 8 [January 1827], *Korespondencja*, 1:74.

[47] Ferdynand Hoesick, *Warszawa: Luźne kartki z przeszłości syreniego grodu* [Warsaw: Loose leaves from the past of the "mermaid city"] (Poznań: Księgarnia Św. Wojciecha, 1920), 154.

[48] Chopin, Berlin, to his family, Warsaw, 20 September 1828, *Korespondencja*, 1:84.

In Search of Polish National Opera

The question of language was pivotal to the debate on opera in the first decades of the nineteenth century. The earliest Polish operas in the vernacular were written in the eighteenth century. Kamieński's *Misery Made Happy* (*Nędza uszczęśliwiona*) of 1778 was the first such work, but the true success came in Jan Stefani's *Cracovians and Highlanders* (*Krakowiacy i Górale*) of 1794. Within a decade of the premiere of *Cracovians*, Elsner brought issues concerning the musical prosody of the Polish language into the public eye: his earliest thoughts on this subject were published in 1803 and later reprinted in the *Allgemeine musikalische Zeitung*.[49] The discussion on the use of the Polish language in opera focused on the need for the articulation of Polishness through opera and on opera's role as a tool for educating audiences in Polish history and proper moral values. In more practical terms, the proponents of Polish libretti, Kurpiński among them, emphasized that the language was useful for attracting wider audiences, claiming in 1823 that "from very long ago until the present, wherever Italian operas are maintained, the populace does not frequent them, for it does not understand the language."[50] For the same reason, Kurpiński not only advocated the use of the Polish language in native operas but also encouraged the staging of foreign works in translation. In the composition of Polish operas, Kurpiński did not oppose taking foreign works as musical models but urged that the new works be idiomatic, saying "let us imitate, where possible, the exquisite flexibility of Italian singing, but the melody shall be sketched by the words of our language."[51]

The appropriateness of the Polish language for singing was questioned by some participants in the debate. Kurpiński and Elsner, as well as the poets and writers who supported vernacular opera, had to face the prevailing tradition that claimed that the Polish language, unlike Italian, was unsuitable for singing. The task to prove them wrong fell to Elsner, who did so by explaining the prosody of the Polish language and demonstrating specific methods of setting it to music through examples in his 1818 *Treatise on Meter and Rhythm of the Polish Language* (*Rozprawa o metryczności i rytmiczności języka polskiego*).[52] *Der Freischütz* addressed similar concerns

[49] "In wie weit ist die polnische Sprache zur Musik geeignet," *Allgemeine musikalische Zeitung*, 1821, no. 40, 682–684.

[50] Karol Kurpiński, *Dziennik podróży* [Diary of a journey], ed. Z. Jachimecki (Kraków: Polskie Wydawnictwo Muzyczne, 1954), 43.

[51] Kurpiński, *Dziennik podróży*, 44.

[52] Around the same time, other works on the same subject appeared: J. F. Królikowski's *Rozprawa o śpiewach polskich* (Treatise on Polish chants) and J. Kruszyński's *O prozodii i pokładaniu słów pod muzykę* (On prosody and text underlay in music). Elsner continued his work on this subject, but he wrote to Chopin in 1832 that the censor suppressed the publi-

raised in the debate on the use of the vernacular in opera in German-speaking lands and conclusively proved that such work can be highly successful, not just at home but also abroad.

Like *Der Freischütz*, the earliest Polish libretti, in the eighteenth century, were inspired by the simpler opera genres in the vernacular—Singspiel, Liederspiel, vaudeville, and melodrama. Directed at wider audiences, they traditionally featured common people and simple plots featuring the everyday world. The plots of those works often derived from folk tales and included the supernatural and fantastic elements. However, they arose out of the philosophy of the Enlightenment and conveyed messages other than that of *Der Freischütz*, in which the supernatural shaped the human destiny and was inexplicable by reason. In them, the fantastic served to amuse, or was explainable by reason, or was used to teach a moral lesson. Moreover, the use at the vernacular and of identifiably Polish music, as well as the portrayals of native traditions, served to further the goal of making opera national.

Most notable of those early operas was Jan Stefani's 1794 Singspiel *The Supposed Miracle, or the Cracovians and the Highlanders* (*Cud mniemany, czyli Krakowiacy i górale*), with a libretto by Wojciech Bogusławski.[53] This simple love story set in a village outside of Kraków featured common people speaking in stylized peasant dialect. On the surface a naïve pastoral comedy, *Cracovians and Highlanders* was written in the eve of the Kościuszko Insurrection by Bogusławski, who was a member of the conspiracy: the staging was meant to incite audiences to take up arms. It did so then, and for decades after. The libretto, a tour de force of allusions, hinted at current events, and without an explicit call to arms, it awakened the Polish thirst for independence. In the person of the itinerant student Bardos, who settles a dispute between the Cracovians and the Highlanders, Bogusławski embodied a model intellectual who used his education in service of the national cause. Bardos rejects his classical education not only as useless but also as harmful: the study of ancient

---

cation of the completed three (he says) volumes, rejecting any works containing references to national issues. The rejected manuscript, actually a single volume, is entitled "Treatise on Melody and Chant" (see discussion of this work at length in chapter 4).

[53] There is vast literature in Polish dedicated to this work. Among most significant studies are Jerzy Got, *Na wyspie Guaxary: Wojciech Bogusławski i teatr lwowski 1789–1799* [On Guaxara's island: Wojciech Bogusławski and the Lwów Theater 1789–1799] (Kraków: Wydawnictwo Literackie, 1971); Ryszard Wierzbowski, *O "Cudzie czyli Krakowiakach i Góralach" Wojciecha Bogusławskiego* [On Wojciech Bogusławski's *Miracle, or the Cracovians and the Highlanders*] (Łódź: Wydawnictwo Uniwersytetu Łódzkiego, 1984); and Mieczysław Klimowicz, "'Cud mniemany' Wojciecha Bogusławskiego w 200-lecie premiery. Rozwiązane zagadki i nowe pytania," [Wojciech Bogusławski's *The Supposed Miracle* on the 200th anniversary of the premiere: resolved puzzles and new questions], in the issue *Wojciech Bogusławski i teatr polski w XVIII wieku* in *Wiek Oświecenia* 12 (1996): 11–25.

writers has only distanced him from his own language. Thus when others use rhetoric and philosophy to corroborate Machiavellian doctrines, he employs Machiavelli's ideas to alleviate the sufferings of his fellow human beings. The supernatural, the "supposed miracle," is easily explainable by science: Bardos uses an electricity-generating machine to bring about reconciliation between the two quarrelling sides. Bardos's optimism and call to action energized the populace, downtrodden by the fall of the Constitution of May 3. The original performance, in particular Bogusławski's unambiguously political acting in Bardos's role, delighted them, but it also caused the play to be taken off the stage just a few days after the premiere. The songs with their provocative texts, however, had already begun circulating and quickly entered the Polish patriotic repertory.

The popularity of *Cracovians and Highlanders* continued (the work remains in the performing repertory in today's Poland), and in 1816 Kurpiński offered a new version of the opera entitled *Superstition, or Cracovians and Highlanders, or The New Cracovians* (*Zabobon, czyli Krakowiacy i górale, albo Nowe Krakowiaki*).[54] In addition to subtle political references, much of the popular appeal of both works came from the ear-catching music. The melodically simple arias of Stefani's and Kurpiński's scores articulated the national character of the story through music by emulating folk idiom. For the audiences, the krakowiaks, polonaises, and mazurs from these operas *became* Polish folk music.

The tunes from *Cracovians* and *New Cracovians* were often reworked by other composers. The acclaimed violinist Karol Lipiński during his 1827–1828 Warsaw concerts played a potpourri on Bardos's cavatina "Cruel World" (*Świat srogi*) and "Let Us Love One Another" (*Kochajmy się*), perhaps identical with his op. 33 *Fantasia on Motives from the Opera* Krakowiacy: Górale. Chopin used "Cruel World" from *Cracovians and Highlanders* (ex. 7.1) and Jonek's song "In Town Strange Customs" (*W mieście dziwne obycaje*) from *New Cracovians* (ex. 7.2) as themes for his improvisation during his second spring concert, on March 22, 1830. With these he replaced his Fantasy op. 13, which failed to make a strong impression on the public. It appears that Chopin was hoping for the popularity and intensely patriotic connotation of these songs—"Cruel World" is Bardos's first monologue encapsulating his views—to contribute to achieving a persuasive musical oration. After all, he was already known and admired for his ability to capture the imagination of his listeners with dramatically charged improvisa-

[54] Similar was the appeal of the ballet *Wesele w Ojcowie* (Wedding in Ojców), which was created by Kurpiński and Damse, based on Stefani's *Cracovians*, and staged in 1823 as the first national ballet. The history of ballet in Poland is beyond the scope of this discussion, but it is important to mention that the National Theater during the period under discussion premiered dozens of foreign and Polish ballets (as many as ten new works a year). See Sieradz, "Kultura muzyczna Warszawy w latach 1815–1830," app. 4, 219–225.

tions. Unfortunately, in a large hall, with dilettante audiences, even these masterful improvisations made only a moderate impression, and using universally loved songs from landmark operas made very little difference.

A large group of operas composed in early nineteenth-century Warsaw involved exoticism and magic. The fashion for works of this kind came to Warsaw with the local productions of foreign works of this sort: for instance, *Die Entführung aus dem Serail* of Mozart, *Le Calife de Bagdad* of Boieldieu, *La clochette, ou Le diable page* of Hérold, and compositions from the Viennese magic opera tradition. Among Polish works of this sort were *Sultan Wumpum, or Unwise Wish* (*Sułtan Wumpum, czyli Nieroztropne życzenie*) or *Nurzahad, or Immortality and Riches* (*Nurzahad, czyli Nieśmiertelność i bogactwa*) of Elsner, and *Lucifer's Palace* (*Pałac Lucypera*) and *The Charlatan, or The Raising of the Dead* (*Szarlatan, czyli Wskrzeszenie umarłych*) of Kurpiński. These works were seemingly entirely apolitical and not carrying any message of consequence; they appeared to simply be aiming to amuse. While this might have been true for some, others had another layer of meaning underneath the charming music and entertaining plot. Many of the Polish intelligentsia and artists—Kurpiński, Elsner, and their librettists, Żółkowski (the librettist of *The Charlatan* and the translator of *Lucifer's Palace*), among them—were active members of Warsaw's Masonic lodges until 1822, when Freemasonry was forbidden; Elsner even published a collection entitled *Music to Freemasonic Songs* (*Muzyka do pieśni wolnomularskich*; Cybulski, 1811). Kurpiński's magic operas, in particular, show affinity with Masonic themes and symbolism. It is not coincidental that *Lucifer's Palace* was the nickname given to the Mniszech palace, the quarters of Warsaw's Masonry; moreover, the plots of *Lucifer's Palace* and *The Charlatan*, in the Masonic manner, focused on the dismantling of fallacies and endorsing the morality of the Enlightenment. Modeled after Mozart's *Die Zauberflöte*, which was being performed and published in Warsaw, these operas served to affirm Masonic philosophy: underneath the magic and laughter, the audiences found lessons on reason and moral law.

The most directly politically conceived Polish operas engaged historical themes. They were to serve as a vehicle for raising the historic awareness of the audiences, and in subtle or not so subtle ways they drew parallels to Poland's present situation. These works began to appear on the national stage in the first decade of the nineteenth century. Elsner first approached historical topics after the French forces entered Warsaw, perhaps as a reaction to the new political circumstances. The composition of the earliest of these operas coincided with Niemcewicz beginning his work on *Historical Chants*, and probably stemmed from the same impulse: to put poetry and music in the service of raising national historical awareness. An operatic inspiration for Polish political operas came from the rescue opera tradition, most notably from Cherubini's *Lodoïska*, which enjoyed immense popular-

Example 7.1. Jan Stefani, Bardos's cavatina "Świat srogi" [Cruel world] from *Cud mniemany, czyli Krakowiacy i górale* [*Supposed miracle, or Cracovians and the Highlanders*].

ity in Poland after its first Warsaw performance in 1804. The libretti of *Lodoïska* and Cherubini's later work *Faniska* provided specifically Polish contexts; enjoyed in Paris for their exoticism, they were seen in Poland through the prism of national identity.

During the period of the Congress Kingdom, national operas were mostly composed by Elsner and Kurpiński. Among Elsner's operas, *King Łokietek, or The Women of Wiślica* (*Król Łokietek, czyli Wiśliczanki*, 1818) and *King Jagiełło in Tenczyn* (*Jagiełło w Tenczynie*, 1820) were most successful. The most celebrated of Kurpiński's historical operas were *Jadwiga, the Polish Queen* (*Jadwiga królowa polska*, 1814), and *The Castle of Czorsztyn, or Bojomir and Wanda* (*Zamek na Czorsztynie, czyli Bojomir i Wanda*, 1819). The prevailing musical idiom of these works was that of a Singspiel: vocal style employed by both composers was simple and direct, with strophic settings dominating. But operas on national themes featured large numbers of songs and dances emulating native folklore, which gave them a specifically Polish flavor. The preponderance of folklike material in these op-

Example 7.1. *continued*

eras largely contributed to the construction of musical Polishness though dance idiom—the polonaise, krakowiak, and mazur, in particular.

The national fervor generated by the subjects and musical Polishness of these works justifiably alarmed the Russian authorities. A witness of a performance of Elsner's opera *Leszek the White, or The Witch of the Bald*

Example 7.2. Karol Kurpiński, Jonek's song "W mieście dziwne obycaje" [In town strange customs] from *Zabobon, czyli Krakowiacy i górale, albo Nowe Krakowiaki* [*Superstition, or Cracovians and Highlanders, or new Cracovians*].

Mountain (*Leszek Biały, czyli Czarownica z Łysej Góry*), which took place during the 1827–1828 season, describes the public's enthusiastic response, which bordered on political demonstration:

> The noise quieted down. One could hear the first solemn chords of the orchestra. Someone yelled out: "Polish music!" and this cry was repeated with vivid approval by a thousand voices. "Polish music!" "Polish music" sounded from all sides. The music quieted down. Then someone called out: "krakowiak"—and to the public's great delight the orchestra played the national folk dance krakowiak. After that, mazur, the very boisterous dance of the inhabitants of Mazovia, was requested in unison. Suddenly, one could see Kapellmeister Elsner getting up with inspiration, sign with the baton for the orchestra to stop playing, after which his baton moved in solemn tempo: the mighty tones of Kościuszko's Polonaise carried minds into highest awe, and continuing applause accompanied this wonderful musical composition. Everybody was overcome by emotion that defies description. Silence fell for a few minutes, after which everybody stood up, as if previously arranged, and the entire crowd intoned the national anthem, the magnificent Dąbrowski polonaise [*sic*], to boisterous orchestra accompaniment. Legs moved as in dance, spurs rang, hearts were filled with emotion, and eyes glistened with tears. The exalted moment affected everyone. Only after the love offering to the homeland was completed could the overture of the opera be performed.[55]

The most seriously conceived of these works were more elaborate, through-composed, in Italianate style and with musically related overtures. Kurpiński's *Jadwiga, the Polish Queen* (1814), on a libretto by Niemcewicz, was the most ambitious of them in scope and design.[56] Although *La vestale* did not premiere in Warsaw until 1821, the composer of *Jadwiga* was obviously familiar with Spontini's grand operas on historical themes, which already attained stunning successes in Paris. The stage sets for Kurpiński's opera were spectacular: in place of the traditionally neutral backgrounds, the three scenes received new paintings by Antonio Scotti that placed the opera's action in the nation's beloved Kraków. The costumes were lavish and attempted to accurately place the events in the fourteenth century (fig. 7.2). In the manner of grand opera, the large chorus employed by Kurpiński was integral to the narrative. Most important, the composer took great care to express the spirit of the text through music and to provide the work with an overture that was integral to the drama. Some critics, preferring solemn simplicity, found the florid coloratura arias that reflected the influ-

[55] W. Zawadzki, "Bogusławski w oczach obcych," *Pamiętnik Teatralny*, 1954, no. 3–4, 331–332, quoted after Nowak-Romanowicz, *Klasycyzm 1750–1830: Historia muzyki polskiej*, 180.

[56] On the reception of the opera see Chachaj, "*Jadwiga, królowa polska*," 1–15.

Figure 7.2. Konstancja Dmuszewska in the title part in Kurpiński's *Jadwiga królowa polska* [Jadwiga, the Polish Queen]. Aquafort color, after 1814. Biblioteka Narodowa, Warsaw, G. 2905 (Zb. Krasińskich).

ence of Rossini troubling, but overall Kurpiński's music was well received. A review written by a member of the Society of Exes concluded that

> The overture immediately announces the character of the poem. One can sense in it something solemn and grand. In concurrence with the rules of art, the seeds of ideas and images that are to be developed are being sown. In the recitative of Jadwiga's first aria, music is in per-

fect accord with the words. Every motion from tone to tone depicts the succession of thoughts and various stirs of Jadwiga's heart.[57]

Indeed, the recitative and aria "The Words of Beloved Mother" [*Słowa matki ulubionej*] from *Jadwiga* show Kurpiński's skill providing dramatic emotions in the text with musically expressive setting (fig. 7.3). The reviewer also praised Kurpiński's music for the chorus, as possessing the same dramatic power as his solo writing:

> Most outstanding is the end of the second act; it always makes a great impression. The chants that arise from the people falling on their knees and imploring their queen are in harmony with the words and emotions that bring it to life. How well the music imitates the queen's hesitation, confusion, and the secret torture! In the end, the sense of duty prevails, and the last sound of the chorus is the sound of joy and thanksgiving.[58]

The debate about the relationship of music and text in *Jadwiga* often stressed the appropriateness of using a religious musical idiom to express the time period as well as the person of the queen (the historical Jadwiga was known for her piety and after centuries of efforts was canonized in 1997). Furthermore, there was much discussion about the national character of sacred music and its ability to express Polishness. Like the religious *topoi* found in the songs from *Historic Chants* and in narrative instrumental pieces (including Chopin's works), the national opera would speak of Polishness through Catholic Christianity and its music. Such approach was also consistent with the nascent political messianism.

Nowhere else were these trends more explicit than in the pivotal scene of Elsner's *King Łokietek, or The Women of Wiślica* of 1818. This opera, composed in a much simpler idiom than that of *Jadwiga* (the grander, through-composed style is found in Elsner's *Andromeda* with its coloratura arias and musically integrated overture), told the story of Poland's thirteenth-century exiled king through the folkloristic idiom Warsaw enjoyed so much. In a messianic gesture, the legendary king's central aria and the ensuing *scena*, during which the humble pilgrim reveals himself as the savior of Poland, quote and develop the then well-known religious hymn "I Stand at Your Door, O Lord" (*U drzwi Twoich stoję Panie*) (fig. 7.4).

The composition and production of intensely national and political works as well as the enthusiasm with which they were received by audiences began to wear thin for the czar and his officials. As a measure of Novosil'cov's crackdown on political activities, freedoms of expression began to be curbed with unprecedented intensity. *King Jagiełło* was deemed too patriotic by the censor and was closed down soon after its first per-

[57] *Gazeta Warszawska*, 21 May 1816, no. 41, after Chachaj, *"Jadwiga, królowa polska,"* 7.
[58] *Gazeta Warszawska*, 21 May 1816, no. 41, after Chachaj, *"Jadwiga, królowa polska,"* 7.

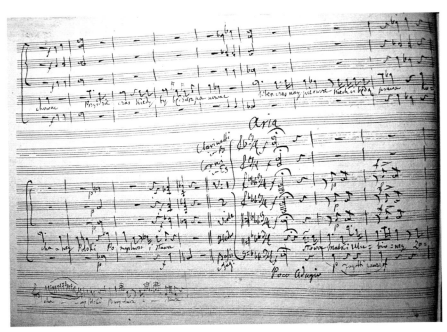

Figure 7.3. Karol Kurpiński, recitative and aria "Słowa matki ulubionej" [The words of beloved mother] from *Jadwiga królowa polska* [Jadwiga, the Polish Queen], autograph manuscript. Biblioteka Warszawskiego Towarzystwa Muzycznego, Warsaw, R 1036.

Figure 7.4. Józef Elsner, King Łokietek's aria with choir "Dziatki, Pan Bóg z wami" [Children, Lord be with you] from *Król Łokietek, czyli Wiśliczanki* [King Łokietek, or The women of Wiślica], the religious hymn "U drzwi Twoich stoję Panie" [I stand at your door, O Lord] appears in the woodwinds and later in the strings and voice, autograph manuscript. Biblioteka Narodowa, Warsaw, Mus. 91/1.

formance, triggering a demonstration by academic youth. *King Łokietek* enjoyed numerous performances in Warsaw and in Lwów, but after 1822 it was forbidden in Warsaw; an attempt to revive it in 1827 was curtailed. Although *King Łokietek* was not on stage during most of the 1820s, the opera was well remembered. Among its many melodies the most popular was the mazurka "Young Peasants from Połaniec" (*Parobcaki od Połańca*), which already in 1818 served as a theme for variations by Würfel (see fig. 3.14). During his 1829 stay in Warsaw, Paganini performed in concert introduction and variations on the same theme (probably identical with the *Sonata Varsavia*, variations on a mazurka by Elsner), a gesture that gained him the heartfelt gratitude of his listeners. Chopin still referred to *King Łokietek* in an 1831 letter to Elsner from Paris, in which with typical wit and humility, he expressed the hope that one day he would be able to approach models set by Elsner; and if he could not create *The Midget King* (*Łokietek* is actually a nickname referring to the sovereign's small stature) at least he would create *King Bony Legs* (*Król Laskonogi*).[59]

The production of historical operas halted after the Russian authorities tightened their control of politically provocative topics. Not until 1829 did Kurpiński embark on a historical subject—this time it was the opera *Cecylia Piaseczyńska*, composed and performed for the festivities held for the coronation of Czar Nicholas I, on May 31, 1829. The work was approved by the censor, who found the subject matter appropriate for the occasion: the story focused on the reconciliation between a patriotic father and a daughter he disowned for marrying a foreigner. Cecylia's husband, though a foreigner, fought bravely to secure Poles' freedom, and at the conclusion of the opera, Cecylia's father (presumably representing an outdated model of Polish patriotism), realizing how unfair he was, forgave and embraced his daughter and her family. In spite of the opera's conciliatory political context, the overture to *Cecylia Piaseczyńska* was very popular, and it was chosen for Chopin's debut concert on March 17, 1830, along with the overture from Elsner's 1809 opera *Leszek the White* (*Leszek Biały*), which during the 1827–1828 season instigated the political outburst described earlier.

The politically charged atmosphere of the year preceding the outbreak of the November Uprising encouraged Kurpiński and the National Theater team to turn to the most controversial of contemporary operas: Auber's work *La Muette de Portici*. With a libretto carefully toned down by Scribe to meet the French censor's demands, this opera was premiered in Paris in 1828. It was already in rehearsal at the National Theater in September 1830 when the Russian authorities halted the premiere: the opera's asso-

---

[59] Chopin, Paris, to Józef Elsner, Warsaw, 14 December 1831, *Korespondencja*, 1:204. Whereas the Midget King was a real historical figure, King Bony Legs is a pun on the nicknames of several Polish kings that refer to their physical characteristics.

ciation with a revolt that took place that August in Brussels was quickly turning it into the symbol of a revolution. Although Kurpiński was not allowed to stage the opera, its music was already known in Warsaw. For instance, in August Chopin heard General Szembek's band play a brass orchestra arrangement of a cavatina from *La muette*, and at a concert featuring musicians from Chopin's circle—Brzowski, Teichmann, Mejer, and Aszperger—that took place on November 12, 1830, shortly before the onset of the November Uprising, an aria from *La muette* was performed. A few days earlier, on November 8, already on route to Vienna, Chopin played a concert in Wrocław—the town where Elsner spent his youth—in Silesia, outside Russian control. During the concert, Chopin improvised on themes from *La muette*, an opera banned by the czar's censorship, in a gesture of solidarity with the revolutionary sentiments of Varsovians. The Warsaw premiere of Auber's opera, along with the long-awaited revival of Elsner's *Król Łokietek* and his new work entitled *The Insurrection of the Nation* (*Powstanie narodu*) finally took place once the Russian censor was silenced, after the onset of the November Uprising.

Parisian Romantic Opera in Warsaw: Spontini, Boieldieu, and Rossini

During the 1820s, the repressed impulse toward Polish historical opera was replaced by inclination for Spontini, Boieldieu, and Rossini, in particular the works that heralded the new Romantic trends. Gaspare Spontini's *La vestale*, which was staged in Warsaw in 1821, was a great success. It appealed to the new tastes with its pageantry and the use of a large orchestra, but also through the character of melodic lines resulting from Spontini's avoidance of coloratura. Chopin heard *La vestale* in Warsaw, and he made it a point to attend a performance of Spontini's *Ferdinand Cortez* and possibly *Olimpie* during his 1828 trip to Berlin; in fact, this trip to Berlin appears to have been centered around hopes of seeing Spontini's operas and even meeting the composer himself.[60]

The operas of Adrien Boieldieu enjoyed special popularity in Warsaw, partly because of his connection to the court of Czar Alexander I (he worked in St. Petersburg from 1804 to 1811), and his works were performed there with very little delay. Chopin must have been familiar with

---

[60] Chopin, Berlin, to Woyciechowski, Poturzyn, 9 September 1828, *Korespondencja*, 1:77–78. The visit proved to be a musical feast; not only did Chopin see *Ferdynand Cortez* (Fryderyk Chopin, Berlin, to his family, Warsaw, 16 September 1828, *Korespondencja*, 1:81) but also he attended several other musical events: Cimarosa's *Il matrimonio segreto*, Onslow's *Le colporteur*, and an oratorio performed by the Singakademie. Chopin, Berlin, to his family, Warsaw, 20 September 1828, *Korespondencja*, 1:83.

several operas by Boieldieu that were performed in Warsaw, the most popular being *Télémaque, Le petit chaperon rouge, Les deux nuits,* and *La dame blanche.* In his correspondence, Chopin mentions Boieldieu's *Télémaque,* and during his first Vienna concert in 1829, he improvised on a theme from Boieldieu's phenomenally popular *La dame blanche.*[61]

The story of *La dame blanche,* set in a distant past reminiscent of Walter Scott's Scotland, and its melancholic music appealed to Romantic tastes. Chopin's friend Maurycy Mochnacki skillfully captured the sentiments aroused by this opera: "When tones—fittingly arranged through singing or harmony—stir such feelings, they are like rays of light, which suddenly bring forth buried things and obscure apparitions from shadows into brightness."[62] Like Weber's *Der Freischütz, La dame blanche* elevated a popular vernacular genre to new heights. The Romantic nature of the libretto, based on two of Sir Walter Scott's novels, along with the Rossinian melodiousness and dramatic intensity attained by the music in places were unusual for opéra comique of the period.

The middle section of Chopin's *Fantaisie-Impromptu* op. 66 (ex. 7.3) bears a very strong resemblance to Brown's cavatina "Viens gentile dame" from *La dame blanche* (ex. 7.4), opening some curious possibilities for discussion. Opus 66—not intended by Chopin for publication and published posthumously—survived with the heading "Allegro Agitato" as the composer's inscription into the *Stammbuch* of Baronne d'Est. The Théâtre Italien context of this album has already been discussed by Jean-Jacques Eigeldinger, who emphasized the d'Est family's patronage of this institution, as well as Chopin's involvement with this particular circle of musicians and patrons.[63] If my assertion that the middle section of the piece echoes Boieldieu's "Viens gentile dame" is correct, then the Théâtre Italien connection ceases to be straightforward. After all, Boieldieu's *La dame blanche* was written as a response to Rossini's staggering triumph at the Théâtre Italien and became itself an unprecedented triumph for the Opéra-Comique. Boieldieu died in October 1834 and, as the foremost champion of the French operatic tradition, was given a state funeral at Les Invalides. The manuscript of Chopin's *Allegro Agitato* bears the date "Vendredi/1835." Perhaps it is worth exploring the possibilities that Chopin's inscription and the veiled quotation somehow resonate with the aesthetic debate about the French

<hr>

[61] Chopin, Warsaw, to Woyciechowski, Poturzyn, 2 September 1828, *Korespondencja,* 1:78; Chopin, Vienna, to his family, Warsaw, 12 August 1829, *Korespondencja,* 1:93. During the 1829 concert in Vienna he also improvised on the Polish folk song "Chmiel" (Hops), which shocked the ears of the Viennese, unaccustomed to such harsh sound.

[62] Mochnacki, *Pisma,* 402.

[63] Jean-Jacques Eigeldinger, "Chopin, Bellini et le Theatre Italien: Autour de l'album de Mme d'Est," in *D'un opera l'autre: Hommage a Jean Mongredien,* ed. Jean Gribenski, Marie-Claire Mussat, and Herbert Schneider (Paris: Presses Universitaires de France, 1996), 347–369.

Example 7.3. Adrien Boieldieu, Brown's cavatina "Viens gentile dame" from *La dame blanche*, mm. 1–8.

Example 7.4. Fryderyk Chopin, Impromptus-Fantaise op. 66, mm. 43–46.

versus the Italian tradition or that the piece is an homage to the just-departed French master whose music Chopin admired as a young man.

The composer who truly dominated the Polish operatic scene of the 1820s was Gioacchino Rossini. His operas were staged in Warsaw already during the second decade of the century, but by the late 1820s each year saw one or more new productions of Rossini's operas. Excerpts of his works were published locally by the dozen. And his music was featured in concert more often than that of any other composer: overtures were featured as openers of virtuoso concerts, and individual arias or scenas were selected by singers for virtuoso concerts and soirées or matinees. Scarcely a performance went by without including excerpts from those of Rossini's operas that had been staged in Warsaw or others that had been made fashionable through imported and locally published scores. For his last concert in Poland, one over whose programming he had full control, Chopin selected two pieces by Rossini: the overture from *Guillaume Tell* and a scena from *La donna del lago*, another opera based on Sir Walter Scott's poem. The scena from *La donna del lago*, beginning with the recitative "Mura felici, ove il mio ben" and ending with the cabaletta "Oh quante lagrime finor versai," was sung by Chopin's adored Konstancja Gładkowska, who was preparing to

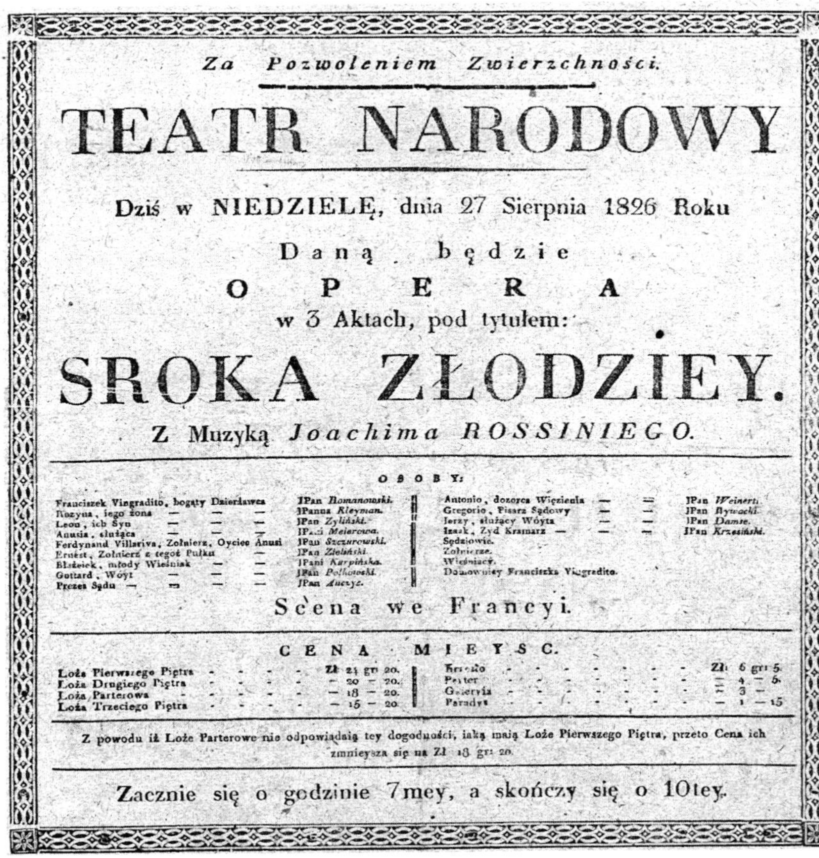
Za Pozwoleniem Zwierzchności.

TEATR NARODOWY

Dziś w NIEDZIELĘ, dnia 27 Sierpnia 1826 Roku

Daną będzie

O P E R A

w 3 Aktach, pod tytułem:

SROKA ZŁODZIEY.

Z Muzyką *Joachima ROSSINIEGO.*

O S O B Y:

Franciszek Vingradito, bogaty Dzierżawca — JPan *Romanowski.*
Rozyna, iego żona — JPanna *Kleyman.*
Leon, ich Syn — JPan *Zyliński.*
Anusia, służąca — JPani *Meierowa.*
Ferdynand Villariva, Żołnierz, Oyciec Anusi — JPan *Szczurowski.*
Ernest, Żołnierz z tegoż Pułku — JPan *Zieliński.*
Błażeick, młody Wieśniak — JPani *Karpińska.*
Gottard, Wóyt — JPan *Polkowski.*
Prezes Sądu — JPan *Aucżyc.*
Antonio, dozorca Więzienia — JPan *Weinert.*
Gregorio, Pisarz Sądowy — JPan *Bywacki.*
Jerzy, służący Wóyta — JPan *Damse.*
Izaak, Żyd Kramarz — JPan *Krzesiński.*
Sędziowie.
Żołnierze.
Wieśniacy.
Domownicy Franciszka Vingradito.

Scena we Francyi.

C E N A M I E Y S C.

Loża Pierwszego Piętra - - - Zł 24 gr 20.
Loża Drugiego Piętra - - - — 20 — 20.
Loża Parterowa - - - — 18 — 20.
Loża Trzeciego Piętra - - - — 15 — 20.
Krzesło - - - Zł 6 gr 5.
Parter - - - — 4 — 5.
Galerya - - - — 3 —
Paradys - - - — 1 — 15

Z powodu iż Loże Parterowe nie odpowiadaią tey dogodności, iaką maią Loże Pierwszego Piętra, przeto Cena ich zmnieysza się na Zł 18 gr 20.

Zacznie się o godzinie 7mey, a skończy się o 10tey.

Figure 7.5. Announcement of a Warsaw performance of Gioacchino Rossini's *La gazza ladra*, 27 August 1826. Biblioteka Jagiellońska, Kraków, DŻS 224678 IV.

appear in the new production of this opera. There are also nearly continuous references to Rossini's operas in his letters: *La donna del lago, Comte Ory, La gazza ladra, Turco in Italia, Guillaume Tell, Tancredi, Maometto II, Il barbiere de Siviglia,* and so on. His preoccupation with Rossini was to some degree a result of his intense interest in Gładkowska, but on another level it reflected the fame Rossini's music enjoyed at the time. If a single sound could be said to have dominated the Warsaw operatic universe of Chopin's adolescence, it was the sound of Rossini (see, e.g., fig. 7.5).

In these early years, Chopin frequently improvised and composed on themes by Rossini. Already in 1825, he had composed a polonaise on *Il barbiere de Siviglia* which he intended to publish; no such work is known today.[64] A year later, he included a quotation from Gianneto's aria "Vieni fra queste braccia," from act 1 of *La gazza ladra* (fig. 7.6), in the B-flat

[64] Chopin, Warsaw, to Białobłocki, Biskupiec, [November 1825], *Korespondencja,* 1:60.

Figure 7.6. Gioacchino Rossini, Gianneto's aria "Vieni fra queste braccia" from act 1 of *La gazza ladra*, from "Philomele" (Vienna: Diabelli, [1825]), p. 2. Biblioteka Narodowa, Mus. III 112.585 Cim.

Minor Polonaise (ex. 7.5) offered to his childhood friend Wilhelm Kolberg. The gift marked Chopin's departure to Reinerz (Duszniki) and referred to a performance of *La gazza ladra* that the two boys had attended a couple of days earlier (and about a month earlier than the one announced in fig. 7.5). The reference to the opera, in the trio, was indicated by Chopin's inscription "Au revoir! After an aria from *Gazza ladra*." Some years later, during his 1829 visit to Teplitz (Teplice) on his way back from Vienna, he reported improvising on *Mosè in Egitto* and *Il barbiere de Siviglia* in a letter to his parents.[65] Angelina's "Non più mesta" from *La cenerentola* served as the theme of the Flute Variations dedicated to Count Cichocki (see chapters 3 and 6), which are possibly also the work of young Chopin.

The Romantics did not shy away from lighter operas by Rossini. Even in them they were able to find Romantic qualities, mostly in his choice of subjects, as well as his cantilena and ability to startle. Thus *La cenerentola* was viewed as Romantic by Mochnacki, who felt that "Here, Rossini is unconstrained, capricious; here he completely gives into the Romantic fantasy,

[65] Chopin, Dresden, to his family, Warsaw, 29 August 1829, *Korespondencja*, 1:101.

Example 7.5. Fryderyk Chopin, B-flat Minor Polonaise, trio, mm. 34–43.

though more similar to the Romanticism found in the stories of Sche-
herazade in *Thousand and One Nights* or in the poetry of Ariosto."[66] Still,
they were particularly drawn to Rossini's darker, more emotional works,
especially his *Otello*, which premiered in Warsaw in 1828. In this work
Rossini reached for a plot befitting the younger generation's need for intense emotions: Shakespeare's passionate story of Othello. Mochnacki,
who adored Shakespeare, welcomed Rossini's *Otello* with special enthusiasm. Although he recognized the shortcomings of the libretto, he admired
the mastery of the music: "Like the sky of Africa, Rossini's composition is
inflamed and fervent; passionate like the impulsive love of Otello and in
many places savage, like the Moor's passions—when he is motivated in
turn by jealousy, vengeance, and later despair and regret."[67] This emotional complexity of the Moor's character was in large measure a credit to
Polkowski's magnificent execution of Otello's part, which, according to
Mochnacki and Chopin, made the Warsaw staging of Rossini's masterpiece
especially effective.[68] Mochnacki noted that some fragments of the opera
were particularly significant "for their novelty, for sudden displays of the

[66] Mochnacki, *Pisma*, 432.

[67] Mochnacki, *Pisma*, 397.

[68] Mochnacki, *Pisma*, 399, and Chopin, Warsaw, to Woyciechowski, Poturzyn, 9 September 1828, *Korespondencja*, 1:78.

author's genius, for departures from the ordinary pathway . . . e.g., at the end of the first act, when the sinister curse of the father is imitated and clearly marked in a certain discord of the harmony."[69]

Indeed, in works like *Otello*, the music of Rossini reached beyond the clichés of the "Rossini crescendo," vocal fireworks, and rhythmic vitality, to introduce the musical vocabulary of Romanticism. In its best lyrical moments, Rossini's cantilena epitomized the bel canto style, serving as a model for Bellini, Donizetti, and Verdi. To understand the true nature of Rossini's impact on Chopin requires us to revisit the time-honored *topos* of Bellini's influence on Chopin. While the artistic relationship between Bellini and Chopin should not be overlooked, Chopin, whose musical language was essentially developed by the time he left Poland, became acquainted with Bellini's works only after arriving in Paris. During the Warsaw years, Chopin gained a profound knowledge of Rossini by attending performances of his operas in the Polish capital and while traveling abroad, as well as listening to his works in concert and in the salon. Some of these operas contain sections of very subtle bel canto, which would have inspired both Chopin and Bellini. At times, Rossini proves capable of unexpectedly moving portrayals of characters and emotions, and of building intense drama through startling harmonic passages and moments of dissonant suspense.

The last tragic act of *Otello* contains some of the most dramatically and lyrically persuasive music Rossini wrote. *Otello*'s libretto follows Shakespeare in channeling Desdemona's fears and presentiments into her Willow Song, "Assisa a piè d'un salice," set by Rossini as a scena with the strophic setting of Shakespeare's poem in its center. Desdemona shares her fears with Emilia in an exquisite bel canto aria (ex. 7.6)—whose delicate cantilena resonates in Chopin's posthumously published C Minor Nocturne, most likely dating to his Warsaw years (ex. 7.7). Each successive stanza of Desdemona's song becomes more poignant through expressive use of ornamentation. To further intensify the portrayal of the heroine's emotions, Rossini interrupts the narrative with dramatic accompanied recitative depicting her panic caused by the window knocking in the wind. When she resumes her song, it is transformed—the fear lending the music a greater urgency and sense of despair. This sort of dramatic theme transformation, as well as the use of ornamentation integrated into the melodic line and serving expressive purposes, became the hallmark of Chopin's style, for instance in his nocturnes. In the early Warsaw years, the finest example of this nocturnal bel canto style was Chopin's Larghetto from the F Minor Concerto—shaped, perhaps not accidentally, like Desdemona's Willow Song, speaking though expressive ornamentation and recitative that are integrated into the Larghetto's formal design.

[69] Mochnacki, *Pisma*, 398.

Example 7.6. Gioacchino Rossini, Desdemona's Willow Song, "Assisa a piè d'un salice" from *Otello*, mm. 4–12, 22–29, and 39–46.

In Chopin's narrative, as in Rossini's, the return of the cantilena cannot escape being transformed by the disturbing intrusion of the recitative.

As a touch of genius, in *Otello's* last act, Rossini introduced a fleeting but memorable offstage gondolier's song, which serves as another premonition of things to come. The song, which has no precedent in Shakespeare's play, quotes Dante's *Inferno*, specifically the celebrated canto 5, which focuses on Francesca di Rimini's adulterous love story:

Nessun maggior dolore
che ricordarsi del tempo felice
nella miseria

Chopin returned to this quotation in one of his last works: the song usually known as "Melody." He inscribed this song sometime in 1847 into a
Stammbuch (no longer extant) of his close friend Countess Delfina Potocka.[70] Underscoring the parallel states of desolation he and Delfina

---

[70] Fontana's inscription in the Stichvorlage indicates that the song was composed in
1847, and according to Fontana's and Jane Stirling's correspondence, it was written into
the *Stammbuch* of Delfina Potocka. The whereabouts of this *Stammbuch* are not known, but
it still existed at the beginning of the twentieth century. The Stichvorlage is in Fontana's
hand (Music-Sammlung Österreichische Nationalbibliothek, Vienna). Kobylańska, *Rękopisy*

were experiencing, Chopin added to his signature in the *Stammbuch* the words "nella miseria," evoking associations not only with Dante's *Divine Comedy* but also with Rossini's *Otello*. The tradition has it that Rossini was one of the composers whose music Chopin asked to hear on his deathbed, and that the weeping Delfina sang Rossini for her dying friend.

The vibrant opera scene in Warsaw gave Chopin access to the most important operas of the time and gave him with the grounding for developing aesthetic judgment of repertory and performances that he continued to use in his adult life abroad. These early experiences developed in him a lifelong love for opera. When he first arrived in Paris, he was excited at the chance to participate in its splendid opera life: "I am quite content with what I found here; I have the leading world musicians and the first orchestra in the world. I know Rossini, Cherubini, Paër, etc."[71]

But soon his hopes concerning the eminent musicians of the older generation were disappointed: "These gentlemen [Reicha and Cherubini] are dried up old prunes; one can only look at them with reverence and learn from their works."[72] The music resounding in the theaters of the French capital, however, did not disappoint him: the world of Parisian opera continued to beguile him, and he continued to draw musical lessons from the work of opera singers and composers, who were often his friends.

Warsaw's opera could not match the greatest theaters of Europe; it paled in comparison with performances at the Viennese Kärntnertortheater, Parisian Opéra, and the Théâtre Italien in Paris. But according to Kurpiński, who in 1823 traveled with the purpose of visiting major European opera theaters and transplanting to Warsaw any improvements he observed, the Polish National Theater proudly stood up to comparisons with established opera houses in several other countries.[73] Chopin concurred with him when it came to evaluating some performances in Berlin or the one he attended in Dresden, where he found the quality of opera unsatisfactory: "Yesterday I went to the Italian opera, but it was poorly performed; there would have been nothing to hear if not Rolla's solo and the singing of Miss Hähnel from the Viennese theater, who yesterday sang her debut as *Tancredi*."[74]

---

utworów Chopina: katalog [The manuscripts of Chopin's works: a catalogue], 2 vols. (Kraków: Polskie Wydawnictwo Muzyczne, 1977), 1:454–455.

[71] Chopin, Paris, to Norbert Alfons Kumelski, Berlin, 18 November 1831, *Korespondencja*, 1:186.

[72] Chopin, Paris, to Elsner, Warsaw, 14 December 1831, *Korespondencja*, 1:206.

[73] In his *Dziennik podróży* of 1823, Kurpiński talks with little enthusiasm about opera performances in Leipzig (31) and Frankfurt (36–37); he finds Geneva's opera poor (93) and Rouen's insufferable (84). Even the Milanese La Scala (96) and Parisian Opéra-Comique (40) are disappointing.

[74] Chopin, Berlin, to his family, Warsaw, 27 September 1828, *Korespondencja*, 1:84; Chopin, Dresden, to his family, Warsaw, 14 November 1830, *Korespondencja*, 1:151–152. Antonio Rolla, director of Italian opera and concert master in Dresden, was an excellent violinist.

Kurpiński, of course biased by his affiliation with the National Theater, had a positive view of his theater: "I will continue to repeat, that we have splendid talents, but (with the exception of some persons) we still have some neglect in learning roles and particularly in communicating with each other."[75] His sentiments are echoed five years later in the tribute Maurycy Mochnacki wrote to the Warsaw opera and to Kurpiński:

> It would be unjust to be unable or unwilling to recognize the work, skill or even mastery of our artists. It would be unjust not to bestow real merit upon the one who through his enthusiasm and illumination in such short time accomplished almost impossible deeds; who most contributed to elevating opera from its quiet origins to a European level. May the respect and gratitude of his countrymen be his reward.[76]

If Chopin never wrote an opera, it was not for lack of exposure to musical theater during his youth in Warsaw. To some degree, the reason must be sought in his inherent predilection for the piano. Moreover, since he settled in Paris, it became highly impractical to dedicate time and energy to the creation of a Polish-language opera on Polish themes with hopes of staging it in the French capital. Composing a Polish-language opera to be staged in Warsaw was similarly unrealistic: such a performance would not have been allowed in the political climate of post–November Uprising Poland, in which even the name "Warsaw Theater" became preferable to "National Theater" and the production of national operas was at a complete halt. Instead of composing a Polish opera, Chopin concealed national texts within the cosmopolitan medium of instrumental music: in his polonaises and mazurkas, but no less in his nocturnes, scherzos, ballades, and the Fantasy op. 49.[77] Instrumental music's metaphoric narrative appealed more directly to Romantic sensibilities and to the composer who seldom expressed his most passionate thoughts in words. Chopin's piano pieces became a compromise that allowed him to sing Polish tales in a universal language.

[75] Kurpiński, *Dziennik podróży*, 37.

[76] Mochnacki, *Pisma*, 399; written after a performance of Rossini's *Otello*.

[77] Jeffrey Kallberg, "The Rhetoric of Genre: Chopin's Nocturne in G Minor," in *Chopin at the Boundaries: Sex, History, and Musical Genre* (Cambridge, Mass.: Harvard University Press, 1996), 3–29, and "Hearing Poland: Chopin and Nationalism," in *Nineteenth-Century Piano Music*, ed. R. Larry Todd (New York: Schirmer, 1990), 221–257; James Parakilas, *Ballads without Words; Chopin and the Tradition of the Instrumental Ballade* (Portland, Or.: Amadeus Press, 1992), 23; Karol Berger, "Chopin's Ballade Op. 23 and the Revolution of the Intellectuals" in *Chopin Studies 2*, ed. John Rink and Jim Samson (Cambridge: Cambridge University Press, 1994),72–83; Mieczysław Tomaszewski, "Fantazja F-Moll op. 49: Struktura dwoista i drugie dno," in *Muzyka Chopina na nowo odczytana* [Chopin's music read anew] (Kraków: Akademia Muzyczna, 1996), 73–93; and Halina Goldberg, "'Remembering that Tale of Grief': The Prophetic Voice in Chopin's Music," in *The Age of Chopin: Interdisciplinary Inquiries*, ed. Goldberg (Bloomington: Indiana University Press, 2004), 54–92.

8

CONCERT LIFE

The term "concert" carries many meanings today—it denotes orchestral and choral performances, recitals, and chamber and even church music—but during the early nineteenth century the term "concert" was reserved for a specific event: a public virtuoso performance. For Chopin's contemporaries, the virtuoso concert represented the newest performance trend, favored by general audiences; connoisseurs, however, viewed it as a public display of superficial skill not to be mistaken for meaningful music making. The other type of performance, focused on repertory judged worthwhile by connoisseurs, was referred to as "soirée" or "matinée." The distinction between the two categories of musical events is made clear in an article in *Ruch muzyczny*, the music periodical published by one of conservatory students of Elsner, Józef Sikorski:

> A *matinée* is not a concert. The latter is intended mainly for introducing an artist, even [if] already known to the public; thus it forces him into somewhat self-indulgent splendor. One might say the point is not so much music, but the artist, the show, even in the noblest sense, regarding the virtuoso or the composer. . . . The distinction between a concert and a *matinée* is subtle, though real and deserving consideration while determining the designation which will denote the nature of the artist's principal aims and the relationship in which he stands to his audience.[1]

The negligible aesthetic value accorded to the public concert by contemporary musicians explains Chopin's later decision to limit his public performances: his choice was motivated as much by his artistic standards as by

[1] *Ruch muzyczny*, 1859, no. 49, 417.

the lukewarm reception of his public concerts, stage fright, or poor health. In the process of defining his own artistic goals, it must have become obvious to Chopin that to avoid succumbing to vain virtuosity, a musician had to elude the entrapments of the concert stage. The salon was a rational alternative, since it provided the atmosphere of privacy and sophistication necessary for the presentation of more intimate and conceptual works.

Before he had arrived at such a negative view of the virtuoso concert, Chopin spent years preparing for the career of a touring composer-virtuoso. This formative period of Chopin's life coincided with an upsurge of public performances in the Polish capital, and the young pianist enthusiastically took part in this dynamic concert scene. Warsaw's public concerts were of diverse types. In addition to performances featuring local and foreign virtuosi, there were also matinées and soirées organized by various societies, church concerts, and performances in local cafés. A chronicle of concerts that took place in Warsaw during the years 1815–1830 shows a gradual increase in the number of musical events, culminating by the 1820s in a quite active musical scene.

The history of the public concert in Warsaw follows the same path as elsewhere in Europe.[2] The conservative social structure of eighteenth-century Poland helped cultivate private rather than public musical performances. Before the fall of independent Poland, the royal palace and many noble courts had maintained good orchestras, and thus the patronage came mostly from the highest strata of the aristocracy. However, the beginning of the nineteenth century saw an emergence of new social attitudes: "Music became very common and there was almost no household without music. . . . Also composers appeared, since there were enough music lovers. . . . Never until now was a Pole such a music connoisseur."[3]

---

[2] Some of the topics addressed in this chapter are explored in the three master's thesis from the University of Warsaw: Magdalena Kwiatkowska, "Kultura muzyczna Warszawy w latach 1795–1806" [Musical culture of Warsaw in the years 1795–1806] (master's thesis, University of Warsaw, 1981); Anna Bućko, "Kultura muzyczna Warszawy w latach 1807–1815" [Musical culture of Warsaw in the years 1807–1815] (master's thesis, University of Warsaw, 1982); and Halina Sieradz, "Kultura muzyczna Warszawy w latach 1815–1830" [Musical culture of Warsaw in the years 1815–1830] (master's thesis, University of Warsaw, 1983). There are many inaccuracies and lacunae in previous research concerning concert life in Warsaw, for instance in the early history of Warsaw's music societies, and this chapter involves an effort to correct or complete some of them. The history of musical performances in Warsaw's churches remains to be written; therefore, most of the information presented here comes directly from primary sources. It is not, however, a primary objective of this chapter to write a comprehensive and systematic history of Warsaw's musical life in the nineteenth century.

[3] Antoni Magier, *Estetyka miasta stołecznego Warszawy* [The aesthetics of the capital city of Warsaw] (1830 manuscript), ed. Hanna Szwankowska (Wrocław: Wydawnictwo Ossolińskich, 1963), 143.

The earliest type of public concert was connected to theater performances—during intermissions, vocalists, orchestra, and sometimes solo instrumentalists performed short concert works. Warsaw theaters, quite typically, had a tradition of performing symphonic movements between the acts of a drama, though the audience paid no attention to what was being played or who the composer was.[4] Another type of concert was also connected with theater—the first part of the performance was taken by a one-act opera, the second devoted to a concert. Some of the early public concerts were associated with charity events, balls, or lotteries, and only in the case of the most distinguished visiting performers did a concert fill up a complete evening. In addition to these, individual Polish entrepreneurs tried sponsoring musical performances, a concept well known elsewhere in Europe. Already at the beginning of 1817 the *Gazeta warszawska* announced that one Tonnes was hosting famous virtuosi during musical Mondays and Fridays.[5] In 1824, one Stadnicki placed an advertisement in the daily press announcing concerts of which the first one was to take place on December 1, 1824, at a location on Krakowskie Przedmieście street: "The undersigned, having as his goal combining (in every respect) the pleasure and comfort of his Honorable Guests, has decided to give at his place so-called Musical Soirées involving the finest artists of this vocation."[6]

Tonnes's and Stadnicki's ventures appear to have been unsuccessful; much better success in promoting concerts was achieved by music societies—organizations with dues-paying members, sponsoring performances by professional and amateur musicians. In addition to these specialized organizations, various societies, whose primary goals were other than fostering music, provided occasions for musical events. In fact, Chopin's first public appearance in 1818 was as a part of a charity event organized by the Warsaw Benevolent Association, and many of his youthful concerts took place during events hosted by the Merchant Club. These two institutions were especially active on Warsaw's musical scene during Chopin's time, serving, along with associations dedicated specifically to the advancement of music, as venues for performances of solo, chamber, and orchestral repertories.

[4] *Ruch Muzyczny*, 1859, no. 29, 256.

[5] Though at first this press announcement might be mistaken for a press notice of a salon concert, in fact it is an advertisement for public concerts. In it Tonnes, describing himself as an entrepreneur, offers single tickets or subscriptions for four concerts, which are to take place in his home at Sto Jańska Street no. 24. *Gazeta warszawska*, 7 January 1817, no. 2, 35. No further information about Tonnes's venture can be located, so the fate of his concert series remains unknown.

[6] *Kurier warszawski*, 28 November 1824, no. 284, 829.

Figure 8.1. The Mniszech Palace, residence of the Harmonie Gesellschaft and later the Merchant Club. Copper engraving by Nicholas Chalmandier, after Rizzi Zannoni, 1772. Muzeum Fryderyka Chopina w Towarzystwie im. Fryderyka Chopina w Warszawie, Warsaw, M/615. Photo by Andrzej Ring & Bartosz Tropiło.

Music Societies

The earliest music society in Warsaw, the Musikalische Institut der Harmonie-Gesellschaft, was created during the Prussian administration of Warsaw and housed in the early eighteenth-century Mniszech Palace, specially restored for this purpose (fig. 8.1).[7] The idea of creating the Harmonie-Gesellschaft came in 1801 from a member of the Prussian administration, Oberfiskal Wilhelm von Mosqua. The society adopted an ambitious program, sponsoring concerts—at times several of them taking place simultaneously in different rooms—that consisted of oratorios, symphonies, quartets, trios, sonatas, sometimes even songs.[8]

The Harmonie-Gesellschaft survived until 1808, but according to the published statutes, in 1805 a group of members split away from the original institution to create another affiliated society, the Musik-Gesellschaft. Although it is not clear what relationship existed between the two societies, the additional statutes of the Harmonie-Gesellschaft published on July 17, 1805, suggest that it remained in rivalry with the new organiza-

[7] Magier, *Estetyka miasta stołecznego Warszawy*, 156.

[8] Franciszek M. Sobieszczański, *Rys historyczno-statystyczny wzrostu i stanu miasta Warszawy od najdawniejszych czasów aż do roku 1847* [Historic-statistical outline of the growth and state of the city of Warsaw from the oldest times until 1847] (Warsaw: S. Strąbski, 1848), 150.

tion created by Oberfiskal Mosqua, Józef Elsner, and E. T. A. Hoffmann.[9] Hoffmann, the famous music lover, poet, and musical critic, was stationed in Warsaw from 1804 until 1807 as a member of the Prussian administration, and his efforts were central to the creation of an active musical scene in Warsaw.[10]

This new Musik-Gesellschaft involved members of the Prussian administration and Polish musicians, artists, intelligentsia, bourgeois, and aristocratic amateurs. The intent was to create a music society that would not only organize concerts but also offer vocal training for amateurs. With this goal in mind, the necessary funds were raised to provide for performing space in the Ogiński Palace and for two voice teachers—one for the soloists and one for the choir.[11] Members of the society organized lectures, discussions, and concerts featuring local and foreign performers. Music performed during concerts included symphonies, concertos, and chamber music, especially quartets, by composers like Mozart, Haydn, Gluck, Cherubini, and Beethoven. Although Józef Elsner became the so-

---

[9] *Ruch muzyczny*, 1861, no. 12, 181–182. According to Józef Elsner, *Sumariusz moich utworów muzycznych* [A summary of my musical works], ed. Alina Nowak-Romanowicz (Kraków: Polskie Wydawnictwo Muzyczne, 1957), 78 in 1806 the "newly created music club" was initiated by Kuhlmayer, a lawyer and amateur musician, and had Mosqua, Hoffmann, and Wobser as directors.

Aleksander Poliński, *Sprawozdanie jubileuszowe komitetu Towarzystwa Muzycznego w Warszawie* [Anniversary report of the Music Society in Warsaw Committee] (Warsaw: Kowalewski, 1896), 9, claims that the initiative to start this organization came from Count Krasiński, E. T. A. Hoffmann, and W. Mosqua, and names the same directors as does Elsner. The statutes of this society, in the *Allgemeine musikalische Zeitung*, October 1805, 43–48, name Mosqua, Hoffmann, Count Krasicki, and Major Lessel.

[10] Hoffmann had settled in Poland already in 1800, when he married a Polish woman, Michalina Trzcińska. Born in 1776, in Königsberg, he entered the law profession, following his ancestors, but he had loved music since his childhood, and his dream of devoting his entire time to his true vocation became a reality after he left Poland in 1807, retiring from his profession and working in music from then on. Hoffmann became involved with the Harmonie-Gesellschaft after it purchased the Mniszech Palace, destroyed by fire shortly before. He worked out sketches and architectural plans for the rebuilding and personally participated in repairs. In May 1805, the statutes of the Musik-Gesellschaft were published, and Hoffmann was named second director ("zwejter Vorsteher," supervising the library, the musical inventory) and censor (deciding which Polish, German, or French literary-musical works would be read during the public reading sessions). After much preparatory work, the first concert took place on August 3, 1806—the birthday of the Prussian king. A detailed story of Hoffmann's stay in Poland and his musical involvement in Warsaw is Jan Kosim, "Ernest Theodor Hoffmann i Towarzystwo Muzyczne w Warszawie" [E. T. A. Hoffmann and the Music Society in Warsaw], in *Szkice o kulturze muzycznej XIX wieku* [Essays on the musical culture of the nineteenth century], ed. Zofia Chechlińska, 5 vols. (Warsaw: Państwowe Wydawnictwo Muzyczne, 1971–84), 2:105–179.

[11] *Ruch muzyczny*, 1861, no. 12, 181.

ciety's official conductor, sometimes performances were led "with great skill" by E. T. A. Hoffmann.[12]

The first *regular* musical evenings during which amateurs presented "respectable performances of noble compositions" took place in the Dulfus House (at Freta Street across from the Dominicans) in "a kind of a club from which ladies were excluded."[13] The host of these musical evenings, taking place twice a week, was Antoni Wejnert, the future Conservatory professor.[14] These might have been identical with the performances reported by the press in 1815, when quartets were to be performed every Monday and Friday evening at six by amateurs and musical artists at an eatery located at the same address.[15] However, according to the historian of Warsaw Ferdynand Hoesick, these musical evenings, to which the public were admitted for a small fee, first took place very early on in the century (sometime after 1803).[16] Soon after, they were moved to the Salwator House in Nowe Miasto, and here women were allowed to join.[17] None of the historians' accounts report on the name or organizational structure of this "club."

By 1817 (or even as early as 1815), the meetings in Salwator House were under the aegis of the Music Amateur Society (*Towarzystwo Muzyczno-Amatorskie*).[18] Each member had to pay an initial fee and dues (12 złoties every quarter) in order to attend concerts that took place every Wednesday evening. The orchestra was made up of members with musical skills, supplemented by hired professional wind players, and performed programs selected by an elected board of directors.[19] At first, the programs consisted of symphonies by Haydn, Mozart, and Beethoven; later the repertory was enlarged by symphonic works of Romberg, Méhul, Reicha, and Krommer, and some overtures and Lessel's oratorio were presented.[20] For the more demanding music lover, there was no more pleasurable way

[12] *Ruch muzyczny* 1861, no. 10, 148; and 1861, no. 12, 181–183.

[13] Magier, *Estetyka miasta stołecznego Warszawy*, 156.

[14] Kazimierz Władysław Wójcicki, *Cmentarz powązkowski w Warszawie* [The Powązki Cemetery in Warsaw] (Warsaw: Gebethner i Wolff, 1855), 1:217.

[15] *Gazeta warszawska*, 31 October 1815, no. 87, 1768.

[16] Ferdynand Hoesick, "Luminarze warszawscy w roli przyjaciół i znajomych F. Chopina" [Warsaw luminaries as Chopin's friends and acquaintances], in Hoesick, *Warszawa: Luźne kartki z przeszłości syreniego grodu* [Warsaw: loose leaves from the past of the "mermaid city"] (Poznań: Księgarnia Św. Wojciecha, 1920), 258.

[17] Magier, *Estetyka miasta stołecznego Warszawy*, 156.

[18] Łukasz Gołębiowski, *Gry i zabawy różnych stanów* [Games and amusements of various classes] (Warsaw: Glücksberg, 1831), 255.

[19] Sobieszczański, *Rys historyczno-statystyczny wzrostu i stanu miasta Warszawy od najdawniejszych czasów aż do roku 1847*, 221.

[20] *Rozmaitości*, 1820, no. 20, 74–75.

to spend an evening, and listeners were frequently delighted with the level of execution and the emergence of local talent.[21]

During the last two years of its existence, the Music Amateur Society's concerts took place in the building of the Benevolent Association at Krakowskie Przedmieście Street.[22] An 1820 article speaks highly of the society's achievements—especially the most recent concert, during which Piotr Kaczyński, an amateur violinist, performed difficult works by Rode and Lafont—and expresses hope that concerts will resume after summer vacations.[23] Unfortunately, despite all these praises, in 1820, only few years after its creation, the society ceased to exist because of insufficient funds.[24]

To replace the Music Amateur Society and make concerts more popular through combining them with other goals and pleasurable activities, a new society was created in January 1821. This new institution was established under the aegis of the Merchant Club, located at Miodowa Street, and later moved to the Mniszech Palace. The merchants of Warsaw saw promotional and social opportunities in providing the organization and space for art, culture, and entertainment serving the capital's upper classes.[25]

The first confirmed Chopin concert at the Merchant Club is his performance at the club on December 19, 1829 in a joint concert that also involved Bielawski, Copello, Dorville, and Soliva. The young pianist accompanied the singer, Copello, and played fantasias on various themes including melodies from the melodrama *Der Bauer Millionär,* which had had its Warsaw premiere just a month earlier and immediately attained extraordinary popularity.[26] More specifically, Fryderyk improvised on "The Broom" from *Der Bauer Millionär* and accompanied an aria from Paër's *Achille;* in addition, an unidentified quintet by Beethoven was performed.[27]

Before that Chopin mentioned a performance by his older friend, Kessler, of the Hummel's E Major Concerto that took place on a Saturday in January, 1829, at the club. From the same letter we learn that there was

[21] Sobieszczański, *Rys historyczno-statystyczny wzrostu i stanu miasta Warszawy od najdawniejszych czasów aż do roku 1847,* 221.

[22] Magier, *Estetyka miasta stołecznego Warszawy,* 156.

[23] *Rozmaitości,* 1820, no. 20, 74–75.

[24] Sobieszczański, *Rys historyczno-statystyczny wzrostu i stanu miasta Warszawy od najdawniejszych czasów aż do roku 1847,* 221.

[25] Sobieszczański, *Rys historyczno-statystyczny wzrostu i stanu miasta Warszawy od najdawniejszych czasów à do roku 1847,* 221–222.

[26] *Kurier Polski,* 20 December 1829, no. 19; *Kurier Warszawski,* 23 December 1829, no. 343.

[27] Sieradz, "Kultura muzyczna Warszawy," 191.

talk of Fryderyk performing his Variations op. 2 at the club on the following Saturday.[28] No such performance is confirmed by other sources.

Musical events intended to raise money for various altruistic purposes were common in Warsaw, and Chopin participated in many of them.[29] Fundraising for charitable aid was in particular the primary purpose of musical events sponsored by the Warsaw Benevolent Association (*Warszawskie Towarzystwo Dobroczynności*). This association was created by Countess Zofia Zamoyska with the help of Maria Gutakowska, Maria Würtemberg, Teresa Kicka, and Józef Lipiński in 1814 in response to a humanitarian crisis caused by wars and intensified by the unusual flooding of the river Vistula (*Wisła*). Local musicians immediately joined in the cause. The *Allgemeine musikalische Zeitung* reported that

> The misery caused by the overflowing of Vistula in Warsaw and Praga [a suburb of Warsaw], in October 1813, prompted numerous friends of music to a decision that in order to assist families afflicted by the flood, an open concert in the local Piarists' Church be performed on the 14th of September [1814] under the direction of the Music Director Mr. Elsner.[30]

Soon the founding members were joined by other prominent members of the Warsaw community: Stanisław Staszic, Stanisław Zamoyski, and Stanisław Grabowski, to mention a few.[31] Initially, the society used various halls for its concerts. When on February 24, 1818, little Fryderyk—invited on the behalf of the Benevolent Association by Julian Ursyn Niemcewicz and Zofia Zamoyska—played his first public concert, the location was the Radziwiłł Palace. This must have been one of the last public concerts there, since during this year this palace became the official residence of the vice-regent and thereafter was closed to public events.

[28] Fryderyk Chopin, Warsaw, to Tytus Woyciechowski, Poturzyn, 14 January 1829 [1830], in *Korespondencja Fryderyka Chopina* [Fryderyk Chopin's correspondence], ed. Bronisław Edward Sydow, 2 vols. (Warsaw: Państwowy Instytut Wydawniczy, 1955), 1:114.

[29] Among others, Magier reports an important charity event that raised funds for Warsaw's hospitals, during which Haydn's *Die Schöpfung* was performed by three hundred people at the National Theater. Unfortunately, the historian provides no further information. Magier, *Estetyka miasta stołecznego Warszawy*, 143. Shortly before his departure from Poland, Chopin took part in another kind of altruistic event, the benefit concert. On 8 July 1830, in the hall of the National Theater, a group of musicians, including Chopin, presented a fundraiser concert for the purpose of aiding Barbara Mejer, whose weak health required a trip to a health resort. Mejer was a well-known singer with whom Chopin worked on several occasions. During the benefit concert he accompanied her and performed his B-flat Major Variations, op. 2. *Kurier warszawski*, 7 July 1830.

[30] *Allgemeine musikalische Zeitung*, September 1814, 653.

[31] Franciszek Salezy Dmochowski, *Wspomnienia* [Memoirs] (Warsaw: Jaworski, 1858), 276–277.

Chopin's performance of the E Minor Concerto by Vojtěch Gyrowetz under the auspices of the Benevolent Association was well received, and Niemcewicz thanked the young pianist personally. The revered poet, however, apparently maintained some healthy skepticism, and he satirized the event and the excitement created around a child virtuoso named Chopin in a miniplay that was found in manuscript among Niemcewicz's papers after his death.

Chopin performed again for the Benevolent Association in 1823. This time, the association organized a series of concerts in the concert hall of its new building, the old convent of the Carmelite Nuns at Krakowskie Przedmieście Street, acquired in 1821. The young virtuoso played in the sixth and ninth concerts of the series. On February 26, 1823, he performed Ries's piano concerto "with the greatest ease, precision and feeling."[32] The last concert of the series took place on March 17, 1823, and the performer of a Hummel's concerto was most likely Chopin.[33]

The existence of the Conservatory in Warsaw necessitated the establishment of an appropriate venue for student performances. In 1824, the Conservatory was given a building that had previously served as a convent for the Bernardine Sisters; it was quickly converted to a concert hall that became a stage of concerts by conservatory students and music professionals. Chopin performed at the Conservatory on several occasions. In all probability, he participated in choral concerts; for instance, in April 1828 the students performed Cherubini's *Ave Maria* and fragments of other religious works.[34] A year later, in April 1829, the program of a conservatory concert included Cherubini's *Pater noster.*[35]

In two concerts Fryderyk was a soloist. In the concert of May 27, 1825, he played a Fantasia for eolipantalion. The concert was received very warmly by Warsaw's music lovers, and as a result a second concert was organized. This performance featured Antonia Bianchi (an Italian singer and a friend of Paganini, who sang for the first time in Warsaw, presenting arias from Paër's *Achille* and Rossini's *Otello*), a flutist named Kresner, and Chopin, who played Moscheles's Concerto on the piano and improvised on the eolopantaleon. The concert took place at the Conservatory on June 10, 1825, and Chopin was especially applauded for his performance on the eolopantaleon.[36] The concerts were very successful, and

[32] *Kurier dla płci pięknej* 1 (1823), reproduced in Krystyna Kobylańska, *Chopin w kraju: Dokumenty i pamiątki* [Chopin in his own land: documents and souvenirs] (Kraków: Polskie Wydawnictwo Muzyczne, 1955), 61.

[33] Kobylańska, *Chopin w kraju*, 61.

[34] Sieradz, "Kultura muzyczna Warszawy," 186.

[35] Sieradz, "Kultura muzyczna Warszawy," 188.

[36] *Kurier Warszawski*, 11 June 1825, no. 137, reproduced in Kobylańska, *Chopin w kraju*, 105.

even the *Allgemeine musikalische Zeitung* published a favorable mention of Chopin's performance (see chapter 2).

Concerts addressed to connoisseur audiences, properly falling into the category of matinées and soirées, had the same characteristics in Poland as abroad. They featured a diversified repertory that could include compositions typical of the virtuoso concert—concerti and improvisations, other short instrumental compositions, and vocal selections from operas—but unlike the virtuoso concert, these performances also presented choral works, chamber pieces, and complete symphonic compositions. Society concert series would sometimes concentrate on a specific genre (symphony or string quartet, for instance), and unlike the virtuoso concert that highlighted the performer's own pieces and popular works of living composers, they would often focus on cherished works of the recent past, especially Mozart and Haydn.

Typically, these events took place in performing spaces smaller than those used for virtuoso concerts, primarily because audiences interested in the repertory they featured were smaller (hence larger spaces were economically not feasible) but also because the intimate sound and atmosphere were preferable. The performers of these concerts were an amalgamation of amateurs (often quite capable) and professionals, combined in proportions that depended on the occasion and venue. Given the circumstances and auditoria in which these concerts took place, the performing forces could not be large and did not need to be. In these concert spaces, like in the salons, pieces for orchestra were often executed by a chamber ensemble of nine or fewer players or by a chamber orchestra of about thirteen (rather than the twenty-five to thirty that were customary for a full orchestra in the early nineteenth century)—contemporaries often referred to both categories of ensemble by the term "quartet" (see chapter 6). The chamber orchestra, as a rule, consisted of four violins, one viola, one cello, one bass, one flute, two oboes or clarinets, two French horns, and one bassoon. Kurpiński, who describes such an ensemble in an 1821 article, explains that this small orchestra is capable of performing symphonies by Mozart and Haydn with the greatest accuracy and that excellent performers are capable of achieving powerful results because good musicians (especially wind players, who can control their sound) can overcome the imbalance in numbers.[37]

Given the custom of using chamber ensembles to stand in for a full orchestra, it is probable that when Chopin performed concert works in smaller venues—the Gyrowetz, Ries, and Hummel concerti for the Benevolent Association, and the Moscheles Concerto for the Conservatory event—or when he heard his friend Kessler play the E Major Concerto by

[37] *Tygodnik muzyczny i dramatyczny,* 23 May 1821, 26.

Hummel at the Merchant Club, the piano was accompanied by one of such ensembles. When his own concert works were issued abroad, the publishers also offered a chamber option for purchase. In the case of Chopin's works, a very common and very inexpensive manner of producing such arrangements was selected: the printing the orchestral string parts with wind solos already transcribed into them in small print, to be sold separately (and at a price lower than that of the full set of orchestral parts) for performance by a string quintet or a double quartet with a bass. The piano part included reductions of orchestral tuttis to enable the pianist to participate in them and provide for any missing wind parts. While in Warsaw, Chopin publicly performed his own concerti with a full orchestra (though he rehearsed the E Minor with a chamber ensemble in front of a small audience in his parents' salon, as discussed in chapter 6); the 1832 Salle Pleyel concert and an 1838 performance in Rouen both likely featured chamber ensemble accompaniment.[38]

By altering the sonority of the original symphonic work, these performances compromised an indispensable component of the aesthetic whole. But Chopin's contemporaries agreed that the goal justified the means, even in a symphony, where the aesthetic transgression caused by the reduction of sonority to a chamber ensemble was more discernible:

> Naturally an engraving, even the best, is not able to replace a painting, which contains the other half of meaning in its color; however if the painting is not available, it is better to at least have an engraving, as long as the thought and contour of the original are faithfully rendered.[39]

Ultimately such transcriptions were the most realistic rendition then available of the original sonority, and an important vehicle for the dissemination of orchestral music prior to the advent of the phonograph. Attending soirées and matinées allowed the young Fryderyk not only to hear and perform a repertory of concertos, symphonies, and other orchestral works, albeit in chamber transcriptions, but also to become acquainted with chamber and choral masterpieces of past and contemporary composers.

[38] For an in-depth discussion of this subject see Halina Goldberg, "Chamber Arrangements of Chopin's Concert Works," *Journal of Musicology* 19/1 (winter 2002): 39–84.

[39] *Ruch muzyczny*, 10–26 April 1857, no. 4, 28. A similar view was expressed earlier by E. T. A. Hoffmann in reference to piano transcriptions of orchestral works. Quoted by Thomas Christensen, "Four-Hand Piano Transcription and Geographies of Nineteenth-Century Musical Reception," *Journal of the American Musicological Society* 52 (1999): 264.

"Handel's *Ode on St. Cecilia's Day* came the closest to the ideal of great music as I have had conceived it," wrote Chopin in 1828 to his family from Berlin.[40] On the subject of his attendance and participation in performances of masterpieces of choral music in Warsaw, Chopin's correspondence is silent; he only enthusiastically reports his own contribution as an organist during the mass at the Visitation Nuns' Church. By comparison with the choral concerts Chopin experienced in Berlin, Warsaw performances of the sacred repertory were very modest; Gołębiowski commented that the monumental concerts of choral masterpieces by Haydn, Handel, Beethoven, and Schneider that took place in England and Germany showed a superior taste for music, but in Poland, influenced by France and Italy, the preference was for dramatic music, "and unfortunately such [music] succumbs the quickest to the whims of fashion."[41] The absence of great oratorio tradition notwithstanding, the most prominent churches in the Polish capital were home to several sacred music societies, educational initiatives, secular concert series, and lavish musical events accompanying services during special tributes and major church feasts.

While Poland was still a sovereign state, regular performances of sacred music took place at the Royal Chapel, the palace chapels of the Polish aristocracy, and churches and convents (high-quality performances of sacred music continued in some churches, in Kraków and Poznań especially, right into the nineteenth century).[42] Naturally, the music for high holy days was the most sumptuous, and thus on Maundy Thursday King Stanisław August always had his orchestra perform at the Royal Castle a large work, usually an oratorio, with the participation of invited eminent foreign soloists. On one such occasion, Paisiello visited Warsaw to conduct one of his own oratorios.[43] After the fall of the Polish state, funds became scarce, and attempts were only gradually made to reintroduce quality music into the churches.

The first efforts to bring good music back into Warsaw's churches took place already at the beginning of the nineteenth century. In 1804, the Church of St. Benon introduced music performed by youths and amateurs for the daily service.[44] The most impressive sacred musical perfor-

---

[40] Chopin, Berlin, to his family, Warsaw, 20 September 1828, *Korespondencja*, 1:83.

[41] Gołębiowski, *Gry i zabawy różnych stanów*, 256.

[42] Gołębiowski, *Gry i zabawy różnych stanów*, 250–252.

[43] *Kurier warszawski*, 16 April 1824, no. 92, 53. According to the sources, most sacred royal concerts took place at the St. John Cathedral or the Holy Cross Church.

[44] Sobieszczański, *Rys historyczno-statystyczny wzrostu i stanu miasta Warszawy od najdawniejszych czasów à do roku 1847*, 149. These concerts have been given careful attention in

mances during this period took place in the spacious and imposing Farny Church (an old term, in Warsaw denoting the Cathedral of St. John the Baptist), which had a large orchestra conducted by one of the capital's most respected and excellent musicians.[45] The musician, Jan Stefani (the composer of *Cracovians and Highlanders*), was a singing teacher at the gymnasium, and his *capella* still existed in 1830, in spite of financial problems.[46]

With time, other churches instituted musical accompaniment to the service, though not always of very high quality.[47] Improvement became noticeable during the years 1822–1825, when amateurs and professionals of the St. Cecilia Society performed Sunday music and Polish devotional chants with the accompaniment of the organ in the Franciscan Church of St. Francis of Assisi.[48] This church also embarked on more ambitious musical projects; for instance in November 1823 a Haydn Mass was heard. The parish church of St. Alexander and the churches of the Capuchins and Canonesses, where Warsaw's aristocracy went to mass, also hosted some musical events on a larger scale.[49]

With every year, the musical events taking place during the Holy Week became more elaborate, and performances of large choral works could be heard around Warsaw. In some churches, it was a custom to arrange for masterpieces of funeral and Passion music to be performed by amateurs on Good Friday. Particular favorites were Mozart's *Requiem* and Haydn's *Die Sieben letzten Worte*.[50] Since the Polish capital had many people with musical skills, such performances were common, and the best ones could be heard in the Piarists' and Carmelite churches.[51] For instance, in 1824, the press announced that "splendid music appropri-

---

Ryszard Miączyński, "Koncerty u benoitów: Z dziejów życia muzycznego Warszawy na przełomie XVIII i XIX w." [Bennonite concerts: from the history of musical life in Warsaw at the turn of the 19th century], *Muzyka* 34 (1989): 65–102. Based on an 1808 inventory, he reports an astounding collection of sacred and secular music associated with performances in this church by some seventy contemporary composers (especially Haydn, Johann Melchior Dreyer, Mozart, and Ignaz Joseph Pleyel).

[45] Antoni Wieniarski, *Warszawa i warszawianie: Szkice towarzyskie i obyczajowe* [Warsaw and its residents: essays on the society and customs], 2 vols. (Warsaw: Bernstejn, 1857), 2:17.

[46] Gołębiowski, *Gry i zabawy różnych stanów*, 252.

[47] *Allgemeine musikalische Zeitung*, April 1822, 276.

[48] Gołębiowski, *Gry i zabawy różnych stanów*, 252–253.

[49] Wieniarski, *Warszawa i warszawianie*, 2:15.

[50] See the *calendarium* of church concerts in Halina Goldberg, "Musical Life in Warsaw during Chopin's Youth, 1810–1830" (Ph.D. diss., City University of New York, 1997), app. 2, 452–459.

[51] Wieniarski, *Warszawa i warszawianie*, 2:36.

ate for the occasion of Good Friday will be performed at the Sepulcher of nearly every church":

> At 3 p.m. in the Visitation Nuns' Church by the professors and students of the Conservatory, conducted by Rector Elsner; at 4, in the Canonesses' [Church] by amateurs and artists, conducted by the Royal Kapellmeister Kurpiński; at 5, at the Piarists' Church by the Society for the Friends of Music; at 7, in the Cathedral supported by the orchestra of this church.[52]

By the mid-1820s, the most musically important churches were the Visitation Nuns' Church at the university, the Piarists' Church, and the Lutheran Church. The majority of the faithful participating in mass at the university church were of the upper classes.[53] Since the church was serving University of Warsaw, it was natural that the initiative to improve the quality of music in this church came from Stanisław Grabowski, who served as the minister of education:

> Minister Count Grabowski, who regularly observes solemn celebrations of the Catholic Mass, is actively engaged in procuring salary increases for church-employed musicians. Also, thanks to him, there already exists in Warsaw the establishment of a University Church and, with it, a regularly observed Sunday Mass [with music], which is performed by music students with the assistance of the Conservatory professors; all under the direction of Mr. Elsner.[54]

Around the time these words were written, following the inclusion of the Conservatory within the university structure in 1821, the students and professors of the Conservatory began attending services and indeed were obliged to provide music for the Sunday 10:30 Mass and for holy days.[55] Chopin, who by 1825 served here as an organist, also was obliged to perform as a member of the Conservatory chorus. He probably participated in the services of October 15, 1826, that included *Vespers* in C Major, *Veni creator*, and the *Te Deum* by Elsner, and it is possible that he was still attending mass during 1830, when a *Stabat mater* by Peter Winter was heard.[56]

Of all Warsaw's churches, the most celebrated for its music was the

---

[52] *Kurier Warszawski*, 16 April 1824, no. 92, 53.

[53] Wieniarski, *Warszawa i warszawianie*, 2:18.

[54] *Allgemeine musikalische Zeitung*, April 1822, 275.

[55] "Antoni Orłowski," *Pamiętnik Muzyczny i Teatralny*, 1862, no. 24, 371–72; and Gołębiowski, *Gry i zabawy różnych stanów*, 253.

[56] Listed in Sieradz, "Kultura muzyczna Warszawy," 182, 192.

Piarists' Church (fig. 8.2). The 1822 *Allgemeine musikalische Zeitung* report noted: "Besides the aforementioned University Church, about which the future will tell of its new direction, that of the Piarists, where a large number of amateurs as well as members of the theatrical establishment are found, remains to be noted."[57] The Piarists' Church was very modest, almost impoverished, but it was known for its dutiful and serious attitude toward religious ritual and the best amateur choirs.[58] Since good music was considered an indispensable element of services at the church, funds were generated for a library, instruments, choir expenses, and even breakfast for the performers.[59] Musicians and amateurs gathered every Sunday morning at ten and were ready to perform at 10:30 under the leadership of Wacław Prohazka, a talented musician and organist. Great music and the character of services attracted music lovers, administrative workers, and youth to Sunday mass.[60]

Period sources refer to two music societies associated with the Piarists' Church and provide a fragmented history of their existence. Sobieszczański informs us that in 1811, Elsner and Kurpiński established a Society for Church Music (*Towarzystwo Kościelnej Muzyki*), which performed music every Sunday during mass in the Piarists' Church.[61] From an article in *Tygodnik dramatyczny*, we learn that in 1814 Elsner established the Society for the Friends of Religious and National Music (*Towarzystwo Przyjaciół Muzyki Religijnej i Narodowej*), and Gołębiowski says that this society ceased to exist in 1829.[62] Unfortunately, on the basis of these passing remarks, it is impossible to establish whether this was one or two separate organizations, and if two societies existed, what the relationship between them was.

The conductors whose names arise in connection with the Society for Church Music were Józef Elsner (the founder of the society), Józef Jawurek (piano professor at the Conservatory), Henryk Lentz (harmony professor at the Conservatory) and Jan Gregorowicz Soloffiew (a fur merchant blessed with a beautiful falsetto voice who sang alto and frequently performed solos). Among other participants were the three brothers Lanckoroński (each specializing in a different musical skill: an opera tenor, a clavichord teacher, and a cellist); a government worker named Mülhausen; the great patron of music and a friend of Chopin, Józef Count

---

[57] *Allgemeine musikalische Zeitung,* April 1822, 276.

[58] Wieniarski, *Warszawa i warszawianie,* 2:14–15.

[59] "Antoni Orłowski," 372.

[60] Wieniarski, *Warszawa i warszawianie,* 2:14–15.

[61] Sobieszczański, *Rys historyczno-statystyczny wzrostu i stanu miasta Warszawy od najdawniejszych czasów aż do roku 1847,* 179.

[62] *Tygodnik Muzyczny i Dramatyczny,* 25 April 1821, no. 3, 11–12; Gołębiowski, *Gry i zabawy różnych stanów,* 252.

Figure 8.2. Długa Street with the Piarists' Church, location of the Society for the Friends of Religious and National Music Engraving by Carl Wilhelm Ullrich. Biblioteka Narodowa, Warsaw, G. 27356.

Cichocki; and his protégées the Turowski sisters and brother, the Orłowski family, and the opera alto Miss Lehman. The little Joanna Orłowska led the children sopranos, the altos were led by Miss Lehman and Gregorowicz, and the students of the Conservatory sang tenor and bass; the orchestra was made up of professionals and amateurs who "gladly worked with the charismatic Elsner."[63] Antoni Wejnert, who never passed up an opportunity to make good music, not only provided sacred compositions for this society but also involved his entire family in the music making.[64] In performances of large works, Elsner and Kurpiński used the help of the army kapellmeister Aleksander Pohlens, who was a virtuoso concert performer on the contrabassoon and a popular composer of dances. In such instances, he usually led his very well-prepared army chorus.[65] All musical celebrities of Warsaw gladly participated in performances, and Polish artists traveling through the capital took the opportunity to contribute their artistic talents.[66]

Among the concerts that took place in the Piarists' Church during the period of Fryderyk's involvement with Warsaw musical scene were the November 1825 performances of a Haydn mass, an Elsner mass, and Bee-

[63] "Antoni Orłowski," 373–375.
[64] Wójcicki, *Cmentarz powązkowski*, 1:217.
[65] *Ruch Muzyczny*, 1859, no. 3, 24.
[66] Wieniarski, *Warszawa i warszawianie*, 2:14–15.

thoven's Mass in C Major.[67] It is plausible that Chopin, involved with the circle of musicians performing at the Piarists' Church, was asked to participate in these concerts, or at least invited to attend them. When Mozart's *Requiem* was played in the Piarists' Church on July 29, 1829, Chopin had already started his first trip to Vienna.[68] Considering, however, that this masterpiece was frequently heard in various Warsaw churches, he doubtless already knew it well.

The Society for the Friends of Religious and National Music not only provided first-rate music for the Piarists' Church but also produced secular performances in other concert venues. In 1817, after many miscarried attempts, Elsner succeeded in instituting subscription concerts under the aegis of the society.[69] These were probably the concert series given in the Casino Room of the Sołtyk Palace during the years 1817–1818: sixteen concerts featuring an impressive repertory of Haydn, Mozart, and Spohr string quartets; piano concertos by Carl Arnold, Jan Ladislav Dussek, Robert Smith, and John Field; and smaller vocal and instrumental works. An even more remarkable concert repertory was reported for the 1819–1820 concert season, when members of the society performed twenty-eight weekly concerts in the Conservatory hall, under the direction of Lessel, Lentz, Würfel, Haase, Jawurek, Stolpe, and Peschke. Each evening included a complete symphony, a concerto, an aria, and a finale. Among the works performed during 1819–1820 season were symphonies by Haydn, Mozart, Beethoven, Romberg, Mehul, Lessel, Lenz, Krommer, and Witt; overtures by Beethoven, Cherubini, Méhul, Romberg, Spohr, Schneider, Elsner, Gerke, Kurpiński, Würfel, Poissl, Böhner, Morgenroth, Küffner, Generali, and Rossini; and concertos by Mozart, Spohr, Rode, Viotti, Lafont, Maurer, Matthaei, von Berbiguier, Lessel, Krommer, Cremont, Pergolesi, Ammon, Tulou, Hummel, Field, Dussek, Ries, and Klengel.[70]

After the 1814 decree of religious tolerance, Warsaw's Lutheran Church of the Holy Trinity (*Kościół Ewangelicko-Augsburski Św. Trójcy*) (see fig. 2.2) was free to add grandeur to its liturgy with music. From then on, special events received adequate musical treatment, and beginning in 1815, the church records indicate a more consistent effort to include musical performances for all high holy days. At first, these musical events consisted of Latin masses performed by amateurs and artists of the National Theater, and were organized by Elsner, who acted at the request of

[67] Sieradz, "Kultura muzyczna Warszawy," 180.

[68] The perfomance of the *Requiem* is reported by Sieradz, "Kultura muzyczna Warszawy," 190.

[69] *Tygodnik Muzyczny i Dramatyczny*, 25 April 1821, no. 3, 11–12.

[70] See *Calendarium* of concerts in Goldberg, "Musical Life in Warsaw during Chopin's Youth, 1810–1830," 398–408.

rector Samuel Bogumił Linde, chairman of the church's board of directors.[71] During the years 1821–1827, the direction of musical events in the church was in the hands of Józef Jawurek, who introduced German cantatas and oratorios, invited conservatory students to join the chorus and orchestra of theater musicians, and in larger works secured the participation of Russian military choirs. The resourceful Jawurek was able to raise funds for the purchase of scores and instruments (twelve violins, two violas, three cellos, and two basses).[72] These were added to the superb Classical organ, as well as the two timpani, five trombones, and four trumpets the church already owned, according to the 1782 inventory.[73] In the years 1828–1829, the direction of music in the church was taken over by another conservatory professor, the aforementioned Antoni Wejnert.

The names "Mlle. Schoppin" and "Herr Schoppin" (Ludwika and Fryderyk) appear several times within the existing documentation pertaining to the operations of the Lutheran Church in the years 1824–1829.[74] On the basis of these documents, Eugeniusz Szulc was able to conclude that Chopin frequently participated in musical events at the church during the years 1824–1825. The same article with some certainty placed Chopin in performance of a duet (with choir?) from Haydn's work *Die Schöpfung* and Eybler's hymn during Easter of 1824 (April 18, 1824); the Bierey *Easter Cantata* and selections from Hummel's Grand Mass (April 2, 1825); and large excerpts from *Die Schöpfung* and Elsner's hymn (May 22, 1825).[75] The improvisation at Brunner's eolimelodicon, mentioned in chapter 2, witnessed by Czar Alexander I took place at the Lutheran Church during the same period, in early May 1825.

The very long list of names compiled by Eugeniusz Szulc—the chorus and orchestra consisted of some two hundred people—includes the names of several conservatory professors (Bailly, Bielawski, Jawurek, Wejnert, and Elsner with his wife); theater musicians (Mrs. Aszperger, Szczurowski, Damse, and Żyliński); music lovers and outstanding ama-

---

[71] The Lutheran church at large maintained vestiges of Latin liturgy, especially the *missa brevis (Kyrie, Gloria)*; in Warsaw, a faction within the Lutheran community favored the introduction of Latin elements into the service; this, combined with the growing tendency toward the Polonization of the German population and the Lutheran church (at times church records and sermons were kept in Polish), made for very inconsistent liturgy. I am indebted for that information to Jerzy Gołos.

[72] Eugeniusz Szulc, "Nieznana karta warszawskiego okresu życia Chopina" [An unknown page from the Warsaw period of Chopin's life], *Rocznik Chopinowski* 18 (1986): 125–127.

[73] Jerzy Gołos, "Organy i muzyka w ewangielickim kościele Św. Trójcy w Warszawie" [The organ and music at the Lutheran Church of the Holy Trinity in Warsaw], *Ruch muzyczny* 15 (1990): 3.

[74] Szulc, "Nieznana karta," 136–150.

[75] Szulc, "Nieznana karta," 129–136.

teurs (Gregorowicz, Ledoux, Mrs. Linde, and Molsdorf); chiefs of military orchestras (Haase and Pohlens); the musical Orłowski family; the wife of the music publisher Brzezina; the violinists and violin builders Jan Michał and Henryk Rudert; as well as Chopin's conservatory colleagues (Józef and Eleonora Stefani, Nidecki, and Nowakowski) and a close friend (Biało-błocki).[76] In the fragmentary information about repertory performed in the Lutheran Church, one finds parts of Beethoven's Mass in C Major (November 11, 1825), portions of Haydn's work *Die Schöpfung* (Easter 1824), Hummel's Grand Mass in E-flat Major (Easter 1825), and works by Romberg, Elsner, Mozart, Wejnert, Himmel, Eybler, and others.[77] The index of scores in the possession of the church—probably including works played during performances—lists, among others, sacred works by Handel, C. P. E. Bach, J. C. Bach, Beethoven, Haydn, and Stadler.[78] Information presented by church records along with the enthusiastic reports in the local and foreign press paint a picture of a musical center on a truly European level— in repertory and performance alike.

The most elaborate schedule of church performances occurred on the somber occasion of the death of Czar Alexander I. Although the czar died some months earlier, the official funeral ceremonies in Warsaw took place in April 1826. On April 7, a solemn funeral mass was celebrated in the Metropolitan Church (St. John's Cathedral), and Józef Kozłowski's *Requiem* was performed by 250 singers.[79] The list of works heard during this service ended with Pergolesi's *Miserere* and Salieri's *Salve Regina*.[80] Services at the St. John Cathedral continued from April 10 through 12 with Kozłowski's *Requiem* performed again, under the direction of Soliva, and Mozart's *Requiem* conducted by Kurpiński. The Lutheran Church had a *Requiem* composed by Elsner, sung and played with the accompaniment of choralion (see fig. 2.2). On April 13, there were also grand musical services in the synagogue (probably the synagogue at Daniłłowiczowska street) and the Metropolitan Church (a Russian Orthodox service, during which a few hundred singers sang Old-Slavonic chant in beautiful harmony).[81] Printed sources document Chopin's presence during the ceremonies.[82] Unfortunately, the sources are silent on the subject of his par-

[76] Szulc, "Nieznana karta," 136–150.

[77] *Calendarium* of church concerts in Goldberg, "Musical Life in Warsaw during Chopin's Youth, 1810–1830," 452–459.

[78] Szulc, "Nieznana karta," 129–131.

[79] *Opis żałobnego obchodu po wielkopomnej pamięci nayiaśniejszym Alexandrze I* [A description of the funeral tribute to His Highness Alexander I of momentous memory] (Warsaw: Glücksberg, 1829), 74.

[80] Sieradz, "Kultura muzyczna Warszawy," 181.

[81] *Opis żałobnego obchodu po wielkopomnej pamięci nayiaśniejszym Alexandrze I*, 82.

[82] *Opis żałobnego obchodu po wielkopomnej pamięci nayiaśniejszym Alexandrze I*, 24.

ticipation in the musical events. Presumably, being an official student of the Conservatory and a recognized member of the Warsaw musical community, Chopin took part in at least some of the musical events.

Active musical schedules during holy seasons and, in particular, the ambitious performances heard during Alexander's funeral ceremonies prove that Warsaw had available the resources and skills needed for presenting large choral works and needed only good organization. Fryderyk, especially in his capacity as gymnasium and later conservatory student, had the opportunity to participate either as a listener or as a performer in numerous events featuring masterpieces of sacred repertory. This interest in religious continued throughout his life: he attended many performances of sacred music in Paris and owned the music for Mozart's *Requiem*, Rossini's *Stabat Mater*, and the just-published piano-vocal score of Bach's St. Matthew Passion, which he received from Schlesinger in 1843. At least in one instance, later on in life, he is reported to have composed a sacred work—a *Veni Creator* (not extant) for the 1846 wedding of his pupil Zofia Rosengardt and his friend Bohdan Zaleski.

The Virtuoso Concert

The newest type of public performance, the virtuoso concert, quickly gained favor in the Polish capital. These concerts of local and visiting master performers served as a context within which Chopin's own virtuosity developed and as a setting for his earliest experiences as a concertizing pianist. His two concerti and the lesser concert works (opp. 2, 13, 14, and 22) arose from the needs of the concert stage, and through virtuoso concerts he became acquainted with the newest technical concepts (for instance, those of Paganini) that he later absorbed into his own compositional language.

The virtuoso concert represented models of music making that were markedly different from those of the soirées and matinées sponsored by the various music societies. The primary goal of the virtuoso concert was financial gain for the star performer and the entrepreneur who provided the venue and organizational skill needed for the event. For this reason, the purpose of the virtuoso concert was to sell the largest possible number of tickets: performances took place in large halls, and concert programs were designed to attract the widest possible audiences. The larger venues required larger performing forces, and the organizers of these events, unlike music societies, were able to hire theater orchestras (which in most cities were the only permanent professional ensembles). Still, in some instances, even for a public virtuoso concert a large orchestra could not be obtained, and a chamber ensemble had to suffice.

In order to capture the interest of audiences that included only a small number of true connoisseurs, the rule of programming was variety—alternating vocal and instrumental pieces, mixing genres—as well as emphasis on virtuoso display. A typical concert would begin with an overture from an opera or the first movement of a symphony, and continue with the presentation of a concerto (preferably composed by the performer), other performers interrupting the concerto after the first movement with a short piece (often an aria from an opera or a brief, brilliant instrumental work). The second part of the concert, constructed in a similar manner, had another virtuoso piece (variations or potpourris on favorite themes), followed by more instrumental or vocal performances by subsidiary soloists, and concluding with the virtuoso extemporizing on themes given by the audience. In the early nineteenth century, the public virtuoso concert would never include chamber works as we know them or short solo piano works: piano miniatures and even sonatas still belonged in the salon, and true chamber music in more intimate venues intended for connoisseurs.

Warsaw had several performing spaces appropriate for virtuoso concerts: the most elegant were at the Town Hall and the Royal Castle, but those were reserved for concerts of the most distinguished musical guests and for carefully selected audiences. During his last year in Poland, Chopin was encouraged to perform in the Town Hall, but he declined, saying, "in Town Hall I would play—with no less stage fright and not much greater effect—for very few but of the highest class or for the city officials."[83] Most typical concerts took place in the National Theater, which in addition to the main stage had a smaller ballroom hall. It was in the main hall of the National Theater that Fryderyk's public virtuoso performances took place. Occasionally, concerts took place in other halls: the French Theater at the Saxon Palace, the Theater in the Orangery at the Royal Łazienki complex (fig. 8.3), or the hall of the Belweder Royal Palace.

Virtuoso concerts featured a variety of star performers: distinguished foreign guests who included Warsaw in their concert-tour itineraries, often on route to Moscow and St. Petersburg, as well as local musicians who had attained international fame and were returning or visiting home. With the establishment of the Conservatory, the ranks of young, skilled local performers increased—among Chopin's peers, Julian Fontana, and the somewhat younger Edward Wolff and Antoni Kątski toured the world as concert pianists. Because of its populist nature, the public virtuoso concert had the tendency to cross the boundaries between art and spectacle. Therefore, like other European cities, Warsaw marveled at ex-

[83] Chopin, Warsaw, to Woyciechowski, Poturzyn, 27 March 1830, *Korespondencja*, 1:116.

Vue du Château et de l'Amphithéâtre à Lazienki
Widok Pałacu i Amfiteatru w Łazienkach w Warszawie.

à Varsovie chez Dal-Trozzo

Figure 8.3. The royal palace and amphitheater at Royal Łazienki complex in Warsaw. Aquatint by Fryderyk Krzysztof Dietrich, *12 widoków* [Twelve vistas], c. 1820 (Warsaw: Dal Trozzo, 1827–29). Biblioteka Uniwersytecka, Warsaw, nr. 1032, tabl. 3.

pert performances by children and disabled musicians, who were judged not just on their musical merit but rather perceived as oddities. Such were the 1828 performances of Peter Simon, a blind virtuoso who served as the guitarist to the king of the Netherlands,[84] or of the blind flutist Grinberg in 1830.[85]

Nineteenth-century listeners particularly enjoyed concerts of young, exceptionally gifted musicians; Fryderyk was not the only *Wunderkind* admired in Warsaw, nor was he the most revered one. Among other Polish child prodigies who acquired fame in public concerts during the 1820s were Antoni Leśkiewicz, Józef Krogulski, Stefan Heller, the Kaczyński brothers, and the Kątski brothers. Chopin's parents and teachers greatly limited his public performances; with the exception of a handful of char-

[84] *Kurier warszawski*, 6 October 1828, no. 272, 1139.
[85] *Kurier warszawski*, 16 April 1830, no. 102, 513.

ity concerts, he did not begin to engage in public performances until, already as a student, he appeared in conservatory concerts. The parents of the other *Wunderkinder* had much fewer scruples about encouraging them to perform in public. In 1825, seven-year-old pianists—Józef Krogulski and Antoni Leśkiewicz—were heard in the Polish capital. The child star of that season was the little Krogulski, of whom the critics said: "More than his proficiency, music connoisseurs are amazed with his remarkable sense of tone color; it gives them hope that if training encourages the development of his talent, he will be regarded among the most prominent artists."[86] In 1830, these two pianists, now twelve-year-olds, were heard again in Warsaw. By then the twenty-year-old Chopin was recognized as Warsaw's best pianist and was often asked his opinion of them, but preferred to express it only privately to Tytus: "The little Leśkiewicz plays very well, though still mostly from the elbow. Yet I believe that he will be a better player than Krogulski."[87] A month later, Chopin shared with Tytus his personal thoughts (ringing with the self-importance of a young expert) about Siegmund Friedrich Wörlitzer, one of the visiting young foreign pianists:

> Mr. Woerlitzer, Pianist of His Majesty [the king of Prussia] is already here two weeks. He plays nicely, the little one. He is a Jew [Chopin uses the condescending diminutive *Żydek*, "little Jew"], therefore by nature very astute, and he rehearsed very well the few things that we have heard. He visited me. He is still a child; only sixteen years old. The Variations on "Alexander" March by Moscheles are his forte. He plays them perfectly; it seems that nothing remains to be desired. He was heard twice publicly and both times played these variations. When you will hear him, his playing will leave you content, although, between us, he has far to go to deserve the title bestowed on him.[88]

During Chopin's Warsaw years, many distinguished musicians visited the city. One of the first public concerts that Fryderyk heard and that left a distinct impression on him was the performance of the legendary Angelica Catalani. The singer came to Warsaw during her last extended tour of Europe. In December 1819 she gave four performances in the Town Hall, and a limited number of rather expensive tickets (30 złoties) were quickly sold; the general agreement was that she had pushed the art of the human voice to its limits.[89] The critics wrote that Catalani distin-

---

[86] *Allgemeine musikalische Zeitung*, November 1825, 761.

[87] Chopin, Warsaw, to Woyciechowski, Poturzyn, 10 April 1830, *Korespondencja*, 1:119.

[88] Chopin, Warsaw, to Woyciechowski, Poturzyn, 15 May 1830, *Korespondencja*, 1:124.

[89] Sobieszczański, *Rys historyczno-statystyczny wzrostu i stanu miasta Warszawy od najdawniejszych czasów aż do roku 1847*, 220.

guished herself with "pleasant appearance, lively performance, extraordinary sonorousness, force and agility of voice, especially in chromatic passages."[90]

Among the piano virtuosi who appeared in Warsaw, two had profound effect on Chopin's pianism: Maria Agata Wołowska-Szymanowska and Johann Nepomuk Hummel. The idol of Chopin's youth, Maria Szymanowska (fig. 8.4), gave a concert in Warsaw on May 6, 1823. She performed a Hummel concerto and the rondo from a Field's concerto. No record of Chopin having heard this performance exists, but a few years later, in when on January 15, 1827, Szymanowska was to perform a single concert in Warsaw National Theater, Chopin with eager anticipation wrote: "This week Mrs. Szymanowska is giving a concert. It is going to be on Friday and the price has been is raised. . . . I will be there without fail and I will inform you about the reception and the performance."[91] According to the press announcement, the concert took place not on Friday but on Monday.[92] The pianist performed a Hummel concerto, variations by Ries, and a potpourri on Weber's *Freischütz*.[93] In a review, Chopin's older friend Maurycy Mochnacki extolled the virtues of her artistry, praising her ability to bring "the illusive imitation of human singing to the highest art."[94]

Johann Nepomuk Hummel's musical vocabulary was perhaps the most direct source of Chopin's pianistic language. His compositions, well known and often performed in Warsaw, were part and parcel of Chopin's youthful performing repertory. The celebrated pianist visited Warsaw in the spring of 1829, and between April 11 and May 2 gave four public concerts. He performed his own compositions as well as pieces by other composers, but on each occasion the large audiences (about 700) attending his concerts were especially impressed with his improvisations. From a review of the second concert, which took place on April 18, we learn that he astonished his listeners with the use of fugues, chords, and bold passages in his improvisation on favorite themes by Mozart and Gluck's overture to *Iphigenia*, with cheerful krakowiak variations in between.[95] Regrettably, there is a hiatus in Chopin's surviving correspondence between

[90] Sobieszczański, *Rys historyczno-statystyczny wzrostu i stanu miasta Warszawy od najdawniejszych czasów aż do roku 1847*, 220.

[91] Chopin, Warsaw, to Jan Białobłocki, Sokołów, 8 [January 1827], *Korespondencja*, 1:75.

[92] *Kurier Warszawski*, 12 January 1827, reproduced in Kobylańska, *Chopin w kraju*, 152.

[93] Sieradz, "Kultura muzyczna Warszawy," 182.

[94] Maurycy Mochnacki, *Pisma* [Writings], ed. Artur Śliwiński (Lwów: Połoniecki, 1910), 378.

[95] *Kurier warszawski*, 19 April 1828, reproduced in Kobylańska, *Chopin w kraju*, 153.

Maria Szymanowska

Figure 8.4. Maria Szymanowska. Lithograph by [Józef] Oleszkiewicz, first half of the nineteenth century. Biblioteka Uniwersytecka, Warsaw, Inw. Gr. 3573.

December 1828 and August 1829, and his reactions to Hummel's performances are not known.

In connection with the two official visits of the new czar, Nicholas I, in 1829 and 1830, other illustrious musicians came to Warsaw, and series of high-profile public concerts took place. The first visit began on May 17, 1829, when the new czar arrived in Warsaw to be crowned king of Poland. The ceremonies surrounding the occasion were accompanied by grand musical events presented by local and visiting musicians who arrived in the city especially for the event, especially the great Niccolò Paganini and the internationally known Polish virtuoso violinist Karol

Lipiński. Already on the eve of the coronation, Paganini performed a private concert for the imperial couple.[96] The coronation took place on May 24, accompanied by a coronation mass composed especially for the occasion by Elsner, Soliva's *Veni creator*, and Kurpiński's *Te Deum*; these were performed by an ensemble of nearly 400 professional and amateur musicians.[97] The official ceremonies were followed by a solemn dinner in the palace, during which the guests could hear Paganini, Lipiński, Soliva, and the young singers Wołkow, Janikowska, and Gładkowska; the orchestra was conducted by Kurpiński. Afterward the Grand Marshal Adam Broniec invited the musicians to his palace, where merrymaking continued: reportedly, the tipsy Lipiński jumped on the table and played his fiddle, while the inebriated Paganini drank to his health in full approval.[98]

During his stay in Warsaw, Paganini played ten concerts, all equally popular (the last concert, in spite of hot weather, had an audience of 600).[99] According to the fragmentary information about the program, Paganini played the Allegro maestoso from a violin concerto by Kreutzer and his own Variations on the G String, and improvised on a Neapolitan song, "Oh, Mamma, Mamma Cara," and on a mazur from Elsner's opera *King Łokietek*: "Young Peasants from Połaniec" [*Parobcaki of Połańca*] (the same song as used as by Würfel in his variations, see fig. 3.15).[100]

Among the many compositional arrangements Paganini's concerts prompted, two survive in the Jagiellonian Library: a gallopade and a polonaise based on themes and motives from his performances (fig. 8.5). Similarly, the A Major Variations *Souvenir de Paganini*, based on the Neapolitan song used by Paganini, if indeed of Chopin's authorship, are believed to have been composed during 1829. In the fall of the same year, Chopin's letters reported the composition of the first études of op. 10, which, like the great violinist's performances, took instrumental virtuosity to a new level.[101]

The performances by Karol Lipiński were also very well received (see fig. 8.6, an arrangement responding to is performance): after his June 5 concert the audiences were in awe, and the gracious Paganini loudly ap-

---

[96] Józef Krasiński, *Pamiętniki* [Memoirs] (Poznań: Kraszewski, 1877), 161.

[97] Gołębiowski, *Gry i zabawy różnych stanów*, 253. For the composition of the mass, Elsner received from the emperor a gold snuffbox. Elsner, *Sumariusz*, 51.

[98] Krasiński, *Pamiętniki*, 161–162.

[99] *Kurier Warszawski*, 15 July 1829, no. 186, after Kobylańska, *Chopin w kraju*, 156.

[100] Sieradz, "Kultura muzyczna Warszawy," 189–190.

[101] Chopin, Warsaw, to Woyciechowski, Poturzyn, 20 October 1829, *Korespondencja*, 1:111; and Chopin, Warsaw, to Woyciechowski, Poturzyn, 14 January 1829 [1830], *Korespondencja*, 1:113.

Figure 8.5. Karol Magnus, *Polonez z motywów Paganiniego* [Polonaise on the motives of Paganini], title page with likeness of Niccolò Paganini (Warsaw: Magnus, 1829). Biblioteka Jagiellońska, Kraków, 528 III Mus.

plauded his younger colleague.[102] Lipiński was known and well received abroad, and his musical visits to his homeland were always welcomed with great enthusiasm. In 1827 Mochnacki wrote of his tone that "It is a timbre artfully differentiated. This sound—sometimes soulful and caressing, and then strong, emphatic, and loud—always bewitches with unspeakable magic and always resembles a spark discharged by a flintstone."[103] Mochnacki was also taken with his technical dexterity in variations on popular themes ("Cruel World" and "Let Us Love One Another")—probably Lipiński's op. 33 Fantasia: "What extraordinary difficulties!" he exclaimed,

[102] *Kurier Warszawski*, 6 June 1829, no. 150, after Kobylańska, *Chopin w kraju*, 157. Lipiński's relationship with Paganini began in Italy in 1817, when with great admiration he first heard the master. Soon afterward he became Paganini's protégé, and the two great violinists frequently played double concerti together. Their relationship took a new turn in the late 1820s, when a conflict between them arose, instigated by an unfriendly outsider. *Allgemeine musikalische Zeitung*, July 1835, 425–426.

[103] Mochnacki, *Rozprawy literackie*, 383.

and "What ease in overcoming them!"[104] All these virtues of Lipiński's art were extolled in a later review in the *Allgemeine musikalische Zeitung:*

> As a violin virtuoso he is truly so outstanding and exceptional that it would not be too much to say that we wish to count him among the very best artists of our time. . . . The greatest difficulties completely surrender their harsh nature under his hands and appear so powerless and malleably docile that, secure in himself like an ancient hero dallying with lions, he can play with them without the tiniest danger. . . . His stroke is long, wide, mighty, and always so tender as distant sighs; always producing [beautiful] tone.[105]

The 1829 Warsaw concerts gave rise to a fierce public debate between Paganini's and Lipiński's enthusiasts. Paganini was magnanimous, but Lipiński, according to Elsner, harbored true bitterness toward his great rival.[106]

The second visit of Nicholas I, during May of the following year, brought to Warsaw two other outstanding musicians: the French pianist Anne Caroline de Belleville and the famous German singer Henriette Sontag. The two distinguished guests were heard in several public performances, and in the end of May de Belleville, Sontag, and the young pianist Wörlitzer performed in Warsaw's Royal Castle for a private audience that included Nicholas I and his wife.[107] Fryderyk witnessed performances the illustrious guests gave outside of the Royal Castle. His opinion of the young Wörlitzer (quoted earlier) was lukewarm, but he thought de Belleville an excellent pianist, who impressed with lightness and elegance.[108] Sontag, the true star of the summer 1830 season, however, enthralled the twenty-year-old Fryderyk.

Only four years Chopin's senior, Sontag was considered one of the greatest sopranos of her time. She was praised not only for her extraordinary vocal agility but also for her musicianship and dramatic skill. By the time she performed in Warsaw, she already had premiered Beethoven's Ninth Symphony and *Missa solemnis* in 1824, made famous the role of Agathe in Weber's *Der Freischütz*, and brought audiences to their knees in Germany, France, and England. Having likely witnessed the "Sontagsfieber" of her admirers during his 1828 visit in Berlin, Chopin eagerly

---

[104] Mochnacki, *Rozprawy literackie,* 385.

[105] *Allgemeine musikalische Zeitung,* July 1835, 427.

[106] Ferdynand Hoesick, *Warszawa: Luźne kartki z przeszłości syreniego grodu* [Warsaw: Loose leaves from the past of the "mermaid city"] (Poznań: Księgarnia Św. Wojciecha, 1920), 113–114.

[107] Krasiński, *Pamiętniki,* 162.

[108] Chopin, Warsaw, to Woyciechowski, Poturzyn, 5 June 1830, *Korespondencja,* 1:128.

Figure 8.6. Karol Magnus, *Polonez z motywów Lipińskiego* [Polonaise on the motives of Lipiński], title page with likeness of Karol Lipiński (Warsaw: Magnus, 1829). Biblioteka Jagiellońska, Kraków, 416 III Mus.

anticipated her arrival in Warsaw.[109] Indeed, Warsaw's public loved Sontag, and her concerts were attended by large crowds of about 850.[110] Her visit was commemorated with compositions and publications celebrating her talent: Kurpiński composed for her a potpourri of Polish songs, which she performed in three of her concerts, and Chopin was asked by Prince Radziwiłł to refine a set of variations on a Ukrainian

[109] Chopin, Warsaw, to Woyciechowski, Poturzyn, 15 May 1830, *Korespondencja*, 1:123.
[110] *Kurier Warszawski*, 28 June 1830, no. 171, after Kobylańska, *Chopin w kraju*, 211.

dumka that this talented aristocrat wrote especially for Sontag.[111] These and several other publications occasioned by the singer's performances are now lost, but we are in possession of *Souvenir à la Sontag*, a polonaise based on works sung by her, composed and published by Karol Magnus (fig. 8.8), as well as Bielawski's arrangement of Pixis's variations on the popular Swiss theme "Schweizerbub" as sung at the National Theater by Sontag.[112] Fryderyk's letter to Tytus, written right after Sonntag's June 4 concert (fig. 8.7) is almost entirely devoted to the famous singer who captivated him with her talent, looks, and personality:

> Miss Sontag is not beautiful, but as pretty as could be. She charms everyone with her voice, whose range is not very large—since usually she lets us hear from A to C/C#—but which is very agile; her *diminuendi* are *non plus ultra*, her *portamenti* beautiful, and her scales (especially upward chromatic) are delicious.[113]

The fact that Chopin was not included in the two rounds of musical performances surrounding Warsaw visits of Nicholas I is puzzling: he was not among the solo performers during the coronation festivities in 1829 and was not invited to the czar's private soirée at the Royal Castle in 1830. Yet just a few years earlier, every opportunity had been seized to show him off to the Russian imperial family during their visits to the Congress Kingdom. In a letter to Tytus, Chopin makes a veiled comment about his absence from the 1830 Royal Castle concert, at which everybody else was present, and people "were surprised that I was not there, but I was not surprised."[114] One can only speculate as to the reason for his absences. Two explanations come to mind: professional jealousies (though Elsner, who would have wholeheartedly supported his favorite pupil, was very much in the center of these events, and no major pianistic stars who might have resented Chopin's competition were featured in the 1829 festivities); or, more likely, Chopin's falling out of favor with the imperial family in some manner, either because of the reshuffling of power within the house of the Romanoffs or because of his personal associations with young people who were viewed as political agitators.

The late 1820s witnessed an increased participation of young conservatory graduates in the capital's professional events. The coronation festivities of 1829 included performances by Chopin's classmates Anna

---

[111] Chopin, Warsaw, to Woyciechowski, Poturzyn, 5 June 1830, *Korespondencja*, 1:127.

[112] Chopin's Variations in E Major on "Steh'auf, steh'auf o du Schweizerbub" were probably composed prior to Sonntag's Warsaw concerts. See chapter 4, note 54.

[113] Chopin, Warsaw, to Woyciechowski, Poturzyn, 5 June 1830, *Korespondencja*, 1:127.

[114] Chopin, Warsaw, to Woyciechowski, Poturzyn, 5 June 1830, *Korespondencja*, 1:128.

Figure 8.7. Announcement of Henriette Sontag's concert, 4 June 1830. Biblioteka Jagiellońska, Kraków, DżS 224678 IV.

Wołkow and Konstancja Gładkowska, the object of his secret adoration. Several other young musicians had their official debuts: among them, two very talented (by his own assessment) composition students of Elsner were presented to the public: Ignacy Feliks Dobrzyński first performed in the National Theater on September 29, 1827, and Antoni Orłowski was heard on the national stage on February 7, 1829.[115] It was time for Fryderyk to appear at Poland's main concert hall.

Chopin's official debut at the National Theater took place on March 17, 1830 (fig. 8.9). The soprano Barbara Mejer and a French horn player, Karl

[115] Kobylańska, *Chopin w kraju*, 154.

Figure 8.8. Johann Peter Pixis, *Waryiacye na thema szwaycarskie Der Schweizerbue* [*sic*] . . . *Śpiewane w Teatrze Narodowym przez pannę Henriette Sontag* [Variations on Swiss themes "Der Schweizerbub" . . . Sung in the National Theater by Miss Henriette Sontag (Warsaw: Vivier, 1830), title page with likeness of Henriette Sontag. Biblioteka Jagiellońska, III 100.

Goerner, joined him in the performance; Kurpiński led the orchestra. Chopin played his Concerto in F Minor op. 21 and the Fantasia on Polish Themes op. 13. Other pieces performed during the concert included overtures from Kurpiński's *Cecylia Piaseczyńska* and Elsner's *Leszek Biały*, and Ferdinand Paër's vocal variations *La biondina*. From the several divergent reports, it can be inferred the concert was a mixed success. Skrodzki, who was a youngster at the time of the event, has given us a rather bleak, and probably inaccurate, description of the performance: "We also remember Chopin's first concert, which was received with indifference. The National Theater was empty, and most of the audience either received free admission, or was connected with him through close acquaintance or friendship."[116] This description is inconsistent with the note in *Kurier Warszawski*: "There were 800 people, which proves that our audience deems to reward true talent. The young virtuoso pleased the guests; it

[116] Wielisław [Eugeniusz Skrodzki], *Wieczory piątkowe i inne gawędy* [Friday evenings and other tales], ed. M. Opałek (Warsaw: Państwowy Instytut Wydawniczy, 1962), 114–15.

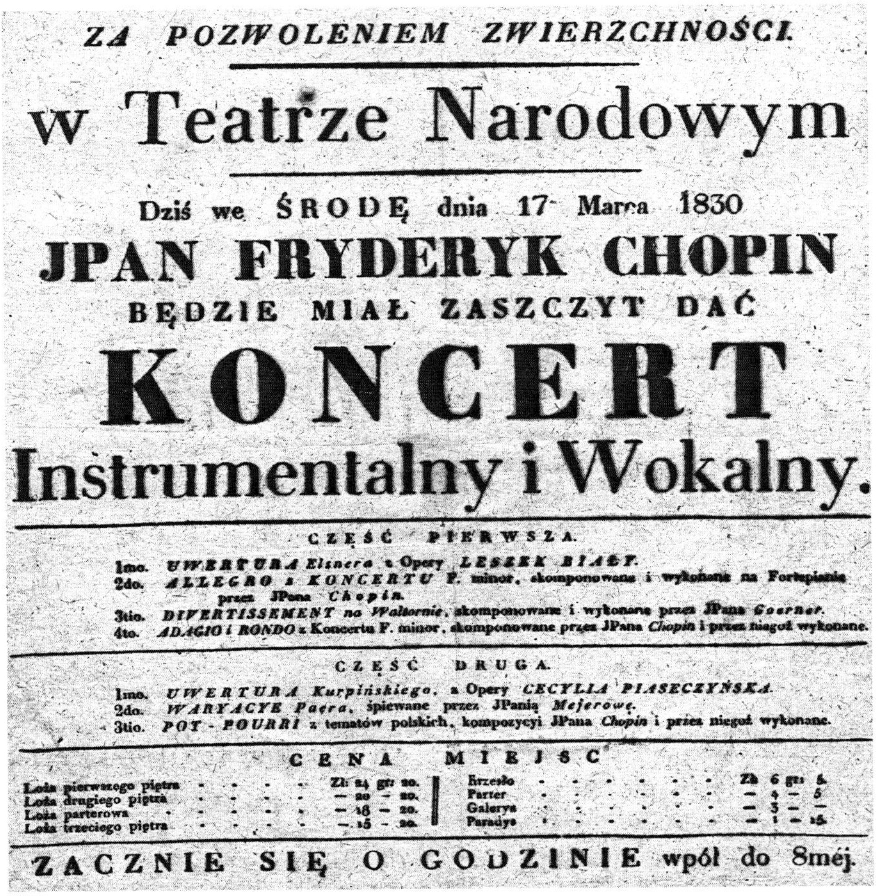

Figure 8.9. Announcement of Fryderyk Chopin's concert, 17 March 1830. Biblioteka Jagiellońska, Kraków, DŻS 224678 IV.

was agreed that he belongs among the greatest masters."[117] The review written by Chopin's close friend Mochnacki, while enthusiastic, offered some basis for criticism:

> This adagio in Mr. Chopin's concerto, this work of an extraordinary musical genius, puts our young virtuoso next to foremost artists of Europe. Truly! One, who so young begins like this will spread his name far. . . . Mr. Chopin's touch is elegant, delicate; maybe in passage-work one could wish more energy and strength; in a salon Mr. Chopin's execution would make a still greater impression.[118]

[117] *Kurier Warszawski*, 18 March 1830, no. 75, 377.
[118] Mochnacki, *Pisma*, 420.

Chopin's own account of the event expressed in a letter to Tytus indicates that he was aware of his listeners' mixed emotions:

> The first concert, although it was full and three days before no more boxes or seats were available, did not leave an impression on the crowd, as I perceived it. The first Allegro, accessible to a small number, received bravos, but it seems to me only because one was expected to be astonished—how amazing!—and to pretend to be a connoisseur! The Adagio and Rondo had the greatest effect—here one could hear more sincere cries—but *Potpourri on Polish Themes,* in my view, completely missed its mark. Bravos were given in the conviction that "before departure we ought to let him know that we were not bored."[119]

In spite of the mixed reception, the public was eager for Chopin to give another concert; many people who tried to obtain loges and seats for the first concert were unsuccessful, so a second concert was scheduled for the following Monday.[120]

The second concert took place on March 22, 1830 (fig. 8.10). The program was changed, probably to better suit the tastes of the audience. It included a new symphony by Józef Nowakowski (a student at the Conservatory), Mrs. Mejer singing Soliva's grand aria from *Helena i Malwina,* Józef Bielawski performing Beriot's violin variations, and the much-anticipated appearance of Chopin. This time he played to an apparently enthusiastic audience of nine hundred. The centerpiece of the performance was still the F Minor concerto, but the *Fantasia on Polish Themes* was dropped, and in its place he improvised on two favorite songs, "Cruel World" and "In Town Strange Customs" (see discussion in chapter 7 and exs. 7.1 and 7.2)[121] In his review of this event, Mochnacki again hinted at superior qualities of Chopin's art that appealed to connoisseurs but could not be appreciated by typical concert audiences: "The improvisation did not and could not achieve the same enthusiastic effect, since it was a genuine not faked improvisation, and as such it could not compare with compositions so happily inspired, so skillfully finished, and supported with utter enchantment of rich harmony."[122]

Chopin was heard at the National Theater once more on October 11, 1830. This time, he invited two colleagues from the Conservatory, the young, talented vocalists Gładkowska and Wołkow, to share the concert with him.[123] The program opened with a symphony by Goerner, followed

---

[119] Chopin, Warsaw, to Woyciechowski, Poturzyn, 27 March 1830, *Korespondencja,* 1:114–115.

[120] *Kurier Warszawski,* 18 March 1830, no. 75, 378.

[121] *Kurier warszawski,* 23 March 1830, no. 80, after Kobylańska, *Chopin w kraju,* 244.

[122] Mochnacki, *Pisma,* 421.

[123] Chopin, Warsaw, to Woyciechowski, 5 October 1830, *Korespondencja,* 1:144.

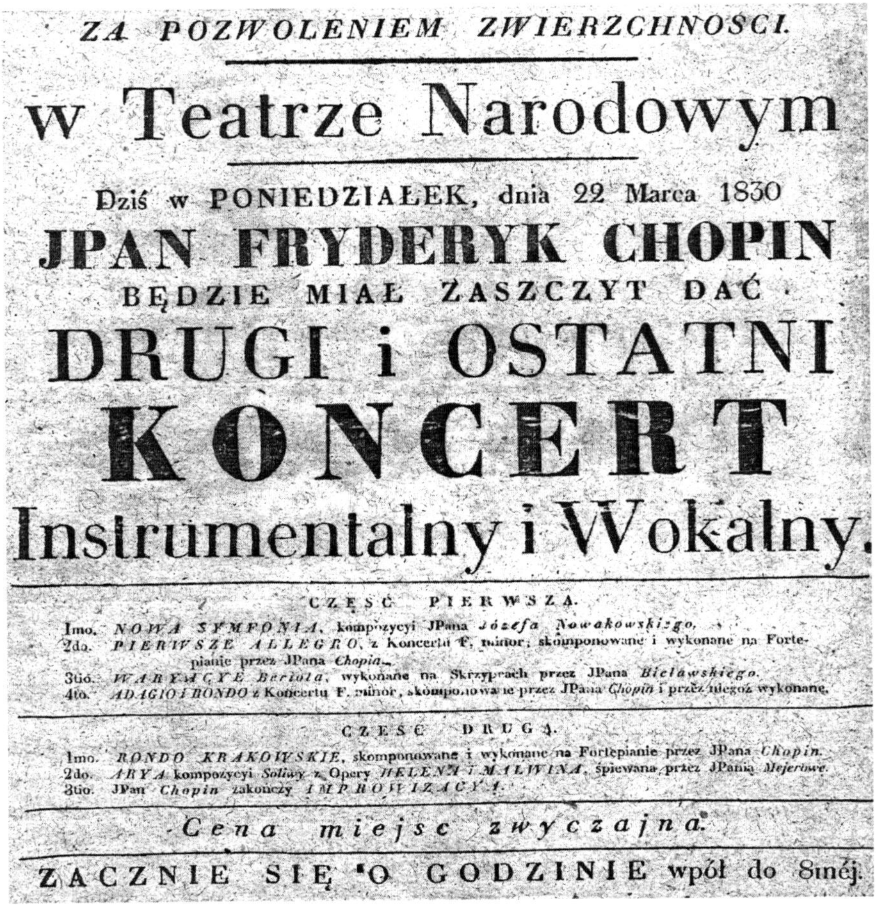

ZA POZWOLENIEM ZWIERZCHNOSCI.

w Teatrze Narodowym

Dziś w PONIEDZIAŁEK, dnia 22 Marca 1830

JPAN FRYDERYK CHOPIN

BĘDZIE MIAŁ ZASZCZYT DAĆ

DRUGI i OSTATNI

KONCERT

Instrumentalny i Wokalny.

CZĘSC PIERWSZA.

1mo. *NOWA SYMFONIA*, kompozycyi JPana *Józefa Nowakowskiego*.
2do. *PIERWSZE ALLEGRO*, z Koncertu F. minor; skomponowane i wykonane na Fortepianie przez JPana *Chopin*.
3tio. *WARYACYE Beriota*, wykonane na Skrzypcach przez JPana *Bielawskiego*.
4to. *ADAGIO i RONDO* z Koncertu F. minor, skomponowane przez JPana *Chopin* i przez niegoż wykonane.

CZESC DRUGA.

1mo. *RONDO KRAKOWSKIE*, skomponowane i wykonane na Fortepianie przez JPana *Chopin*.
2do. *ARYA* kompozycyi *Soliwy* z Opery *HELENA i MALWINA*, śpiewana przez JPanią *Mejerowe*.
3tio. JPan *Chopin* zakończy *IMPROWIZACYĄ*.

Cena miejsc zwyczajna.

ZACZNIE SIĘ O GODZINIE wpół do 8mej.

Figure 8.10. Announcement of Fryderyk Chopin's concert, 22 March 1830. Biblioteka Jagiellońska, Kraków, DŻS 224678 IV.

by the Allegro from Chopin's Concerto in E Minor. After the Allegro, Wołkow sang an aria with a chorus by Soliva (conducted by the composer), and then Chopin played the next two movements of his concerto. The second part opened with Rossini's Overture to *Guillaume Tell*, followed by an exquisite performance of the cavatina "Oh quante lagrime per te versai" from *La donna del Lago* by Konstancja Gładkowska. Fryderyk closed the concert with his *Fantasia on Polish Themes* op. 13.[124]

The pianist's friend Józef Reinschmidt remembered that during this concert Chopin also improvised on a theme given by the audience. Sup-

[124] Chopin, Warsaw, to Woyciechowski, Poturzyn, 12 October 1830, *Korespondencja*, 1:146–147.

posedly, Elsner asked Fryderyk's friends to select and write down a theme, which turned out to be the popular Polish folk song "Hops" (*Chmiel*).[125] Chopin had already improvised on the same theme during his August 11, 1829, concert in Vienna, and thus his task was easier.

The audiences were very pleased, and Kurpiński briefly commented on the performance in his private journal: "This evening a concert consisting of fine pieces was beautifully performed: particularly liked were Mr. Chopin's second concerto and overture from Rossini's opera *Wilhelm Tell*."[126] Moreover, Chopin himself was very content with his performance. Since he was given more control over the program, he was able to select orchestral works he thought suitable and to invite competent vocalists, "so there were none of these unfortunate clarinets or bassoons between piano [numbers]."[127] Soliva's command of the orchestra was so confident that Chopin related to Tytus "never before have I played so calmly with an orchestra."[128] It was undeniably an encouraging experience, and he concluded: "I was not a tiny bit scared and I played as I do when I am alone."[129] Writing these words, he did not know that this performance was fated to be his last public appearance in his homeland. Less than a month later, he set out on his way to Vienna.

The two concerti Chopin composed and presented in concert during his last year in Warsaw were the crowning achievement of his early output. They were quickly absorbed into core pianistic concert repertory, where they remain till today, notwithstanding the critics' bemoaning of their formal and orchestrational deficiencies. Indeed, these works cannot be properly assessed without understanding their original performing contexts and letting them stand within the concerto *brillant* tradition to which they belonged. Records of concert life as well as information about scores available in Chopin's Warsaw indicate that he was familiar with a wide array of concerti by contemporary and past composers. Mozart, Haydn, and their contemporaries were known and performed in Poland, but the attention of audiences and young musicians was captured by a group of contemporary virtuosi: among pianists the most admired were Hummel, Moscheles, and Ries, and to a lesser degree Field, Kalkbrenner,

---

[125] Anna Wóycicka, "Wieczorek pożegnalny Fryderyka Chopina" [Fryderyk Chopin's farewell evening], *Pion*, 1934, no. 24, 2.

[126] "Tadeusz Przybylski, "Fragmenty 'Dziennika Prywatnego' Karola Kurpińskiego" [Fragments of Kurpiński's 'private diary'], *Muzyka* 20 (1975): 108.

[127] Chopin, Warsaw, to Woyciechowski, Poturzyn, 5 October 1830, *Korespondencja*, 1:144.

[128] Chopin, Warsaw, to Woyciechowski, Poturzyn, 12 October 1830, *Korespondencja*, 1:147.

[129] Chopin, Warsaw, to Woyciechowski, Poturzyn, 12 October 1830, *Korespondencja*, 1:146.

and Herz. Chopin's pianistic skill and taste were nurtured through hearing and performing these *stile brillant* works. It is not clear which specific pieces he played, but we know he performed concerti by Gyrowetz, Ries, Hummel, and Moscheles, as well as possibly having played Kalkbrenner's and Field's concerto compositions.

The musical vocabulary of Chopin's two concerti clearly derived from works he heard and played in Warsaw. Like that of Hummel and Moscheles, his piano spoke in vocal operatic idiom—the ornamental melodic lines of concerti *brillant* originated in vocal *fioriture* of Italian opera. Operatic influences were perhaps most pronounced in slow movements of concerti: models for Chopin's slow movements were as much the bel canto lines of Rossini as slow movements of Hummel's Concerto in A Minor op. 85 and Moscheles' Concerto in G Minor op. 58. Especially pronounced as a source of inspiration for Chopin's op. 21 is the recitative interrupting the lyrical narrative in Moscheles' op. 58. Overall, Chopin's figurations are clearly most indebted to those of Hummel; however, in performance, Chopin's figurations were unlike Hummel's, who cultivated a dry, staccato touch. Already enamored with Rossinian bel canto, Chopin wanted his runs to always be rendered cantabile. Perhaps Warsaw audiences' dissatisfaction with Chopin's concerts was influenced by the forced comparison with the recently heard Hummel, whose pianistic style they expected from Chopin as an extension of hearing his compositional language in Chopin's concerti. But Chopin's playing was based on completely different principles. Moreover, Chopin went beyond his models by conceiving figurations that were unconventional and imparted an illusive spontaneity of improvisation, and by using a harmonic language that went beyond that of his prototypes.

The *stile brillant* concerti were composed by touring virtuosi—first and foremost for their own use. Their language and design were dictated by the tastes and whims of concert audiences. Such was the context for the creation of Chopin's opp. 11 and 21. Thus the formal conventions of the concerto *brillant* genre were governed by the desire for virtuoso display; this and the practical obstacles of having to perform in less than perfect circumstance made the role of the orchestra secondary. These conventions were best described in Czerny's model, in which form is determined by melody: the alternation between lyrical themes and virtuoso *Spielepisoden*. Where Chopin really transcended his models was in the overall architectural and tonal coherence of his works, a quality absent in the typical virtuoso concerto.[130]

---

[130] The structure, language, and ancestry of Chopin's concerti are discussed by John Rink, *Chopin: the Piano Concertos* (Cambridge: Cambridge University Press, 1997), with a discussion of the research pertaining to the formal models of the virtuoso concerto, 1–6.

The orchestration of Chopin's concerti has been subject to the most severe critiques: in fact, there have been several attempts to "improve" or "correct" what was deemed "weak orchestration." However, to be adequately judged, the orchestration of Chopin's concert works must be considered within the aesthetics of the early nineteenth-century orchestra and virtuoso concerto, rather than the symphonic concerto tradition that followed, as has been the case. Not just the concerto *brillant* trivialization of the tutti/solo dialogue in favor of virtuoso display but also the demand for interchangeability of performing forces has shaped Chopin's orchestration choices. Because of the various performing ensembles called on to accompany the soloist (depending on the availability of funds and players), Chopin scored his concert works with several performing ensembles in mind: a full orchestra, a chamber orchestra, and string ensembles of four to nine players. His scoring makes much better sense in the context of these diverse performing options, whether he was consciously thinking about the performability of the accompaniment by the various chamber groups or simply was following the contemporary concerto *brillant* models conceived within this tradition. For instance, his sparse writing for the strings in solo accompaniments is unavoidable if strings are to take over the wind parts in quartet performance—in particular during solo sections when the piano, occupied with its own part, could not fill in for the missing winds. It also makes sense that only the wind instruments present in a chamber orchestra are given independent melodic function: Chopin does not write countermelodies involving just any combination of wind instruments, but instead uses the instruments that are available to him in the typical salon orchestra (obbligato); other instruments serve only as reinforcements in tuttis (ad libitum) and their absence from a chamber performance does not effect the musical integrity of the piece. Chopin's orchestration choices can only be understood when seen as reflecting this fluid notion of orchestral sonority and the changeable nature of the relationship among the soloist, the ensemble, the conductor, and the musical text, typical of early nineteenth-century orchestral practices.[131]

Chopin's greatest achievement in his concerti is that, having been borne out of musical practices on the boundaries of art and popular entertainment, they rose above the very genre from which they originated. The characteristics that in the works of lesser composers of concertos became clichés—dazzling figurations, suave melodies, unpredictable har-

---

[131] Goldberg, "Chamber Arrangements of Chopin's Concert Works," 77–79. Modern performances, with the two powerful sound masses of the concert grand piano and a full-sized symphonic orchestra, tend to remove any nuance of sonority interplay. Sound recording touchups often further obscure the role of orchestra.

monies—were elevated by Chopin to the rank of highly individual, elo-quent, and coherent musical language. Because the genre was so much determined by popular taste, Chopin took his earliest opportunity to abandon it and the concert stage. Educated by Elsner, who taught him to uphold the highest principles of art, he was dissatisfied with a genre that was governed by fleeting fashions. This feeling was reinforced by the mixed reception of his art on the part of the typical concert-goers. But it is the freshness of ideas, the subtle lyricism, the formidable pianistic chal-lenges, and the overall coherence that keep Chopin's concerti fresh for each new generation of music lovers and musicians.

Music in Cafés

During his last years in Warsaw, Chopin became a frequent guest in cafés, fashionable with students, intelligentsia, and artists. Musical perfor-mances took place in many cafés. More significant, gatherings in cafés were the pulse of the Polish capital. It was here, especially in the café Kop-ciuszek, that artistic projects were discussed and artistic events, includ-ing Chopin's concert performances, received the most candid reviews. As expected, political debates were just as lively as aesthetic ones. No wonder that in this atmosphere, specifically at the Honoratka café, that plans for armed revolt against Russian occupation were born. And when Chopin left his homeland, it was in a café—U Brzezińskiej (At Brzezińska's), one of his favorite haunts—that the final goodbyes were said between him and his friends.[132]

According to Magier, the first café (coffeehouse) in Warsaw was opened in 1724.[133] Soon there were others, yet only in the first quarter of the nineteenth century did cafés become truly fashionable in War-saw. The *Warsaw Guide* for 1829 lists thirty-three café owners, and Gołębiowski claims that Warsaw had as many as a hundred cafés at the time.[134] There were many elegant cafés frequented mostly by Warsaw's dandies, for example the establishment run by a Swiss named Lourse, which had a very elegant décor and French newspapers available for reading.[135] Chopin was no stranger to places like this, and he was known

[132] Kazimierz Władysław Wójcicki, *Kawa literacka w Warszawie (1829–1830)* [Literary coffee in Warsaw] (Warsaw: Gebethner i Wolff, 1873), 23.

[133] Magier, *Estetyka miasta stołecznegoWarszawy*, 58.

[134] *Przewodnik warszawski 1829* [Warsaw guide 1829], (Warsaw: Glücksberg, 1829), commercial part, 13. Łukasz Gołębiowski, *Opisanie historyczno-statystyczne miasta Warszawy* [Historic-statistical description of the city of Warsaw] (Warsaw: Glücksberg, 1827), 193.

[135] Magier, *Estetyka miasta stołecznegoWarszawy*, 57.

to stop by Lourse's.[136] But of greater interest are the intellectual and artistic cafés of Warsaw, the most famous being Honoratka, Kopciuszek, Dziurka, U Sabatowskiej, U Brzezińskiej, and Suchy Las, and the presence of music in Warsaw cafés.

With the general increase of interest in public musical entertainment, restaurants and cafés began to introduce performances. By midcentury, these were common: "Citizens of Warsaw adore music. . . . The owners of various culinary-leisure establishments are well aware of this and compete in engaging native and foreign orchestras."[137] But the first reference to musical performances in an eating establishment is the aforementioned 1815 report of Monday and Friday quartets at an eatery in Dulfus House. In 1822, the restaurant of Hotel Europa hosted the visiting Italian singers Lucich and Fracassi, who sang Rossini's arias and duets with the accompaniment of violin and guitar.[138] The enthusiastic reception of these concerts prompted the owner to institute Thursday and Sunday garden concerts during the summer of 1823, featuring Italian singers performing arias and duets from the newest operas by Rossini and other composers.[139] Well-played quartets at U Sabatowskiej (At Sabatowska's) attracted an unusual variety of people, a young crowd in particular.[140] New establishments continued to open until the eve of the November Uprising, many with a specific intent to attract guests with offers of good music. Thus when in the fall of 1830 a new café opened in the Chodkiewicz/Kochanowski Palace on Miodowa street, the owners advertised the elegant décor with Corinthian columns surrounding the central salon and a balcony with galleries and loges, as well as the musical entertainment provided daily by Czech musicians.[141]

Cafés were meeting places for the intellectual and artistic avant-garde of Warsaw, providing an atmosphere that fostered new thought and creation. In the best company, in gardens and cafés, one would always hear talk about music, especially the names of famous composers: Paisiello, Mozart, Hummel, Cimarosa, Méhul, and so on.[142] Here was where most

---

[136] Chopin, Warsaw, Woyciechowski, Poturzyn, 4 September 1830, *Korespondencja*, 1:136.

[137] Wieniarski, *Warszawa i warszawianie*, 2:3.

[138] *Kurier warszawski*, 31 May 1822, no. 129, 1.

[139] *Kurier warszawski* 24 May 1823, no. 122, 1.

[140] Magier, *Estetyka miasta stołecznego Warszawy*, 58.

[141] *Kurier warszawski*, 23 November 1830, no. 315, 1645. Initially, performances were to take place on Sundays, Mondays, Wednesdays, and Fridays, but the schedule was adjusted to daily performances right away. *Kurier warszawski*, 24 November 1830, no. 316, 1650–1651. The prospects for this new enterprise were likely confused by the outbreak of the uprising on 29 November.

[142] Magier, *Estetyka miasta stołecznego Warszawy*, 143.

recent musical performances were debated and opinions were formed. After his second concert at the National Theater in the spring of 1830, Chopin, cognizant of the opinion-forming power of café chat, wrote to Tytus: "I would have liked to have been at Kopciuszek to hear the debates that must have surrounded my person."[143]

Music and other arts were often subjects of discussion at Kopciuszek and Suchy Las, the two cafés attended by the circle associated with the National Theater. Kopciuszek (Cinderella), opened in 1817 by the prosperous Warsaw confectioner Józef Baldy, was the first café in the style of the Café Procope in Paris. Kopciuszek moved several times; beginning in 1819 it was located at Długa Street, and during that period it was visited by the entire cultural elite of Warsaw: writers, university professors, actors, and musicians.[144] There nearly every evening one could meet Osiński, Brodziński, Skarbek, Dmuszewski, Kurpiński, Elsner, and other luminaries. Theater was at the center of most conversations, but they would often evolve into disputes of an aesthetic nature.[145] Discussions and exchanges of aesthetic judgments brought together young and old guests; Brodziński in particular was always ready to mingle with the young crowd.[146] The opportunities to share ideas with and draw encouragement from others also nurtured literary and artistic invention.[147] For instance, the opera *Charlatan* (see chapter 7) was conceived in the stimulating environment of a café conversation between Karol Kurpiński and Aloizy Żółkowski (actor and librettist).[148] In 1826, Kopciuszek moved to the Tepper Palace at Miodowa street (also the location of Dziurka [The Little Hole]).[149] At the time when Chopin's concert appearances were debated there, Kopciuszek still was the site of fervent literary disputes, even though it lost some of its clientele.[150]

At the end of the 1820s, a group of Kopciuszek's guests changed their meeting place to Suchy Las (Dry Forest), situated at Długa Street, near the National Theater. After it was taken over by Bautz, this café became a very important meeting place for theater people. It was frequented by, among others, Ludwik Osiński and visited daily by Ludwik Dmuszewski, a cen-

[143] Chopin, Warsaw, to Tytus Woyciechowski, Poturzyn, 27 March 1830, *Korespondencja*, 1:115.

[144] Tadeusz Morawski, *Moje przygody; ustęp z pamiętników* [My adventures: excerpt from memoirs] (Kraków: Leon Paszkowski, 1873), 11.

[145] Dmochowski, *Wspomnienia*, 179–180; and Wójcicki, *Kawa literacka*, 6.

[146] Morawski, *Moje Przygody*, 11.

[147] Magier, *Estetyka miasta stołecznego Warszawy*, 6.

[148] Wójcicki, *Kawa literacka*, 6.

[149] Tadeusz Frączyk, *Warszawa młodości Chopina* [Warsaw of Chopin's youth] (Kraków: Polskie Wydawnictwo Muzyczne, 1961), 321–322.

[150] Wójcicki, *Kawa literacka*, 55.

tral figure in the life of the National Theater: actor, author, director, and member of the board of directors. A creature of habit, Dmuszewski visited Suchy Las before performances, always sitting in the same chair.[151] After his spring 1830 concerts, Chopin, embarrassed, reported to Tytus that Dmuszewski, impressed by his performances, intended to publish sonnets to him in *Kurier Warszawski*.[152] The text was published in *Kurier Warszawski* much later—the day after Chopin left Poland; Elsner set it to music as the "Farewell" Cantata, and it was performed at the city gates as a goodbye to the departing composer.

University students gathered mostly at U Brzezińskiej, located at Krakowskie Przedmieście:

> In this quiet and peaceful corner—filled from seven in the morning with youths, who for breakfast nourished themselves with the superb coffee—from three in the afternoon an ample group of literati gathered, in order to read all the periodicals as much as to visit and chat with each other.[153]

During his last years in Poland, Chopin liked to stop by U Brzezińskiej in the company of his friend Dominik Magnuszewski.[154] Other young men from Chopin's circle also visited the café: Ignacy Feliks Dobrzyński, a conservatory colleague of Chopin, came here often; Kazimierz Wójcicki, the future historian, first met Chopin at U Brzezińskiej. Konstanty Gaszyński, the author of a poem dedicated to Chopin and entitled "Farewell," was also a frequent guest; perhaps the poem was presented to Chopin during his last visit in this café, which took place the day before he left Poland.[155]

While Chopin was preparing to leave Poland to present his musical talents during a tour abroad (at the time he had no intention of remaining abroad), his closest friends were involved in plotting an insurrection against the Russian occupation of Poland. These young men—Maurycy Mochnacki, Józef Bohdan Zaleski, and Seweryn Goszczyński—were already members of the Union of Free Poles (*Związek Wolnych Polaków*), a secret patriotic organization in existence since 1820; they and other friends and acquaintances of Chopin—Konstanty Gaszyński and Joachim Lelewel among them—were at the heart of the plot. A month after Chopin left Poland, they all were bearing arms against the czar. In the years preceding the uprising, the favorite meeting place of these revolutionary ac-

---

[151] Wielisław, *Wieczory piątkowe i inne gawędy*, 69.

[152] Chopin, Warsaw, to Woyciechowski, Poturzyn, 17 April 1830, *Korespondencja*, 1:121.

[153] Wójcicki, *Cmentarz powązkowski*, 2:212.

[154] Wójcicki, *Kawa literacka*, 17.

[155] Wójcicki, *Kawa literacka*, 22–23.

Figure 8.11. The inside of the *Honoratka* café. Oil by Feliks Pęczarski, 1830, from Henryk Piątkowski, *Album sztuki polskiej* (Warsaw: P. Laskauer and W. Babicki, 1901).

tivists was Honoratka café (fig. 8.11), which belonged to Honorata Zimmerman (Honoratka being the diminutive of her given name), and which still exists, having gone through many transformations, at its original Miodowa 14 location. Before his departure from Poland, Chopin was frequently seen there.[156] In fact, the distancing between Chopin and the Russian imperial family that took place in the last years of his stay in Poland and the Russian authorities' subsequent distrust of the composer may have been triggered by his café associations with the revolutionaries at Honoratka.[157] He was not involved in the conspiracy, but he certainly

[156] Magier, *Estetyka miasta stołecznego Warszawy*, 282.

[157] Such sentiments were expressed directly in 1835, when after Chopin's patriotic improvisations at the piano in the salon of the Wodzińskis in Dresden, Count Józef Krasiński was called to the Russian embassy and harshly reprimanded for listening to a demagogue like Chopin. Krasiński, *Pamiętniki*, 162.

was caught up in revolutionary fervor. Once the uprising broke out, he longed to join his friends in combat, and to them he directed all his thoughts: the hopes and fears explicit in his letters and in the so-called Stuttgart diary.

Chopin departed from Poland in the hope of learning more about music and establishing an international career. His expectations were satisfied: in his new home he was able to hear the most splendid performers and compositions, and he reached more than short-lived fame— through his music, he achieved immortality. Yet even Chopin's mature works, composed within the dazzling setting of Parisian concert life, are better understood with the knowledge of the stimuli that nourished his musical imagination when as a young man he attended and participated in the musical life of Warsaw.

SELECT BIBLIOGRAPHY

Secondary Sources

Ballstaedt, Andreas, and Tobias Widmaier. *Salonmusik: Zur Geschichte und Funktion einer bürgerlichen Musikpraxis.* Stuttgart: Steiner Verlag Wiesbaden, 1989.

Bełza, Igor. *Maria Szymanowska.* Translated by Jadwiga Ilnicka. Kraków: Polskie Wydawnictwo Muzyczne, 1987.

Broek, Clara van den. "Le Château des Désertes de George Sand, cours de jeu dramatique: Don Giovanni en prose." *Revue belge de philologie et d'histoire* 76/3 (1998): 687–708.

Bućko, Anna. "Kultura muzyczna Warszawy w latach 1807–1815" [Musical culture of Warsaw in the years 1807–1815]. Master's thesis, University of Warsaw, 1982.

Burkhart, Charles. "Chopin's Concluding Expansions." In *Nineteenth-Century Piano Music: Essays in Performance and Analysis.* Edited by David Witten. New York: Garland, 1997, 95–116.

———. "How Rhythm Tells the Story in 'Là ci darem la mano.'" *Theory and Practice* 16 (1991): 21–38.

Chachaj, Małgorzata. "*Jadwiga, królowa polska* Juliana Ursyna Niemcewicza w ocenie warszawskiej publiczności teatralnej." [Julian Ursyn Niemcewicz's *Jadwiga, the Polish Queen* in the assessment of Warsaw theater audiences] *Annales universitatis Mariae Curie-Skłodowska Lublin-Polonia* 20/21 (2002/2003): 1–15.

Chechlińska, Zofia, ed. *Szkice o kulturze muzycznej XIX wieku* [Essays on the musical culture of the nineteenth century]. 5 vols. Warsaw: Państwowe Wydawnictwo Muzyczne, 1971–84.

———. "Z problematyki badań nad muzyką polską XIX wieku" [On the problems of research in nineteenth-century Polish music]. *Muzyka* 24 (1979): 83–91.

Chodkowski, Andrzej. "Notes on Chopin's Piano Trio." *Chopin Studies* 2 (1987): 55–63.

Chomiński, Józef M. and Teresa D. Turło. *Katalog dzieł Fryderyka Chopina* [A catalogue of the works of Fryderyk Chopin]. Kraków: Polskie Wydawnictwo Muzyczne, 1990.

Christensen, Thomas. "Four-Hand Piano Transcriptions and Geographies of Nineteenth-Century Musical Reception." *Journal of the American Musicological Society* 52 (1999): 255–298.

Cone, Edward T. *Musical Form and Musical Performance*. New York: Norton, 1968.

Cybulska, Janina. *Romans wokalny w Polsce w latach 1800–1830. Z dziejów polskiej pieśni solowej* [The vocal romance in Poland in the years 1800–1830: from the history of Polish solo song]. Kraków: Polskie Wydawnictwo Muzyczne, 1960.

Czekanowska, Anna. *Polish Folk Music: Slavonic Heritage—Polish Tradition—Contemporary Trends*. Cambridge: Cambridge University Press, 1990.

Davies, Norman. *God's Playground: A History of Poland*. 2 vols. New York: Columbia University Press, 1982.

Didier, Béatrice. "George Sand et *Don Giovanni*." *Revue des Sciences Humaines* 226 (1992): 37–53.

Eigeldinger, Jean-Jacques. *Chopin: Pianist and Teacher as Seen by His Pupils*. Translated by N. Shohet, K. Osostowicz, and R. Howat. Cambridge: Cambridge University Press, 1986.

———. "Chopin, Bellini et le Theatre Italien: Autour de l'album de Mme d'Est." In *D'un opera l'autre: Hommage a Jean Mongredien*. Edited by Jean Gribenski, Marie-Claire Mussat, and Herbert Schneider. Paris: Presses Universitaires de France, 1996, 347–369.

Encyklopedia Muzyczna [Music encyclopedia]. Edited by Elżbieta Dziębowska (Kraków: Polskie Wydawnictwo Muzyczne, 1981–)

Engel, Hans. *Die Entwicklung des deutschen Klavierkonzertes von Mozart bis Liszt*. Leipzig: Breitkopf & Härtel, 1927.

Erber, Czesław. "Inwentarz notarialny Lessla" [Notarized inventory of Lessel's estate]. *Muzyka* 34 (1989): 37–57.

Everist, Mark. "Enshrining Mozart: *Don Giovanni* and the Viardot Circle." *19th-Century Music* 25 (2001): 165–189.

Frączyk, Tadeusz. *Warszawa młodości Chopina* [Warsaw of Chopin's youth]. Kraków: Polskie Wydawnictwo Muzyczne, 1961.

Goldberg, Halina. "Appropriating Poland: Glinka, Polish Dance, and Russian National Identity." In *Polish Encounters, Russian Identity*. Edited by David Ransel and Bożena Shallcross, Bloomington: Indiana University Press, 2005, 74–88.

———. "Chamber Arrangements of Chopin's Concert Works." *Journal of Musicology* 19 (2002): 39–84.

———. "Chopin in Warsaw's Salons." *Polish Music Journal* 2 (summer 1999), www.usc.edu/dept/polish_music/PMJ/issues.html.

———. "Musical Life in Warsaw during Chopin's Youth, 1810–1830." Ph.D. diss., City University of New York, 1997.

———. "Narodowość i narracja w polskich fantazjach pierwszej połowy XIX wieku" [Nationality and narrative in Polish fantasias during the first half of the nineteenth century]. In *Topos narodowy w muzyce polskiej pierwszej połowy XIX wieku*. Forthcoming.

————, ed. *The Age of Chopin: Interdisciplinary Inquiries*. Bloomington: Indiana University Press, 2004.

Gołąb, Maciej. *Chromatyka i tonalność w muzyce Chopina* [Chromaticism and tonality in Chopin's music]. Kraków: Polskie Wydawnictwo Muzyczne, 1991.

Gołos, Jerzy (George). "Organy i muzyka w ewangelickim kościele Św. Trójcy w Warszawie" [The organ and music in the Lutheran church of Holy Trinity in Warsaw]. *Ruch Muzyczny* 34 (1990), no. 15, 3.

————. *The Polish Organ*. Vol. 1. *The Instrument and Its History*. Translated by Barbara Dejlidko. Warsaw: Sutkowski Edition, 1993.

————. *Polskie organy i muzyka organowa* [The Polish organ and organ music]. Warsaw: Pax, 1972.

————. "Some Slavic Predecessors of Chopin." *Musical Quarterly* 46 (1960): 437–447.

————. *Zarys historii budowy organów w Polsce* [A historical outline of organ building in Poland]. Bydgoszcz: Bydgoskie Towarzystwo Naukowe, 1966.

Got, Jerzy. *Na wyspie Guaxary: Wojciech Bogusławski i teatr lwowski 1789–1799* [On Guaxara's island: Wojciech Bogusławski and the Lwow Theater 1789–1799]. Kraków: Wydawnictwo Literackie, 1971.

Gradenwitz, Peter. *Literatur und Musik im geselligem Kreise: Geschmacksbildung, Gesprächsstoff und musikalische Unterhaltung in der bürgerlichen Salongesellschaft*. Stuttgart: Steiner Verlag, 1991.

Greive, Tyrone. "A Look at the Violin in 16th- and 17th-Century Poland." *Journal of the Violin Making Society of America* 11/1 (1991): 117–142.

Grey, Thomas S. "Tableaux Vivants: Landscape, History Painting, and the Visual Imagination in Mendelssohn's Orchestral Music." *19th-Century Music* 21 (1997): 38–76.

Grzybowski, Stanisław. *Sarmatyzm*. Warsaw: Krajowa Agencja Wydawnicza, 1996.

Hoesick, Ferdynand. *Chopin: Życie i twórczość* [Chopin: life and works]. 2 vols. Warsaw: Hoesick, 1927.

————. *Pisma zbiorowe* [Collected works]. Vol. 1. *Słowacki i Chopin. Z zagadnień twórczości* [Słowacki and Chopin: on issues regarding oeuvre]. 2 vols. Warsaw: Trzaska, Evert i Michalski, 1932.

————. *Warszawa: Luźne kartki z przeszłości syreniego grodu* [Warsaw: loose leaves from the past of the "mermaid city"]. Poznań: Księgarnia Św. Wojciecha, 1920.

————. *Z papierów po Elsnerze* [From papers left by Elsner]. Warsaw: Hoesick, 1901.

Kallberg, Jeffrey. *Chopin at the Boundaries; Sex, History, and Musical Genre*. Cambridge, Mass.: Harvard University Press, 1996.

————. "Chopin's Last Style." *Journal of the American Musicological Society* 38 (1985): 264–315.

————. "Hearing Poland: Chopin and Nationalism." In *Nineteenth-Century Piano Music*. Edited by R. Larry Todd. New York: Schirmer, 1990, 221–257.

————. "'Voice' and the Nocturne." In *Pianist, Scholar, Connoisseur: Essays in*

Honor of Jacob Lateiner. Edited by Bruce Brubaker and Jane Gottlieb. Stuyvesant, N.Y.: Pendragon, 2000, 1–46.

Kieniewicz, Stefan. *Historia Polski 1795–1918* [A history of Poland 1795–1818]. Warsaw: Państwowe Wydawnictwo Naukowe, 1987.

Klimowicz, Mieczysław "'Cud mniemany' Wojciecha Bogusławskiego w 200-lecie premiery. Rozwiazane zagadki i nowe pytania" [Wojciech Bogusław-ski's *The Supposed Miracle* on the 200th anniversary of the premiere: resolved puzzles and new questions]. In *Wojciech Bogusławski i teatr polski w XVIII wieku. Wiek Oświecenia* 12 (1996) 11–25.

Kobylańska, Krystyna. "Improwizacje Fryderyka Chopina" [Fryderyk Chopin's improvisations]. *Rocznik Chopinowski* 19 (1987): 69–92.

———. *Rękopisy utworów Chopina: katalog* [The manuscripts of Chopin's works: a catalogue]. 2 vols. Kraków: Polskie Wydawnictwo Muzyczne, 1977.

Kraushar, Aleksander. *Polki twórcze czasów nowszych* [Creative Polish women of recent times]. Warsaw: Hoesick, 1929.

———. *Resursa kupiecka w Warszawie. Dawny Pałac Mniszchów (1820–1928)* [The Merchant Club in Warsaw: the old Mniszech Palace]. Warsaw: Hoesick, 1928.

———. *Salony i zebrania literackie w Warszawie* [Salons and literary gatherings in Warsaw]. Warsaw: Towarzystwo Miłośników Historyi, 1916.

———. *Typy i oryginały warszawskie* [Warsaw types and eccentrics]. Warsaw: Towarzystwo Miłośników Historyi, 1912.

Kwiatkowska, Magdalena. "Kultura muzyczna warszawy w latach 1795–1806" [Musical culture of Warsaw in the years 1795–1806]. Master's thesis, University of Warsaw, 1981.

Lisowska, Agnieszka. "Karol Kurpiński jako pisarz, działacz i organizator muzyczny w Warszawie" [Karol Kurpiński as a musical writer, activist and organizer in Warsaw]. Master's thesis, University of Warsaw, 1970.

Lissa, Zofia. "Chopin w świetle korespondencji współczesnych mu wydawców" [Chopin in light of the correspondence of his contemporary publishers]. *Muzyka* 5 (1960): 3–21.

Maunder, Richard. "Mozart's Keyboard Instruments." *Early Music* 20/2 (May 1992): 207–219.

Maunder, Richard, and David E. Rowland. "Mozart's Pedal Piano." *Early Music* 23/2 (May 1995): 287–296.

Miączyński, Ryszard. "Koncerty u benoitów: Z dziejów życia muzycznego Warszawy na przełomie XVIII i XIX w." [Bennonite concerts: from the history of musical life in Warsaw at the turn of the 19th century]. *Muzyka* 34 (1989): 65–102.

Milewski, Barbara. "Chopin's Mazurkas and the Myth of the Folk." *19th-Century Music* 23 (1999): 113–135.

Nathan, Hans. "The Tyrolese Family Rainer, and the Vogue of Singing Mountain-Troupes in Europe and America." *Musical Quarterly* 32/1 (January 1946): 63–79.

Niecks, Frederick. *Frederick Chopin as a Man and Musician*. 2 vols. 1888; reprint, New York: Cooper Square, 1973.

Nowak-Romanowicz, Alina. *Józef Elsner*. Kraków: Polskie Wydawnictwo Muzyczne, 1957.

———. *Klasycyzm 1750–1830* [Classicism 1750–1830]. *Historia muzyki polskiej*. Vol. 4. Edited by S. Sutkowski. Warsaw: S. Sutkowski, 1995.

———. "Nauka teorii muzyki w podręcznikach doby klasycyzmu polskiego (1750–1830)" [The study of music theory in textbooks of the Polish Classical era (1750–1830)]. *Muzyka* 25 (1980): 53–66.

———. "Niektóre problemy opery polskiej między oświeceniem i romantyzmem" [Some problems of Polish opera between the Enlightenment and Romanticism]. In *Studia Heironimo Feicht septuagenario dedicata*. Edited by Zofia Lissa. Kraków: Polskie Wydawnictwo Muzyczne, 1967, 328–336.

———. "Polskie fantazje fortepianowe doby przedchopinowskiej" [Polish piano fantaisias of the pre-Chopin era]. In *Studia musicologia*. Edited by Elżbieta Dziębowska, Zofia Helman, Danuta Idaszek, and Adam Neuer. Kraków: Polskie Wydawnictwo Muzyczne, 1979, 349–358.

Państwowa Wyższa Szkoła Muzyczna w Gdańsku. *Franciszek Lessel: W 200 rocznicę urodzin kompozytora*. [Franciszek Lessel: on the 200th anniversary of the composer's birth]. Gdańsk: Państwowa Wyższa Szkoła Muzyczna, 1980.

Parakilas, James. *Ballads without Words; Chopin and the Tradition of the Instrumental Ballade*. Portland, Or.: Amadeus Press, 1992.

Poliński, Aleksander. *Sprawozdanie jubileuszowe komitetu Towarzystwa Muzycznego w Warszawie* [Anniversary report of the Music Society in Warsaw Committee]. Warsaw: Kowalewski, 1896, 9.

Prokopowicz, Maria. "La musique imprimée de 1800–1831 comme source de la culture musicale polonaise de l'epoque." *Fontes artis musicae* 14 (1961): 16–22.

———. "Musique imprimée a Varsovie en 1800–1830." In *The Book of the First International Congress Devoted to the Works of Frederick Chopin*. Edited by Zofia Lissa. Warsaw: Państwowe Wydawnictwo Naukowe, 1960, 593–597.

Prosnak, Jan. "Karol Kurpiński jako teoretyk" [Karol Kurpiński as a theorist]. *Kwartalnik Muzyczny* 25 (January–March 1949): 138–155.

———. "Krakowiaki z czasów księstwa warszawskiego" [Krakowiaks from the period of the Duchy of Warsaw]. *Muzyka* 5 (1960): 49–59.

———. "Środowisko warszawskie w życiu Fryderyka Chopina" [The Warsaw circle in the life of Fryderyk Chopin]. *Kwartalnik muzyczny* 28 (October–December 1949): 54–55.

———. "Twórczość fortepianowa Karola Kurpińskiego" [The piano oeuvre of Karol Kurpiński]. *Muzyka* 4 (1959): 58–71.

———. "Wariacje fletowe Chopina" [Chopin's flute variations]. *Studia Muzykologiczne* (1953) vol 1: 302–307.

Przybylski, Tadeusz. "Fragmenty 'Dziennika Prywatnego' Karola Kurpińskiego" [Fragments of Kurpiński's 'private diary']. *Muzyka* 20 (1975): 104–113.

———. *Karol Kurpiński*. Warsaw: Państwowe Wydawnictwo Naukowe, 1980.

Rink, John. *Chopin: the Piano Concertos*. Cambridge: Cambridge University Press, 1997.

Rink, John, and Jim Samson, eds. *Chopin Studies 2*. Cambridge: Cambridge University Press, 1994.

Rosen, Charles. *The Romantic Generation*. Cambridge, Mass.: Harvard University Press 1995.

———. *Sonata Forms*. New York: Norton, 1980.

Rothstein, William. *Phrase Rhythm in Tonal Music*. New York: Schirmer Books, 1989.

Rudnicka-Kruszewska, Hanna. *Wincenty Lessel*. Kraków: Polskie Wydawnictwo Muzyczne, 1968.

Samson, Jim, ed. *The Cambridge Companion to Chopin*. Cambridge: Cambridge University Press, 1992.

———. *Chopin*. New York: Schirmer Books, 1997.

———, ed. *Chopin Studies*. Cambridge: Cambridge University Press, 1988.

———. *The Music of Chopin*. London: Routhledge and Kegan Paul, 1985.

Sankowska, Marta. "Studia Fryderyka Chopina w Szkole Głównej Muzyki Króewlskiego Uniwersytetu Warszawskiego" [Fryderyk Chopin's studies at the Main School of Music of the Royal University of Warsaw]. Master's thesis, University of Wrocław, 1994.

Semenovskij, S. A. "Russkie znakomye i druz'ja Šopena" [Russian acquaintances and friends of Chopin]. In *Venok Šopenu*. Edited by Leonid S. Sidel'nikov. Moscow: Muzyka, 1989, 63–68.

Sieradz, Halina. "Kultura muzyczna Warszawy w latach 1815–1830" [Musical culture of Warsaw in the years 1815–1830]. Master's thesis, University of Warsaw, 1983.

Stadnicki, Edwin Kornel. *Walc fortepianowy w Polsce w latach 1800–1830* [The piano waltz in Poland in the years 1800–1830]. Kraków: Polskie Wydawnictwo Muzyczne, 1962.

Strumiłło, Tadeusz. *Szkice z polskiego życia muzycznego XIX wieku* [Essays on Polish musical life in the nineteenth century]. Kraków: Polskie Wydawnictwo Muzyczne, 1954.

———. *Źrodła i początki romantyzmu w muzyce polskiej* [Sources and beginnings of Romanticism in Polish music]. Kraków: Polskie Wydawnictwo Muzyczne, 1956.

Strumiłło, Tadeusz, A. Nowak-Romanowicz, and T. Kurylowicz. *Poglądy na muzykę kompozytorów doby przedchopinowskiej: Ogiński, Elsner, Kurpiński* [Views on music of Polish composers of the pre-Chopin era: Ogiński, Elsner, and Kurpiński]. Kraków: Polskie Wydawnictwo Muzyczne, 1960.

Syga, Teofil, and Stanisław Szenic. *Maria Szymanowska i jej czasy* [Maria Szymanowska and her times]. Warsaw: Państwowy Instytut Wydawniczy, 1960.

Szenic, Stanisław. *Cmentarz powązkowski* [The Powązki cemetery]. 3 vols. Warsaw: Państwowy Instytut Wydawniczy, 1979–83.

Szulc, Eugeniusz. *Cmentarz Ewangelicko-Augsburski w Warszawie* [The Lutheran cemetery in Warsaw]. Warsaw: Państwowy Instytut Wydawniczy, 1989.

———. "Nieznana karta warszawskiego okresu życia Chopina" [An unknown page from the Warsaw period of Chopin's life]. *Rocznik Chopinowski* 18 (1986): 125–150.

Szulc, Eugeniusz, and Jadwiga Szulc. *Cmentarz Ewangelicko-Reformowany w Warszawie* [The Calvinist cemetery in Warsaw]. Warsaw: Państwowy Instytut Wydawniczy, 1989.

Szulc, Zdzisław. "Dwie nieznane kompozycje Chopina na eolopantalion" [Two unknown compositions for eolipantalion by Chopin]. *Muzyka* 1 (1955): 19–20.

Szybruska-Szwed, Małgorzata. "Maurycy Mochnacki jako krytyk muzyczny na tle kultury muzycznej Warszawy pierwszej połowy XIX wieku" [Maurycy Mochnacki as a musical critic against the background of musical culture in Warsaw in the first half of the nineteenth century]. Master's thesis, University of Warsaw, 1987.

Tomaszewski, Mieczysław. "Filiacje twórczości pieśniarskiej Chopina z polską pieśnią ludową, popularną i artystyczną" [Filiations of Chopin's song oeuvre with Polish folk, popular, and art song]. *Muzyka* 6 (1961): 79–89.

———. *Muzyka Chopina na nowo odczytana* [Chopin's music read anew]. Kraków: Akademia Muzyczna, 1996.

Tomaszewski, Wojciech. *Bibliografia warszawskich druków muzycznych 1801–1830* [A bibliography of Warsaw musical prints 1801–1850]. Warsaw: Biblioteka Narodowa, 1992.

———. *Warszawskie edytorstwo muzyczne w latach 1772–1865* [Warsaw music publishing in the years 1772–1865]. Warsaw: Biblioteka Narodowa, 1992.

Vogel, Beniamin (Benjamin). *Fortepian polski* [The Polish piano]. Warsaw: Sutkowski Edition, 1995.

———. "Fortepiany i idiofony klawiszowe w Królestwie Polskim w latach młodości Chopina" [Pianos and keyboard idiophones in the Congress Kingdom in the years of Chopin's youth]. *Rocznik Chopinowski* 9 (1975): 57–61.

———. *Instrumenty muzyczne w kulturze Królestwa Polskiego: Przemysł muzyczny w latach 1815–1918* [Musical instruments in the culture of the Polish Kingdom: music industry during the years 1815–1918]. Kraków: Polskie Wydawnictwo Muzyczne, 1980.

———. "Jeszcze raz o dwóch nieznanych kompozycjach Chopina na eolipantalion" [Once again about two unknown compositions for eolipantalion by Chopin]. *Rocznik Chopinowski* 17 (1985): 124.

———. "Two Tangent Square Pianos in Poland." *Journal of the American Musical Instrument Society* 20 (1994): 84–89.

———. "The Young Chopin's Domestic Pianos." In *Chopin in Performance: History, Theory, Practice*. Warsaw: Narodowy Instytut Fryderyka Chopina, 2005, 57–75.

Walker, Alan, ed. *The Chopin Companion: Profiles of the Man and the Musician*. New York: Taplinger, 1967; reprint, New York: Norton, 1973.

Waśko, Andrzej. *Romantyczny Sarmatyzm: Tradycja szlachecka w literaturze polskiej lat 1831–1863* [Romantic Sarmatism: the noble tradition in Polish literature]. Kraków: Wydawnictwo Arcana, 2001.

Węcowski, Jan. "Religious Folklore in Chopin's Music." *Polish Music Journal* 2 (1999), www.usc.edu/dept/polish_music/PMJ/issue/2.1.99/wecowski.html.

Wierzbowski, Ryszard. *O "Cudzie czyli Krakowiakach i Góralach" Wojciecha*

Bogusławskiego [On Wojciech Bogusławski's *Miracle, or the Cracovians and the Highlanders*]. Łódź: Wydawnictwo Uniwersytetu Łódzkiego, 1984.

Wilhelmy, Petra. *Der Berliner Salon im 19. Jahrhundert: 1780–1914*. Berlin: de Gruyter, 1989.

Wolff, Larry. *Inventing Eastern Europe: The Map of Civilization on the Mind of the Enlightenment*. Stanford: Stanford University Press, 1994.

Zakrzewski, Bogdan. *Boże coś Polskę Alojzego Felińskiego* [Alojzy Feliński's "O God, Thou who hast Graced Poland"]. Wrocław: Ossolineum, 1983.

Zamoyski, Adam. *Chopin*. Translated by Halina Sołdacz. Warsaw: Państwowy Instytut Wydawniczy, 1990.

Select Primary Printed Sources

"Antoni Orłowski." *Pamiętnik Muzyczny i Teatralny*, 1862, no. 24, 371–72.

Bogusławski, Wojciech. *Dzieje Teatru Narodowego* [The history of the National Theater]. Warsaw: Glücksberg, 1820.

Brodziński, Kazimierz. *Pisma Estetyczno-Krytyczne* [The aesthetic-critical writings]. Edited by Aleksander Łucki. 2 vols. Warsaw: Z Zasiłku Funduszu Kultury Narodowej, 1934.

———. *Wspomnienia mojej młodości* [Memories of my youth]. Kraków: Spółka Wydawnicza Polska, 1901.

Chopin, Fryderyk. *Korespondencja Fryderyka Chopina* [Fryderyk Chopin's correspondence]. Edited by Bronisław Edward Sydow. 2 vols. Warsaw: Państwowy Instytut Wydawniczy, 1955.

———. *Korespondencja Chopina z rodziną* [Fryderyk Chopin's correspondence with his family]. Edited by Krystyna Kobylańska. Warsaw: Państwowy Instytut Wydawniczy, 1972.

Correspondence inédite du roi Stanislas-Auguste Poniatowski et de Madame Geoffrin. Edited by Charles de Mouÿ. Paris: E. Plon, 1875.

C[zartoryska], I[zabela]. *Myśli różne o sposobie zakładania ogrodów* [Various thoughts on the method of setting up gardens]. Wrocław: Wilhelm Bogumil Korn, 1805.

Dębicki, Ludwik. *Puławy (1762–1830): Monografia z życia towarzyskiego, politycznego i literackiego na podstawie archiwum ks. Czartoryskich w Krakowie* [Puławy (1762–1830): a monograph on social, political and literary life based on the Princes' Czartoryski Archives in Kraków]. 4 vols. Lwów: Gubrynowicz i Schmidt, 1888.

Dmochowski, Franciszek Salezy. *Wspomnienia* [Memoirs]. Warsaw: Jaworski, 1858.

Dobrzyński, Bronisław. *Ignacy Dobrzyński w zakresie działalności dążącej do postępu muzyki współczesnej jemu epoce* [Ignacy Dobrzyński in the arena of activities aiming at musical progress during his time]. Warsaw: Felicyia Krokoszyńska, 1893.

Elsner, Józef. *O metryczności i rytmiczności języka polskiego* [On meter and rhythm in the Polish language]. Warsaw: S. Dąbrowski, 1818.

———. "O muzyce w ogólności" [On music in general]. *Astrea: Pamiętnik narodowy* 5 (1825): 56–66.

———. *Sumariusz moich utworów muzycznych* [A summary of my musical works]. Edited by Alina Nowak-Romanowicz. Kraków: Polskie Wydawnictwo Muzyczne, 1957.

Encyklopedia Powszechna [Universal Encyclopedia]. 28 vols. Warsaw: Orgelbrand, 1859–68.

Gołębiowski, Łukasz. *Gry i zabawy różnych stanów* [Games and amusements of various classes]. Warsaw: Glücksberg, 1831.

———. *Opisanie historyczno-statystyczne miasta Warszawy* [Historic-statistical description of the city of Warsaw]. Warsaw: Glücksberg, 1827.

Index Praelectionum in Universitate Literarum Regia Varsaviensi, September 15, 1826–Juli 15, 1827. Warsaw: Glückberg, 1826.

Hoffman, Klementyna. *Obiad czwartkowy: Opis wyjęty z nieznanych dotąd pamiętników* [A Thursday Dinner: a description taken from heretofore unknown memoirs]. Warsaw: Gebethner i Wolff, 1917.

———. *Pamiętniki* [Memoirs]. 3 vols. Berlin: Behr, 1849.

Hoffmann, E. T. A. *E. T. A. Hoffmann's Musical Writings: Kreisleriana, The Poet and the Composer, Music Criticism*. Edited by David Charlton. Cambridge: Cambridge University Press, 1989.

Janowski, Jan Nepomucen. *Notatki autobiograficzne 1803–1853* [Autobiographic notes]. Edited by M. Tyrowicz. Wrocław: Wydawnictwo Ossolińskich, 1950.

Karasowski, Maurycy. *Fryderyk Chopin*. 2 vols. 1st German ed., Dresden: F. Ries, 1877; 1st Polish ed., Warsaw: Gebethner i Wolff, 1882.

———. *Rys historyczny opery polskiej* [A historical outline of Polish opera]. Warsaw: Glücksberg, 1859.

Kicka, Natalia. *Pamiętniki* [Memoirs]. Edited by T. Szafrański and J. Dutkiewicz. Warsaw: Pax, 1972.

Kobylańska, Krystyna. *Chopin w kraju: Dokumenty i pamiątki* [Chopin in his own land: documents and souvenirs]. Kraków: Polskie Wydawnictwo Muzyczne, 1955.

Kolberg, Oskar. "Chopin." In *Encyklopedia Powszechna* [Universal Encyclopedia]. Warsaw: Orgelbrand, 1861, 458–463.

———. *Dzieła wszystkie Oskara Kolberga* [The complete works of Oskar Kolberg]. Edited by J. Krzyżanowski. 86 vols. Vols. 61–62. *Pisma muzyczne* [Music writings] parts I and II, edited by M. Tomaszewski, O. Pawlak, and E. Miller. Wrocław: Polskie Towarzystwo Ludoznawcze; Warszawa: Ludowa Spółdzielnia Wydawnicza; Kraków: Polskie Wydawnictwo Muzyczne, 1971–81.

Kowalczykowa, Alina, ed. *Idee programowe romantyków polskich: Antologia* [Program ideas of Polish Romantics: an anthology]. 2nd ed. Wrocław: Zakład Narodowy Imienia Ossolińskich, 2000.

Koźmian, Andrzej Edward. *Listy 1829–1864* [Letters 1829–1864]. 4 vols. Lwów: Gubrynowicz i Schmidt, 1894.

———. "Wizerunki osób towarzystwa warszawskiego" [Images of Warsaw socialites]. *Przegląd Poznański* 24 (1857): 1–28.

———. *Wspomnienia* [Memoirs]. 2 vols. Poznań: Letgeber, 1867.

Koźmian, Kajetan. *Pamiętniki* [Memoirs]. 3 vols. Wrocław: Wydawnictwo Ossolińskich, 1972.

Krasiński, Józef. *Pamiętniki* [Memoirs]. Poznań: Kraszewski, 1877.

Kurpiński, Karol. *Dziennik podróży* [Diary of a journey]. Edited by Z. Jachimecki. Kraków: Polskie Wydawnictwo Muzyczne, 1954.

———. *Krótki rys Teatru Narodowego od roku 1818 aż dotąd* [A brief outline on National Theater from 1818 until now]. Warsaw: J. Węcki, 1831.

———. *Zasady harmonii tonów* [Principles of tone harmony]. Warsaw: Klukowski, 1821.

Liszt, Franz. *Chopin*. Translated by Nicole Priollaud. Paris: Liana Levi, 1990.

Magier, Antoni. *Estetyka miasta stołecznego Warszawy* [The aesthetics of the capital city of Warsaw]. (Manuscript of 1830.) Edited by Hanna Szwankowska. Wrocław: Wydawnictwo Ossolińskich, 1963.

Mickiewicz, Adam. *Ballady i romanse* [Ballads and romances] (Wilno, 1822).

———. *Pan Tadeusz* [Master Thaddeus]. Translated by Kenneth R. Mackenzie. New York: Hippocrene Books, Inc., 1992.

Mochnacki, Maurycy. *Pisma* [Writings]. Edited by Artur Śliwiński. Lwów: Połoniecki, 1910.

———. *Rozprawy literackie* [Literary treatises]. Edited by Mirosław Strzyżewski. Wrocław: Zakład Narodowy Imienia Ossolińskich, 2000.

Morawski, Tadeusz. *Moje przygody; ustep z pamiętników* [My adventures: excerpt from memoirs]. Kraków: Leon Paszkowski, 1873.

Moriolles, Count de. *Pamiętniki* [Memoirs]. Translated by Z. Przyborowska. Warsaw: Biblioteka Dzieł Wyborowych, 1902.

Nakwaska, Anna. "Wyjątki z pamiętników współczesnych" [Excerpts from contemporary memoirs]. *Gazeta Warszawska*, July–August 1852, nos. 198–219.

Niemcewicz, Julian Ursyn. *Śpiewy historyczne: Z muzyką, rycinami i krótkim dodatkiem zbioru historyi polskiéj* [Historical chants with music, engravings, and a brief supplement of the collection of Polish history]. 5th ed. Lwów: Kajetan Jabłoński, 1849.

Odyniec, Antoni Edward. *Poezye* [Poems]. Vol. 1. *Ballady i legendy* [Ballads and legends]. Wilno, 1825.

———. *Wspomnienia z przeszłości opowiadane Deotyemie* [Recollections from the past recounted for Deotyma]. Warsaw: Gebethner i Wolff, 1884.

Ogiński, Michał Kleofas. *Listy o muzyce* [Letters about music]. Edited by Tadeusz Strumiłło. Kraków: Polskie Wydawnictwo Muzyczne, 1956.

Opis żałobnego obchodu po wielkopomnej pamięci nayiaśniejszym Alexandrze I [A description of the funeral tribute to His Highness Alexander I of momentous memory]. Warsaw: Glücksberg, 1829.

Pieniążek, Czesław. *O autorkach polskich a w szczególności o Sewerynie Duchińskiej* [On Polish female writers, especially Seweryna Duchińska]. Poznań: Merzbach, 1872.

Poczet pamiątek zachowanych w Domu Gotyckim w Puławach [Account of mementoes preserved in the Gothic House in Puławy]. Warsaw: Drukarnia Banku Polskiego, 1828.

Posiedzenie Publiczne Królewsko-Warszawskiego Uniwersytetu odbyte 5 października 1818 roku [Public meeting of the Royal University of Warsaw on 5 October 1818]. Warsaw: Glücksberg, 1818.

Posiedzenie Publiczne Królewsko-Warszawskiego Uniwersytetu odbyte 2 października 1820 roku [Public meeting of the Royal University of Warsaw on 2 October 1820]. Warsaw: Glücksberg, 1820.

Potocki, Stanisław. *O wymowie i stylu* [On articulation and style], 4 vols. Warsaw: Zawadzki i Węcki, 1815.

Przewodnik warszawski 1826 [Warsaw guide 1826]. Warsaw: Glücksberg, 1826.

Przewodnik warszawski 1829 [Warsaw guide 1829]. Warsaw: Glücksberg, 1829.

Riemann, Hugo. *Musik-Lexikon*. 6 vols. Leipzig: Verlag des Bibliographischen Instituts, 1882.

Sierawski, Napoleon. *Pamiętnik Napoleona Sierawskiego oficera konnego pułku gwardyi za czasów W. Ks. Konstantego* [A memoir of Napoleon Sierawski, officer of the cavalry regiment of the guard during the times of Great Prince Constantine]. Foreword by Stanisław Smołka. Lwów: Gubrynowicz i Schmidt, 1907.

S[ikorski], J[ózef]. "Narzędzia muzyczne z klawiaturą" [Musical instruments with a keyboard]. *Biblioteka Warszawska*, 1848, no. 2, 378.

———. "Wspomnienie Szopena" [A recollection of Chopin]. *Biblioteka Warszawska*, 1849, no. 4, 510–559.

Skarbek, Fryderyk. *Pamiętniki* [Memoirs]. Poznań: Żupański, 1878.

———. *Pamiętniki Seglasa* [Seglas's memoirs]. Edited by K. Bartoszyński. Warsaw: Państwowy Instytut Wydawniczy, 1959.

Sobieszczański, Franciszek M. *Rys historyczno-statystyczny wzrostu i stanu miasta Warszawy od najdawniejszych czasów aż do roku 1847* [Historic-statistical outline of the growth and state of the city of Warsaw from the oldest times until 1847]. Warsaw: S. Strąbski, 1848.

Sowiński, Albert. *Słownik muzyków polskich dawnych i nowoczesnych* [Dictionary of ancient and modern Polish musicians]. 1st French ed., Paris: Libraire Adrien le Clere, 1857; 1st Polish ed., Paris: Księgarnia Luxemburska, 1874.

Szulc, Marceli Antoni. *Fryderyk Chopin i utwory jego muzyczne* [Fryderyk Chopin and his musical works] (1873). Edited by D. Idaszek. Kraków: Polskie Wydawnictwo Muzyczne, 1986.

———. "Przegląd ostatnich dzieł Chopina" [A review of Chopin's latest works]. *Tygodnik Literacki*, 7 and 14 March 1842, no. 10, 76–77 and no. 11, 82–83.

Tarczewska (Tańska), Aleksandra. *Historia mojego życia* [The history of my life]. Edited by I. Kaniowska-Lewańska. Wrocław: Ossolineum, 1967.

Whistling, Carl Friedrich and Adolph Moritz Hofmeister. *Handbuch der musikalischen Literatur 1829*. 1829; reprint, Hildesheim: Olms, 1975.

Wielisław, [Eugeniusz Skrodzki]. "Kilka wspomnień o Chopinie" [A few recollections of Chopin]. *Bluszcz*, 1882, no. 32, 249–250; no. 33, 257–258; and no. 36, 281–282.

———. *Wieczory piątkowe i inne gawędy* [Friday evenings and other tales]. Edited by M. Opałek. Warsaw: Państwowy Instytut Wydawniczy, 1962.

Wieniarski, Antoni. *Warszawa i warszawianie. Szkice towarzyskie i obyczajowe* [Warsaw and its residents: essays on the society and customs]. 2 vols. Warsaw: Bernstejn, 1857.

Wójcicki, Kazimierz Władysław. *Cmentarz powązkowski pod Warszawią* [The Powązki cemetery near Warsaw]. 3 vols. Warsaw: Gebethner i Wolff, 1855–58.

———. *Kawa literacka w Warszawie* (1829–1830) [Literary coffee in Warsaw]. Warsaw: Gebethner i Wolff, 1873.

———. *Społeczność Warszawy w początkach naszego stulecia* [Warsaw's society in the beginning of our century]. Warsaw: Gebethner i Wolff, 1877.

———. *Warszawa, jej życie umysłowe i ruch literacki 1800–1830* [Warsaw: its literary and intellectual life 1800–1830]. Warsaw: Gebethner i Wolff, 1880.

Wóycicka, Anna. "Wieczorek pożegnalny Fryderyka Chopina" [Fryderyk Chopin's farewell evening]. *Pion,* 1934, no. 24, 1–2.

Zaleski, Józef Bohdan. *Pisma zbiorowe* [Collected works]. 4 vols. Lwów: Gubrynowicz i Schmidt, 1877.

INDEX OF NAMES

GENERAL INDEX

Benevolent Association, 181, 256, 260, 261–262, 263
Gesellschaft der Musikfreunde, 181 n.14
Harmonie-Gesellschaft, 13, 257, 258 n.10
Merchant Club (*Resursa kupiecka*), 76, 77, 184, 222, 256, 257, 260, 264
Music Amateur Society (*Towarzystwo Muzyczno-Amatorskie*), 259–260
Musik-Gesellschaft, 108 n.3, 257–259
Society for Church Music (*Towarzystwo Kościelnej Muzyki*), 268
Society for the Friends of Religious and National Music (*Towarzystwo Przyjaciół Muzyki Religijnej i Narodowej*), 125 n.45, 178, 267, 268, 269, 270
St. Cecilia Society, 266

Nationalism/Patriotism in music, 14, 23–26, 90–95, 106, 180, 235–237, 296. *See also* Patriotic songs
historiography, 5–7
influence on Chopin, 104 (*see also* Chopin, Fryderyk, *in index of names*)
and the November Uprising, 91
in opera, 217–218, 221–222, 226–227 (*see also* Polish Opera)
in poem settings, 100–104
in sacred music, 99–100, 145
National Theater, 13, 15–16, 59, 106, 136, 156, 185 n.27, 218–219, 226–227, 252–253, 261 n.29, 277, 283, 294, 295
administration, 220–221, 223
audiences, 219–220
performers, 112 n.8, 219, 223–226, 270, 271
repertoire, 220, 221–222, 228–229, 232–233, 242–243
ticketing, 220
as a virtuoso concert venue, 274
and the Warsaw Conservatory, 108

Nocturnes
publication, 85, 96, 97–98, 99
vocal origins and characteristics, 95–96, 99
November Uprising, 22, 27, 91, 106, 157, 159, 170, 174, 175

Oberek, 65
Opera, 217–226. *See also* National Theater
French, 243–253
German, 226–229, 230–231
Polish (*see* Polish Opera)
salon performances, 191
transcriptions, 85, 95, 213, 222, 228, 242–243, 245–246
Opéra (Paris), 252
Opéra-Comique (Paris), 245
Orchestral music
and music societies, 256, 257, 264
publication, 61
transcriptions, 213–216, 263, 264
Organ
production, 33–34, 37
pseudo-organs (choralion, eolimelodicon, eolipantalion), 37–41, 157, 197–200, 271–272
Organists' School, 108 n.3
Orgelbrand Encyclopedia, 87

Pamiętnik Muzyczny Warszawski, 186
Pamiętnik Warszawski, 20, 134
Patriotic songs, 23 n.18, 25, 35–36, 63, 75, 86–87, 90–95, 99–104, 106, 232
Dąbrowski Mazurka (hymn), 25, 90–91, 92, 99, 237
Historical Chants (*see* Niemcewicz, Julian Ursyn, *in index of names*)
Kościuszko 's Polonaise, 90–91, 92, 93, 99, 237
"O God, Thou who hast Graced Poland," 35, 36 n.29
Poniatowski's March, 90–91, 92, 100, *102*
Patronage, 184–186, 189, 244, 255, 268–269. *See also* Salons; Soirée/matinée
and concerts, 256
and publishing, 55–56, 61

Pedal piano (Pedalflugel), 35
Philosophical trends, 19
Piano
    amateurs, 179
    Chopin's pianos, 48–52
    Chopin's timbral innovations,
        52–53
    construction, 44–48, 50–52, 196
    domestic use, 29
    education, 42
    grand pianos (pantaleon), 43,
        45–46, 48, 49, 156
    imported foreign works, 192–193
    popularity in Poland, 41–44
    production, 41–48, 50–53, 59
    in salons (see Salons)
    square pianos, 45
    transcriptions for piano, 62, 76,
        213
    upright pianos, 45, 49
    as vocal accompaniment,
        190–191
Piano makers
    Buchholtz, 28, 44, 46–48, 49–51
    Graf, 43–44
    Hochhauser, 44
    Jansen, 44
    Leszczyński, 28, 44, 46–47
    Max, 44
    Pleyel, 28, 44, 53, 105, 194
    Silbermann, 41
    Skórski, 43
    Spiechowski, 44
    Stein, 43
    Streicher, 44
    Troschel, 44
Piano trio, 207–208
Poland
    Congress Kingdom, 16–17, 91
    Duchy of Warsaw, 13–14
    French Occupation, 13
    industrialization, 29
    Prussian Occupation, 11, 257–258
    publishing industry, 56, 59
    Warsaw's cultural significance,
        4–5
Polish Opera, 230–243, 253. See also
    Elsner, Józef, in index of names;
    Kurpiński, Karol, in index of
    names

borrowing melodies from, 86, 88,
    232, 240
chorus, 237
folk idioms (see Chopin, Fryderyk,
    in index of names; Folk music;
    Romanticism in Poland)
foreign models (vaudeville,
    singspiel), 230, 233, 234,
    237–238
and freemasonry, 233
historical themes, 233, 237, 239,
    242
and language, 230–231
national idioms, 232, 234
overture, 237–239
precursors, 231–232
publication, 106
reception, 235–237
sacred music idioms, 239, 241
Singspiel, 231, 234
staging, 237
Polonaise, 24, 63, 76. See also Chopin,
    Fryderyk, in index of names
    as concert music, 78, 80–81
    as a dance, 66
    generic ambiguity, 94
    in opera, 232, 235
    on operatic melodies, 77–78
    publication, 63, 64–65, 181
    in Russia, 63
Potpourri, 88, 93, 233. See also Fantasia
    in salons, 191
    in virtuoso concerts, 274
Powszechny Dziennik Krajowy, 186
Prelude
    generic ambiguity, 194–195
    publication, 85
Public theater, 218. See also National
    Theater; Variety Theater

Quadrille, 63, 65

Romance (as a musical genre)
    publication for piano, 85, 95
    in salons, 190–191
    vocal origins of piano works, 95–96
Romanticism in Poland, 19–24,
    161–168, 173–176, 227, 253
    and cafés, 294

Classical antecedents, 171
folk-inspired, 131, 132 n.63, 138,
    140, 142, 175, 229, 231, 232,
    233, 234
foreign models, 139, 175
and fragments, 20, 163–164
and genius, 201
and history, 24, 163, 165, 169, 175
and improvisation, 200
literary, 20–21, 24, 136–140, 146,
    165, 174
musical, 140, 146
nationalism, 23–26, 137–138, 140,
    142, 143, 163, 174–175
and nature, 20, 162, 163, 164
Ojców, 168–169
and opera, 227–228, 229, 232, 233,
    243–244, 247–249 (see also Pol-
    ish Opera)
ruins, 163
and the supernatural, 169, 175,
    229, 232, 233
Rondo
    dance idioms, 85
    publication, 85, 104
    in salons, 191
Royal Chapel, 265
Ruch muzyczny, 254

Sacred music, 143, 255 n.2, 265–273.
    See also Music societies
    Carmelite Church, 266
    Cathedral of Saint John (Farny
        Church, Metropolitan Church),
        55, 266, 272
    Church of Canonesses, 266, 267
    Church of Capuchins, 266
    Church of St. Alexander, 266
    Church of St. Benon, 266
    at court, 265
    Franciscan Church of St. Francis of
        Assisi, 266
    for Holy Week, 266
    Lutheran Church (Holy Trinity), 34,
        38, 39, 267, 270–272
    and music societies, 143, 257
    and patriotism, 99–100
    Piarists Church, 261, 266, 267, 268,
        269–270
    publication, 95, 106

synagogue, 272
as topos, 99, 100, 101, 104, 144, 239,
    241
University Church, 267, 268
Visitation Nuns' Church, 267
    and Chopin, 33, 34, 35, 267
Salle Pleyel, 264
Salons, 5, 15
    aristocratic, 156
    of the bourgeoisie, 151–156
    chamber music, 200–216 (see also
        Chamber music)
    child prodigies, 182
    dance music, 62 n.16, 63, 72–76,
        85, 191
    dedications of music to hosts, 186,
        188
    eighteenth century, 149–150
    foreign models, 149, 153
    foreign performers, 181, 188, 215
    and gender, 148
    historiography, 8
    instruments, 41, 156
    intellectual salons, 150–151
    and music printing, 61
    and nationalism, 150–151, 169
    orchestral works (transcriptions of),
        213–216
    piano music, 192–200, 213, 274
    and politics, 161
    romantic ideology in (see Romanti-
        cism in Poland)
    virtuoso performers, 215–216
    vocal music, 95–98, 190–191, 213
Sarmatism, 23–24
Singakademie, 108 n.3
Slavophilism, 23, 138–139
Society for the Assistance for Destitute
    Musicians and Their Widows and
    Orphans, 185
Society for the Friends of Learning
    (Towarzystwo Przyjaciół Nauk),
    11–12, 14, 18, 19, 20, 100, 134,
    143, 151, 223
Society of Exes, 171, 172
Soirée/matinée, 254, 255, 256, 263,
    264, 273
    amateur performers, 263
    repertoire, 263
Sonatas, 274

DATE DUE